Peter Mangold is an author and a Senior Associate Member of St Antony's College, Oxford. He is a former member of the Foreign and Commonwealth Office Research Department and the BBC World Service. He is the author of *The Almost Impossible Ally: Harold Macmillan and Charles de Gaulle* (I.B. Tauris, 2006).

# BRITAIN
## AND THE
## DEFEATED FRENCH

*From Occupation to Liberation, 1940–1944*

## PETER MANGOLD

I.B.TAURIS

LONDON · NEW YORK

Published in 2012 by I.B.Tauris & Co Ltd
6 Salem Road, London W2 4BU
175 Fifth Avenue, New York NY 10010
www.ibtauris.com

Distributed in the United States and Canada Exclusively by Palgrave Macmillan
175 Fifth Avenue, New York NY 10010

ISBN: 978 1 84885 431 4

A full CIP record for this book is available from the British Library
A full CIP record is available from the Library of Congress

Printed and bound in Sweden by ScandBook AB

To John Eidinow, friend and critic

'Be patient if you find a Frenchman hard to understand –
he is having difficulties too.'
(*Instructions for British Servicemen in France*)

# Contents

*Contents*

## Part II
### 'Somewhat Difficult People'

# Plates

# Abbreviations

| | |
|---|---|
| AFHQ | Allied Forces Headquarters (Algiers) |
| AMGOT | Allied Military Government of Occupied Territories |
| BBC | British Broadcasting Corporation |
| BCRA | Bureau Central de Renseignement et d'Action |
| BEF | British Expeditionary Force |
| CNR | Conseil National de la Résistance |
| FCNL | French Committee of National Liberation |
| FFI | French Forces of the Interior |
| FNC | French National Committee |
| FO | Foreign Office |
| FTP | Francs Tireurs et Partisans (Communist-led Resistance group) |
| GPRF | Gouvernement Provisoire de la République Française |
| PWE | Political Warfare Executive |
| RAF | Royal Air Force |
| SHAEF | Supreme Headquarters, Allied Expeditionary Force |
| SIGINT | Signals Intelligence |
| SIS | Secret Intelligence Service (MI6) |
| SOE | Special Operations Executive |
| STO | Service du Travail Obligatoire (originally know as la Relève) |
| USAAF | United States Army Air Force |
| WAC | BBC Written Archive Centre, Caversham |

# Operations

| | |
|---|---|
| Attila | Codename for German occupation of whole of France, November 1942 |
| Barbarossa | German invasion of the Soviet Union, June 1941 |
| Catapult | Operation against French fleet, July 1940 |
| Crusader | Attempt to relieve Tobruk, November 1941 |
| Dragoon | Landings southern France, 15 August 1944 (previously Anvil) |
| Exporter | Levant operation, 7 June 1941 |
| Husky | Sicily landings, July 1943 |
| Ironclad | Madagascar, 5 May 1942 |
| Menace | Dakar, September 1940 |
| Overlord | D-Day landings, 6 June 1944 |
| Roundup | Proposed landings in France, 1942 |
| Sealion | German invasion of Britain 1940 |
| Sichelschnitt | German invasion of France, 1940 |
| Sledgehammer | Proposed small-scale attack on the Cotentin Peninsula, 1942 or 1943 |
| Streamline Jane | Occupation of whole of Madagascar, autumn 1942 |
| Supergymnast | Proposed attack on Morocco and Algeria (later Torch) |
| Susan | Proposed operation in Morocco, June 1940 |
| Torch | North African landings, 8 November 1942 |

# Acknowledgements

My thanks to Clare Brown, John Eidinow, Lucian Randall, Tom Purton and John Tod for help with this project.

I am also grateful to Virginia Makins for permission to quote from the Sherfield Papers in the Bodleian Library, Oxford; to Jane Reilly for permission to quote from the Reilly Papers, also in the Bodleian; and to the BBC for permission to quote from material in the BBC Written Archives Centre in Caversham.

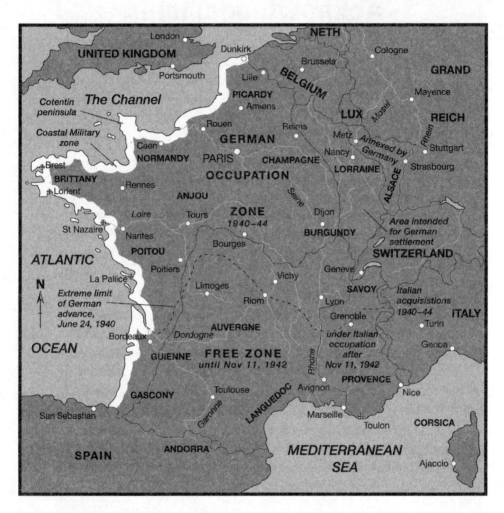

Map 1: Vichy France

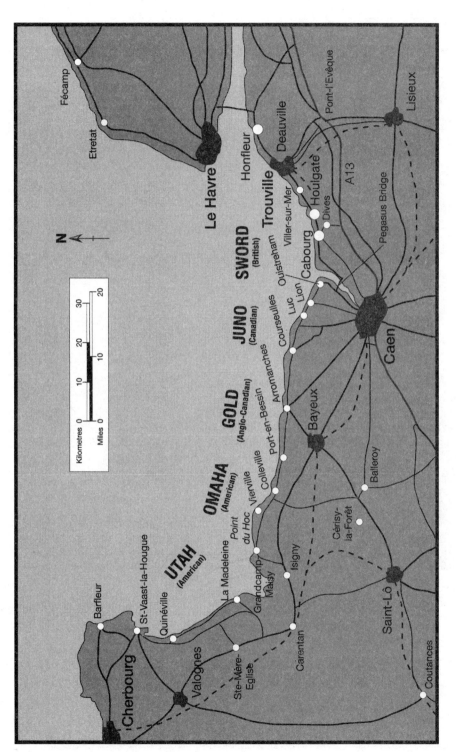

Map 2: D-Day Beaches

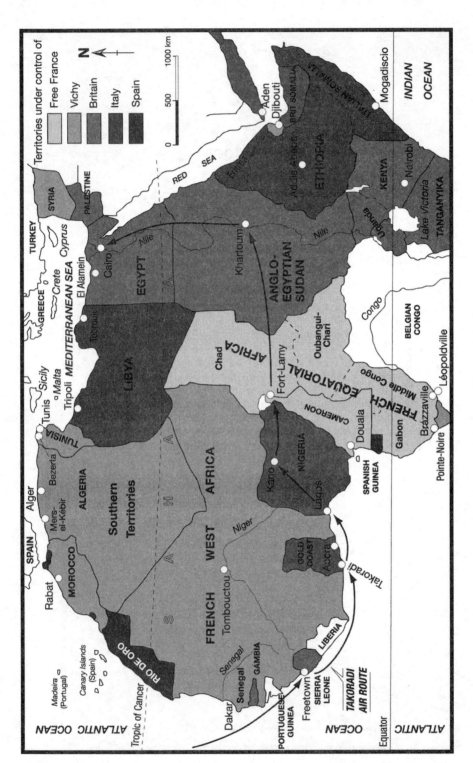

Map 3: African Colonies

# Introductory

# Rival, Enemy, Ally, Friend

# 1

# 'L'Entente Est Morte.
# Vive L'Entente!'

On 14 June 1940, Violet Bonham-Carter, daughter of the Liberal Prime Minister, Herbert Asquith, and a close friend of Winston Churchill, visited her son at Winchester. It was, she recorded in her diary,

> a radiant day. The buildings rose in silvery beauty from amongst the trees … The stream along the edge of Meads flowed crystal clear. Boys passed through War Memorial – raising their straw hats as they went. Very old dons crawled about in the sunshine. All unchanged – and seemingly unaware. We lunched at school-shop on buttered eggs and strawberries. The young waitress bringing in the strawberries suddenly said to us with a bright uncomprehending smile on her face 'The Germans have entered Paris.'[1]

Across the Channel, a remarkable military campaign was reaching its climax. Five weeks earlier, in the early hours of 10 May, Germany had attacked the Low Countries. On the 13th, German armoured forces spearheaded by General Erwin Rommel had surprised the French at Sedan and crossed the Meuse. From here they advanced at such speed that they had not bothered to take prisoners, simply telling captured French troops to throw away their arms and head south so as not to clutter up the roads.[2] By 20 May, German forces had reached the Channel coast, surrounding the Allied armies in Belgium and forcing the evacuation of the British Expeditionary Force (BEF), minus its equipment, at Dunkirk.

The next German offensive, launched on 5 June, had been south-west towards Paris. The French government, headed by the Anglophile Paul Reynaud, retreated first to Tours on the Loire, and then to Bordeaux. It was here that on the evening of 16 June Reynaud resigned, to be succeeded by the octogenarian First World War hero Marshal Philippe Pétain. The new government wasted no time in suing for an armistice. The night before it came into effect, a strange scene was played out in the peasant house where Hitler was staying near Sedan. The German leader ordered the lights to be turned out. 'Silently,' his architect Albert Speer recorded,

> we sat in the darkness, swept by the sense of experiencing a historic moment so close to the author of it. Outside, a bugler blew the traditional signal for the end of fighting. A thunderstorm must have been brewing in the distance, for as in a bad novel occasional flashes of heat lightning shimmered through the dark room. Someone, overcome by emotion, blew his nose. Then Hitler's voice sounded, soft and unemphatic: 'This responsibility ...'[3]

The shock waves generated by this sudden and totally unexpected collapse of France reverberated across Europe and over to America and the Far East.[4] Paris was widely seen as the capital of Western culture, while France had been regarded as a formidable military power, whose army even the German High Command had held in respect. 'The one firm rock on which everybody has been willing to build for the last two years,' the Foreign Secretary Lord Halifax noted in his diary on 25 May, 'was the French army, and the Germans walked through it like they did through the Poles.'[5] Not since the Prussian defeat by Napoleon at the battle of Jena in 1806 had a Great Power met its doom so quickly and inexorably. Like Prussia, France had been 'struck from the roster of nations,' with no further voice over the conduct of the war.[6] Hitler was now the dominant force in Europe from the Bay of Biscay to the Black Sea. More than anything else, it was the collapse of France that helped turn what had begun nine months earlier as a European conflict into a world war that would reshape the international politics of the second half of the twentieth century.[7]

Nowhere, of course, was the sense of disaster more acute than in France. There is, as Andrew Shennan notes,

> probably no more terrible a trial for a people than the defeat of its armies: in the scale of crises, this is the supreme catastrophe ... It wounds something essential in each of us: a certain confidence in life, a pride in oneself and in the group to which one belongs, an indispensable self-respect.[8]

'I had been reared,' wrote Robert Marjolin, a French civil servant and later Vice President of the EEC Commission, 'on the idea that France was a great military Power, that she was in fact the arbiter of peace in Europe. Those illusions were dispelled in the space of a few days.'[9]

The terms of the Armistice were in many respects harsh. Hitler was settling scores for the German defeat of 1918. The French army was limited to 100,000 men, the same number the Germans had been reduced to twenty-two years earlier, while occupation payments were set at the same inflated level as the 1919 reparations imposed on Germany (which had followed a four-year war). One million, six hundred thousand French prisoners of war would be transferred to Germany pending the conclusion of a peace treaty, where they would in effect be held hostage against good French behaviour. At the same time, the Armistice reflected Germany's strategic needs for the next phase of the current war, namely the invasion of England. Some two-thirds of the country, including Paris and the main northern industrial areas, as well as the whole of the Atlantic and Channel coasts, were thus occupied. But in contrast to the fate which had befallen Poland and the other countries occupied by Germany, the French were allowed to maintain a nominal independence.

Pétain's government quickly established itself in the small, provincial spa town of Vichy in the Auvergne, a town whose main attraction, other than its rather unpleasant medicinal waters, was the ready availability of accommodation to house government ministries in a certain degree of comfort. Pétain and the Foreign Ministry established themselves in the Hotel du Parc. The Ministry of the Interior settled into the Casino. The Colonial Ministry, ironically enough given the long history of Anglo-French imperial rivalry, was housed in the Hotel des Anglais.[10] Vichy – the name quickly became synonymous with that of the Marshal's administration – was recognised as the legitimate government of France. Various foreign embassies and legations followed, notably that of the USA. The diplomats found the new capital to be an isolated and introverted place. Intrigue flourished and rumours swirled, and it was wise to keep a suitcase permanently packed in case of a sudden German occupation.[11]

The impact on the French people was grim. 'The dark years,' *les années tragiques*, as they became known, saw a closing down of horizons. 'People came and went in a world which no longer seemed real, cut off from normal human feelings.'[12] There was hardship, deprivation and silence:

the silence of the dark mornings and the blackouts at night, of the streets after curfew. The silence between people faced with the worst in human nature; the silence of a population doing what it was told, doing what it was safest to do, and the mirror image of this in the mountains of denunciatory letters which poured onto office desks. Faced with betrayals, disloyalties and greed, with trust gone, it was always dangerous to speak your mind.[13]

The moral certainties of peacetime had disappeared. In the philosopher Jean-Paul Sartre's words, 'Everything we did was equivocal. We never quite knew whether we were doing right or wrong. A subtle poison corrupted even our best actions.'[14]

The defeat exacerbated divisions going back to the Revolution of 1789, and Vichy provided an excellent vehicle for settling old scores.[15] In pursuit of a policy of national regeneration, Vichy abolished the Republic and liquidated France's democratic institutions. It persecuted Freemasons, Communists and Jews, some 75,000 of whom were to die in Auschwitz. Some 30,000 French civilians were to be shot as hostages or as members of the Resistance; some 650,000 civilian workers were compulsorily drafted to work in German factories. Vichy leaders, such as Admiral François Darlan, clung to the fiction that France was still a Great Power and hoped to establish a privileged place in the New European Order. The Germans had other ideas. France's role, in the words of the German Propaganda Ministry, was to be confined to that of 'a greater Switzerland, a country of tourism ... and fashion.'[16]

If defeat represented catastrophe for France, it precipitated the worst crisis in modern British history. Along with the 1942 fall of Singapore, the fall of France marks a nadir in Britain's war, but one which, much more than Singapore, was a military and strategic game-changer. Deprived of its forward line of defence in Continental Europe, Britain faced air attack and invasion. As early as 20 June, newspapers had carried the sinister silhouettes of German troop-carrying aircraft. General Sir Alan Brooke was Commander-in-Chief, Southern Command, which would bear the brunt of any German attack. 'All reports,' he noted in his diary for 7 September, 'look like invasion getting nearer. Ships collecting, dive bombers being concentrated, parachutists captured.'[17] Kent and East Anglia seemed the two most likely targets.[18] But the invasion never came. Britain enjoyed several critical advantages over France, the most important of which was geography. The Channel constituted a much more formidable anti-tank trap than the

Meuse. Despite its remarkable showing on the Continental battlefield, the German army was neither equipped nor trained for amphibious warfare. The invasion of Britain, in Hitler's own words, represented 'an exceptionally daring undertaking,' which could only be contemplated if air superiority had been achieved.[19] While they had conspicuously neglected their Continental Expeditionary Force, the British had taken care to establish the world's most effective air defence system. Unlike the French army, which had been outclassed by the Wehrmacht, the Royal Air Force (RAF) proved a match for a Luftwaffe overconfident from its victories on the Continent but handicapped by the losses it had sustained in the battle of France.[20]

Britain's final advantage over its ally was moral. Unlike France, the crisis of June 1940 pulled the British together, producing a climate of defiance articulated by a strong leader in the form of Churchill and symbolised by David Low's cartoon of a British soldier standing on the cliffs of Dover, shaking his fist at the menace on the Continent, with the caption, 'Very well, alone!' Senior British ministers, as General Catroux, the former French High Commissioner in Indochina, noted on his arrival in Britain in September 1940, had confidence in Churchill, in themselves and in victory. France's defeat had produced Britain's 'finest hour,' the phrase which Churchill used for the title of the second volume of his war memoirs. (For its French edition, the title was changed into *L'Heure tragique.*)[21]

While Hitler's immediate purpose was thus deflected in the late summer and early autumn of 1940 with the German defeat in the battle of Britain, the underlying strategic situation remained grim. The whole of the west European continent, from the North Cape to the Spanish frontier, remained in hostile hands, and Britain found itself in the historically unique position of facing a European enemy without significant Continental allies. To add to Britain's difficulties, Italy had taken advantage of France's collapse and had declared war on 10 June. The combination of the defection of the powerful French navy, with which Britain had shared the defence of the Mediterranean, and the threat posed by Italy's numerically impressive fleet and strong air force, meant that all convoys to the Middle and Far East had to be routed via the Cape.[22] Other pre-war defence plans, which had been made in conjunction with the French, were also turned upside down. A German move against the important West African port of Dakar was expected. To the east, the defection of French Somaliland compromised the security of the Horn of Africa. Italian troops in Abyssinia threatened Kenya, Sudan and Aden. In September 1940, at the start of what was to prove a more than two-and-a-half-year war in North Africa, six Italian divisions from Libya crossed the border into Egypt. Small wonder that Churchill described British strategy in 1940 and 1941 as a matter of 'KBO: Keep Buggering On.'[23]

If rarely centre-stage in Britain's war after June 1940, France, or at least French territory, was nevertheless of considerable importance. The Germans used bases in France in the battle of Britain, which was in effect the continuation of the battle for France, as well as in their prolonged naval campaigns against British supply lines in the Atlantic. In November 1942, French North Africa was the scene of the first Anglo-American operation of the war, Operation Torch, and it was here that the invasion of Sicily was launched eight months later. The road to Germany in 1944–5 lay across the Normandy beaches. Churchill and Eden never forgot that the restoration of France would be an essential element in the post-war balance of power.

Yet the reason why France commanded such continuous time and attention in Whitehall lay with the political divisions in the country which had opened up the defeat of June 1940. With Vichy withdrawn into a sullen and potentially hostile neutrality, Britain was forced to look for new French allies, whether in France, the French Empire or London, who were prepared to continue the war. Over the next couple of years, a series of informal new Anglo-French alliances sprang up, in effect a new post-Armistice entente. Their overlapping and at times cross-cutting relationships took Britain geographically and politically deep into France. The BBC, which quickly emerged as an important new instrument of policy, gave Britain a 'virtual' presence in towns and villages across the Occupied and Unoccupied Zones, where British influence had never previously penetrated. Agents from the Special Operations Executive (SOE) established links with, and entrusted their lives to, members of the various French Resistance movements which began to emerge in 1941.

London became a French capital, where for three years a hitherto-unknown French general, Charles de Gaulle, had his headquarters within walking distance of Downing Street and the Foreign Office. Later it became a hub for the Resistance. And it was in London that the 1942 Allied landings in French North Africa and the D-Day landings were planned.

Meanwhile, Britain had become an important factor in the post-Armistice French political equation. De Gaulle was regarded by Vichy as a rebel, and indeed he directly challenged Vichy's authority and legitimacy. His recognition by the British as early as 28 June 1940, as 'leader of all Free Frenchmen, wherever they may be, who rally to him in support of the Allied cause,' was thus a direct and ultimately highly subversive intervention in French politics.[24] But it offered the French a critical alternative to Vichy, the importance of which was to grow, as the General's voice and message became familiar to BBC listeners.[25] Following the North Africa landings, and in the face of French deep-seated rivalries and American obstructionism, British diplomats helped to mediate the emergence of a de-facto provisional government.

These were conditions in which personalities loomed large. Two men, both of whom would have been worthy of the imagination of Tolstoy or Shakespeare, stand head and shoulders above the Anglo-French cast. Winston Churchill had long been a familiar figure on the British political stage. Born in 1874, the son of the Tory politician Lord Randolph Churchill and an American mother, he had entered parliament at the age of twenty-six. Within eight years he was in the Cabinet, and over the next quarter century he held a succession of high offices, including First Lord of the Admiralty, Home Secretary, Colonial Secretary and Chancellor of the Exchequer, in first Liberal and later Conservative governments. The 1930s, however, proved to be wilderness years. Out of office, and often out of step with his party, his reputation languished. In 1938, it was Chamberlain's pursuit of 'peace in our time,' rather than Churchill's dire warnings over the rise of the new German threat, that resonated with the public. But Chamberlain was wrong, and when war broke out in September 1939, Churchill returned to government as First Lord of the Admiralty.

Eight months later, Chamberlain was forced to resign following the failed Anglo-French expedition to Norway. The choice of his successor, made coincidentally the day before Hitler's assault on the Low Countries, lay between Churchill and the Foreign Secretary Lord Halifax. Halifax, by his own private admission, was a 'layman' in all things military and was bored by military strategy. Churchill by contrast thrived on war and was fascinated by it.[26] His drive, energy and indomitable will were at once evident in the Continental European crisis that now broke. They certainly impressed the young French Under-Secretary of War who first met him in early June. 'Mr Churchill,' de Gaulle wrote in his war memoirs,

> seemed to me to be equal to the rudest task, provided it had also grandeur. The assurance of his judgement, his great culture, the knowledge he had of most of the subjects, countries and men involved, and finally his passion for the problems proper to war, found in war their full scope. On top of everything, he was fitted by his character to act, take risks, and play the part out-and-out and without scruple.[27]

Yet, while every inch the war leader, Churchill's strategic judgement, as had already been evident over the failed Gallipoli campaign during the First World War, was by no means always sure. Impulsiveness, along with a gambler's spirit and a natural belligerence, constantly threatened to override sound calculation of risks. It could make the Prime Minister extremely difficult to work with. So too did his highly emotional and mercurial temperament. The South African Prime Minister, Field Marshal Jan Smuts, once told de Gaulle not to give too much importance to Churchill's frequent changes of mood. What de Gaulle ignored at his peril was the importance Churchill paid to personal relations. Intensely loyal to his friends, the Prime Minister reacted with corresponding anger when he felt that friendship to have been spurned or betrayed.[28]

In marked contrast to his predecessor, Churchill was Britain's leading Francophile. The young Winston had first visited France, where his mother had been brought up, at the age of eight. He would spend much more time there than in any other foreign country, making many French friends.[29] His command of the language was somewhat idiosyncratic. 'Et, marquez mes mots, mon ami,' he once told de Gaulle, 'si vous me double-crosserez, je vous liquiderai.'[30] But he had a deep knowledge of French history and an enduring sense of French greatness. Already before the First World War he had come to the conclusion that Britain could not be secure without a strong France, and during the inter-war years had pressed from both within and outside government the need for a treaty protecting France against unprovoked aggression. 'Some people,' he presciently warned Parliament in March 1939,

> talk as if it is fine and generous of us to go to the help of France. But I can assure you that in the pass to which things have come, we stand at least as much in need of the aid of France as the French do of the aid of Britain.[31]

Like Churchill, de Gaulle's career merged into the history of his country.[32] Fifteen years younger than the British Prime Minister, prior to 1940 Charles de Gaulle had pursued a military career. Described by Pétain, whose protégé he had originally been, as 'the most intelligent officer in the French army,' this was a man who impressed.[33] Philippe Serre, a French deputy and later minister, wrote of de Gaulle's 'Olympian side.' He had 'an authority, a command and an eloquence that compelled recognition straight away. He spoke with a kind of majesty, like someone who feels he is invested with a lofty mission.'[34] When, in 1936, the French Prime Minister Léon Blum invited de Gaulle to meet him, he found a man

> whose height, breadth and bulk had something gigantic about them: he walked in with an easy, placid calmness. Straight away one felt that he was 'all of a piece.' He was so in his physical being, and all his gestures seemed to move his body as a whole, without friction. He was so in his psychological behaviour.[35]

De Gaulle was a man of immense self-confidence and of great moral and physical courage. He had an iron will, a strong sense of history and a unique self-identification with France. If not a military leader of the first rank, his grasp of strategy was outstanding.[36] But he was also a man who polarised opinion. As Harold Nicolson's neat description of 'an eagle with bad habits' suggests, de Gaulle's virtues were also offset by some very notable vices.[37] His military superiors had quickly discovered that he was no easy subordinate, being a natural rebel, with an itch to challenge hierarchies of any description. 'Cantankerous,' 'damned awkward' and 'one of the most difficult people I have ever had to deal with,' were just some of the comments made about him by British ministers and officials. A man of heavy weather, happy only in squalls, he was aloof and arrogant, and, as the unfortunate BBC producer who had to tell him that no recording had been made of his first broadcast discovered, he had a foul temper.[38] British wits in North Africa in 1943 nicknamed him 'Charlie Wormwood' and 'Ramrod,' on the grounds that he had all the rigidity of a poker with none of its warmth.[39] He could show an intolerance for the opinion of others. More important, he was intensely suspicious. De Gaulle seemed unable to come across a muddle without seeing a conspiracy behind it. In contrast to Churchill, who was a bad hater, de Gaulle nursed grievances.

One other contrast to Churchill must be noted. While the British Prime Minister was a Francophile, de Gaulle was of an Anglophobe inheritance. An ancestor had reputedly been one of the knights attendant on Joan of Arc, and, according to Harold Macmillan, who got to know the General in North Africa in 1943, in moments of antipathy against the English, de Gaulle seemed 'almost physically to feel the hot, singeing fire of those burning flames.'[40] Born in 1890, he has been described as a man of the generation of the Anglo-French Entente Cordiale of 1904, which was signed when he was fourteen.[41] But he had also grown up during a period of acute Anglo-French imperial rivalry, epitomised in France by the Fashoda Incident of

1898. Anglophobe sentiment had been rife in the army officer corps which he joined in the early twentieth century. His interest in French history made him all too well aware of the defeats France had suffered at British hands, and on more than one occasion he referred to Britain as France's hereditary enemy. Nothing in British policy of the inter-war years served to undermine his suspicion of 'les Anglais.'[42]

A third actor needs to be introduced at this point. Although the USA did not enter the war until after the attack on Pearl Harbor in December 1941, its importance had been evident since at least May 1940. Asked by Churchill whether Britain could continue the war without France, the Chiefs of Staff had replied that without full American economic and financial support, 'we do not think we could continue the war with any chances of success.'[43] In his first broadcast on 18 June, de Gaulle cited the vast industrial resources of the USA in justification of his claim that the war could still be won. At Vichy, the seventy-seven-year-old Joseph Caillaux, who had been Prime Minister in 1911, advised the Foreign Minister, Paul Baudouin, to 'cultivate the US. The future is there.'[44]

What nobody in the early summer of 1940 foresaw was the permanency with which the 'special relationship' with Washington, which Churchill now assiduously set out to cultivate, would eclipse the Entente. Nor could anybody anticipate how the Americans would complicate British policy towards France, particularly regarding de Gaulle, for whom Roosevelt developed a visceral dislike. Where French ministers had in the 1930s been criticised for following the 'British nanny,' by the end of 1942, de Gaulle, along with senior Foreign Office figures, accused Churchill of subservience to the USA. The Anglo-French relationship had become a triangle.

Any account of Anglo-French relations must inevitably reflect the side of the Channel on which it is written. The official British records, while incomplete on intelligence matters, are nevertheless extensive. They underscore the fact that the British were often uniquely close and shrewd observers of the French wartime scene. The official voice, normally measured and controlled, at times condescending and exasperated, gives us a good reading of the emotional temperature of a relationship in which sympathy mingled with contempt. But it is, of course, only one side of the story. French perspectives on their former allies, intermittent adversaries and potential liberators are even more ambivalent, not least because of the divisions within France opened up by the defeat. Some admiring and hopeful, others hostile, resentful and suspicious, they were heavily influenced by lacerated pride. This was not simply a matter of the defeat itself but of its consequences –

the low esteem in which the French were often held, their dependence on the British and the extraordinarily unequal relationships this entailed, as well as their exclusion from the councils of the war. All this in turn put a heavy burden on British tact and understanding. In the words of a letter quoted in the BBC's bimonthly intelligence reports,

> profoundly wounded in her sense of honour ... France has failed in her historic mission. Morally, she will be a convalescent, infinitely sensitive. What tact the British – rightly proud of their admirable resistance – will need not to hurt our fellow countrymen, not to adopt towards them an attitude of superiority which French sensitivities would not accept.[45]

A British diplomat, Roger Makins, made much the same point when he wrote that 'our relations with the French require the skill of the psychiatrist as much as the experience of the diplomat.'[46]

Seen within the wider perspective of the history of Anglo-French relations in the twentieth century, the years of occupation are very much 'the best of times ... the worst of times,' a period of both unprecedented intimacy as well as a hostility not known since the end of the Napoleonic wars.[47] Between July 1940 and November 1942, Britain launched five attacks on Vichy French forces. Relations with the Free French were often characterised by suspicion, tension and frustration as both sides worked under intense stress, with emotions close to the surface, on occasion boiling over in spectacular fashion. Britain and the French were travelling very different journeys. For the British, who had lost a battle, the journey was clear: the continued prosecution of the conflict, which, if they were to win, must sooner or later bring their forces back to France. The French, who had lost a war, faced two radically different alternatives: accommodation with Germany, which was an obvious corollary not so much of defeat as defeatism, or de Gaulle's mission, which seemed quixotic in June 1940, to find a way back from defeat and to re-establish national dignity and self-respect. Paradoxically, both choices created tension with Britain.

In some respects, these wartime years feel distant. They are set on a cusp, at the end of Europe's long era of global pre-eminence and of that period of sea power in which battleships were of vital strategic importance. The Anglo-French wartime disputes over Syria and Lebanon belong to a forgotten world of colonial rivalries. Mindsets, as also language, particularly in the case of Churchill, are unfamiliar. Yet this is a chapter in the history of a war, which, albeit for very different reasons, continues to preoccupy both the British and the French into the twenty-first century, almost to the point of obsession.[48] The quarrels between Churchill and de Gaulle belong to the great dramas of the conflict.

What is more easily overlooked in a country for which the retreat from Dunkirk and the battle of Britain served to reinforce its sense of apartness from the mainland is that the close wartime involvement with France constitutes one of the most constructive and significant chapters in Britain's long relationship with Continental Europe. As Churchill had remarked on 20 August 1940, with Hitler 'sprawled over' the Continent, 'we have the honour to be the sole champion of the liberation of Europe.'[49] France was the most important of the countries to be liberated, and Britain's brief wartime role as a power in French affairs deserves to be highlighted.

# 2

# Historical Baggage

The English Channel – *La Manche,* or sleeve, as it is known in France – is one of Europe's smaller waterways. Only 21 miles wide at its narrowest point between Dover and Calais, it extends for some 350 miles west, with a maximum breadth of some 110 miles. For those living on its northern shore, the Channel, with its White Cliffs, is a peculiarly emblematic as well as absolute border. It has kept invaders at bay in a way which other European borders, such as the Rhine, have conspicuously failed to do. At the same time, it has also helped to shape a sense of insular identity, most famously celebrated in Gaunt's dying speech in Shakespeare's *Richard II,* making Britain a semi-detached European power.

> This fortress built by Nature for herself
> Against infection and the hand of war
> This happy breed of men, this little world
> This precious stone set in the silver sea,
> Which serves it in the office of a wall,
> Or as a moat defensive to a house,
> Against the envy of less happier lands.[1]

In her novel *The Children's Book,* A. S. Byatt describes the scene from a village on the south coast:

> a wild beach that looked across the Channel to France, which was sometimes visible as a shadowy strip in the sky, and sometimes hidden in mist or cloud, and now and then a lit, creamy line of solid rock, just distinguishable from bright cloud and wave crest.[2]

The political weather of the relationship between Britain and its nearest Continental neighbour could often seem as changeable as the elements. Historically, Anglo-French relations have been stormy and complex. Britain has of course had its Francophiles who have liked the French, admiring their culture, country and food, just as France has had its Anglophiles, who have admired British institutions and liberties. Even when relations have been bitter, commentators in England and France have recognised the other as in some ways a model, with both sides often reading, applauding, disagreeing with, copying and responding to each other in a constant exchange. Both countries tended to see themselves as joint leaders of civilisation, even though they sought to lead in different directions.[3]

Mutual fascination, however, always vied with suspicion, hostility and incomprehension. Over and above the obvious linguistic barrier are the differences of temperament and culture. 'When one crosses the Channel,' wrote General Victor Huguet, who had been French Military Attaché in London between 1904 and 1914, 'one finds oneself suddenly without any transition in contact with habits, customs and a cast of mind which are not only different in essence from ours, but are sometimes directly opposite.'[4] Or, as a British general put it, British and French minds are 'of a different texture. When the same problem is put to both they rarely produce the same answer.'[5]

More important than incomprehension and difference has been the blunt fact of mutual antipathy. Hostile stereotypes have been long entrenched on both sides of the Channel, and the two countries seemed to like each other as little as cat and dog. The French viewed the English – the term *les Anglais* (the English) was normally used rather than *les Britanniques* (the British) – as arrogant and haughty. England, in the words of Théophile Declassé, Foreign Minister at the beginning of the twentieth century, was 'the most domineering and violent of countries.'[6] The English were also seen as supremely egoistic, pursuing a policy of narrow self-interest clothed in high moral purpose (a complaint in turn often made by the British about the French).[7] The English were widely viewed as *perfide*. The term 'perfidious Albion' was originally religious in connotation – a reference to England's lapse from Rome in the sixteenth century – but its associations in later years were with duplicity and hypocrisy. 'Perfidious?' de Gaulle's father is reported as saying. 'The adjective hardly seems strong enough.'[8]

For their part, the English, never overly fond of any foreigners, could be rude and patronising. Queen Victoria complained that the French were 'so fickle, corrupt and ignorant, so conceited and foolish that it is hopeless to think of their being sensibly governed.'[9] Lord Palmerston bemoaned French vanity and unreliability. 'You can't trust them from one week to another, or even from one day to the next.' Undependability, sometimes expressed in the crude adage 'Never trust a Froggy,' was to prove something of a leitmotif in British Francophobia.[10]

The roots of this antipathy go back to the Hundred Years' War. The French countryside had been systematically ravaged in this fourteenth-century conflict, which saw the growth of nationalist feelings on both sides, laying down what one historian describes as a 'particularly luxuriant seedbed of nationalist prejudices.'[11] The English came to regard the French as their natural prey, developing feelings of hatred and contempt for them. The French brooded for centuries over the consequences of defeat and the iniquities of the invaders. When, in the spring of 1944, in the run-up to the D-Day landings, the RAF bombed Tours, the gossip among the locals was that the English were systematically bombing the towns through which Joan of Arc had passed.[12]

In succeeding centuries Anglo-French conflict variously took dynastic, religious, commercial, imperial and, after the French Revolution, ideological form. Another particularly acute phase, known as the second hundred years' war by historians, opened in 1689, ending only with Napoleon's defeat in 1815. France was by far the stronger party, with twice the territory and gross national product and three times Britain's population.[13] Britain suffered a major reverse in the War of American Independence of 1776–83, when the French took a dazzling revenge for their defeat in the Seven Years' War twenty years earlier. In 1804, Napoleon concentrated an invasion force of some 165,000 troops along the Channel coast from Etaples to Antwerp. On clear days, French troops could be seen drilling, and panicky residents deserted Eastbourne.[14] But the British did very well out of this final cycle of Anglo-French wars. Conflict with Catholic France saw the emergence of Britain as a Great Power and helped cement a sense of Protestant British identity in the wake of the 1707 Union with Scotland.[15] The British Empire was significantly enlarged at French expense. By the time of Waterloo, Britain had established a permanent ascendancy in an Anglo-French duel which had lasted almost five centuries. Trafalgar and Waterloo, which today provide the names of two of London's main landmarks, joined a roll-call of British victories, stretching back to Agincourt. Small wonder if French Anglophobia often seems tinged not just with dislike but with fear and a sense of aggrievement.

After 1815, attempts were made to end this cycle of hostility, and in the 1840s there was already talk of an *entente cordiale*. The two countries entered into an alliance against Russia during the Crimean War of the mid-1850s, and an 1860 commercial treaty was intended to promote friendship as well as trade. French political refugees continued to come to Britain, as they had done since Huguenot times. But Anglo-French relations during the nineteenth century were a matter of coexistence rather than friendship, and the mid-century decades were marked by a succession of crises and war scares.[16] Imperial rivalry continued unabated. French proponents of expansion in Africa regarded the more powerful British Empire as a constant threat. A note written in 1890 by two French authorities on the trans-Saharan railways complained that with European Powers claiming spheres of influence in Africa,

> As always Britain is getting the lion's share. Britain, the great insatiable Britain, not content with its Asiatic Indies, with its Dominion of Canada, with its Australian Empire, with its vast possessions in South and East Africa, wishes to snatch from us Central Sudan and dreams of establishing its economic supremacy not only northward from the Great Lakes to Egypt and southward to the Cape, but westward also to Timbuctoo.[17]

Eight years later, the two countries nearly came to blows at Fashoda, an abandoned mud-built fort in the Sudan. Forced to withdraw, the French felt angered and humiliated. The nationalist press charged the British with arrogance, bullying and hypocrisy, with Albion being depicted in one leading humorous journal as a bird of prey. The outbreak of the Boer War the following year poured yet more oil onto the Anglophobe fire.[18]

What finally brought the two enemies together was, in classical fashion, the rise of a new European power. The wars of German unification in the 1860s had culminated in the French defeat at Sedan in 1870. British public sympathies at the outset of the Franco-Prussian War had been against the French, but the rapid Prussian victories had led to a shift of support in favour of France, and British volunteers had fought on the French side. 'The balance of power,' Disraeli declared, 'has been entirely destroyed and the country that suffers most is England.'[19] But it was only at the beginning of the new century, with the emergence of a German battle fleet designed to challenge the predominance of the Royal Navy, that the British became sufficiently anxious to enter into secret Anglo-French staff talks to discuss the help they might provide France in the event of a land war in Europe. The Entente Cordiale of 1904, which was originally a settlement of colonial disputes, now developed into something much more serious.

From its outset, however, the Entente had a fissure, or flaw, which was to be brutally exposed in the crisis of 1940. Britain and France faced a common threat, but the danger to France, with its land border with Germany, was greater and more immediate than the threat facing Europe's off-shore power. The British had a constant tendency to overestimate the margin of security, and, in consequence, the freedom of diplomatic manoeuvre, which the Channel conferred. Although, as one senior Foreign Office official admitted as early as 1911, Britain was no longer strong enough to stand alone, ministers insisted that no commitments were entailed, and in the absence of anything in writing, French war planners assumed that they could not count on British cooperation.[20] When the crisis triggered by the assassination of the Archduke Ferdinand at Sarajevo on 28 June 1914 led to the mobilisation of the Continental Powers, the British Cabinet hesitated, causing the French Ambassador to ask bitterly 'whether the word "honour" should not be struck out of the English vocabulary.'[21] But Britain entered the war on 4 August, and the BEF was rapidly despatched across the Channel.

All roads now seemed to lead to France. Parts of Picardy were to become a British graveyard, while the names of some of its villages, and above all one river – the Somme – were to become etched into the British consciousness. It took four years of gruelling and often gruesome trench warfare before the British and French armies, supported after 1917 by the Americans, were able to defeat the formidable German war machine. The BEF expanded from an initial five to some sixty divisions, some 2 million British soldiers, plus another 700,000 Indian and Dominion troops.[22] With British and French armies fighting side by side, their commanders had to learn to work together. Politicians had to get used to frequent Channel crossings and to doing business face to face. Gradually, the machinery of Anglo-French economic, as well as political and military cooperation, was put into place. A Supreme War Council was established, and by the end of the war there was even a supreme allied commander, in the form of a French general.[23]

Yet these remained two armies, fighting what seemed to be separate wars. In 1915 and 1916 French troops were often unaware that British units were fighting only a mile away, and no real sense of solidarity emerged from the ordeal.[24] On the contrary, there were accusations that each party was bearing an insufficient part of the burden, while failures to respond to requests for help at times of particular danger created a new set of grievances. The French complained that the British would fight to the 'last Frenchman' and were always looking for an opportunity to scuttle to the Channel ports. The British complained that the French were irreducibly selfish.[25]

Nor did the massive British presence create any real new bonds. Until the summer of 1918, this was a static war, with the BEF confined to three north-western departments of France. The majority of French people never saw any British soldiers. In those areas where the British were stationed they seemed at once omnipresent and apart. The Tommies kept to themselves, as Edward Spears (then a British liaison officer with the French army, who was to play a more prominent role in the Second World War) later put it, 'uninquisitive and detached, insular even when overseas, preserving their own habits and secure in their own routines.'[26]

Thus, while the 'Great War,' as it was then known, had created an important strategic precedent, it had not created any lasting Anglo-French friendship nor broken down the traditional distrust the two sides felt for one another. Returning to Oxford after the war, the poet Robert Graves found that anti-French feeling among undergraduates back from the trenches amounted almost to an obsession.[27]

None of this boded well for the decidedly unequal post-war relationship, in which the French constantly seemed to be getting the worst of the deal. Britain and France might both be Great Powers, but France had much the smaller empire and economy. Its share of world manufacturing output in 1929 was 6.6 per cent compared with Britain's 9.4 per cent. By 1938, the year of the Munich Crisis, this had shrunk to 4.5 per cent, compared with Britain's 9.2 per cent. Of the major powers, its relative war potential for 1937 was less than half that of Britain.[28] Although France maintained one of Europe's largest armies, the sense of insecurity left by the war made it desperately anxious for the British military guarantee which was never forthcoming. If France, which had lost 1,327,000 lives had been 'biologically exhausted' by the experience of the trenches, the British, whose losses – some 723,000 dead – amounted to just over half this figure, had been psychologically scarred by a war of attrition which had produced so little in terms of tangible territorial gains. The war memorials which now appeared in villages and towns across the country overshadowed any memory that, as a 1915 General Staff paper put it, 'in the most literal sense ... we are defending England in France,' let alone an appreciation that the seeds of the German defeat had been sown in the mud of the Somme.[29]

Unhelpful to the French on land, the British seemed to lord it over their neighbours at sea. The French felt humiliated by their treatment at the 1921 Washington Naval Conference, where Aristide Briand, the only head of government leading a delegation, could not find a seat among the

Great Power delegates and was forced to sit with the British Dominions. The British, Americans and Japanese then proceeded to exclude the French from discussion of the ratio of capital ships. In the final accounting, the French, along with the Italians, were allowed 1.75 capital ships to Japan's three and Britain's and America's five each. French naval sensitivities were again hurt at the London Naval Conference of 1930, where a French delegate, Rear Admiral François Darlan, complained of sitting opposite large pictures of Trafalgar and Waterloo during the opening session in the House of Lords.[30]

More bad blood was created by British policy in the Middle East, which had been a source of Anglo-French rivalry since the time of Napoleon. In 1915, Britain and France had signed the Sykes–Picot agreement covering the future of part of the Ottoman Empire, which had allied itself with Germany. This provided for French control of the whole of Lebanon and Syria. But at the Versailles Peace Conference Britain had sought to water down the arrangement, abrogating French control of Syria in favour of an Arab kingdom. Tempers ran high, and Clemenceau at one point accused Lloyd George of being a cheat. The British thought the French impertinent to interfere in an area which did not concern them, while the French were determined to make clear that they were not British satellites. Eventually France gained League of Nations mandates for Lebanon and Syria.[31] But suspicions of British intentions in the region remained high among local French officials during the 1920s and 1930s, a point reflected in the report of a French commander in the Levant:

> Everywhere from Aden to Alexandretta, England is, perhaps through the activity of her local agents rather than in the execution of a general plan, engaged in activities every day and in every way, which are tending to undermine and cramp French influence, to destroy our traditional position and to eliminate us from the East.[32]

Hitler's advent to power in 1933 was slow to revive Anglo-French cooperation. There was a mutual reluctance to face up to the reality of the renewed German threat, a reluctance exacerbated by dislike and distrust. During the initial crises of the 1930s – Mussolini's war in Abyssinia and the 1936 German reoccupation of the Rhineland – both sides were quick not just to blame the other but to use them as an excuse for inaction.[33] A dependency culture was developing in France, which, in the words of one French critic, was constantly looking for an English lead. For their part, the

British saw France, wracked by political instability and in apparent economic decline, as not a very desirable ally. And yet they continued to use France, with its network of East European alliances, as the shield behind which they maintained themselves in Europe.[34] With the financially straitened British rearmament effort giving priority to the RAF and Royal Navy, and a new BEF ruled out on political grounds, what else could they do?

The picture of British policy to France which emerges during this period is not an attractive one. The British took the French for granted, often seeming high-handed and condescending and giving the French frequent cause for complaint.[35] Having agreed with London a few months previously on the principle of joint negotiations with Germany of any armaments agreements, the French were taken aback in 1935 at the signature of an Anglo-German naval treaty. 'If the French are nasty,' the Secretary of the Cabinet, Maurice Hankey, minuted, 'we must put the strongest pressure on them ... they cannot do without us. We are the soundest, the solidest, and the most reliable people in Europe, as well as potentially the strongest – and the French know it.'[36]

More serious was the Anglo-French rift over Abyssinia. The two countries had secretly negotiated a settlement that ceded much of the territory to Mussolini. When details of the Hoare–Laval pact, named after the British Foreign Secretary Sir Samuel Hoare and the French Prime Minister Pierre Laval, were revealed in the French press, there was an outcry in Britain, forcing the government to repudiate the deal and Hoare to resign. A ferocious outburst of Anglophobia followed. The British were accused of being a nation of hypocrites, only out for their own interests. 'I hate these people,' wrote the Anglophobe Henri Béraud, in a series of articles which were reprinted in pamphlet form. 'I say and I repeat that England must be reduced to slavery, since in truth the nature of the Empire consists in oppressing and humiliating other peoples.'[37]

So long as British policy remained dominated by the search for a political settlement with Germany, consideration for France was inevitably limited, while Francophobe prejudices could be given rein. The point was clearly underscored by the Munich Crisis of September 1938. Czechoslovakia was one of France's key East European allies, but the diplomacy with Hitler was dominated by Neville Chamberlain, who appears hardly even to have spoken to his French opposite number during the Munich Conference.[38] It was only in the autumn of 1938 that the British finally began to realise that France could no longer be taken for granted. The Foreign Secretary, Lord Halifax, warned of the danger that the French might become so defeatist

22

as to give up the struggle to maintain adequate defences, leaving Britain to face alone 'the weight of German military power in the West.'[39] A few months later the Chiefs of Staff advised that it was hard to see how the security of the British Isles could be maintained if France were forced to surrender. In February 1939, therefore, the Cabinet authorised the creation of a Continental-style army of thirty-two divisions.[40] The following month, when Hitler violated the Munich Agreement, Chamberlain responded with British guarantees to Poland. Conscription, which the French had long been urging, was announced in April.

When the final crisis, over Danzig, finally broke in the late summer, it was Britain that took the lead in the historic decision forcibly to oppose this German expansionism. Both countries entered the war reluctantly: Chamberlain's broadcast of 3 September was that of a tired, dispirited and indeed defeated man. But there was an ominous difference between London and Paris. The British, buoyed in part by the sense of security provided by the Channel, believed that they would win and that their victory would somehow attain a better world. The mood in France, sapped by political divisions of the 1930s and the memories of the terrible losses of the last war, was one of deep pessimism, making France particularly vulnerable to a major military reverse.[41] Given that France provided Britain's forward line of defence, as well as being its main ally, the British had more reason for unease than they may have realised.

With the outbreak of the new war, the cooperative machinery built up during the previous conflict, including the Supreme War Council, was quickly re-established. A unified military command was set up again under a French general, while arrangements for economic cooperation were also resumed. On 28 March 1940, the two countries agreed not to negotiate an armistice or peace settlement except by mutual agreement, nor to discuss peace terms before agreeing to conditions necessary for their long-term security. In a broadcast a week later, Churchill spoke of the two countries being 'joined together in indissoluble union.'[42]

Anglo-French strategy, meanwhile, remained purely defensive. The British had no option. The new BEF, which was quickly despatched to France, was originally only four divisions strong and was badly trained and equipped. It was short of artillery, radios and modern maps; its armour only arrived in May 1940. On the eve of the German attack, the British still had only ten divisions on the Western Front, compared with 104 French divisions.[43] But having invested heavily in the defensive doctrines quite literally embodied in the Maginot Line, the French were psychologically unprepared to take the offensive. Both countries feared a repetition of the carnage of the previous war. For the time being, therefore, pressure on Germany was to be maintained by way of an economic blockade.[44]

The Allies maintained their defensive complacency into the spring. 'We cannot ignore the possibility of the main German attack being directed against France,' a British assessment of 4 May 1940 noted. 'In this eventuality we estimate that there are sufficient land forces to maintain the security of French territory against both Germany and Italy, if adequate air protection is provided.'[45] Belief in the French ground forces was an article of faith for most British army figures, although not everybody agreed with this convenient consensus. They included a corps commander, General Sir Alan Brooke, and the Chief of the Imperial General Staff.[46] An inspection of French forces in January 1940 did not reassure General Sir Edmund Ironside. Nothing seemed amiss on the surface:

> The Generals are all tried men, if a bit old from our view-point. None of them showed any lack of confidence. None of the liaison officers say they have seen any lack of morale after the long wait they have had, after the excitement of mobilisation. I say to myself that we shall not know till the first clash comes. In 1914 there were many officers and soldiers who failed but old Joffre handled the situation with great firmness. Will the *Blitzkrieg* when it comes allow us to rectify things if they are the same? I must say I don't know. But I say to myself that we must have confidence in the French army. It is the only thing in which we can have confidence. Our own army is just a little one and we are dependent on the French. We have not even the same fine army we had in 1914. All depends on the French army and we can do nothing about it.[47]

Yet, despite this reference to *Blitzkrieg*, there was an almost complete failure to take account of the daring and ambition of the enemy. Hitler had given orders for an attack on the west, aimed at the 'complete annihilation' of British and French forces, shortly after the successful conclusion of the Polish campaign in the autumn of 1939. The plan, which had eventually emerged, was based in part on a careful study of British and French weakness, notably their difficult in responding rapidly to surprises.[48] It departed radically from the conventional thinking which the British and French appear to have anticipated. Operation Sichelschnitt was designed to outflank the Maginot Line through the thickly wooded hills of Ardennes and then to overwhelm French forces through the combined use of armour and airpower.

The plan succeeded brilliantly. Assuming that the main thrust of the German attack lay to the north, the French and British armies moved into Belgium. But the centre-point of the German attack was on the Meuse. Here some of the best units in the German army had little difficulty in defeating the second-ranking French reserve units defending the crossings at Sedan, scene of a French defeat in 1870. Reynaud spoke of the hard point of the German lance having gone through the French troops 'as through a sand-hill.' A contemporary commentator likened the German advance to the coast to that of the Martians in H. G. Wells's *The War of the Worlds*.[49]

The moral impact on the French was crippling. A mood of defeatism quickly gripped the French High Command and seemed to spread to the whole of the country. Oliver Harvey, who was Minister at the British Embassy in Paris, was struck at 'the lack of holy wrath among the French. No blood seems to be boiling at the thought of the invader on French soil.'[50] Spears, who was a friend of Churchill's and was now appointed as his special representative to Reynaud, wrote of 'the mainspring of France's psychological mechanism being broken.' At a meeting of the French War Cabinet on 25 May, the French Commander-in-Chief, General Maxime Weygand, described the situation as impossible and hopeless.[51]

Britain in turn faced a worst possible case scenario against which no contingency plans had been made. The prevailing assumption, shared by senior ministers such as Halifax and Chamberlain (who was still a member of the Cabinet), and indeed by Churchill, was that Britain could not survive the fall of France.[52] But it was an assumption that had never been subject to rigorous analysis. With British backs to the wall, the Chiefs of Staff were now asked to examine whether it really held good. Their response, contained in a paper coyly entitled 'British Strategy in a Certain Eventuality,' made for what Churchill later described as 'grave and grim' reading. Assuming that air superiority could be maintained, it concluded that Britain had a fighting chance of survival if France fell, although, as noted in the previous chapter, the prospect of ultimate victory was dependent on an increasing cooperation with the USA.[53]

This document was essential briefing for the crucial meetings of the War Cabinet held between 26 and 28 May against the background of the increasingly desperate position of the BEF in France, when the question of whether to investigate the possibility of a negotiated peace via the Italians was debated. The idea, advocated by the French, was supported by Halifax. Churchill did not exclude this, saying that he would jump at the chance of getting out of this mess by giving up Malta, Gibraltar and some African colonies. But he warned that this would only be possible once Hitler had been convinced that Britain could not be beaten. The debate became at times heated, with Halifax at one point threatening resignation and Churchill declaring 'that the nations which went down fighting rose again, but those which surrendered tamely were finished.'[54] Churchill won the argument. This effectively closed the question, which was not reopened in the wake of the French surrender three weeks later.

Events continued to move swiftly. Belgium had capitulated by 28 June, and by 4 June some 224,301 men of the BEF, along with 111,172 French and Belgian troops, had been successfully evacuated from Dunkirk. It was in announcing this news that Churchill had told Parliament that Britain would fight on in France and on the seas, and defend their island, 'whatever the cost may be ... we shall never surrender.'[55] These last four words are engraved under the statue of Churchill that stands in Paris today. On 5 June, the Germans began a new offensive south of the Somme which within a week would bring them to Paris. Churchill now sought to square a circle, trying to 'help the French in the battle without hurting ourselves mortally, and in a way that will encourage the French to feel that we are doing all in our power.'[56] But the French needed far more than the essentially symbolic support that Britain could now safely provide. Only one division, along with some 100,000 line of communications troops, had been left in France after Dunkirk, and although Churchill had agreed to send a new BEF, the timetable was totally unrealistic. 'Our intention,' he cabled Roosevelt on 11 June, 'is to have a strong army fighting in France for the campaign of 1941.'[57] The crisis, however, was at hand, and the commander of the new force, General Sir Alan Brooke, estimated that two complete armies would have been required to exert any influence on the military situation. In the event, Brooke, who arrived in France on 12 June, was forced to withdraw a mere six days later.[58]

Nor could Britain meet the even more insistent demands for more aircraft, for which the French had been pressing ever since the Germans first crossed the Meuse. Britain simply did not have enough fighters to help France and to ensure its own defence in the increasingly likely event of French defeat. The question highlights the difference in Anglo-French perspectives opened up by the crisis. In French eyes, the battle for France was decisive, and all British aircraft should therefore be committed to it. 'If France falls,' as Jean Monnet, Chairman of the Franco-British Economic Coordinating Committee, put it, 'all fall.'[59] Churchill bluntly dissented. Britain, with what Weygand called its powerful anti-tank trap in the form of the Channel, and which Churchill described as that 'priceless twenty miles of salt water which separated us from the Continent,' could, and indeed must look beyond the battle for France. As the Prime Minister had earlier put it to the Cabinet, if Britain was beaten, France became 'a vassal state; but if we won, we might save them.'[60]

This position did not come easily to Churchill, who in the great crisis of modern Anglo-French relations showed an imaginative sympathy for Britain's ally conspicuously lacking from earlier phases of British policy. Spears describes the Prime Minister as 'haunted and tortured by watching the martyrdom of the people he liked so well.'[61] Besides, Churchill was all too well aware of the French feeling that the British were not pulling their weight. It was on the Prime Minister's insistence that substantial numbers of French troops had been taken off the beaches at Dunkirk, even though the British Force Commander had signalled that 'every Frenchman embarked is at [the] cost of one Englishman.'[62] This did not stop the French, who were also all too conscious of British contempt for their strategy and conduct of the crisis, seeing Dunkirk as a needless and perfidious betrayal.[63]

The niggardly nature of subsequent British help only made things worse. Paul Baudouin, Reynaud's *chef du cabinet*, described by Harvey as 'a sinister man, ignorant of foreign affairs,' recorded in his diary for 6 June that the French Prime Minister 'is fated every morning for an hour or more to obtain British help which, in spite of his efforts, does not materialize. There can be no doubt but that if this fact were not carefully concealed from the public there would soon be a violent outbreak of Anglophobia.'[64] Pétain complained bitterly about the British to the American Ambassador, William Bullitt, while General Weygand spoke darkly about Churchill playing a 'double game' and abandoning France to her fate.[65]

In a letter written on 11 June, Lord Beaverbrook, the Minister of Aircraft Production, likened Churchill to Atlas 'with two worlds to carry. With one hand he bears up the British Empire and with the other he sustains the French Republic. And the French Republic takes a bit of supporting too, let me tell you.'[66] The Prime Minister remained tireless in his exhortations that Britain would fight on and that the French should continue resistance, whether from a redoubt in Brittany, by guerrilla warfare or from the French Empire. 'Go on reiterating that we shall carry on, whatever they do,' he told Spears. 'If they have lost faith in themselves, let them develop faith in us and in our determination. We will carry them, as well as everything else, or,' he added presciently, 'we will carry those who will let themselves be carried.'[67]

But by the end of the second week of June, French defeatism was well advanced. The situation was worsened by an extraordinary exodus of refugees fleeing in the path of the German advance. The shock of a defeat for which they had been totally unprepared, combined with fear of bombing and memories of German behaviour in previous Franco-German wars, led between 6 and 10 million people, many from the Paris region, to abandon their homes. As Helen Diamond notes, more people were on the move 'than at any time in previously recorded history, probably since the Dark Ages.'[68] France, in the words of the novelist, Antoine de Saint-Exupéry, seemed to be displaying 'the sordid disorder of a scattered ant-hill,' and Weygand, fearing social anarchy, began to press ever more insistently for an armistice.[69] Memories of disturbances and revolution sparked by previous defeats, including the Paris Commune of 1871, loomed large, as did the need to keep the army from disintegration.[70] Against this background, Churchill's eloquent words cut little ice, and promises that we will 'win it all back for you' were met with incredulity. In Pétain stark words, 'You have no army. What could you achieve where the French army has failed?'[71] At the last meeting of the Supreme War Council at Tours on 13 June, the French asked Britain to release them from their undertaking not to seek a separate peace. By 15 June even Churchill seemed close to despair.[72]

The Prime Minister had two final, albeit very long shots in his locker. One was American intervention, which at this stage in the war was politically completely unrealistic. The second was an initiative born of a combination of desperation and imagination. The idea of an Anglo-French union had been hatched in London over the previous few days by a group of British and French officials. They included two French figures later closely involved in the European integration movement, René Pleven and Jean Monnet, as well as Sir Arthur Salter, who had worked with Monnet on the creation of an Allied Wheat Executive during the First World War. On 14 June, Leo Amery, the Secretary of State for India, forwarded to Churchill a memorandum by Arthur Salter in which the latter warned that the French would only continue the struggle if they felt that Britain and France were 'fighting as one country.'[73] Severed from France and deprived of its help, Salter also warned, the British people may well feel that 'they cannot continue the struggle in isolation with any hope of victory.'[74] Amery also added another consideration. The French might well fear that a government in exile would lose status and be looked upon as a poor relation. That might be remedied if a standing Supreme War Cabinet, along with an Anglo-French General Staff were established on their arrival in Britain.[75]

Churchill was understandably sceptical, but the need for a dramatic gesture to help Reynaud hold his wavering cabinet together was pressed on him by the visiting French Under-Secretary for War, Charles de Gaulle. In the afternoon of 16 June, therefore, the Cabinet agreed a far-reaching, if vaguely defined proposal, which included the creation of joint organs of defence, foreign, financial and economic policies, a single war cabinet and common citizenship.[76] John Colville, Churchill's secretary, recorded the extraordinary scene in No. 10 Downing Street, as the Cabinet meeting

> turned into a sort of promenade … Winston beginning a speech in the Cabinet room and finishing it in Morton's room, and everybody has been slapping de Gaulle on the back and telling him he shall be Commander in Chief (Winston muttering, *Je l'arrangerai*).[77]

Nothing is more eloquent of the sense of desperation created by the imminent collapse of France than that a British Cabinet should, after only brief deliberation, have approved so far-reaching a document.

De Gaulle immediately telephoned an enthusiastic Reynaud on a line which, presumably unbeknownst to him, was being tapped on the orders of Weygand.[78] But the French Prime Minister gained little support for a proposal which most of his ministers regarded as coming too late as well as being ill prepared and totally irrelevant to France's situation. The French had lost confidence in Britain. They feared that if they accepted they would pay the price when Britain, as was widely expected, sued for peace. Anglophobia was on the rise in Bordeaux, and old suspicions were resurfacing, reflected in fear of suffocation in the proffered British embrace and becoming 'a British dominion.'[79] Such *arrière-pensées* scarcely boded well for the future of Anglo-French relations.

It was the end of the road for Anglophile Reynaud, as indeed for the Entente. Pétain, who had described the Anglo-French union as "a marriage with a corpse" had for some time been arguing the need to put French interests before those of the Anglo-French alliance.[80] At one o'clock on the morning of 17 June, the new Foreign Minister, Paul Baudouin, informed the British Ambassador, Sir Ronald Campbell, that France would seek an armistice. This time, however, there was no attempt to gain British acquiescence to release France from its undertaking not to accept a separate peace. Although the Permanent Under-Secretary at the French Foreign Office, François Charles-Roux, describes Campbell as very calm and avoiding all recrimination, Baudouin was evidently uneasy. 'The stiffness of our nocturnal conversation,' he recorded in his diary, 'was terrible.'[81] This was scarcely surprising. The French were abandoning an alliance which they saw as having failed them in their hour of need, and in the process leaving their ex-allies open to attack. Each side felt the other had let them down.[82] There would be no amicable separation.

# Part I

## Hitler's *Diktat*

# 3

# A Ruthlessly Aggressive Act

On 15 June, the day before Reynaud's resignation, the Foreign Office had issued a circular telegram stating that in the event of France's collapse, everything possible would be done to prevent French naval, military and air equipment falling into enemy hands, as well as to encourage 'any elements we can to join our forces.'[1] One of the copies surviving in the official files bears an undated pencilled note that 'virtually none of this has come off.'[2] In the third week of June 1940, the future of Anglo-French relations was effectively in Hitler's hands. The Italian Foreign Minister, Count Galeazzo Ciano, who met the German Führer on 18 June, compared him to a gambler 'who has made a big scoop and would like to get up from the table risking nothing more.'[3] Having knocked France out of the war, Hitler's immediate objective was to consolidate his victory, so as to be able to pursue the war against England. To this end he was ready to concede a 'lenient' peace.[4] Anxious to prevent the Pétain government following the Norwegian, Danish and Dutch examples and fleeing to London, from where they could formally continue resistance, Hitler was ready to allow a nominally independent French administration to function in an Unoccupied Zone in the south of the country.[5] The French would thus also assume part of what Hitler described as 'the unpleasant responsibility' in the administrative sphere, which the Germans would otherwise have had to take over. A small army would be able to maintain order during the final assault against England.[6]

Concern about Britain explains another of Hitler's 'concessions.' The German navy was very much the Cinderella of the German services. It had lost heavily in the Norwegian campaign and would have liked to have got its hands on French ships, just as it would have liked to have gained access to French overseas bases such as Dakar in West Africa.[7] But in purely practical terms the Germans could not have manned the French vessels, which had in any case been moved from the Channel and Biscay ports as the Germans advanced along the coast, with orders to scuttle should the Germans try to seize them. Control of the navy was the one issue over which France was prepared to break off the Armistice talks.[8]

This was precisely what Hitler did not want. According to the explanation he gave Mussolini, he was particularly concerned to prevent the Royal Navy gaining access to French destroyers, which would facilitate convoy work, allowing Britain to supply itself without difficulty and transport troops to

> all sorts of places (from Egypt to Portugal), thus maintaining or creating a series of theatres of operation. The result would be a long war and the impossibility of striking the enemy decisively ... That being so, it would not be well to demand purely and simply that the French surrender their fleet. France will not agree to that and, as against the very slight probability that the French may sink the Fleet, there would be the much greater probability that they would send it to join the British fleet. It will be better, therefore, to demand that they assemble the fleet in such a way that it cannot be moved or dispersed, either in French ports under control or in neutral ports (preferably Spanish). Furthermore, it seems wise to leave France the hope of regaining her fleet once peace has been made. Once England has been defeated and we come to the making of the peace, we shall see.[9]

Under Article 8 of the Armistice the French were thus allowed to retain possession of a disarmed fleet, with all ships demobilised at their peacetime stations, two-thirds of which were within the German-occupied zone, under German or Italian supervision. The Germans solemnly declared that they would not use the vessels, other than some coastal craft, for their own purposes for the duration of the war.[10]

Like the fleet, the French Empire lay largely beyond Hitler's reach. Following the heavy losses the Germans had incurred during the battle of France and the threat posed by the RAF, even with Italian naval support, a German landing in North Africa in the summer and autumn of 1940 would have been very difficult. Besides, Hitler's interest lay in Europe and in the east rather than in Africa and the Mediterranean. (The question of former German colonies lost in 1918 could be left until the final peace treaty.) Far better therefore to subcontract the task of keeping their empire out of British hands to the French government.[11]

It was thus in large part thanks to the British determination to fight on that France escaped the fate of Poland. The signature on 23 June of the

Armistice was widely welcomed in a country which had already lost more than 100,000 dead and had no taste for continued resistance. It was in any case viewed as a purely temporary arrangement which would be replaced by a peace treaty as soon as Britain had withdrawn from the war. Once this happened, Darlan informed his officers, the area of German occupation would be reduced.[12] Meanwhile, the fleet remained as a valuable potential bargaining chip. It also provided the means of defending an empire which would allow France to compensate for at least some of its losses of manpower, territory and resources while also sustaining its decidedly dubious claims to remain a Great Power. Despite the magnitude of their defeat, the French could yet hope to recover, as they had done after their defeat of 1870.[13]

For Britain, too, the Armistice had advantages. It kept vital French residual assets out of German hands, and also, according to the Foreign Office, helped keep the Iberian Peninsula out of the war.[14] This, however, was not how things were seen at the time. Campbell described the Armistice as 'diabolically clever.'[15] In a broadcast on 23 June 1940, Churchill declared that he had heard 'with grief and amazement' that the French had accepted terms dictated by the Germans, which must compromise their 'freedom, independence and constitutional authority.' His comments to the War Cabinet were even more scathing. Britain could not maintain relations with a government which had broken its 'pledged word as an ally, placed a large part of French territory under German control and surrendered a great quantity of military material which will now be used against Great Britain.'[16] The French government was now completely under the German thumb, and Britain must expect to become 'the object of the deepest hatred of France.'[17]

It was in this frame of mind that the Cabinet sought to grapple with the most immediate threat posed by the French defection: the future of the large and modern French fleet. While Hitler worried about the British gaining control of French destroyers, the British worried about French capital ships falling into German hands. The *Strasbourg* and the *Dunkerque* were faster than any British battle cruiser, except possibly the *Hood.* In the view of the Chiefs of Staff it was of paramount importance that the uncertainty regarding these ships should be dissipated as soon as possible so that the British vessels following them should be released to defend against the imminent threat of invasion. Churchill believed if they fell under German control that the two most modern French battleships, the *Richelieu* and the *Jean Bart,* might alter the whole course of the war.[18]

Concern about the future of the French fleet had already begun to be voiced in late May. By 16 June, with a French collapse imminent, the British government was sufficiently worried to consider releasing France from its obligation not to make a separate peace with Germany, on condition that the fleet sailed for British ports, a concession subsequently superseded by the Anglo-French union offer.[19] With the Armistice, the key figure was the new Minister of Marine, Admiral Darlan. Described by one British naval officer as a typical French sailor, short, sturdy, tanned and smoking a pipe, Darlan was an ambitious naval officer who had been closely involved with the modernisation of the French fleet in the 1930s. Although he supported the Entente as a necessary alliance, he was, as already noted, acutely conscious of the French navy's historic rivalry with the Royal Navy. Indeed, at a dinner at the Admiralty in 1939 he had reminded his hosts that his great-grandfather had been killed at Trafalgar. Darlan had, however, established formal if cordial relations with Churchill on the latter's return to the Admiralty in September 1939, and privately welcomed his appointment as Prime Minister.[20] He had earlier talked about the possibility of sending the fleet to British ports. Now, however, the Admiral had changed his mind.

In Churchill's eyes, Darlan had made a capital mistake.

He had only to sail in any one of his ships to any port outside France to become the master of all French interests beyond German control. He would not have come, like General de Gaulle, with only an unconquerable heart and a few kindred spirits. He would have carried with him outside the German reach the fourth Navy in the world, whose officers and men were personally devoted to him. Acting thus, Darlan would have become the chief of the French Resistance with a mighty weapon in his hand. British and American dockyards and arsenals would have been at his disposal ... The French gold reserves in the United States would have assured him, once recognised, of ample resources. The whole French Empire would have rallied to him.[21]

That was not how Darlan saw it. He had not, as he was reported to have remarked later, created a fleet in order to hand it to the British, nor had he any intention of putting himself under British command. An opportunist rather than a gambler, he lacked Churchill's faith in British victory and was determined to ensure that this vital French asset remained in French hands. He was happy to give Britain assurances that the Germans would be prevented from gaining the French ships. 'So long as I can issue orders you have nothing to fear,' he had said. But that was as far as he was prepared to go.[22]

Darlan, however, had miscalculated. London and Bordeaux were living in different worlds, with increasingly poor communications between them, particularly after Campbell had left France immediately after the signature of the Armistice.[23] French ministers, gripped by the trauma of defeat, failed to take the measure of their former ally's anger and determination. To Pétain and Weygand, Churchill's rhetoric was simply a matter of words. Nor could the leaders of a country which put so much store by land power appreciate the threat their fleet posed to a sea power. They could not see their navy as the British saw it, namely as that very rare and dangerous phenomenon: a powerful fleet under the control of a very weak state.

French assurances were not dismissed out of hand. Senior Royal Navy officers in the Mediterranean believed that there was in fact little risk of the French allowing the fleet to fall under German control.[24] The Cabinet, however, felt, or at least was persuaded by Churchill, that it could not afford to be so sanguine. 'In a matter so vital to the safety of the whole British Empire,' the Prime Minister told the Cabinet, 'we could not afford to rely on the word of Admiral Darlan. However good his intentions might be, he might be forced to resign and his place taken by another minister who would not shrink from betraying us.' Even if they did not, what assurance was there that the Germans would not seize French ships before they could be scuttled?[25]

The French had had due warning of the British mood. Already on the day of the Armistice, the First Sea Lord, Sir Dudley Pound, told Admiral Odend'hal, the French Naval Attaché in London, that 'the one object we had in view was winning the war ... all trivialities such as questions of friendship and hurting people's feelings must be swept aside.'[26] Several days later, a French naval squadron in Alexandria, which had been operating with the Royal Navy against the Italians, was prevented from sailing to Beirut. Darlan responded by calling for 'crippled France to be treated not as an enemy but as a neutral Power.' The same day he warned the fleet not to listen to the appeals of 'outside interested parties,' which would lead to French territory becoming a German province. 'Our former allies are not to be listened to. Let us think French, let us act French.'[27]

In London, meanwhile, the War Cabinet, under strong pressure from Churchill, was thinking and acting British. Having considered such unlikely alternatives as buying the fleet or getting the Americans to do so, ministers decided on Operation Catapult: 'the simultaneous seizure, control or effective disablement or destruction of the accessible French Fleet.'[28] Britain and France were set for what was potentially their first military confrontation since 1815. A great deal now depended upon the diplomatic skill with which the operation was conducted.

Catapult was a very complicated operation. The French fleet was by now well dispersed. The ships concentrated at Toulon, as well as the cruisers at the heavily protected port of Algiers, were effectively beyond British reach. Some 200 vessels, mostly small craft but including two old battleships which had been unable to make for Casablanca or West Africa, were in British ports. These were seized in the early morning of 3 July. According to Churchill, with one exception, the transfer was 'amicable, and the crews came willingly ashore.' In fact, the crews, who had been roughly handled, were highly indignant. Spears describes the way in which the operation was carried out as 'inexcusable.' The ships' crews were then interned at Aintree under conditions lacking comfort and dignity.[29]

Much more finesse was shown in the treatment of the French squadron at Alexandria. Force X, under the command of Admiral René-Emile Godfroy, consisted of a battleship, four cruisers and a number of smaller vessels. Good relations had been established between Godfroy and the British Commander, Admiral Sir Andrew Cunningham, and the latter was now determined to avoid a confrontation. 'The officers and men in the French squadron,' as he later wrote,

> were our friends. We had many most cordial social contacts with them, and they had fought alongside us. Vice-Admiral Godfroy, moreover, was a man of honour in whom we could place implicit faith. Suddenly and without warning to attack and board his ships and in the course of it probably to inflict many casualties on his sailors, appeared to me to be an act of sheer treachery which was as injudicious as it was unnecessary.[30]

Cunningham was anxious to avoid a battle inside the port, which would damage his naval installations, or to have the harbour fouled with wrecks should Godfroy scuttle his ships. He was also concerned about the danger of alienating French sympathies in the Middle East, including the vital Suez Canal zone, French Somaliland and Syria.[31]

Godfroy was an Anglophile, whose wife had been Scottish, and who had his clothes made in Savile Row. Like Cunningham, he was willing where necessary to ignore orders in the interests of a peaceful outcome.[32] The situation nevertheless became extremely tense, with British liaison officers at one point seeking to suborn French officers and crews from their allegiance to their commander. In the end, however, Godfroy bowed to *force majeure*, and a typically British compromise was negotiated, whereby the French agreed to immobilise their ships. Godfroy discharged his fuel oil, removed certain important parts of his gun mechanisms and repatriated some of his crew. He also agreed not to scuttle his ships, to attempt to leave port or to commit any hostile action against Britain. For his part, Cunningham agreed that pay for the remaining officers and men would be forthcoming from British funds.[33] The British admiral had scored a diplomatic triumph. Churchill grumbled and the Germans complained about the deal; neither, however, pressed their point.[34]

The full extent of the responsibility that Catapult placed on individual naval commanders is underscored by the very different events that took place at Mers-el-Kébir, the naval port of Oran. The French force here included the *Strasbourg* and the *Dunkerque*. Like Godfroy, its commander, Admiral Marcel-Bruno Gensoul, was an Anglophile. He had participated in Anglo-French operations in the Atlantic in which Royal Naval vessels, including the battleship *Hood*, had been under his command. Unlike Godfroy, Gensoul was on French territory and was also much less given to bold or original initiatives.[35] That, however, was what the British were now demanding of him. Gensoul found himself sandwiched between obedience to the orders of his own government and Britain's insistence on fighting on. It was impossible, Gensoul was told,

> for us, your comrades up to now, to allow your fine ships to fall into the power of the German or Italian enemy. We are determined to fight on to the end, and if we win, as we think we shall, we shall never forget that France was our Ally, that our interests are the same as hers, and that our common enemy is Germany. Should we conquer, we solemnly declare that we shall restore the greatness and territory of France.[36]

The French admiral was given three options: to fight with Britain; to sail with a reduced crew to a British or American port or to the French West Indies; or to scuttle his ships. Otherwise, he was warned that the British would use 'whatever force may be necessary' to prevent his ships falling into German or Italian hands.[37]

Gensoul reacted badly. Poorly informed about the situation in Metropolitan France and, like so many other French officers, traumatised by defeat, he bridled at an ultimatum which would involve a breach of the

Armistice terms, with the likely consequence that the whole of Metropolitan France would be occupied and the war possibly extended to North Africa.[38] Nor did he appreciate the fact that Cedric Holland, the officer sent to negotiate with him, although a Francophile and personally known to him, only held the rank of captain. While relations between the French and British navies were much better than those between the two armies, French awareness that theirs was the smaller fleet with the less successful history meant that patronising slights were often perceived where none were intended.[39]

The afternoon of 3 July was one of acute tension. Churchill waited impatiently in the Cabinet Room, in constant telephone contact with the Admiralty, as Holland sought desperately to persuade Gensoul to accept British terms. It was only at the last moment, and quite possibly with the aim of playing for time, that he came up with his own alternative that the ships should be disarmed *in situ*. This idea had in fact been earlier raised in London by Sir Dudley Pound, but turned down by the War Cabinet on the grounds that this would look like weakening. The British had subsequently intercepted news of the movement of the French reinforcements, and the British Admiral, Sir James Somerville, was ordered to open fire.[40] Some 1,297 men were killed and another 351 wounded, the large majority when the battleship *Bretagne* exploded and capsized. These were the worst French naval losses of the war. Gensoul has been harshly criticized for showing insufficient flexibility to defuse the crisis, but, as Lord Ismay wrote in his memoirs, 'it spoke for his stubborn courage and the robust discipline of the French Navy, that in spite of the hopelessness of their position they did their duty as they saw it.'[41] Catapult, however was still not quite finished. On 8 July the battleship *Richelieu* was attacked and damaged at Dakar.

Mers-el-Kébir was not an operation in which the British took any pride. They had never previously made war on a beaten ally. The navy hated it, although, according to Somerville, it didn't seem to worry the sailors as they 'never 'ad no use for them French bastards.'[42] Churchill is said to have been physically sick when he heard the news. He later described it as the most 'unnatural and painful decision' in which he had ever been involved, which, as one of his biographers, Geoffrey Best, remarks, was saying something.[43] Of France's nine capital ships, one had been sunk at Mers-el-Kébir, one damaged at Dakar, two seized in British ports and one immobilised at Alexandria. The *Strasbourg* and the *Dunkerque*, however, had escaped. By Somerville's own private admission, he had been half-hearted in carrying out the operation.[44] In addition, some 450,000 tons of French merchant shipping had been seized.[45] The net result was to defuse the immediate sense of crisis surrounding the French fleet, although it continued to give anxiety to British naval planners until November 1942, when half the fleet was scuttled at Toulon.

The political effect was as significant, if not more so. Churchill's great speeches after Dunkirk, and the announcement that the French were suing for an armistice, had galvanised the British public. But the Prime Minister's words badly needed to be bolstered by action to efface the record of Appeasement followed by the debacle in Norway and the retreat from Dunkirk. The unexpectedness and ruthlessness of Mers-el-Kébir thus had a symbolic impact out of proportion to the amount of military damage it caused. The news was wildly cheered when it was announced in the House of Commons. 'It is not often the House is so deeply moved,' *The Times* reported. The reaction greatly distressed Churchill.[46] According to the Ministry of Information's Home Intelligence reports, the attack had been good for morale, although there was little evidence its consequences were fully considered. 'Aggressive actions in themselves,' it was noted on 8 July, bring forth public appreciation and enthusiasm. Verbatims indicated public temper. 'Well, we've shown them what we can do,' and 'That'll give Hitler a surprise for a change.'[47] The irony that this effect was achieved against a country which less than three weeks earlier had been an ally does not appear to have been noted.

International reaction was also positive. Ciano's diary describes Mers-el-Kébir as showing that the Royal Navy 'still has the aggressive ruthlessness of the captains and pirates of the seventeenth century.'[48] General Lee, the US Military Attaché in London, made a similar observation, describing the operation as 'a dashing, old-fashioned, Nelsonian, cutting-out expedition.' But, although the Americans applauded, Roosevelt was not immediately convinced of Britain's prospects; indeed, on 7 July the President is reported as describing Britain's chances as 'about one in three.' It was not until August that he was prepared to provide significant American assistance.[49] The operation, however, did convince a number of European countries, including Greece, Turkey, Yugoslavia and Spain, whose continued neutrality was vital to Britain, that it would fight on, making them more resistant to Axis pressure.[50]

Hitler was taken aback. Four days later he congratulated himself to Ciano, saying that the decision not to demand the surrender of the French fleet had been vindicated. By this 'intelligent handling' of the naval question, Britain and France had been turned into mutual enemies.[51] The Führer was sufficiently impressed by French determination to defend themselves, to suspend the naval clauses of the Armistice in the Mediterranean – but not the Atlantic – ports. But he had also been put on notice that, contrary to his hopes, Britain was determined to continue the war, whatever the cost. This may have had wider strategic implications than were appreciated at the time. In Hitler's eyes, London was banking on an eventual Soviet entry into the war. The Soviet Union had always been his main target. Coming on top of the huge success of Operation Sichelschnitt, Mers-el-Kébir brought the fateful German attack on Russia a year later, in June 1941, that much closer.[52]

Meanwhile, the cost for this exercise in British ruthlessness fell full square on Anglo-French relations. In a journal entry for 7 July, the French writer André Gide compared England and France to 'two puppets in the hands of Hitler, who now amuses himself, after having conquered France, by aligning against her, her ally of yesterday.'[53] Mers-el-Kébir drew a line of blood between Britain and the French government.[54] Although Darlan had warned of the possibility of an attack, in the event both he and the whole of the French government were taken completely by surprise. The response to what was sometimes described as the 'assassination of Oran,' was one of shock, outrage and humiliation. France, Pétain declared, 'defeated in heroic combat, abandoned yesterday, attacked today by England, for whom it had made so many and such hard sacrifices, remains alone in face of its destiny.'[55] Any sense of residual unease at abandoning its former ally now evaporated. In the words of two French naval historians, 'We were freed. The English had only thought of themselves. We had only to imitate them in thinking first of all of ourselves.'[56] Anglophobia now became deeply entrenched in the most senior reaches of the government.

Darlan took the attack on his fleet very personally. A cabinet colleague, Yves Bouthillier, describes him on 4 July as a man

> seized by a terrible passion which he concealed by settling down into a state of apparent composure and internal frenzy. Mentally he was no longer the same. Physically, too, he had changed. His speech was sharper and choppier, his voice was muffled, his hand trembled. His lips disappeared in his face, and his expressionless eyes, turned towards his interior being, seemed to contemplate his devastated soul.[57]

The Admiral's initial reaction was to draft orders for the French navy to attack Somerville's force. Subsequently, he proposed a joint Franco-

Italian operation to attack Cunningham at Alexandria. There was talk of an attack on the British colony of Sierra Leone and the seizure of the Mosul oilfields in Iraq. But France was in no position to fight a war against Britain, which, in Baudouin's words, would 'deliver us hand and foot, to Germany and Italy who would finally extinguish us.'[58] The French were thus forced to confine themselves to an ineffective attack on Gibraltar and to the breaking of diplomatic relations. All British consulates were withdrawn from Metropolitan France, as well as from Dakar and the coastal towns of French North Africa, thereby depriving Britain of valuable listening posts in the French Empire, although those in Beirut and Tangiers remained.[59] These measures did not stop Darlan from nursing his grievance and passing on to the Germans information about the Royal Navy learned during the period of the Entente.[60]

Mers-el-Kébir also played into the hands of a professed Anglophobe of older standing: Pierre Laval. A lawyer by training, Laval had been elected to Parliament as a socialist deputy, but by the time he first became Prime Minister in 1931, he was heading a right-wing government. He had quickly gained a reputation for unscrupulousness and for putting personal contacts before ideology. Some of the British and American cartoons of Laval are grotesque.[61] Laval had borne the British a grudge since the collapse of the Hoare–Laval pact in 1935 and had been arguing for a breach with Britain following Campbell's departure from Bordeaux on 23 June.[62] Now he declared that France

has never had and never will have a more inveterate enemy than Great Britain. Our whole history bears witness to this. We have been nothing but toys in the hands of England, who exploited us to ensure her own safety … I can see only one way to restore France … to the position to which she is entitled: namely to ally ourselves resolutely with Germany and to confront England together.[63]

Mers-el-Kébir created the climate in which such a reversal of alliances became that much more palatable.[64] As he worked towards this goal, Laval lost no opportunity to press his anti-British views. At the end of July he was telling an American diplomat that he ardently hoped that Britain would be defeated. In late August, Laval offered French participation in the Luftwaffe's bombing campaign against Britain. Shortly afterwards, he proposed to the Council of Ministers that France should declare war on England.[65] Operation Catapult had made Britain some powerful French enemies.

Of more immediate concern to London, the attack on the French fleet had undermined the prospects, admittedly never good, of promoting continued French resistance. Initial hopes in the wake of the announcement that France was suing for an armistice had focused on the continuation of resistance from North Africa, and a British minister, Lord Lloyd, had been dispatched to Bordeaux with an offer to transport French troops to North Africa and to help with its defence.[66] The question of whether to move the government to North Africa had been the subject of heated debate, with Pétain and Weygand strongly opposed. To these soldiers, abandoning France in its hour of need was tantamount to desertion in the face of the enemy. Pétain believed that France's revival should be sought 'from the soul of our country,' which would be preserved by staying there rather than by reconquest 'by allied cannon, under conditions and after a delay impossible to foresee.'[67] It was a widely shared view. 'Run away?' asked Jean Moulin, then Prefect of Chartres but later a key Resistance leader. 'Wouldn't that be to act like the others, like all those who have run away from responsibilities, hunger or danger?'[68]

Although the Armistice terms effectively resolved the matter, a ship, the *Massilia*, carrying a number of French deputies, including the former Prime Minister Edouard Daladier and former Interior Minister Georges Mandel, had already left for Casablanca. Duff Cooper, the Minister of Information, along with the former commander of the BEF, Lord Gort, made a non-stop ten-hour flight to try to make contact with the group, which was wrongly believed to include Reynaud. The hope was for the establishment of a government in North Africa or Syria which would be given disposal of the stocks of French gold in Britain. But the deputies were arrested, and the British delegation was prevented from making contact. Churchill subsequently gave orders to the Admiralty to try to rescue the prisoners, but this proved impossible.[69] By 26 June, Hugh Dalton, the Minister of Economic Warfare, was complaining in his diary that Frenchmen had 'all become sawdust ... we see before our eyes nothing less than the liquification of France.'[70]

# 4

# Rebel and Empire

In the immediate aftermath of the defeat, all the male inhabitants of the Île de Sein off the coast of Brittany came to the Cornish port of Newlyn. The lighthouse keeper had heard de Gaulle's first broadcast appealing for Frenchmen to join him in Britain. Breton fishermen had been fishing off the Cornish coast since the beginning of the century and had made many friends there.[1] But with the northern coastline cut off, it was logistically difficult for most French men and women to make the journey. Nor do many appear to have been disposed to leave family and friends to come to a country which was widely expected to follow the French example into defeat. Others blamed Britain for leading them into the war and then deserting them at Dunkirk and now for shelling their fleet at Mers-el-Kébir. To accept exile for many French men meant breaching a taboo, and the number of French refugees in Britain was never more than around 4,000.[2]

Not only did few French people come to Britain, but many of those who were already there left. A few of these were diplomats who went to the USA. The majority, however, were among the 12,000 French servicemen and sailors who had found themselves in Britain at the time of the Armistice: soldiers who had been rescued from Dunkirk and Narvik and sailors whose ships had been seized on 3 July. They had not been made particularly welcome. The British army's priority was now the expected German invasion, and they looked askance at their former allies who had collapsed so precipitously. General Sir John Dill told the Chiefs of Staff that he would like to get rid of the French troops as soon as possible, and the British authorities did little to dispel the fears of those who believed that in joining de Gaulle they would lay themselves open to charges of treason or endanger their families in France.[3] In addition, some French soldiers and sailors saw de Gaulle as a dangerous element, viewed the British as untrustworthy, or came under peer pressure to avoid enlisting with 'perfidious Albion.'[4]

De Gaulle had shown none of the doubts or inhibitions of his compatriots. The most junior general in the French army, he was a largely unknown figure. On his appointment as Under-Secretary of War, an article in *The Times* had described him as a man 'with an enlightened and penetrating mind, a man of action and at the same time of dreams and abstraction.'[5] Major Desmond Morton, who dealt with intelligence matters at No. 10, described him somewhat inaccurately as 'a magnificent crook ... another Max Beaverbrook, just what we want.'[6] Colville wondered whether he was a new Napoleon, noting that he was reputed to treat Reynaud like dirt.[7]

The French were not much wiser. 'Who is this general?' was the question asked in France in the wake of his first broadcast appeal.[8] Yet the very fact that he had been willing to defy orders and to come to Britain marked de Gaulle as a figure out of the ordinary. True, he risked arrest in France or North Africa and had not expected to find himself alone in London. He also had the advantage of a British plane at his disposal, the one which had taken him back to France on the evening of 16 June with the offer of Anglo-French union.[9] But Churchill's capital was the obvious destination for a Frenchman determined to continue the war, as the Benelux, Czech, Danish, Polish and Norwegian governments in exile who had set themselves up in London had also recognised. In contrast to Pétain, de Gaulle believed that were France to be the only country to accept capitulation, 'it would be the end of honour, unity and independence.'[10] The result could only be that self-disgust, as well as the contempt it would inspire, 'would poison [France's] soul and its life for many generations.'[11] Totally untainted by defeatism, de Gaulle had the strategic vision which other members of the French government lacked and understood that Germany had not yet won the war. In common with other French figures already in London, such as Jean Monnet, Robert Marjolin and René Pleven, he had confidence in Britain's capacity to survive under Churchill's leadership.[12]

De Gaulle's welcome, however, was by no means unqualified. In the chaotic few days before the terms of the Armistice were known, British ministers and officials were naturally wary of a man who might complicate their relation with the Bordeaux government. The Cabinet, chaired not by Churchill but by the Lord President of the Council, Neville Chamberlain, had initially turned down de Gaulle's request to broadcast to France 'as long as it was still possible that the French Cabinet would act in a way conformable to the interests of the Alliance.'[13] Although his broadcast on 18 June, which ironically was the 125th anniversary of the battle of Waterloo, went ahead, the Foreign Office warned of the need to be careful 'not to ride two horses at the same time. So long as we are gingering up the present French government, and with some success, it would be disastrous if we should appear at the same time to be coquetting with a possible successor in London.'[14] De Gaulle was first 'muffled,' being allowed only to broadcast in general terms, and then briefly kept away from the BBC microphones.[15]

The day after the signature of the Armistice, the Cabinet agreed in principle to a proposal from de Gaulle to recognise a London-based French Committee of Liberation to pursue the war in cooperation with Britain.[16] But the General failed to gain the support of potential members, including the French Ambassador in London, Charles Corbin, and Jean Monnet. The latter had reservations about de Gaulle, who, he complained, listened to no one and was unlikely to share power. But Monnet also believed that there was no chance of the French in their present strained and wounded condition accepting any kind of government established under British protection.[17] Once again it was decided to keep the General in the background. But as nobody else came to the fore, the British found that they had no alternative to de Gaulle.[18]

This did not particularly please those in Whitehall who thought him too junior a figure, who were unsure about who or what he represented and, most significantly, who worried that he had a tendency to rub people up the wrong way. The latter idea was publicly rejected by Captain Cyril Falls, the Military Correspondent of *The Times,* who declared that 'strong men of action of his sort inevitably rub people up the wrong way,' a view the General himself would echo to Churchill during their first major row fifteen months later.[19] In June 1940, the Prime Minister took a distinctly favourable view of the energetic French general who he had first met on the 9th and who he had already referred to as *l'homme du destin.* 'You are all alone?' the Prime Minister asked, when he saw de Gaulle on 27 June. 'Well, then, I recognize you all alone.'[20] The die had been cast, as Spears, who had been appointed as liaison officer with the Free French, later wrote:

> It had been recognised that no more notable man and certainly no one more wholeheartedly in favour of fighting on was likely to join us. The fact that de Gaulle had burnt his boats and had been condemned by Bordeaux played its part in taking the decision … There was both gratitude and admiration in the government for this lonely and courageous man.[21]

The practical effect of Churchill's decision was that de Gaulle was to be granted facilities to establish a French legion in Britain. Whether he could later set up a central political authority must, in the view of the Foreign Office, largely depend on the support he received from the French.[22] Nevertheless, this was an act of considerable political import. The British were giving public support to a Frenchman whose actions and, more immediately important, words, relayed to France by the BBC, constituted a direct challenge to the policy and legitimacy of Pétain's government. In a diary entry of 23 June, Colville describes de Gaulle's broadcast as preaching sedition. The General had denounced the Armistice as an enslavement, proclaiming the need to continue the fight, and announced the formation of a French fighting force.[23] In allowing him to do so, the British were helping to sow the seeds of political division which Pétain believed to be fatal to France.

The General's immediate value to the British was symbolic. Along with the European governments in exile, de Gaulle helped give a continued international character to the war. The General represented a thread of continuity, however tenuous, of the Entente, which might help soften the shock to British public opinion of the collapse of France.[24] The romantic image of this lonely soldier defying the menace of Nazism and the cowardice of Vichy appealed to a country which had as yet few, if any, of its own heroes. The *Daily Sketch* likened him to Robinson Crusoe 'washed up on his island.'[25] There were cheers in cinemas when de Gaulle appeared on newsreels, which also treated as heroes the handful of Free French pilots who fought with the RAF in the battle of Britain.[26] And there was a further consideration: knowledge that Free French opinion was siding with Britain could influence public opinion not just in France but also in the French colonies.[27]

Hopes that the French Empire might continue the fight had been high in the immediate wake of Pétain's announcement that France was suing for an armistice. The empire had been untouched by the defeat, and governors and senior officers were quick to declare their willingness to fight on. The most important of these was General Auguste Noguès, the French commander in North Africa. The Governor of French Equatorial Africa, Pierre Boisson, reported that he was receiving reports from across the territories of the determination to continue the struggle 'alongside our allies.'[28] From Lebanon, the High Commissioner, Gabriel Puaux, telegraphed that continued resistance in the empire seemed to him the way of coming to the aid of British arms, which offered the only means of delivering France from the *asservisement définitif* with which it was threatened.[29]

Already on 17 June British representatives in French territories overseas had been instructed to tell the local French authorities that British forces would do all in their power to assist against enemy attack and that requests for economic and financial aid would be very sympathetically received. These offers were renewed following the Armistice, but by then the British had been effectively outbid by Hitler.[30] The fact that the empire was to remain free from German and (in French eyes even more important) Italian incursions took much of the wind out of the sails of those who had previously been talking of continuing the war. De Gaulle's audacity was not shared in the colonies. The American Consul in Casablanca noted a lack of initiative on the part of senior officials, describing them as 'the purest conventionalists who will probably follow whatever order they get, even to fight for Hitler. This applies to all services.'[31] A telegram from the Head of the British Military Mission in Beirut, Colonel Salisbury-Jones, dated 25 June, reported that General Eugène Mittelhauser was feeling the enormous weight of responsibility which would result from any decision to break with Weygand or Pétain. He was expecting the telegram naming his successor at any moment. There would be difficulties from some reservists cut off from their families in France. 'Did I appreciate the vastness of his task?' Mittelhauser has 'the right idea of honour,' Salisbury-Jones concluded, 'but I regret he is not younger.'[32]

Mittelhauser had raised another concern with Salisbury-Jones. He wanted assurances that Britain would not take over the Levant at the end of the war. In doing so he was reflecting suspicions of British imperial designs widely felt by French officials in the Levant and North Africa, suspicions which were not shared by the Dutch or Belgians.[33] Yet perhaps the most important barrier to the revolt against the Armistice which the British wanted to promote was the fact that the French chain of command remained intact. All the instincts and training of both officers and officials was to obey the orders from Weygand and Pétain. In the words of one senior French officer in the Middle East, 'I do not approve of the present government, but that is beside the point. I did not swear to obey the government which I approved.'[34] In a period of chaos and confusion, the oath of obedience was the remaining sheet anchor to which people clung. Even for a man of de Gaulle's rebellious temperament, the act of breaking with France had been, in his own word, 'appalling.'[35] The point was not always readily appreciated by British officials, with their single-minded determination to continue the war, who had never been faced with a similar dilemma. The loyalty of the French officer corps was a stumbling block that would bedevil British policy towards France over the next two and a half years.[36]

Churchill, of course, was not a man to take no for an answer. The idea of a British military expedition to Morocco had been suggested by Duff

Cooper on the return from his abortive visit to Rabat. The Prime Minister was attracted. De Gaulle would be sent to set up a French administration and to rally French forces, including the still-unfinished battleship *Jean Bart*. In the process, the British would gain a base on the Atlantic. The 25,000 troops required would be provided by the Free French, the Commonwealth and possibly also the Poles. But the plan was strongly opposed by the Chiefs of Staff, who argued that Britain must now give priority to its own defence rather than embarking on French colonial ventures which would require long-term British commitments.[37] Any lingering hopes the Prime Minister may have had about Morocco disappeared in the wake of Mers-el-Kébir, which effectively ended all hope of any French colony rallying to the British cause.[38]

Undeterred, the Prime Minister looked around for alternative places to establish a French government friendly to Britain. The Cameroons, which continued to be sympathetic towards the British cause, did not interest him. Consideration was given to landings in Algeria and Tunisia, but these were dismissed at least in part because they would require the use of British forces and Britain did not want to embark on a course of active conquest of the French Empire.[39] West Africa seemed to offer a more promising prospect for a British-backed Gaullist landing. Dakar, the capital of Senegal, possessed the best equipped and most modern harbour in the area. It commanded British imperial communications routes around the Cape to the Middle and Far East, which had become of critical importance now that the Mediterranean was closed to British convoys. Churchill was anxious to pre-empt the German navy. 'Unless we act with celerity and vigour,' he minuted to General Ismay on 8 August, 'we may find effective U-boat bases, supported by German aviation, all down this coast and it will become barred to us, but available to the Germans in the same way as the western coast of Europe.'[40] Dakar's proximity to the Western Hemisphere meant that this was also of concern to the USA. Roosevelt, who had been Assistant Secretary of the Navy, shared Churchill's interest in sea power. (Churchill's letters to the President were signed 'Former Naval Person.') This American factor was a consideration of some importance to Churchill at a time when he was trying desperately to get the USA to become more involved in the war.[41]

The seizure of Dakar offered additional advantages. The *Richelieu* would be taken over under the French flag. Access would be gained to some 65 billion francs worth of Belgian and Polish gold which had been transferred there by the Banque de France for safe keeping. And Churchill hated staying on the defensive. Vichy's empire seemed to offer an easy target for a diversionary expedition which, like Mers-el-Kébir, would boost international prestige and home morale. Once installed at Dakar, the hope was that the whole of West, and possibly also North, Africa would rally to the Allied cause.[42] The prospect that the Germans would react by moving into North Africa does not seem to have entered into British calculations.[43]

Churchill had first looked at the Dakar option in early July, when he had proposed that de Gaulle should fly out to Gibraltar and embark on a British ship for Senegal, escorted by French troops which were then being repatriated back to North Africa. The plan had what the historian Desmond Dinan describes as 'all the hallmarks of a Churchillian adventure: short on detailed planning and long on wishful-thinking,' and it was successfully opposed by the Chiefs of Staff.[44] That did not, however, mean that Churchill abandoned the idea. On 6 August, the Prime Minister outlined to de Gaulle, in beguiling detail, a plan whereby the sudden arrival of a large British fleet off Dakar would overawe the Vichy governor, who, after little more than token resistance for honour's sake, would rally to the Gaullist cause. By de Gaulle's account it was a bravura performance, with the Prime Minister 'brimming over with conviction' and miming 'one by one, the scenes of the future, as they spurted up from his desire and his imagination.'[45] His visitor was happy to cooperate. De Gaulle saw Africa as the theatre in which France should continue the war. He was anxious to set up the seat of government on French soil and to make the Free French less dependent on his British hosts. He may well also have shared the view of the former senior French diplomat to London, Roger Cambon, that if the Free French remained in Britain doing nothing they would become demoralised and disintegrate.[46]

The British military planners were much less happy about Operation Menace. Here was an immensely tricky and hazardous operation thousands of miles from home, effectively dependent on the cooperation of the enemy, being launched at a time when invasion threatened at home and the Italians were poised to attack Egypt. The parallels with the 1915 Dardanelles fiasco were all too obvious. Menace was nevertheless duly authorised by the War Cabinet, subject to consideration by the Foreign Secretary of the chances, which Churchill discounted, of Vichy declaring war.[47] On 31 August, the force set sail. It was rather less impressive than the one which Churchill had so imaginatively described to de Gaulle three weeks earlier. It also had a rather larger British contingent than had been intended. The original plan had been for Britain to provide only the equipment, transports and escorts. Now there were also two British brigades. Some, including the novelist

Evelyn Waugh, serving with the Royal Marines aboard a converted P&O passenger ship, travelled in style, the officers being called in the morning by a liveried steward carrying a tray of tea, an apple and a slice of thin brown bread and butter.[48]

Nothing else went as smoothly. The first major problem was caused by the appearance of the French navy. At the end of August, de Gaulle had scored his first success. A Free French force of a mere twenty men had, with British logistic support, succeeded in rallying Chad, Cameroons and the French Congo.[49] This outbreak of 'dissidence' alarmed Vichy.[50] It also disturbed the Germans. Admiral Erich Raeder warned that the unrest might spread to other French colonies in West Africa, jeopardising German chances of controlling 'the African area; the danger exists that strategically important West African ports might be used for British convoy activities and that we might lose a most valuable source of supplies for Europe.'[51] Vichy was duly put on notice to keep its African house in order, on pain of German intervention. It was also authorised to send a force of six cruisers, whose immediate task was to dissuade Gabon from joining the Gaullists.[52]

News of the French ships' unexpected arrival at Dakar reached London at a very bad time. The battle of Britain was at its height. On 15 September, when Churchill had visited the headquarters of Air Vice Marshal Keith Park at Uxbridge, he had found Fighter Command stretched to its very limits.[53] Small wonder therefore that when the following day the War Cabinet discussed the new situation created by the arrival of the French cruisers, which were presumed to be carrying troop reinforcements, thereby putting paid to the hope of a bloodless landing, it decided to give orders to abandon the operation. De Gaulle should instead be landed at Duala in the Cameroons, to consolidate his position in Equatorial Africa and to extend Gaullist influence to Libreville. But de Gaulle and the British force commanders were given an opportunity to object to this change of plan, which they duly did. General Spears, who was accompanying de Gaulle, was particularly vocal. De Gaulle's future, Spears warned, was at stake. Should he fail to seize the opportunity,

so obviously in his grasp, of rallying West Africa ... his power to rally any other part of the French empire is gone for ever. If the Fleet departs leaving de Gaulle here, the accusation of abandoning him to his fate will swing French opinion totally against us in France as well as in Africa.

This argument was supported in London by both Chamberlain and the Secretary of War, Anthony Eden. Operation Menace was allowed to proceed.[54]

The force duly arrived off Dakar on 23 September. What now ensued was, in Churchill's words, 'a glaring example of miscalculation, confusion, timidity and muddle.'[55] The fundamental British mistake was the failure to appreciate that Vichy continued to command the loyalty of its troops and that they would resolutely resist incursions into the French Empire (encouraged, at least as far as the sailors of the *Richelieu* were concerned, by a desire for revenge for the earlier British attack on their ship). De Gaulle's presence did nothing to improve Britain's chances. To the Governor of Dakar, Pierre Boisson, the General was a rebel. A clumsily worded ultimatum issued by the British Force Commander, General Noel Irwin, alleging that Dakar might be handed over at any moment to the Germans, met with a defiant response.[56] By 24 September, London was sufficiently concerned by the situation to request Washington to put pressure on Vichy not to declare war. The next day, by which time two British battleships had been damaged, one seriously, the operation was broken off. As Halifax put it to Cabinet, the only way to turn failure into success was to engage in a major operation, and Britain had too many commitments elsewhere.[57] French casualties amounted to some 500 killed and wounded, including civilians. British and Free French suffered forty-four killed and wounded.[58]

*Paris Soir* of 26 September carried the headline 'Gibraltar Pays for Dakar!' According to the paper, 45 tonnes of bombs had been dropped on the colony, with four large ships hit and a large numbers of fires started. This was wishful thinking. Gibraltar had indeed been bombed, but the damage had been minimal. It scarcely mattered. Britain, along of course with de Gaulle, was the clear loser in this second round of Anglo-French fighting, and the two sides were now quits.[59] For the French navy, Dakar had been more than a valuable morale booster; the Germans, impressed by French determination to keep out the British, responded by allowing the rearming of the *Strasbourg*, along with six cruisers and a number of other smaller ships.[60] The affair was also valuable in reinforcing French arguments at the Armistice Commission in Wiesbaden against the establishment of a German control commission at Dakar (which paradoxically can also be regarded as a British gain). Vichy was able to turn Dakar to good propaganda effect. The attack played readily to French suspicions that Britain had designs on their empire. Last, and by no means least, Vichy had the satisfaction of seeing both the British and 'de Gaulle and his clique' worsted.[61]

De Gaulle's behaviour had impressed British commanders. In the words of Vice Admiral Sir John Cunningham, the General's attitude 'when he was naturally suffering from the terrible disappointment which his reception undoubtedly gave him, was that of a great man.'[62] The affair had indeed been a grievous personal blow to de Gaulle, who was deeply depressed in its aftermath. According to one of his French biographers, de Gaulle may actually have contemplated suicide.[63] In London, the Free French had the disagreeable experience of finding that they were suddenly viewed with the same lack of confidence previously reserved for Vichy.[64] In Washington, Roosevelt drew the conclusion that de Gaulle was an adventurer, willing to advance his own career at the expense of French unity.[65]

Churchill, who came under heavy criticism, defended the General. But he was forced to accelerate a cabinet reshuffle to divert attention from the affair.[66] More important, Dakar precipitated a reassessment of British policy towards France. Vichy was proving a more intractable proposition than Churchill had bargained for, and the debacle played into the hands of critics in the Foreign Office and the Services opposed to the aggressive policy towards France which the Prime Minister had been pursuing since the Armistice. As one Vichy minister later put it, the guns of Dakar opened the eyes of the English.[67]

# 5

# Modus Vivendi or Collaboration?

By the autumn of 1940 Britain and France had reached a stalemate. Back in the last week of June 1940, the expectations in Bordeaux had been that Britain would quickly follow France into making terms with Germany. A certain element of *Schadenfreude,* as much as strategic miscalculation, had informed this assumption. In a conversation with the American Ambassador, William Bullitt, two days before Mers-el-Kébir, Darlan remarked that he did not believe the British people would have the courage to stand up to air attacks and would surrender. When Bullitt replied that the Admiral seemed to regard this prospect with considerable pleasure, the latter smiled.

> I said that it seemed to me that I had observed that the French would like to have England conquered in order that Germany might have as many conquered provinces to control as possible, and that France might become the favourite province, he smiled again and nodded.[1]

Darlan had again misjudged his former allies. Britain had not only fought off the Luftwaffe, thereby postponing indefinitely the day when the Armistice would be turned into a peace treaty; it had also inflicted a good deal of pain on the vulnerable rump French state. Even before the attack on the fleet, Britain had imposed a blockade on Metropolitan France, and at the end of July this was extended to French North Africa. The French were deeply worried. France depended on imports for all of its petrol and petroleum product, along with a range of minerals and considerable quantities of foodstuffs.[2] Darlan's initial response was to press for naval escorts for French convoys and for another attack on Gibraltar. Baudouin, by contrast, sought negotiations; the Ministry of Foreign Affairs was in constant apprehension of naval or colonial incidents with Britain. But he was also influenced by rivalry with Laval; playing the English card while Laval was trying to negotiate in Paris with the Germans afforded Baudouin a means of trying to stay in the political game at Vichy.[3]

The case for negotiations with the British was reinforced by the defections of French colonies to de Gaulle at the end of August.[4] On 3 September the French Foreign Minister wrote to Halifax, warning that if the Gaullist movement were successful it would provoke Axis intervention in Africa and bring Spain, which had its own claims in Morocco, into the war. Ten days later, Baudouin proposed an Anglo-French colonial modus vivendi.[5] Meanwhile, the French Naval Attaché in Madrid was summoned back to Vichy, where Darlan told him to keep in discreet touch with his British opposite number. The message passed on to the British was that the French spirit of resistance had improved and that disarmament would not be real. But this appears to have been largely an attempt to gain amelioration of the blockade.[6]

Pressure for a change in British policy came from two main sources. One was the Services, which believed that Britain should concentrate on fighting Germany rather than France. This view was particularly strongly held by the Royal Navy, which, hard pressed against both Germany and Italy, had borne the brunt of the fighting with France. The navy's priority was to keep France from joining the war and to avoid what it regarded as secondary commitments. It was also nervous about Gibraltar. While they had done little damage, the French bombing raids had caused disruption and had shown up the Rock's vulnerability to attack from North Africa. Having 'tasted blood,' as an Admiralty memorandum put it, the fear was that the French would make more raids. If Gibraltar became untenable, the whole strategic position in the western Mediterranean would be lost and that in the eastern Mediterranean seriously compromised.[7]

Such pessimism was scarcely calculated to commend itself to Churchill. The Prime Minister did not believe that Vichy had the power to wage war against Britain and warned against accepting the position that 'we must yield to the wishes of Vichy out of fear, lest they make air raids on Gibraltar; for there would be no end to that.'[8] He had rather more difficulty in resisting pressure from the Foreign Secretary. Lord Halifax had never been enthusiastic about the Prime Minister's aggressive strategy towards France, privately believing that both Mers-el-Kébir and Dakar had been mistakes.[9] In a Cabinet paper written immediately after the Dakar fiasco, Halifax raised the question of Baudouin's colonial modus vivendi and the problems this might raise in relations with de Gaulle. While there could be no question of going back on the promises given to the General, Halifax opposed any further military operations unless it was 'clear beyond reasonable doubts' that French colonies were willing to come over. Meanwhile, de Gaulle should be content with the territories he already had and should turn his attention to Syria and the Middle East.

Halifax developed his thinking in Cabinet on 1 October, when he argued that the important thing was that the French Empire resisted German and Italian pressure; so long as it did, it was immaterial whether it did so under de Gaulle or a Vichy leader. There was a risk of Britain and France drifting into hostilities. While nobody wanted to start eating out of 'the uncertain hand of Vichy,' there was a 'considerable case for informing Vichy what we wanted, what we would stand and what we would not stand.'[10] Churchill acquiesced, if without particular enthusiasm.[11] What followed was three months of complicated, murky and, in the end, frustrating diplomacy, in which the British constantly seemed to be running after the French. Though London did not immediately appreciate the point, this was part of a political struggle over Vichy neutrality. Could Vichy be induced to accommodate Britain or would it gravitate into the Axis camp?

Since there were no direct contacts between London and Vichy, negotiations were initially carried out in Madrid. Here the Anglophile French Ambassador, the Comte de la Baume, had already established a good working relationship with his British colleague, the former Foreign Secretary, Sir Samuel Hoare.[12] Hoare's first priority was to prevent Spain from entering the war and allowing German troops to transit the Peninsula to take Gibraltar. Since the Spanish regarded Pétain as the only hope against a total occupation of France, the Ambassador believed that some kind of British relationship with Vichy would be helpful in this regard. The Ambassador had in any case been instructed by Halifax to 'keep the ball moving' between the British and French governments and not to bring relations to a stop.[13] De la Baume sounded conciliatory, arguing that it was essential to heal rather than to extend Anglo-French breaches, with a view to Britain and France being firmly together for the later chapters of the war. Hoare's problem was that he was unsure how far de la Baume represented opinion at Vichy, while being completely baffled as to whether London wanted to keep Pétain or to destroy his government.[14]

The answer, as contained in the instructions issued after Dakar, appeared to be the former. Hoare was told that Britain was willing to discuss trade between France and its colonies. But it needed guarantees that neither the empire nor the fleet would fall under German or Italian influence or control.

There was also no question of abandoning the commitment which Britain had recently made to the naval defence of de Gaulle's colonies, which were entirely dependent on British economic and military support.[15] Churchill subsequently wrote to Hoare, urging him to tell de la Baume that 'we will let bygones go and work with anyone who convinces us of his resolution to beat the common foe.' 'It passes my comprehension,' the Prime Minister added, 'why no French leaders secede to Africa, where they have an Empire, the command of the seas and all the foreign gold in the United States.'[16] Shortly afterwards, on 21 October, Churchill took the unusual step of making a personal broadcast to France.[17]

The French response was decidedly cool. The Ministry of Foreign Affairs was interested, having already sought to enlist the good offices of South Africa, Canada and Ireland in support of an Anglo-French détente. But there remained a deep reservoir of anti-British feeling in Vichy. Laval continued openly hostile, while Pétain was only interested in a commercial agreement, while wanting to maintain a free hand for reprisals against de Gaulle and the British.[18] It was against this background that an unofficial French intermediary arrived in London on 22 October. Louis Rougier was a French professor of International Relations with a taste for unofficial diplomacy. He had conceived the idea of a personal mission to London, for which he had gained the approval of Baudouin as well as a note to the effect that his visit was known to Pétain. The importance the British attached to this first Vichy envoy can be gauged from the fact that his journey, via Geneva, Madrid and Lisbon had been facilitated by the Secret Intelligence Service (SIS [MI6]). He was received by both Halifax and Churchill, the latter anxious, as he later put it, 'that no road that led to France should be incontinently barred.'[19]

Rougier seems to have made a rather mixed impression on his hosts. Major Desmond Morton, who dealt with relations with the Free French at No. 10, described him as 'very, very naïf,' a verdict borne out by ensuing events.[20] For Rougier returned to Vichy with what he wrongly claimed was a comprehensive draft Franco-British agreement.[21] Precisely what happened to this dubious document in Vichy is unclear. Baudouin claims that Pétain ratified it, but there is no independent evidence for this, and, according to a letter from Pétain to Weygand, the former seems to have suspected Rougier of being a British agent.[22]

The diplomatic confusion of the autumn of 1940 did not end here. While one arm of the French government had been secretly pursuing a modus vivendi with its former ally, another arm was pursuing a new relationship with its recent enemy. The term 'collaboration' had entered the vocabulary in July. Highly ambiguous – its attraction lay precisely in the fact that it conveyed a very precise idea while still remaining extremely vague – its implications for Britain were ominous.[23] France was moving from neutrality towards cooperation with the enemy and even a possible reversal of alliances.

The leading proponent of this radical shift in Vichy policy was Pierre Laval. A militant pacifist, Laval had long championed the principle of Franco-German reconciliation. He both hoped and believed that Germany would win the war. 'Look at the map. See how far away America is,' he told a journalist. If France held back and waited until the end of the war before making peace, Laval believed it would be in a bad bargaining position.[24] The difficulty with this policy was that Hitler distrusted France, believing that sooner or later there would be an Anglo-French rapprochement. Hitherto, he had shown no interest in cooperation with his most prominent victim.[25] But as the prospects of a rapid German victory against Britain receded in the autumn of 1940, the German leadership began casting around for alternative means of breaking British resistance. Attention now began to focus on trying to force Britain from the Mediterranean, with an operation against Suez in cooperation with the Italians. The capture of Gibraltar would deprive Britain of a key base in the battle of the Atlantic.[26]

The service with the greatest interest in cooperation with France was the German navy. On 26 September, the day after Dakar, Admiral Raeder had an unusual private interview with Hitler at which he argued the case for the incorporation of the French as full allies in the war against England. In addition to the help this would provide in pushing Britain out of the Mediterranean, alliance with France would open the prospect of securing French colonial possessions and their raw materials. Britain would be forced out of Central Africa, including the strategically important port of Freetown in Sierra Leone, thereby causing serious problems for convoys from the South Atlantic and those routed around the Cape.[27] Hitler was sympathetic, but he faced a dilemma. To take Gibraltar he needed Spanish cooperation, but this was only likely to be forthcoming in return for German support for Spanish claims against Morocco. This in turn risked alienating France and encouraging a North African defection to de Gaulle. The question was whether some kind of deal could be fashioned, possibly compensating the French with Nigeria.[28]

In the last week of October, therefore, just as Rougier arrived in England, Hitler paid a visit to Franco. En route he saw Laval, who, 'full of unctuous humility, opened up the prospect of close French cooperation with Germany, hoping for France's reward through retention of its African possessions and release from heavy reparations – both at the expense of Great Britain – once a peace settlement could be concluded.'[29] Hitler made no specific demands, but he made clear that the terms France would get in any peace treaty would depend on the extent of French cooperation and the rapidity with which British defeat would be attained. Hitler then went on to see Franco for what proved a completely unsuccessful meeting. Franco, Hitler subsequently complained, did not seem to have 'the same intensity of will for giving as for taking.'[30]

On his way back through France, Hitler held a second meeting, this time with Pétain, at the small town of Montoire-sur-le-Loir, near Tours. Having spoken two weeks previously of France's desire to free itself from its traditional friendships, Pétain assured the Führer that he had always been opposed to the English and readily committed himself to the principle of 'collaboration,' while remaining studiously vague on the details. This does not appear to have worried Hitler, who described the Marshal as giving the impression of a 'very decent, reliable character.'[31] Three days later, Laval told the German Ambassador, Otto Abetz, that he planned to implement France's 'alignment against England.' The point at which British forces offered resistance to a French offensive against the Gaullist colonies might, he suggested, be the moment for an open declaration of war.[32]

This was going rather further than Hitler wanted. French entry into the war not only risked the defection of more French colonies to the Gaullist cause, it also seriously risked upsetting the Italians, who had their own territorial claims against France.[33] Germany, Hitler now told Mussolini, did not need direct French aid. Rather, what he wanted were bases for the Luftwaffe and the commitment of parts of the fleet, particularly submarines operating from ports in West Africa, against England. But he saw symbolic value in France's integration into the 'Front against England,' since 'the whole of Europe, including the former ally, would thereby be solidly arranged against the English.'[34] Germany and Italy needed to support the Pétain government by assuring it that they would make only modest demands, would not destroy its empire and would compensate colonial losses at Britain's expense. 'If France knew this, the knowledge would mean the end of de Gaulle.'[35] In a directive dated 12 November 1940, Hitler described France's role as that of a 'non-belligerent power' which will have to tolerate German military measures on her territory ... and to give support, as far as possible, even by using her own means of defence. The most pressing task of the French is the defensive and offensive protection of their African colonies ... against England and the de Gaulle movement.[36]

During the Franco-German negotiations which took place in late autumn, the French Defence Minister, General Léon Huntzinger, declared that the English should be kicked out ('Il faut chasser les Anglais'), and there was talk about a French expedition to retake Chad. But it was soon evident that there was serious unease in Vichy about any military operations.[37] Over and above the logistic difficulties, there was a strong reluctance to risk further fratricidal French conflict, or indeed war, with de Gaulle's backers. According to Admiral Charles Platon, the Minister for the Colonies, 'the English factor' was decisive. War with England would make France totally dependent on Germany, threaten links with the USA (which Vichy valued) and risk the loss of further colonies.[38]

The British had been taken by surprise by this apparent Franco-German rapprochement. It was extraordinary, Churchill told the War Cabinet when the news of the Montoire meeting reached London, that neither Britain nor the Americans had received any information about the Franco-German negotiations nor knew whether collaboration would extend into the military sphere.[39] In Madrid, de la Baume warned Hoare of the possibility that Vichy intended to sign a peace agreement with Germany on 11 November, the anniversary of the 1918 Armistice, and that Laval wanted to use the French fleet to recover the colonies lost to de Gaulle.[40] Writing to Roosevelt on 27 October, the Prime Minister painted a grim picture. If the Axis submarines were to gain access to Oran (in Algeria) and Bizerta (in Tunisia), hopes of impeding Italian reinforcements, which were currently attacking Egypt, would be destroyed and the situation in the western Mediterranean seriously undermined. A draft of a subsequent letter to the American President summarised the real danger in a single sentence: 'We have no margin at all.'[41]

Having reacted so strongly to the Armistice, Britain's response to this new and more immediate threat was therefore much more hesitant. At Britain's request, the Americans, who were themselves much exercised over the fate of the French fleet, duly warned Vichy that were the force to be used against the Royal Navy Vichy would lose all prospects of American economic aid. Furthermore, the USA would make no efforts to ensure the restoration of the French Empire at the end of the war.[42] The unusual step was also taken of sending a letter from King George VI to Pétain, professing confidence that the Marshal would reject all terms dishonouring France's name and damaging 'a late Ally.' 'The disaster that overwhelmed France,' the King continued, 'deprived us of her assistance, but it would indeed be a sombre event in history if France were to range herself against us and afford direct assistance to our enemy.'[43] It cut little ice in Vichy.

No less telling of this new consciousness of British weakness was the attempt in the wake of Montoire at distancing Britain from de Gaulle. On 1 November, the Cabinet decided not to give de Gaulle the same measure of support for an attack on Libreville in the French Congo as they had previously done at Duala in Cameroons.[44] The Colonial Office, the Foreign Office and the Admiralty were all against further de Gaulle operations in West Africa, and Churchill told British naval commanders in the Gulf of Guinea that Britain did not want to compromise the outcome of a power struggle between Laval and Pétain by local action at Libreville. Vichy reinforcements should be made to turn back without actual fighting if possible.[45] The same day, Churchill referred to de Gaulle as 'an embarrassment to us now in our dealings with Vichy and the French people,' and shortly afterwards Halifax suggested that the General might not be allowed to re-establish his headquarters in London.[46] The view in London was that the General, who had just issued a declaration in Brazzaville declaring Vichy unconstitutional, while himself assuming the 'sacred duty' of directing the French war effort, should eschew politics and stick to soldiering.[47] In the event, de Gaulle succeeded in taking Gabon with his own forces, and he was invited back to London, so the uneasy duality of British policy – of supporting de Gaulle while not burning its bridges with Vichy – continued.

Churchill remained suspicious. A paper circulated to the War Cabinet on 14 November set out his views in typically trenchant and elegant fashion.

Laval is certainly filled with the bitterest hatred of England, and is reported to have said that he would like to see us *'crabouillés,'* which means squashed so as to leave only a grease spot. Undoubtedly, if he had had the power, he would have marketed the unexpected British resistance with his German masters to secure a better price for French help in finishing us off. Darlan is mortally envenomed by the injury we have done to his fleet. Pétain has always been an anti-British defeatist, and is now a dotard.[48]

The best way of promoting 'favourable tendencies,' in the Prime Minister's view, was to make sure that 'the Vichy folk are kept well ground between the upper and nether millstones of Germany and Britain. In this way they are most likely to be brought into a more serviceable mood during the short run which remains to them.'[49]

Halifax, by contrast, preferred to treat Vichy 'kindly' and to multiply contacts.[50] His immediate concern was to defuse the risk of the Germans manipulating the French fleet into a clash with Britain, thereby forcing Britain to choose between abandoning de Gaulle or fighting Vichy. Were Britain to be assured of Vichy's determination to defend French overseas territories against Germany and Italy, it would be prepared 'to facilitate the task of the Vichy government in organising such defence of the Empire.'[51] If the French did not attack the territories which had declared for de Gaulle, Britain would refrain from attacking Dakar; and, on the explicit understanding that the above conditions were met, there could be economic discussions, starting with a review of trade between French North Africa and ports in unoccupied France.[52]

By December, it looked as though Halifax's policy might be paying dividends. A letter from Rougier outlined a set of assurances which he claimed had been given personally by Pétain. France would not make a separate peace with the Axis before the end of hostilities. It would not cede either the fleet or naval and air bases to the Axis and would resist Axis or Spanish attempts to seize French colonies in North Africa. And it accepted the submission of French Equatorial Africa to de Gaulle as a fait accompli until the end of the war on the understanding that the territories would then be restored to France and that there would be no attack on French West or North Africa. 'All this is most encouraging,' Cadogan, who was Permanent Undersecretary at the Foreign Office, minuted. 'If these reports are to be believed, we have already got more than we expected out of the French.'[53] Details were circulated to the Cabinet, and Rougier was subsequently paid an allowance for his decidedly questionable services.[54]

Even more encouraging was news of Laval's sudden dismissal on 13 December. This resolved one of the odder debates within Whitehall: whether it was worth trying to bribe him. Cadogan had been opposed, arguing that 'even if we get Laval on our side, we should have handicapped ourselves with an incubus. So long as he stayed there, though, once the Germans are out of France, the French people will see to it that he goes too. There is not enough market value in him.'[55] Much more important, as Churchill noted, the dismissal meant that, for the time being at least, the limits of collaboration had at last been reached.

According to General Halder, Hitler now had doubts whether he still needed France and was 'always thinking' of making peace with England at France's expense.[56] Two days previously, Hitler had given the order for plans for the occupation of the whole of France. Operation Attila, which was to be ready by 22 December, was intended partly to support German negotiations with Vichy but also as a corollary to the planned German capture of Gibraltar, which would require extensive German troop movements through France. The resultant German military movements were noted by General Huntinger, who drew up plans to move the French administration to North Africa.[57]

A second element of the Attila operation is noteworthy in the light of Churchill's fears expressed at the time of Mers-el-Kébir. Discussing the possible occupation of Toulon with his military commanders in early January 1941, Hitler warned that if France became troublesome

> she will have to be crushed completely. Under no circumstances must the French Fleet be allowed to get away from us; it must be either captured or destroyed. Hence Toulon must be occupied at the very outset by means of airborne troops and transport gliders. The harbour and coastal batteries must be taken immediately.[58]

Although the British appear not to have been aware of these developments, they drew encouragement from a visit to Vichy by a Canadian diplomat, Pierre Dupuy. Unlike Britain, Canada still maintained diplomatic relations with France, and Dupuy's visit to Vichy at the beginning of December was the first by a 'British' envoy to France since Campbell's departure from Bordeaux. Dupuy had been briefed to tell the French that the British understood the French feelings of resentment against them. The British were fighting for French lives as well as their own, and their actions in Africa were due not to doubts as to French good faith but to fear that they would not be able to resist German pressure to use French resources against Britain. Dupuy saw Pétain, Darlan and General Huntzinger.[59] His reliability as an intermediary was subsequently questioned in the Foreign Office. 'He hasn't much native sense, his head was rather turned, and he hasn't the knack of very accurate reporting,' was Cadogan's damning later verdict.[60] At the time, however, some importance was attached to his reports that the French had hinted at cooperation in North Africa and Continental

France under a smoke screen of tension (a phrase which in French accounts is attributed to the British), behind which contacts could be made and information exchanged.[61]

Such remarks reflected little more than a French attempt to win time and hedge bets against what was still seen as the unlikely prospect of a British victory. Secretive and opportunist, Pétain was a master of dissimulation who disliked adopting clear-cut policies. Having told Hitler at Montoire that he had always been opposed to the English, he now told Dupuy that he desired British success but was not in a position to help other than by resisting German pressure to use France against Britain. 'I am obliged officially to maintain the balance between both sides,' the Marshal is quoted as saying, 'but you know where my sympathies lie.' Or, as the French historian Claude Huan writes, while disliking the English, Pétain detested the Germans.[62]

This was enough to encourage Churchill to make a bid to bring France back into the war. British military fortunes had revived during the autumn. The Royal Navy had scored an important victory over the Italians at Taranto in mid-November, while British land forces had defeated the Italians in Libya, stimulating an anti-Italian revolt in Abyssinia. The German naval staff was alarmed, reporting to Hitler that 'the enemy has assumed the initiative at all points, and is everywhere conducting successful offensive actions – in Greece, Albania, Libya and East Africa.'[63] Anxious, as he engagingly puts it in his memoirs, 'to give Vichy the chance to profit by the favourable turn of events,' Churchill now addressed a letter to Pétain offering to send 'a strong and well equipped Expeditionary Force of up to six divisions to aid the defence of Morocco, Algiers and Tunis' should the French government decide to cross to North Africa and resume the war there.[64] This was whistling in the wind. But Churchill was ever hopeful, not least because the stakes were so high. Were the French to come over, it would become possible to resist indefinitely a German attack on Gibraltar, and the situation in the Mediterranean would be improved to the point where it could be reopened for convoys to the Middle East.[65]

A similar letter was addressed to General Weygand, whom Hitler regarded as 'unreliable and dangerous' and who, since September, had been Delegate-General in Africa.[66] Churchill had already been trying to get in touch with the French general in July with the object of getting him to try to set up a government in North Africa, which Britain would recognise and support militarily.[67] At the end of October, information was being passed to him via the British Consul-General in Tangiers. The Prime Minister also entrusted Rougier with a message for Weygand, asking him to send an officer to Gibraltar to provide details of the arms he would need to resume fighting against the Germans and Italians. This was another reason for going slow on de Gaulle. Weygand was bitterly hostile to de Gaulle, and Churchill worried that the Free French might become 'an obstacle to a very considerable hiving off of the French Empire to our side.'[68]

Several other emissaries were subsequently commissioned to try to make contact with Weygand, including General Catroux, the most senior general in the Free French movement. In his letter to Weygand, Catroux invoked confidence in Britain's fighting spirit. But he also put forward the argument that Weygand should join the war to ensure that the eventual victory should not be exclusively due to the British. Here, as on so many other occasions in this story, the sense of Anglo-French rivalry was never far from the surface.[69] While denying that he was an Anglophobe, Weygand expressed the typical French concern that Britain was seeking to take Dakar and other French bases which would be lost to France at the end of the war when the French would receive as compensation '500 square miles of desert.'[70]

Churchill described the opportunity open to Weygand as 'the most splendid ... ever offered to daring men.'[71] Not everybody in Whitehall, however, was convinced that the seventy-four-year-old Weygand, who described himself as too old to be a rebel and who was a loyal supporter of Pétain, fitted this bill.[72] Having just lost one major battle, Weygand was determined to avoid a premature declaration in favour of the Allies, which would bring German forces into Africa. 'If the British come to North Africa with four divisions,' he remarked, 'I shall fire on them; if with twenty divisions, I shall welcome them.'[73] The message that came back to London was that while there could be no question of the cession of the French Empire to Germany or Italy, a premature move on Weygand's part would be disastrous. He had a point. When the British Chiefs of Staff again considered the matter, they decided that only two divisions would be available to help him. Weygand wanted to rejoin the war, but only after the balance of power had shifted in the Allies' favour, with the prospect that the remaining conflict would be sufficiently short not to impose any constraints on French sovereignty or the empire's loyalty.[74]

The British received no further encouragement from Vichy. Anglo-French economic discussions, which opened in Madrid in January 1941, proved a failure. The French were by now becoming far less worried about the impact of a blockade, which was proving decreasingly effective.[75] Finding the French demands at Madrid unreasonable, and furious to discover that the French had leaked the discussions to the Germans, the British broke off the talks. The attempts to negotiate a modus vivendi had run into the sands. It should, however, be noted that the French made no further attempts to retake de Gaulle's colonies, and there was no more British military action in Africa until November 1942.

British optimism lingered until February. By the middle of the month disillusion had set in. Unlike Halifax, now exiled to the embassy in Washington, Anthony Eden, his successor, had no time for Vichy. This was Eden's second stint at the Foreign Office, where he had succeeded Samuel Hoare in December 1935, resigning in disagreement over Chamberlain's handling of relations with Italy in 1938. Like Churchill, Eden was a Francophile. Unlike Churchill, Eden spoke fluent French and took a much more pragmatic, impersonal view of foreign policy. He was to prove himself more than ready to fight his corner when sentiment threatened to gain the better of the Prime Minister's judgement, becoming a key figure in the conduct of Anglo-French wartime relations.

For the time being, however, Eden and Churchill were in agreement over France.[76] 'Not one scrap of nobility or courage has been shown by these people [Vichy] so far,' Churchill complained to the Foreign Office on 12 February, 'and they had better go on short commons till they come to their senses.'[77] A week later he declared that it was impossible to 'base policy upon this grovelling crowd. Events may move them, but they have not the slightest concern for us.'[78] In early March the Foreign Office complained that Vichy's policy of subservience to the Germans and the presence of German commissions at bases in France and North Africa threatened to nullify Pétain's undertaking 'that in no circumstances will bases be surrendered to the enemy.'[79]

Anglo-Vichy relations had passed a point of no return, with France drifting, in the words of one senior British officer, 'more and more into becoming our enemy under a very thin disguise.'[80] Darlan's appointment in late February as Vice-President was a significant milestone. Churchill was rightly disturbed, describing Darlan as 'a bad man, with a narrow outlook and a shifty eye,' who nourished 'abnormal and professional resentment' against Britain.[81] Harold Nicolson records Churchill as saying that he would like 'to break that man.'[82] The ill-feelings were fully reciprocated. At the end of 1940, Darlan had described Churchill to an American diplomat as a drunkard.[83]

Darlan's elevation coincided with a more aggressive British enforcement of the blockade, and, by the spring, a virtual Anglo-French naval war seemed to be taking shape as a result of continuing British arrests of French merchant vessels. When a French ship was detained off South Africa in March, Darlan threatened to convoy supplies across the Atlantic. This alarmed London. The war was again going badly for Britain. Italy's reverses in North Africa had drawn in the much more formidable German army, under Rommel. Spanish neutrality remained uncertain. With British naval resources stretched to the limit, a Vichy naval action threatened to tip the war in Germany's favour. A serious naval clash was only narrowly averted at the end of the month following an exchange of fire between a British naval patrol and an escorted French convoy near Oran, and the Cabinet decided temporarily to cease interceptions.[84]

Earlier in April a further crisis threatened following secret reports that Darlan intended to move the *Dunkerque*, which had escaped the bombardment at Mers-el-Kébir, to Toulon, where, for all practical purposes, Churchill believed, it would be in German hands. The Prime Minister remained intensely sensitive over the possible threat posed by France's remaining capital ships. In October 1940 he had been expressing concern over the possible movement of the *Richelieu* and the *Jean Bart* for completion at Toulon. Churchill now seemed to relish the prospect of action against the French warship. If sunk 'neatly and cleanly,' i.e. without heavy loss of life, he wrote, it would increase British prestige and be viewed as a 'natural sequel' to Mers-el-Kébir, which had been so 'generally acclaimed here and in the United States.'[85] This worried the Admiralty, who remained most reluctant to take action that might lead to hostilities against yet another adversary. The French, the First Sea Lord pointed out, remained strong in destroyers and submarines, while the *Strasbourg*, which had also escaped at Mers-el-Kébir, could be 'used with effect' on British trade routes.[86] In the event, however, Churchill was to be deprived of his easy victory, since, following American intervention, the *Dunkerque* stayed put.[87]

The real danger for Britain in the spring of 1941, however, lay in the revival of Franco-German collaboration, for which the German navy was pressing in a last-ditch attempt to wean Hitler away from his planned attack on Russia. Shortly before becoming Vice-President, Darlan had described collaboration as 'indispensable not only for the recovery, but for the very life of the nation.'[88] Britain had no direct means of countering this danger. An offer in late April, passed on by the Americans, to provide the French with all possible assistance if they resisted pressure going beyond the terms of the Armistice elicited no response.[89] By early May there were newspaper reports that Germany was seeking facilities in Syria and Morocco, while, according to an intelligence source, Darlan had come to some agreement about North Africa. This followed reports earlier in the year of German pressure to gain the use of Tunis or Bizerta.[90] Pétain's assurance to the American Ambassador, Admiral Leahy, in May, that he would not give any 'voluntary' military aid to Germany, was regarded in London as ominous. 'Hitler has cracked the whip and the men of Vichy have offered their backs,' one official minuted, while Eden described the Vichy attitude as 'abject.'[91]

What made this succession of rumours and reports particularly ominous was the deteriorating strategic situation in the Mediterranean. Rommel was advancing in the Western Desert. By the beginning of May he had established a foothold in Egypt, and the British had been forced to evacuate Greece following the intervention, a month earlier, of German forces. To compound Britain's difficulties, a revolt now broke out in Iraq. 'These dirty Iraquis [sic] are attacking us at Habbaniya [Britain's main air base in the country],' Cadogan noted in his diary on 30 April.

Talk with A[nthony Eden] ... about Syria (the great danger) Iraq and N[orth] Africa. Met P.M. who said 'So you've got another war on your hands tonight!' News awful. Bad sinkings again in Atlantic. Libya-Egypt seems to be going badly – at least according to the Germans – and Plymouth wiped off the map.[92]

The leaders of the Iraqi revolt appealed for German support, but Iraq was only accessible by way of either neutral Turkey or Vichy-controlled Syria. Provision of such transit facilities went well beyond the terms of the Armistice. In theory, the Germans might have seized what they wanted. In practice, they felt the need to negotiate for fear of stimulating the defections of the French colonies of de Gaulle.[93]

For Darlan, this was an opportunity to be grasped. Hitherto it was always the French who had been *demandeurs*. Now the German were unexpectedly making requests of the French. With no sign of an early peace treaty, Syria provided the Admiral with a new bargaining card.[94] Darlan's aim was a rapprochement with Germany, which would minimise French territorial losses and give France what he described as 'an honourable' role in the future Europe.[95] Behind this lay the assumptions not just that Germany would win the war but that such an outcome would be more favourable to French interests than a British victory. In a bitterly Anglophobe speech, delivered in the wake of a British attack on the port of Sfax in Tunisia on 28 May, Darlan warned that a British victory would settle France's fate whether it was a question of our colonies or our metropolitan territory, guided only by her interests, whatever might have been our attitude during the war … In a triumphant Anglo-Saxon world, France would be only a second-rate dominion, a foreign body in a system in which she could play no honourable role.[96]

Whether Britain treated France as 'a kind of Continental Ireland' or even as a colony, the Admiral declared that he would ensure that France took up her position of a Great Power in Europe and the world, which meant participating in the construction of the new, i.e. German, order.[97]

Darlan therefore had wasted no time in agreeing to German requests for the use of Syria by German aircraft, on the condition that they should have no markings and that the crews should not be recognisable as military personnel. In return, the French believed, in the event wrongly, that they had received German concessions, including the return of French prisoners of war, an easing of controls on the demarcation line between the Occupied and Unoccupied Zones and a promised reduction in reparations.[98] On 11 May, Darlan was received by Hitler at Berchtesgaden. This was the feast day of Joan of Arc, who, as the Admiral pointed out, had chased the English out of France. If Hitler's interest in Anglo-French history was limited, he did tell Darlan that France could help speed up German victory and that for every large concession France made, Germany would make a large concession in return.[99]

More interesting, from the Anglo-French perspective, were Darlan's talks with Joachim Ribbentrop. The German Foreign Minister promised France an 'honourable place' in the new Europe and, possibly with an eye to diverting Hitler from his planned move against the Soviet Union, pressed France to enter the war against England 'in the near future.'[100] Ribbentrop was not the only senior German interested in this possibility. General Wilhelm Keitel talked about embroiling France in war with Britain, while proposals put forward by Otto Abetz, German Ambassador to France, included a French offensive in Africa, support for German operations against the Suez Canal and French naval support for operations against Gibraltar and the Canary Islands.[101] According to the German record, which is in contradiction to the Admiral's subsequent claims to Vichy ministers and diplomats, Darlan agreed to Ribbentrop's proposals, though he was careful to add that France would need more arms.[102]

In the event, the 'Paris Protocols' concluded on 27–8 May reflected a rather less ambitious German agenda, which nevertheless covered three of the main theatres of the current conflict, underscoring the importance of French colonial territories in a world war. In the Levant, the French agreed the delivery of arms from Syrian stocks and an exchange of intelligence over British strengths and defence measures in the Middle East. The second protocol, which was potentially more damaging to Britain, covered North Africa, where France had already supplied Rommel with some trucks while shutting its eyes to the use of the Bizerta–Gabès railway in support of German operations in Libya. France now agreed to the delivery of additional French equipment to Rommel and, more significantly, the use of the Tunisian port of Bizerta, commanding the Straits of Sicily. This was important to the Germans since this sea passage would be much safer than that to Tripoli and Benghazi, which was subject to serious interference from the Royal Navy.[103] The third protocol covered West Africa. German submarines had recently begun operating off the Azores and the West African coast but had been hampered by the Spanish refusal to allow the use of the Canary Islands for victualling and supplies. As of 15 July, German submarines would be allowed access to Dakar. Coming at a time when Britain was suffering severe losses in the battle of the Atlantic, the outcome of which was quite literally a matter of national survival, this was potentially highly damaging to Britain.[104]

All this, as the French negotiators were well aware, involved risks, particularly with respect to German operations from Dakar. But they seemed more than outweighed by the potential gains outlined in a fourth protocol under which Germany agreed to make unspecified 'political and economic concessions' to give the French government the means of 'justifying to the public opinion of its country the eventuality of an armed conflict with England and the United States.' Besides, by struggling with Germany against a common adversary, the French hoped that the Franco-German relationship would change from that of victor and vanquished to one of partners 'honourably associated.'[105] The term 'honourable' is used suspiciously often.

The Paris Protocols represent a nadir in modern Anglo-French relations. Mers-el-Kébir had been an act of self-defence, committed in sorrow rather than anger. The Paris Protocols were a deliberate attempt to buy German concessions at British expense, as well as an act of revenge. But they were also an agreement too far. Ministers at Vichy baulked at allowing the Germans into the French Empire. The opposition was led by General Weygand, who threatened resignation and warned that the French army in Africa would never accept collaboration 'with our enemies.'[106] The Germans in turn failed to follow through with the fourth protocol. What Hitler wanted was the maximum of French concessions without committing himself in any way. However much the German military wanted facilities in Tunisia and Dakar – their forces had been withdrawn from Syria in early June following the collapse of the Iraqi revolt – Hitler had no desire for the complications of a Franco-British war in the run-up to the impending Operation Barbarossa, the attack on Russia on 22 June. The Germans still lacked confidence in a country which Ribbentrop described as exhibiting the uninspiring spectacle of 'courting their conqueror in order to fight their ally of yesterday.'[107] The deal was never implemented. This, however, did not mean that France would be absolved of the consequences of Darlan's opportunistic diplomacy. On 7 June, British-led forces entered Lebanon, precipitating the bloodiest Anglo-French military encounter of the war.

# 6

# Unfriendly States

During Darlan's visit to Berchtesgaden on 11 May, there had been an exchange between Hitler and Jacques Benoist-Méchin, one of the leading French proponents of collaboration, about the chances of British intervention in the Levant. Hitler had dismissed the prospect, arguing that the British already had their hands full in Africa and in the Middle East. Benoist-Méchin disagreed. This was partly because he shared the widely held French belief that the British had long-term designs on Syria. But he had also taken note of the precedents of Norway and Greece, where Britain had sought the pre-emptive occupation of territories which they believed the Germans intended to attack.[1]

Syria and Lebanon had not hitherto been a major priority, the British aim having been limited to ensuring that the war effort should not be hampered by the two countries without having to tie up British troops.[2] Hopes of a Free French coup in the autumn of 1940 had not materialised. Subsequently, Britain had sought to keep local Vichy authorities in line by means of a partial blockade, an approach that frustrated more aggressively minded figures such as Sir Edward Spears and de Gaulle.[3]

The collapse of Greece at the end of April 1941, however, along with the Iraqi revolt, forced the territories to the top of the British agenda. One possibility, tentatively explored at the end of April, was to sound out the French High Commissioner, General Henri Dentz, about the prospects of British support in the event of a German incursion. Dentz was an Alsatian, with no love for the Germans, who had annexed Alsace-Lorraine in 1940. But as a former Chief of Army Intelligence in the Middle East after the First World War, he had also become highly suspicious of the British, to the point where he had several times been passed over for promotion because of his Anglophobe sentiments. Above all, he was a loyal and disciplined French officer who obeyed orders.[4] According to the British Consul-General in

Beirut, Geoffrey Harvard, the approach had obviously interested Dentz. Although insisting that he had sufficient forces to deal with a German attack, he did not entirely rule out the offer. But the matter was not pursued for fear that military information provided to Dentz might be passed on to Vichy and thence to the Germans. Desperately short of troops, the Commander-in-Chief in the Middle East, General Archibald Wavell, was anxious to avoid disclosing 'the nakedness of the land.'[5]

The initial British response to the arrival of German aircraft in Syria on 9 May was to bomb the airfields where they were based. But this was only a preliminary, for with Vichy having, in Eden's words, 'sold out,' direct British intervention now became inevitable.[6] Benoist-Méchin had been right. Britain would not allow the Germans to gain control of what had suddenly become a very important piece of strategic real estate. Airbases were critical at this point in the Middle East war. Over and above the danger to Iraq, once installed in Syria German airpower would threaten Egypt and the Suez Canal, as well as Palestine and Iran, with its oil production facilities.[7] There was also an important political consideration. The Iraqi revolt had aroused considerable enthusiasm throughout an Arab world where British prestige was dangerously low. A German incursion into Syria threatened serious repercussions in Egypt and Arabia as well as the position of neutral Turkey.[8]

'We are surely not going to allow the Germans to take over Syria by default, like a property at a sale for which there are no bidders?,' General Spears thundered from Cairo on 18 May.[9] As this was very much Churchill's view, Wavell's objections to taking on yet another commitment while fighting in Crete and preparing for an offensive in the Western Desert were overruled. A scratch force of some 30,000 men consisting of British, Australian and Indian troops, along with the Transjordan Frontier Force, was duly mustered. The Free French provided six battalions for Operation Exporter, which was launched on 7 June. 'No one can tell which way the Vichy cat will jump, and how far the consequences of this action will extend,' Churchill had written to his son, Randolph, and British commanders in West Africa and the South Atlantic were warned that there was 'a strong possibility' that Vichy would act against British territories in Africa. The greatest danger, if France moved closer to Germany, was to Britain's Atlantic communications, with Gibraltar and Freetown again at risk.[10]

These concerns proved unwarranted. Vichy had no interest in widening the war; the French Ambassador in Madrid was instructed to make the point clear to Hoare. But Vichy was equally determined to defend its territory, not least for fear that the Germans would otherwise take North Africa. In his address to the army of the Levant, Pétain drew on French suspicions of British colonial designs, declaring that, as at Dakar, Mers-el-Kébir and Sfax, England was seeking to realise its old project of dismantling the French Empire, with the Free French acting as British acolytes.[11]

According to the journalist Alan Moorhead, everyone on the British side hated this campaign. The novelist John Masters, then an officer with a Gurkha regiment, came across some graffiti scrawled on an abandoned French post, which read, 'Wait, dirty English bastards until the Germans come. We run away now, so will you soon.' 'I love France,' he recorded, 'and it made sad reading, in a way sadder than the actual fighting and that was tragic enough.'[12]

The French, however, felt that they had no choice. Moorhead describes the view of the better-informed French as one of 'why shouldn't we fight?'

'We're professional soldiers obeying orders and you came here on a deliberate aggression. You think it would have been easy for us just quietly to submit: but what about our friends and relatives imprisoned in Germany? The Boche keep threatening us. They say they will take reprisals, and they mean it. We have to fight.'

And there was another subtler impulse. It was expressed perfectly by a French sergeant near Sidon. 'You thought we were yellow, didn't you? You thought we couldn't fight in France. You thought we were like the Italians. Well, we've shown you.' They were fighting for something which was as fundamental as self-preservation – for human dignity, for the right of walking among others as an equal. And since we brought against them forces much inferior in numbers to their own, the French could not out of a sense of pride surrender at once.[13]

Yet, for all its determination, the army of the Levant could do no more than slow their enemies' progress. Reinforcements proved impossible. Attempts to reach Syria by land were blocked by the Turks; the Royal Navy prevented any Vichy warships reaching the Levant by sea. Consideration was given to mobilising the French fleet at Toulon, but the force lacked air cover and had only a week's supply of fuel. France could not afford to risk its fleet, and, in the final analysis, the Levant was less important than the African empire.[14]

Nor could the French afford to ask for German support. German Stuka dive-bombers had proved highly effective against British forces in Crete.

But the idea of calling in the Germans, especially in a fight involving fellow Frenchmen, was morally repugnant. The presence of German aircraft on French territory would be regarded as treasonous by the French air force and could only increase the risk of defections to the Free French.[15] If German aid were accepted in Syria, what good reason could be found for refusing it elsewhere in the empire, such as Bizerta or Dakar? And there was the immediate risk of widening the war against Britain. Caught between two enemies, the French, in the words of one senior commander, preferred 'to succumb fighting alone.'[16]

It was, nevertheless, an agonisingly difficult decision. Dentz had been torn, at one point asking for German support then withdrawing his request.[17] Towards the end of the war, bitterness at the prospect of a second defeat got the better of the Defence Minister, General Huntzinger, who asked the Luftwaffe to raid British airfields in Palestine and Jordan. This time the Germans refused, citing the demands of the Russian campaign, which had begun on 22 June, the day Damascus had fallen. Operation Barbarossa, for which an army of some 3.2 million men with 3,350 tanks had been assembled, dwarfed the fighting in the Middle East. But when, on 7 July, the Germans changed their minds, the French refused the German offer.[18] Two days later, Dentz was finally authorised to negotiate an end to hostilities.

Dentz had initially put out peace feelers on 18 June but had been prevented from pursuing these by Vichy, which was anxious not to be seen to be violating the Armistice. His instructions now made clear that he was not to negotiate with the Gaullists, described as 'the French who are traitors to their country.'[19] A surrender to the British was not only less distasteful but had the potential advantage that in the event of the British defeat, which Darlan still expected, France might be able to recover its rights in the territory.[20] This entailed the indignity of negotiations on 14 July, Bastille Day, in the Sidney Smith Barracks in Acre, named after the man who had halted Napoleon's advance there in 1799. Symbolism apart, the subsequent convention – Darlan had objected to calling it an armistice on the grounds that France and Britain were not at war – otherwise took full account of French susceptibilities and national pride. The French were allowed to repatriate all of their troops – some 37,500 – who did not want to go over to the Free French.[21] Churchill had spoken respectfully in the House of Commons of the fighting qualities shown by the French, and at the last meeting of the Anglo-French Armistice Commission the British general declared that 'All of us know and love France. Many of us have served alongside her gallant soldiers. All of us look forward to the day of her restored greatness.'[22] When the final French forces embarked at Beirut, they did so to the sound of 'La Marseillaise' played by a British military band.[23]

According to Churchill, Operation Exporter had greatly improved Britain's strategic position in the Middle East, closing the door on the possibility of further Axis penetration eastward from the Mediterranean. The defence of the Suez Canal had been moved northwards by 250 miles, while Turkey was relieved of anxiety from its eastern border.[24] But the immediate threat to Syria had probably lifted even before the campaign began, as a result of the heavy losses suffered by German forces in Crete and the preparations for Barbarossa. In a directive issued on 23 May, Hitler had decreed that any further operations in the Middle East must wait until after the Russian campaign.[25]

The five weeks of fighting had cost some 4,600 casualties on the British-led side – including 1,300 Free French. Vichy casualties amounted to some 4,200 killed, wounded or deserted.[26] Only one in seven men joined the Free French, and de Gaulle's prestige declined in the Unoccupied Zone in Metropolitan France. The General was accused of being responsible for a fratricidal French conflict that served only British interests, and there was a new outbreak of Anglophobia. The repatriated troops were received with astonishing demonstrations of sympathy in France. In November, the German Armistice Commission authorised the transfer of 15,000 repatriated Syrian veterans, along with their equipment, to North Africa. It was an astute move, reinforcing an area already deeply suspicious of British colonial intentions with units which had battle scars inflicted by *les Anglais*.[27]

That said, Vichy was the main loser from the Levant affair. The events of May to July 1941 had once again underlined the unenviable nature of France's position, caught between the German devil and the deep blue English sea. The French did not give up on collaboration. On 21 October, the anniversary of the Montoire meeting, Pétain wrote to Hitler declaring that there 'was so much high-mindedness in your gesture of last year that I feel it my duty to emphasise with words of my own the historical significance of our talks.'[28] Increasingly embroiled with Russia on the Eastern Front, Hitler showed little interest. At the end of 1941, the Germans did revert to the question of whether Vichy would be prepared to enter the war, this time in return for a peace treaty. General Halder's diary of 9 December, the day after Pearl Harbor, refers to Hitler wanting to win France over and using it in Africa and the Mediterranean in the struggle with Britain and the USA.[29] Darlan was again prepared to explore the possibility. Over the two previous months he had hinted that France might move against British colonies in Africa and offered to provide the Germans with intelligence on the British fleet.[30]

As in the past, the Germans quickly backtracked. After being on the defensive in the rapidly moving battle in the Western Desert, Rommel was re-establishing his position in Libya, and Hitler reverted to his distrust of France, which, he told Joseph Goebbels on 22 January 1942, 'renders us certain services in Africa, but not of sufficient importance for us to offer concessions.'[31] Darlan complained privately that during the year in which he had pursued a policy of rapprochement he had received nothing but distrust from the Germans and Italians.[32] Meanwhile, the French were left feeling acutely vulnerable to German pressure – and with good reason. On 29 May 1942, Hitler signed the order updating the contingency plan for the occupation of the whole of France, a possibility never far from the Führer's mind.[33]

Yet despite this catalogue of setbacks in the pursuit of collaboration with Germany, there was little disposition at Vichy to seek rapprochement with Britain. A close reading of the course of the war in the wake of the German attack on Russia and the Japanese attack on Pearl Harbor might suggest a French interest in seeking some kind of reinsurance against the prospect of German defeat. In his final report on 16 July 1941, the French representative to the Armistice Commission at Wiesbaden, General Paul Doyen, argued that increased German demands were a sign of weakness, a demonstration that Germany's chance of victory were 'more and more dubious.'[34] At the beginning of the new year, a memorandum drawn up by the Armistice army staff argued that of the three solutions which could end the war in 1942 – Axis victory, compromise peace or Anglo-Saxon victory – 'the first may be set aside with certainty. The war may drag on for a long time, but the Anglo-Saxon block can no longer be defeated.'[35]

This did not, however, mean that the British were winning. On the contrary, Japan's advances in 1942 in south-east Asia resulted in a string of major British reverses: the fall of Malaya, Hong Kong, Burma and, most humiliatingly, Singapore. Hervé Alphand, a French civil servant who had joined the Free French in London, described the scene in the St James's Club, as members listened on 15 February to Churchill's broadcast describing the grim situation facing Britain in the wake of Singapore's surrender.

I watch the face of the English. Not a muscle flinches. They are heavy and silent. This is the moment, says Churchill, for England to show its genius, its capacity for recovery in adversity.

Then he stops. The old men get up, silent. No word is exchanged. They leave without mentioning the traditional place of their reunion. This silence has its grandeur.[36]

In April 1942, the British seemed, in one British general's phrase, to be hanging on by their eyelids. Australia and India were threatened by the Japanese, Britain had temporarily lost control of the Indian Ocean, the Germans were threatening Persia. In the Western Desert, the British position was precarious.[37] The year 1942 was by far the worst for shipping losses in the battle of the Atlantic. Between January and June, Allied losses rose from 327,357 to 700,235 tons.[38] All this undermined British prestige and cast doubts on its military abilities. There was, as Harold Mack, the Head of the Foreign Office's French Department, noted at the end of May, no prospect of help from France until it was clear to them 'beyond a peradventure that we are winning the war very rapidly.'[39]

Under these circumstances, Anglo-Vichy contact was infrequent and inconclusive; indeed, in pursuing the latter history of this doomed relationship, there is a sense of grappling with spectres and shadows. Indirect communications could be maintained via the Americans, whose embassy at Vichy provided Britain with what Churchill described as 'a window on that courtyard which otherwise would not have existed.'[40] In Madrid, Hoare kept in frequent touch with his French opposite number, François Piétri. In his memoirs, Piétri suggests that the two men maintained a cordial relationship, but Hoare certainly found him far less sympathetic than de la Baume. A telegram from Madrid in November 1941 reported that the French Ambassador had called on Hoare 'with his usual sheaf of protests. I told him that if I started putting our complaints into the form of notes he would be inundated with them.'[41] There were also contacts with French diplomats in other neutral capitals, notably Berne, where the British gained in information from friendly French diplomats. In an emergency, SIS could facilitate rapid communication via its contacts with Vichy intelligence (discussed in Chapter 7).[42]

Occasionally there were more direct, albeit highly clandestine contacts. In June 1941 there was a visit to London by Colonel Groussard, Inspector General of the Sûreté Nationale, who had previously made contact with Resistance groups in France. Groussard claimed that his mission had been authorised by General Huntziger, who had agreed to convey to Pétain any acceptable proposals which Groussard might bring back but who had also made clear that he would be disavowed if the mission came to light. Like

Rougier the previous autumn, Groussard was seen by Churchill, to whom he outlined plans for the expansion of British intelligence operations in France and the means by which the Armistice army could assist if and when the Allies landed in France. Unlike Rougier, Groussard also met with Colonel Dewavrin, also known by his codename, Passy, head of the Free French intelligence.[43] British officials, however, were by no means impressed with a visitor who seemed to ask rather too many questions. Colonel Groussard, William Strang, assistant under-secretary at the Foreign Office, minuted, 'is Teutonic in appearance. His questionnaires are Teutonic in thoroughness, and some of his enquiries and comments are Teutonic in their tactlessness: but I suppose some Frenchmen are like that.'[44] While he was not given the secret information he had asked for the personal use of Pétain and Huntzinger, he was shown something of the British war effort. The British were anxious 'to maintain every contact we may have with Vichy,' and Groussard was given a cipher with which to keep in touch.[45] According to Groussard's own account, on his return to Vichy he secured Pétain's agreement for a continuation of the talks. But when he was subsequently arrested by Darlan, Pétain took no steps to secure his release. He later escaped to Switzerland and continued to provide valuable intelligence to SIS.[46]

Other contacts were sporadic. Now and then, an enigmatic comment from Pétain would be reported to London. In December 1941, Colonel Burckhardt, the former League of Nations Commissioner for Danzig, quoted Pétain. 'Si seulement les Anglais pouvaient voir le fond de ma pensée.'[47] The following month the Duke of Nemours told Hoare that Pétain, whom he had seen, had shown much greater friendliness to Britain but could not collaborate with the British so long as the latter maintained relations with de Gaulle. The Marshal claimed that the two members of his family of whom he was most proud were two nephews serving with the RAF. (The Foreign Office unchivalrously suggested that the relationship was rather closer.)[48] Pierre Boisson, the Governor of Dakar, put out vague feelers to the British in February 1942.

Two months earlier, an officer from the Troisième Bureau of the French General Staff had arrived in Britain and submitted a proposal that when the Allies finally arrived on the Continent relief convoys should be despatched from the UK to Bordeaux and La Rochelle for the support of the Armistice army, which would seize these ports and establish a corridor to unoccupied France. Subsequent communications suggested this plan had the support of General Weygand, who had been dismissed from his African post under German pressure and who was now living in retirement in Provence. This is debatable; a French envoy commissioned in February 1942 to sound out

Weygand about taking command of a landing in North Africa was told that the General was unable to do so since he had given his word to do nothing to embarrass Pétain. What is quite clear, however, is that all contacts with the Armistice army underscored the importance of excluding de Gaulle from any plans.[49]

More intriguing, though at the time equally unproductive, were the feelers put out by Darlan in the autumn of 1941. This contact appears to have begun in September 1941 via Captain Holland who had negotiated with Gensoul at Mers-el-Kébir and who was now Chief of Staff to the Governor of Gibraltar. Although Darlan would not allow Holland to come to Vichy, the Admiral subsequently asked an SIS contact to find out how the British government felt about him and whether, when the war came to an end, they would refuse to treat with a French government of which he was a member.[50] The British response was positive. 'If the French fleet at Toulon were to sail to North African ports and be prepared to resist German attacks,' Churchill replied,

> that would be an event of the first order. Whoever commanded or effected such a great stroke of policy and strategy would have made a decisive contribution to the Allied cause which carries with it the restoration of France as one of the leading powers in Europe. Such a service would entitle the author to an honourable place in the Allied ranks.[51]

This response, which was approved by the Foreign Office and the Chiefs of Staff, reflected Churchill's pragmatic approach to a government for whom he had little but contempt. He variously referred to Britain's 'desertion' and 'betrayal' by a 'caitiff' government which had committed 'acts of baseness.'[52] In a speech to the Canadian Parliament delivered shortly after his reply to Darlan was drafted, Churchill contrasted the behaviour of the 'valiant stout-hearted Dutch' with the 'men of Vichy' who 'lay prostrate' at the conqueror's feet and fawned on him.[53] But as he had already made clear in autumn 1941, Churchill was firmly of the opinion that revenge had no part to play in politics. Vichy was the only government that could deliver the fleet and entry into the French North African provinces, and the Prime Minister was not going to give up on it.[54]

The hard immediate reality, however, was that Vichy was a threat. Not as much of a threat as Britain was to Vichy, but nevertheless an unwelcome distraction and additional source of anxiety during one of the most difficult periods of Britain's war. Vichy was unpredictable. Admiral Leahy complained in July 1941 that it was 'impossible to guess what will happen tomorrow or the day after.'[55] Its senior leadership was avowedly Anglophobe. Laval's return to power in April 1942 was regarded in London as particularly ominous. For a moment it seemed possible that Pétain might be induced to flee to Africa and set up as head of a pro-Allied government there, but this hope soon passed. 'We can hope for nothing good from this government,' Harold Mack wrote in a paper which was circulated to the Cabinet. Laval has 'staked his life on German victory and will do all that he can to bring it about.'[56]

In fact, Laval, who had little interest in military collaboration, was less of a danger than Darlan, who remained Commander-in-Chief of the French armed forces. The Admiral had military information about Britain which was of interest to the Germans, some dating back to the period of the Entente, some derived from French listening posts. As early as 1940, reports on British naval movements through Suez and the Red Sea were being passed from French Somaliland to Vichy and then on to the Germans and Italians. Some additional information on British warship movements appears to have been provided in 1941 as a result of the Paris Protocols.[57] In December 1941, the Admiral offered the Germans information about British naval bases and the establishment of a teleprinter link between the French naval command at Vichy and German naval authorities in Paris. In response, Hitler sanctioned an exchange of intelligence about the Royal Navy. Franco-German naval cooperation only ended with the scuttling of the French fleet at Toulon in November 1942.[58]

With Japan added in December 1941 to the list of its enemies, what primarily concerned the Royal Navy was to avoid hostilities with the French. When, in December 1941, officials discussed possible French reactions to a proposed ultimatum by Churchill to Vichy, a senior naval officer warned that an all-out French attack on British convoys in the Atlantic risked a major disaster. This danger was in fact remote; the French were short of manpower, fuel, ammunition and equipment and were anxious to avoid a clash with the British.[59] But there were periodic scares over the reported movement of France's remaining capital ships resulting in the dislocation of British naval plans, which, at worst, caused the postponement of other arrangements and at best gravely increased anxieties. The British were particularly concerned to avoid the concentration of French forces at Toulon, where it could be used against the Allies or more easily seized by the Germans, and orders were issued to use all means to prevent the battleships *Richelieu* and *Jean Bart* from entering the Mediterranean.[60]

One group of French ships remained within British control: Admiral Godfroy's Force X interned at Alexandria. Relations between the local British and French naval commanders remained good, with the French treated with courtesy and consideration. Force X, however, was not entirely harmless. It provided intelligence to Vichy, with which it had been allowed to retain radio contact, and, according to Spears, its sailors surreptitiously circulated pamphlets attacking de Gaulle and the British and 'creating a dangerous element of dissatisfaction among the mixed, uncertain population' of Alexandria.[61] Churchill, who had never really liked Cunningham's deal with Godfroy, remained restless. In a bloodthirsty note to Ismay and the Chiefs of Staff on 23 May 1941, the Prime Minister asserted that the arrangements regarding Force X had been superseded by Vichy actions in 'destroying the basis of the Armistice terms' (i.e. allowing the Germans into Syria).[62] Britain should therefore now seize the ships, which he described as an indispensable replacement reserve for the Mediterranean fleet, 'killing without hesitation all who withstood us.'[63] In the event, Godfroy's conduct at the time of Operation Exporter was, in the Admiralty's words, 'immaculate,' and on 14 July Cunningham ordered his own ships to fly the French flag.[64] In March 1942, the Prime Minister was again on the offensive. With British forces in the Mediterranean heavily reduced, Britain must make sure that Force X was 'put on a safe basis, even if rough measures have to be used.'[65] Wiser Admiralty counsels again prevailed.[66]

Three months later there was a crisis. Following the fall of Tobruk on 21 June, news of which a badly shaken Churchill received while in the White House, Rommel's incursion into Egypt momentarily threatened to force the evacuation of Alexandria. Here was a contingency unforeseen by the original Cunningham–Godfroy accords. The British wanted Godfroy to follow the Royal Navy through Suez to a British port, an action the Germans insisted would be regarded as a rupture of the Armistice. Vichy wanted to exploit the situation to regain control of its ships, and Godfroy was instructed to try to go to a French port, preferably Bizerta.[67] This was rejected in London where Cadogan complained that 'our naval officers are too prone to trust the "honour" of other naval officers.'[68] But there was also reluctance to take violent action for fear that 'another Oran' would give Laval the excuse to move even closer to Germany, or possibly to declare war. This prospect worried Churchill not so much because of its immediate military consequences but because of long-term political repercussions. How could Britain restore France's empire after the war if it had fought Britain during it?[69] The Americans became involved, proposing that the ships might be sent to a harbour in the Western Hemisphere. The problem effectively disappeared with the halting of Rommel's advance at the first battle of El Alamein at the end of July.

More serious than the French naval danger was the continued risk that one or more of Britain's enemies might gain access to bases in the French Empire. Despite the collapse of the Paris Protocols, the German services continued to show interest in Dakar and Bizerta, where Darlan had already conceded the Axis resupply facilities.[70] Pressure increased at the end of 1941 in response to reverses suffered by Rommel in Libya and successful attacks by the Royal Navy on Axis Mediterranean supply routes. Mussolini urged the seizure of Bizerta, but Hitler demurred, arguing that France could only be approached after the Axis had regained command of the central Mediterranean. A premature demand might lead to British intervention in North Africa.[71]

This did not, however, stop the Germans putting pressure on France, not just for resupply facilities through Bizerta but also for Franco-German military cooperation in the event that the Germans were forced to retreat into Tunisia. Darlan conceded both demands, although conditions were attached to the latter. Privately he claimed that Rommel was unlikely to need to fall back on Tunisia and that resupplying him was in French interests in order to avoid the arrival of British troops on the Tunisian border and to prevent French Africa from becoming a battlefield.[72] A subsequent agreement on French supplies for Libya was signed with the Italians in early February 1942. American pressure helped to end this operation.[73]

The difficulty for the British was that while aware of German pressure they were unsure of what Vichy had conceded. In a general directive dated 22 September 1941, Churchill warned that 'at any moment' Britain might be faced with German penetration of Morocco, Algeria and West Africa.[74] A meeting between Marshal Hermann Göring and Pétain and Darlan on 1 December was followed by a spate of contradictory intelligence reports as to whether or not France had conceded base facilities in North Africa. Trying to assess the evidence ten days later, Harold Mack concluded that 'the balance of evidence and probability' supported the view that France had indeed agreed to place North African bases at German disposition. This was incorrect; a subsequent SIS report that the meeting had been frigid and had led to no important results was much nearer the mark. The French Naval Attaché in Madrid was instructed to deny the reports to his British opposite number.[75]

Germany was not the only threat. In July 1941, France had been forced to concede bases in Indochina to Japan, though this time without the counter of any kind of concessions. A cartoon by Low showed a Japanese soldier goose-stepping into a door marked 'Indo China Gateway to Mastery of the Far East,' while Pétain stood to attention. From the British point of view it was to prove the single most damaging French action of the war. The Japanese air attack on 10 December 1941 that sunk the *Repulse* and the *Prince of Wales*, Britain's most modern battleship, was launched from Indochina. Bases in Indochina were also used by Japanese air, naval and ground units in the attack on Malaya.[76]

In the wake of Pearl Harbor, attention in London quickly turned to another French territory, where it was feared the Japanese might seek bases. Almost equidistant between Aden, Cape Town and Colombo, the Indian Ocean island of Madagascar commanded key British communications routes to the Middle East and India, routed via the Cape and East Africa.[77] The Japanese had toyed with the prospect of seizing a base on the island, an idea to which Laval appeared receptive. Despite assurances conveyed to the Americans and to the British via Madrid, Laval had raised the issue in discussions with the Germans in April.[78]

British opinion was divided over whether or not to take the island. The Chiefs of Staff were not convinced that Japan would venture some 4,000 miles into the Indian Ocean, while Wavell, now the Indian Commander-in-Chief, was opposed to an operation that would divert resources from the defence of India. Churchill, although sharing some of the Chiefs of Staff's doubts, was in favour. His reasons were by no means exclusively military. In addition to the Prime Minister's incurable addiction for adventurous military undertakings, Churchill was aware of a need to boost British morale, as well as his own political standing after a run of military reverses.[79] France, in other words, once again appeared to offer the prospect for a relatively easy victory. The decision for Operation Ironclad was taken by the War Cabinet on 12 March.

An amphibious operation in the Indian Ocean was not something to be undertaken lightly in the spring of 1942. Because of the extensive naval movements required at a time when the German battleship *Tirpitz* was posing a serious threat in home waters, the British needed to ask for temporary American reinforcements in the Atlantic.[80] Laval's return to power in April heightened concern over possible French retaliation. The list was by now familiar. The French might grant the Germans access to Bizerta, or, more worrying, because of the difficulty it would cause in running convoys around the Cape, to Dakar. They might bomb Gibraltar or Freetown, or even hand over the fleet.[81]

The planners considered their options. Retaliation would not be easy. Attempts to bomb Vichy by daylight would result in heavy losses – 'wastage' is the term used in the official documents – while night bombing was complicated by the absence of topographical identifying features. The Chiefs of Staff discussed bombing Paris, but this was rejected on the grounds that it would alienate French opinion.[82] In the event, the French were taken completely by surprise by the assault on the deep-water port of Diego Suarez in the north of the island on 5 May, the fourth British attack on Vichy forces in two years. Whatever the anger at what even pro-Allied Frenchmen saw as a premature and useless attack against French territory, as usual Vichy was anxious to localise the conflict. There were three days of heavy fighting, with British casualties amounting to 20 per cent of the attacking force – some 380 men killed and wounded. The French suffered 510 casualties and lost three submarines and a frigate.[83]

The British now faced a dilemma. Ideally the whole of Madagascar island should be secured to prevent the Japanese taking any other of the harbours, but with troops badly needed for the defence of India there was a natural reluctance to become involved in what Eden described as 'a new, small and vexatious war on this large island.'[84] The idea of bringing in Belgian troops, albeit for garrison duties, was strongly opposed in the Foreign Office. Britain, one official argued, would be accused of inflicting 'yet another indignity on conquered France. Beaten as they have been the French still maintain their pride, and they would regard the presence of Belgian troops, whether white or coloured, in Madagascar, as a further humiliation.'[85]

More serious attention was thus paid to the idea of a local modus vivendi, with money and trade being used as bargaining counters. Immediately after Pearl Harbor, Churchill had raised with Roosevelt the rather implausible possibility of an Anglo-American approach to Vichy for the amicable transfer of the island's ports to British control. Now he suggested that money and trade facilities might be used to facilitate a local arrangement.[86] Others were doubtful if not downright hostile. South Africa had a close interest in the operation, and its Prime Minister, Field Marshal Jan Smuts, was unable to understand the reason for 'the continued policy of appeasement of Laval's henchmen whose clear aim it is to help the Axis in every way possible.'[87] There was concern in the Foreign Office about further upsetting de Gaulle, who was already furious at having been excluded from the operation and the bad example such an arrangement would set to resistance movements in

Europe. Besides, it was doubtful whether the attempt would succeed. The record of trying to negotiate with Vichy was, to say the least, unimpressive, and the French were unlikely to agree to anything to which the Armistice Commission at Wiesbaden did not consent.[88]

The sceptics were proved right. The French Governor of Madagascar, Armand Annet, took full advantage of British weakness, feigning an interest in negotiation, which he hoped to drag out until the rainy season in October would make further operations on the island impossible.[89] By July, the British military authorities had tumbled to the Governor's tactics, and as the Japanese threat to India appeared to recede Churchill became anxious to 'tidy up' Madagascar.[90] Once it was clear that the new operation would not divert shipping from the impending Anglo-American landings in North Africa, which were now dominating British strategic considerations, Operation 'Streamline Jane', to take control of the whole island, was given the go-ahead. Darlan ordered resistance to the end. Even if the British could not be thrown into the sea, they could be taught to leave the French Empire alone. The French put up a skilful, but relatively bloodless defence, blocking the advance of motorised columns along the island's poor road system, which allowed Vichy to play up the resistance to the Germans.[91] Eventually, on 6 November, an armistice was signed, putting the island under British control while preserving French sovereignty. The resistance had continued just long enough to entitle French soldiers for a military medal and possible cash rewards. The penultimate Anglo-Vichy clash, described by one historian as an absurd little Anglo-French war within a world war, was over.[92]

# 7

# Enemy-Controlled Territory

Concerned as the British were over the future of the French fleet and empire, they were even more exercised by the fate of Metropolitan France. A country of some 40 million people with a land mass of around 212,000 square miles, nearly twice the size of Britain, it represented a potentially lethal threat in the hands of Germany. French territory provided the Germans with bases in the two battles most vital to British survival: the battles of Britain and of the Atlantic. Air defence planning had assumed that enemy bombers would come from Germany. But the Luftwaffe now had access to French bases, which were much closer to Britain, for the aerial onslaught to which, following the fall of France, the whole of its bomber force could be concentrated. The large majority of the German bombers, along with their all-important fighter escorts involved in the battle of Britain, which had started at the beginning of August, had taken off from French airfields.[1] Had the Germans succeeded in achieving air superiority, then Operation Sealion, the proposed landing on the British south coast between Ramsgate and the Isle of Wight, would have depended heavily on the use of the French Channel ports, including Cherbourg, Boulogne, Le Havre, Calais and Dunkirk.[2]

The battle of Britain was over by the autumn, although the Blitz, the attacks on London as well as ports and industrial targets, continued until May 1941. During the worst attacks on the capital, German aircraft flew double and even treble sorties from airfields in France and Belgium.[3] The battle of the Atlantic, which British propaganda to France referred to as 'our Verdun,' dragged on until 1943.[4] This was another battle Britain simply could not afford to lose. Churchill later described it as 'the dominating factor all through the war.'[5] Britain lost more than a third of its gross shipping tonnage in the second half of 1940, and the mortal danger to Britain's lifelines 'gnawed' at the Prime Minister's bowels.[6] Here again access to

French bases and territory gave the Germans an important advantage. A series of large modern airfields were built at Bordeaux, Cognac, Vannes, Dinard, Rennes and Evreux. German dive bombers flying from northern France attacked British convoys in the Channel; long-range bombers based at Bordeaux reached out into the Atlantic; and reconnaissance aircraft based at Lorient sought out convoys for attack by U-boats. The German navy gained access to the French Atlantic ports. These were used by both powerful surface raiders, such as the cruisers *Scharnhorst* and *Prinz Eugen*, as well as by Italian and the all-important German submarines. Access to France allowed these vessels to operate well beyond the range of British air and naval escorts, as well as to avoid the long and dangerous transit from the North Sea to the Atlantic. Submarines could stay longer on patrol, thus increasing the numbers available to attack British ships.[7] Major building works were undertaken at the Atlantic ports of Brest, La Pallice, Saint-Nazaire and Lorient, the headquarters of the U-boat command, including the construction of heavily protected submarine pens, which were to prove bomb-proof. In November 1942, naval intelligence estimated that there were some seventy-five submarines currently in the French harbours, with another ninety vessels at sea. From the naval point of view, the west coast of France was thus 'of overwhelming importance.'[8]

France made another significant contribution to the German war effort. In the first three months of the occupation, the Germans placed orders worth over 12 billion francs with French companies. By 1943, Germany was taking 40 per cent of France's total industrial output, including 80 per cent of its vehicle production. The French aviation industry became an important supplier for the German air transport fleet: some 27 per cent in 1942, rising to 49 per cent in 1944. Planes produced in France supplied Rommel's army in North Africa. By the end of 1941, the Germans were taking 40 per cent of French bauxite, 55 per cent of its aluminium and 90 per cent of its cement. Tens of thousands of France's most advanced machine tools were shipped to Germany, as well as locomotives and large numbers of rolling stock to supplement the inadequate German railway system.[9] As the German labour shortage began to bite in 1942, France was forced to provide labour to German industry. The following year, some 600,000 men were drafted to work in Germany under Laval's Service du Travail Obligatoire (STO). Together with French prisoners of war, there were some 1,388,000 French workers in the Reich in the autumn of 1943.[10]

Reaching back into France, whether to attack the enemy, mobilise the French population or exfiltrate agents, escaped British airmen and intelligence, posed formidable challenges. At the outset, even information was sparse. France had not been a major intelligence target before the war. Partly due to French sensitivities, attempts to establish stay-behind operations had been frustrated until May 1940, by which time it was too late. Initially the main source of military information was air reconnaissance, which was still a young art, while SIS was relying on Michelin tourist maps of France.[11] This was scarcely reassuring at a time when German invasion seemed imminent. Such was the desperation for intelligence about the planned German invasion that, aware of Hitler's interest in astrology, attention was even paid to his horoscope. But between October 1940 and April 1941, SIS managed to infiltrate fifty-seven agents into France.[12]

SIS's main partner in its intelligence-gathering operations was the Bureau Central de Renseignement et d'Action (BCRA), the intelligence arm of the Free French. In early 1942, SIS estimated that 40 per cent of its intelligence on France came from the Free French.[13] Personal relations between the two services were good, a reflection of Colonel André Dewavrin's pragmatic approach to cooperation with the British, who, in turn, showed understanding for the Free French. In July 1941, SIS offered a system that would allow the French to code and decode non-military intelligence from their own agents in recognition of the Free French desire to feel their messages were going directly to their own countrymen in London. Nevertheless, tensions inevitably arose, not only from BCRA's dependence on SIS for equipment, communications and transport, but also from SIS insistence on the right to work with non-Gaullist elements and its refusal to help BCRA in any kind of political work in France. These frictions accentuated BCRA suspicions of British motives when there were problems over the supply of equipment to BCRA or air pick-ups in France.[14]

A second British intelligence asset consisted of Polish networks which had managed to stay behind after the French defeat.[15] But the majority of the networks were French. They drew on a wide cross-section of French society, including government officials, businessmen, factory workers, railway officials and prostitutes.[16] Recruitment, certainly of serving officers, was by no means always straightforward. One French naval officer, who was to prove a particularly valuable source, initially hesitated; his reasons are familiar: Mers-el-Kébir and concern about violating his oath of allegiance to Pétain.[17]

Not all were savoury characters. Claude Lamirault, who ran the important 'Fitzroy' network, was described by a SIS officer as being 'as tough as any Chicago gangster and rather an ugly customer.'[18] Like the leaders of two other important networks, Lamirault was on the political right. Many of the members of the Confrérie de Notre Dame had strong religious leanings. Its leader was a former film producer, Gilbert Renault, who had been a far-right political activist before the war. Renault had joined the Free French in June 1940. In the autumn he was infiltrated back into France via Lisbon and Spain and built up a network which eventually consisted of some 2,000 agents.[19] A second network was set up by Georges Loustaunau-Lacau, an extreme right-winger with good contacts at Vichy. On his arrest, it was taken over by his secretary, Marie-Madeleine Fourcade. In 1942, the network, which had some 3,000 contributing agents, of whom nearly 500 were killed, was receiving some 2 million francs a month from the British.[20] Sometimes known as Noah's Ark, since its agents were given the code names of animals, Fourcade preferred the name L'Alliance in order to make clear that, like the Free French, its members were allies rather than agents of SIS.[21]

The point is worth stressing. Members of these networks, along with the French postal engineers, who in 1942 tapped one of the main German communications lines from France to German defence headquarters in Potsdam and Berlin, were among the most valuable of Britain's new French allies, contributing directly to the British war effort. Although it is impossible to build up a comprehensive picture of the intelligence flow from France, it is clear that a great deal of information was obtained. Perhaps the most important information provided in the early years concerned the German naval presence along the Atlantic coast. French agents furnished information about German naval movements. Between the end of March and June 1941, daily reports were received regarding the position and seaworthiness of the battlecruisers *Scharnhorst* and *Gneisau* in Brest. There were again warnings about the imminent movement in early 1942 of the *Scharnhorst* and *Prinz Eugen*. These, however, were not acted on, allowing the ships to escape up the Channel to Germany. But the complete plans for all the submarine bases in France were acquired at the cost of six bottles of good wine.[22]

Other information from French agents concerned Luftwaffe bases in France and early warning of the development of the V1 Flying Bombs, which began attacking London in June 1944. Joseph Brocard, who worked for the Agir network, travelled around France, often by bicycle, looking for wood for a front company. He was one of a number of French agents who helped provide maps and detailed drawings which allowed the RAF to destroy most of the early fixed V1 sites.[23] Details of German coastal defences, including complete plans of the 'Atlantic wall,' which the Germans began building in 1942, proved invaluable for the planning of D-Day.[24]

More politically intriguing was the material provided by Gustave Bertrand. Like the British, before the war the French had got hold of an Enigma decoding machine. In the wake of the collapse, the French equipment, along with its decoding personnel, was moved by the section head, Gustave Bertrand, to the Unoccupied Zone and set up at a chateau not far from Nîmes. This was vitally important to Britain, because it ensured that the Germans did not learn that Enigma, the critical mainstay of British wartime Signals Intelligence (SIGINT), had been compromised. Bertrand then re-established contact with Britain and began providing advance warning of Abwehr and Gestapo operations against SIS officers, along with information about German and Italian troop and ship movements into North Africa, German dispositions in the Balkans and losses on the Russian front. Before the German occupation of the whole of France in November 1942, when the chateau had to be hastily evacuated, there were reported to have been eight to ten daily transmissions to Bletchley Park. Contacts with SIS, however, continued into 1943.[25]

Bertrand's role raises the intriguing question of the intelligence relationship between Britain and Vichy, or, more accurately, elements within Vichy. Contact with the French military Deuxième Bureau had been re-established by September 1940, and a special section of SIS, separate from the one dealing with the Free French, was created to work with Vichy.[26] Intelligence is an inherently murky business, reflecting, on the French part, divided loyalties and very complex calculations of interest. Vichy intelligence, which covered both Metropolitan France and the Empire, faced an unprecedented number of potential enemies. The Service de Renseignement (SR) under whose auspices Bertrand's cryptologists fell, saw the Axis as the primary enemy. According to Bertrand, the only limitation imposed in the wake of Mers-el-Kébir on his cooperation with London was the supply of 'operational' intelligence, a limitation which he ignored. Bertrand is also said to have acted as a contact point between the Head of SIS, Sir Stewart Menzies, and Louis Rivet, head of the Deuxième Bureau.[27] SR Air, which centred its attention on the Luftwaffe, also relayed material to London. Commandant Paul Paillole, the head of the Travaux Ruraux, a counter-espionage service which disguised itself as an agricultural association, maintained contacts with London – while at the same time collecting information on Allied agents in France.[28]

Although the exchange of intelligence between Vichy and Britain was limited, Vichy authorities tipped off members of L'Alliance regarding raids on their clandestine radio transmitters. The network was useful as a means of maintaining a potential link with Britain, if only as a form of insurance, a point certainly not lost on Darlan.[29] Further information came via Bertrand from the Ordre de la Résistance de l'Armée (ORA), an intelligence organisation that included regular French officers on 'armistice leave.' While their members considered themselves anti-German, anti-British, anti-Communist and 'purely and traditionally French,' their main task was to be capable of rapid reactivation in the event of a British landing.[30] For those in Britain amassing intelligence on France after the Armistice, the lines separating friend from enemy were hazy. The same was even more true for the myriad Vichy intelligence organisations. As Paillole remarked in a 1942 lecture, Germany was the No. 1 and England the No. 2 danger. 'Everyone is working against us. France is all alone.'[31] It was the Vichy cry of lamentation.

None of this, of course, prevented British intelligence from targeting Vichy, any more than alliance with de Gaulle prevented them targeting the Free French. The fact that British intelligence gained a copy of Rougier's report from Pétain's office suggests that Britain had informants there as early as 1940.[32] But the main source of political information on Vichy came from the breaking of the diplomatic codes of some of the foreign embassies there. Higher priority was given to this task following the signature of the Paris Protocols in May 1941, a copy of which was obtained in October, and by autumn Churchill was receiving regular SIGINT on the growing factionalism in Vichy. The breaking of Japanese ciphers proved particularly productive. The Japanese Embassy sent extremely accurate and thorough reports on Vichy foreign policy and the relationship with the Germans. Japanese cable traffic from Madrid, the favourite Vichy neutral capital for covert contacts with Britain, was also useful. Telegram traffic from the Turkish Embassy provided another invaluable source of information, most notably following Weygand's dismissal in autumn 1941 and regarding the Vichy response to the Anglo-American landings in North Africa in November 1942.[33] Intelligence on French naval movements, gained, inter alia, from diplomatic and consular officers in Berne, Lisbon, Madrid and Tangiers, as well as sources in Unoccupied France and Casablanca, was consistently good. Britain had prior warning of all major French naval movements.[34]

All of this was supplemented by open source material. The Foreign Office Research Department's French Section employed 150 people, monitoring and interpreting French radio broadcasts and newspapers, along with confidential reports from agents and official reports on French public opinion from friendly sources in Vichy. They even recovered and analysed newspapers used as wrapping paper. A more orthodox source of French papers was provided by the British embassies in Stockholm and Lisbon.[35] The BBC issued a bimonthly intelligence report that drew on a wide range of sources. These included interviews with travellers from France, listeners' letters (some of which seem to have been allowed through by sympathetic Vichy censors), radio monitoring, French newspapers, copies of letters opened by British postal censors and letters seized at sea en route from French territories to and from France.[36] Intelligence-gathering on France had become a major industry.

As well as information, plans, documents and, on one occasion, components for the V1 rocket, people needed to be brought out of France. Numerous informal and ad-hoc escape lines sprang up in the autumn of 1940 for British servicemen left behind after Dunkirk and aircrews shot down over enemy territory. Most ran either to Marseilles or to the Pyrenees. Across France, men and women took immense risks to help over 3,000 Allied airmen escape.[37] Agents and Resistance leaders as well as people joining the Free French were brought out. They included men who became well known in the post-war world. In November 1943, a future French president, François Mitterrand, was flown to Tangmere airfield in Kent, before being interrogated at the special intelligence holding centre for foreign arrivals at the Royal Victoria Patriotic school in London.[38] Mitterrand, like many others, came by a small single-engined aircraft, the Lysander, which was capable of landing at night on fields or improvised air strips. The night-time flights across the Channel into a darkened France by these slow, gawky aircraft, which resembled a partridge in flight, graphically symbolise the tenuous nature of the physical links between Britain and France.

The Lysander could carry two or, at a pinch, three passengers. In notes for pilots, a senior RAF officer advised that

Pick-ups have long been outstanding for the good will which exists between pilots and agents, founded during the agents' Lysander training and continued before and after pick-ups. This is most important and all pilots should realise what a tough job the agents take on and try to get to know them and give them confidence in pick-up operations. This is not easy if you don't speak French and the agent doesn't speak English, but don't be shy and do your best to get to know your trainees and passengers and to let them get to know you.[39]

This advice seems to have been heeded. Some of the personal Anglo-French friendships formed in the process, as well as between members of the Resistance and comrades in the SOE, lasted a lifetime.[40]

Not everybody could be successfully evacuated. In March 1943, a message reached London suggesting that the lives of Reynaud and Georges Mandel, the former Minister of the Interior who had advocated fighting on in June 1940, might be in danger. Eden minuted Churchill that he was reluctant to do nothing for the two but that he could think of no useful action. Churchill asked whether SOE could not make a plan of escape. But the difficulties of getting Reynaud and Mandel out of the fortress where they were being held were insuperable. Mandel was executed by the Vichy Milice in July 1944.[41] There was an odd incident in autumn 1943, when a message arrived in Algiers that Pétain was willing to come out of France. For reasons that remain unclear, the information was suppressed by Harold Macmillan, the Minister Resident in Algiers.[42]

Important as it was to get information and people out of France, the key challenge was to reach back into the country. The prospects of any kind of land operation were remote. Despite Churchill's enthusiasm, it was not until 1942 that any British raids were launched against French territory. The first of these, in March at Bruneval on the French coast, succeeded in capturing a radar station used for guiding German bombers to Britain. The following month, a commando raid which, as at Bruneval, utilised intelligence provided by French sources, blew up a dry dock at Saint-Nazaire, which it was feared might be used by the German battleship *Tirpitz*.[43] But the raid created unforeseen political difficulties. No warning had been given to the local population, which had assumed this to be part of a larger invasion. The consequent French support had resulted in brutal German reprisals, for which the British were subsequently blamed. The much larger Dieppe raid of August 1942 raised similar hopes, but proved a hapless failure.[44] No serious land operation against Metropolitan France was undertaken before the 1944 D-Day landings.

The RAF, by contrast, had little difficulty reaching German military targets in France as well as French factories working for the German war effort. But there was a serious political problem of which British ministers and officials were acutely aware. Collateral damage to French residential quarters close to the targets risked alienating French sympathies and providing a propaganda gift to Vichy and the Germans.[45] Daylight attacks on French factories in northern France were only authorised in June 1941, and it was not until early the next year that night-time bombing raids were agreed by the War

Cabinet. One of the arguments put forward in their justification was that to refrain would be regarded by many French as a sign of weakness.[46] Bomber Command was, however, warned that much of the value of the attacks would be lost, and British prestige and good will amongst the French people would suffer, if there were large numbers of civilian casualties and the target attacked not decisively damaged.[47] Instructions for Bomber Command for one series of raids on French industrial targets thus laid down that they were only to be made in favourable weather conditions by reliable and experienced crews and that bombs were only to be released if targets were definitely identified.[48] The fact that public opinion was believed to be more pro-German helped deter any attacks in the Unoccupied Zone.[49]

The first major test of French reaction came with the bombing of the Renault works at Billancourt on the outskirts of Paris on the night of 3 March 1942. This was the RAF's largest raid against any single target in Europe so far in the war, aimed against a factory estimated to be producing some 18,000 lorries a year for Germany. Production was halted for a period of weeks, but, despite precautions, 367 French people were killed, with 341 badly injured. Some 9,250 people lost their homes.[50] The initial reaction in Vichy, as reported by the Americans, was bitter, with complaints that the British 'who cannot win a battle anywhere wished a cheap victory against a defenceless city to present to the British public.'[51] Pétain and Darlan attended a memorial service for the victims in Vichy, and the German Commander in Paris attended a service at Notre Dame. Churchill was accused of having 'the emotional life of a butcher.'[52]

This propaganda barrage masked the fact that the attack had produced significantly less anger than the British had originally feared. According to a source in the French police, some 75 per cent considered it 'normal' for the RAF to have bombed the Renault factory.[53] The moral drawn by Eden was that bombing was acceptable provided that it was powerful, accurate and 'reasonably economical of civilian life.'[54] Three months later, Mack noted that the French response to the bombing left nothing to be desired, adding that he sometimes wondered 'if in similar circumstances we ourselves would take the same view of such raids.'[55] In some cases, bombers were escorted by Free French aircraft serving with the RAF.[56]

Yet the unease remained. In May, a proposed attack on the Schneider armaments and locomotive workers at Le Creusot was turned down, this time in part because of the political situation in Vichy in the wake of Laval's return to power, though the decision was reversed two months later.[57] The Free French expressed concern when the Cabinet authorised night-time attacks on trains. (The Germans had been reported as experiencing a shortage of railway engines and rolling stock.) SOE too voiced doubts about the attacks which caused relatively little damage while killing and injuring French railwaymen, and they were discontinued the following year.[58] In June 1942, the Secretary of State for Air, Sir Archibald Sinclair, voiced concern over proposals to bomb the Atlantic submarine bases. His language is telling. If the air staff were convinced that this would reduce the maritime threat to manageable proportions, Sinclair was willing to ask Cabinet whether it was worthwhile to incur the 'political odium' for such an important objective. Otherwise, it was useless to ask Cabinet to embark on a policy of 'ruthless attacks' on French towns.[59]

The matter was raised again in late autumn. This time it was Eden who voiced reservations, citing the likely impact on de Gaulle's Fighting French in North Africa and the harm it could do Britain with public opinion in France both during and after the war.[60] Now military considerations won out over political concerns. The battle of the Atlantic was reaching a climax. November 1942 saw the highest Allied losses of the war – 860,000 tons, more than 720,000 of which had been sunk by submarines.[61] Under strong pressure from the Admiralty, the War Cabinet authorised attacks designed to devastate 'the whole area in which are located the submarines, their maintenance facilities and services, power, water, light, communications etc.'[62] The result was five weeks of intensive attacks that consumed half Bomber Command's total bombing efforts and did heavy damage to Lorient and Saint-Nazaire. A raid on 28 February 1943 destroyed three-quarters of the town and drove out the 12,000 people who still lived there, although none of the submarine pens were penetrated.[63] But the fact that for the first, and only, occasion 'area bombing' of French towns had been authorised is a reflection of the gravity of the threat Britain was facing in the Atlantic.

If France was difficult to attack directly, it was much easier to infiltrate. The most geographically accessible of the states occupied by Germany, it had land frontiers with two neutral countries – Switzerland and Spain – as well as long and open coasts, suited to secret landings by saboteurs or intelligence agents. The Special Boat Service operated a small flotilla from Cornwall and the Scilly Isles. The port of Newlyn had what one Free French officer described as an odour of secrecy and espionage. A boat could leave the Helford river at 5.30 in the afternoon and reach the Breton coast by midnight, allowing an hour ashore for delivering stores and meeting and collecting people. At least one convenient Breton cove had been used during the Napoleonic wars. Operations from Gibraltar were rather easier. Here submarines could be used, as well as feluccas, which, while exceedingly uncomfortable, could carry more than thirty passengers. This allowed agents of the various secret services to be transferred to and from the south of France.[64]

Although France was in easy air range of England for parachute or clandestine landings, in practice these were often far from straightforward. Everything depended on the weather. Lysander pilots had to read their maps with the help of the moon. Landings had then to be made on unfamiliar small fields, guided in by hand torches manipulated by partisans, who had been alerted by messages sent out by the BBC French Service. Parachute drops were no easier. The task of the French landing committees, as SOE's official historian, M. R. D. Foot notes, bristled with difficulties:

> Three men held torches or bicycle lamps out in a row, along the direction of the wind, in the middle of a flat space of open ground about half a mile across. The commander of the party stood with a fourth torch so that the lit torches looked from the air like a reversed capital L. When a distant rumble in the sky announced that an aircraft was near, all the torches were pointed towards it; the leader's torch flashing a previously announced morse letter. Provided the aircraft did see the lights and the letter was correct, it released its load above them and was gone as soon as it could, so as to attract as little local attention as possible.[65]

But the lights were by no means always visible. A combination of navigational difficulties in the air and police activity on the ground, plus the risk that the dropping zone could be clouded over in a few minutes, meant that some 40 per cent of the sorties flown to France by aircraft of the Special Duties squadron, formed in 1942 to provide an air link with France, proved abortive.[66]

Most of the men and also women, who along with their vital radio transmitters were being infiltrated into France, belonged to SOE, which had been set up in July 1940 in response to the German occupation of much of the Continent. Although it would not, in Churchill's flamboyant words, 'set Europe ablaze,' it was to play an important part in the creation of a nucleus of trained men and women who would be able to assist as 'fifth columns' in the liberation of their countries – a task, it was believed, which would be best promoted by committing or instigating acts of sabotage. 'Tales of derring-do for the reading of a school boy,' to quote Foot again, became entangled with 'tales of intrigue and treachery of Proustian complexity.' This was an 'essentially unorthodox formation created to wage war by unorthodox means in unorthodox places.'[67] Continental Europe suddenly offered much the same opportunity for adventure as the Empire had traditionally done.

Second to Yugoslavia, France would prove SOE's most important theatre of operations, with six sections dealing with the country. Like SIS, SOE deemed it prudent to create different units to deal with Gaullists and non-Gaullists. The main work was done by F-Section which had been established in October 1940. Its existence was originally concealed from de Gaulle, who was furious when he found out and would have been even more furious had he read an SOE minute of December 1940, stating that F-Section should know everything the Free French were doing, but that the latter should know nothing of SOE operations. The General complained bitterly and continuously about the existence of an organisation acting independently of the Free French, insisting he must be the coordinating authority of all subversive and secret work in France.[68] But de Gaulle's view may also have been coloured by a paranoid view of the British intelligence services, popularised by inter-war Anglophobic writing. The British stood their ground. De Gaulle, it was pointed out, was demanding a degree of autonomy not even accorded to an independent government. Besides, SOE did not want to place all underground operations in Free French hands, insisting on also being able to work with those who did not support the General. SOE did not share the General's political agenda in France and regarded Gaullist attempts to centralise resistance activities as dangerous from a security point of view.[69]

In March 1941, a separate section was set up to provide backing for the Free French. R/F-Section's principal task was to stimulate, guide and service the creation of a unified resistance movement and a secret army in France. The operational orders of its agents were normally drafted by de Gaulle's service and then sent to R/F-Section for agreement, but both de Gaulle's and SOE's staff had to agree the wording down to the last letter. R/F-Section did not, however, have full operational control. Although it handled, or at least believed it handled, all de Gaulle's wireless traffic, it might not know the full directives or reports of all the men it carried. Indeed, it remained a cardinal point of de Gaulle's policy that he should put his own men in by his own means where he could and evade as much British supervision as possible.[70] Although it deployed fewer agents than F-Section, until well after D-Day its importance was sometimes as great, indeed – with the sparking of a French national uprising in the summer of 1944 – it came to be greater.[71]

The rivalry with F-Section could be intense, and the two sections operated out of separate buildings in London.

By January 1944, SOE's tentacles stretched into virtually every part of France.[72] But its operations had been slow to get going. Initially there had been a problem of recruitment. To operate effectively and relatively safely in France, agents needed to pass as French, or at least as Swiss or Belgian, in terms both of appearance and linguistic fluency. Several agents whose voices were detectably not French died as a result. Most members of R/F-Section were French citizens. Given the paucity of English speakers with impeccable command of French, F-Section tended to recruit British subjects from international business circles or from Anglo-French families.[73] Some of these were the product of the First World War, being the children of British soldiers in France. The agents' backgrounds ranged from pimps to one Indian princess, who died in Dachau. Motives, Robert and Isabelle Tombs note, are difficult to assess, but 'Franco-British patriotism, a taste for adventure and personal animus against the enemy made an effective combination.' Of some 1,000 agents sent to France, fifty were women, who tended to attract less suspicion, and worked as couriers and radio operators.[74]

Finding such people, however, took time. SOE operations were further hindered by logistic bottlenecks – until August 1941 there were fewer than five planes available for operations in north-west Europe. There was also a certain amateurish quality in F-Section's work, which remained evident up until 1942, and the official history exposed what was privately described as the 'repeated incompetence' of the Head of F-Section, Maurice Buckmaster.[75] Tactics were developed by a process of trial and error, security was at times defective, networks were penetrated and destroyed by the Germans. In one case, a Frenchman recruited by SOE, Henri Déricourt, who conducted seventeen operations involving twenty-one aircraft, appears to have been operating for the Germans.[76]

Fraud sometimes posed a problem. In 1941, SOE discovered an organisation based on the Côte d'Azur, led by a French painter named André Girard. Code-named Carte, Girard claimed to have hundreds of thousands of men at his disposal and to be in contact with elements of the Vichy military, notably Weygand. SOE and SIS agreed that Carte was either a cover for the Vichy Armistice army created for its secret organisation or a private venture closely related to it. Arms and money were supplied, and a special black radio station, Radio Patrie, set up, much to the annoyance of the Free French, since Girard was anti-Gaullist. But it was a sham. Girard, who was living in a delusional world of his own, allowed the British to fool themselves. When he arrived in Britain in 1943, SOE decided he was 'virtually mad' and forbade his return to France.[77]

Getting help on the ground in France could be difficult, particularly in the early years of the war, when Britain was doing badly. As one SOE agent later noted of the situation in 1942, 'They wanted to back the winner and that's why they were not prepared to cooperate. They weren't pro-German but they were certainly not prepared to back us.'[78] Things got easier as the war progressed and support for the Resistance grew. That said, even at the start offers to help were more common than attempts to betray, and some of SOE's earliest efforts depended on clandestine French police cooperation. In many cases, particularly in the country, ordinary policemen looked the other way, even advising agents to get themselves better forged identity cards or to carry their pistols less conspicuously.[79]

The first F-Section agents were only infiltrated into occupied France in spring 1941.[80] In June there was a successful sabotage operation against an electricity transformer station at Pessac near Bordeaux. This fed the railway line between Bordeaux and Irun, which the British feared might be used by the Germans if they decided to move forces through France to Spain en route to Gibraltar. By September twenty-one agents and organisers had been sent, and thirteen organisers and subagents recruited locally. As of August 1942, six organisers had been installed in the Occupied Zone, while twenty-five SOE-trained organisers were operating in the Unoccupied Zone. In addition, SOE had sent in some 42 million francs, the equivalent of around £150,000.[81] These were not large numbers, and the results were correspondingly limited. Although sabotage, along with murders and attacks on members of the Wehrmacht, was becoming common, and trains were frequently derailed, these did not as yet constitute a serious danger for the Germans.[82]

It was only in 1943, later described by the German Supreme Commander in the West, Field Marshal Gerd von Rundstedt, as a 'serious turning point in the internal affairs of France,' that SOE could claim to be making the sort of impression on the enemy high command that it had been set up to achieve.[83] Serious damage was done to the French inland waterway system, disrupting normal German traffic as well as the despatch of German E-boats and miniature submarines from the North Sea to Italy at the time of the Allied landings at Anzio and Salerno in early 1944. Carried out by the BCRA and R/F-Section, this was one of the few Resistance operations that can claim to have had a significant strategic impact on the war.[84] Sabotage attacks on the transport system were more effective than those by the RAF and did not involve the same French casualties. By late 1943 targets were increasingly divided up between the British and American air forces and SOE. In other instances, SOE was given a limited period to secure the cooperation of management or the workforce for factory sabotage, under the threat that these would otherwise be bombed.[85] But the bulk of industrial sabotage was only carried out in 1944 in coordination with the Allied landings in Normandy and in the south of France.

SOE's other main role was to provide help for the French Resistance. 'Give the French time,' Churchill had told an American journalist in July 1940. 'I just cannot see the French people going on submitting to the Nazis.'[86] The Resistance emerged by way of a series of disparate and uncoordinated groups in both zones, which only finally coalesced under the Conseil National de la Résistance (CNR) in May 1943. Most began when a handful of friends got together, decided they had to do something and found ways of producing leaflets, stickers or a newspaper.[87] Their activities were essentially political. Attacks on Germans, which began in 1941, were aimed at individual soldiers and drew fierce reprisals on the French population. Large-scale sabotage operations only began in 1943. Estimates of the size of the Resistance vary, in part according to definitions of what constitutes resistance. They were certainly very much a minority, less than 2 per cent of the population, according to Matthew Cobb – a maximum of 500,000 people, strong in some areas of the country, while weak in others.[88]

Getting through, or at least being seen to get through to Britain was a gauge of serious intent in the early days of the Resistance. Alban Vistel, a Resistance leader in the south-east, said he formed the first nucleus in his Lyon factory by claiming to have contact with London.[89] In fact, the British knew relatively little about the Resistance before the visit to London in autumn 1941 of Jean Moulin, the former Prefect of Chartres. Moulin was a man of fearless integrity. Physically stocky and inconspicuous, he had a commanding presence and gifts of drive and leadership.[90] He had made his own way to Lisbon, from where he was flown on to Britain by the RAF. He came with what he described as an SOS from three Resistance movements operating in the Unoccupied Zone: Libération, Libération Nationale and Liberté. The French will to resist, he reported, had reached the point where arms, money and cohesion could be usefully applied to assist the German downfall when the time came and preserve civilised society at the point of transition from a German-dominated to a free society. Failure to provide this support could only benefit the Communists. At the same time, Moulin complained that while 'the Anglophile movements in France' were without any communications with London, Pétain had been able to send a secret agent to London, in the form of Colonel Groussard.[91] In talks with Major Morton, Moulin stressed that with the great decline of Pétain's prestige, de Gaulle's name had now become real to the large majority of Frenchmen.[92]

Moulin's visit set a precedent. In 1942, a series of Resistance leaders began to come to London for talks with de Gaulle, and Moulin himself returned to London for a short rest in February 1943.[93] He had returned to France the previous year with a message from de Gaulle to Resistance leaders, along with the General's mandate to control and coordinate their activities. Until his arrest in June 1943 he controlled the radio links between London and the Resistance, as well as allocating the large amounts of money which now began to be sent out from London, and which, although channelled through the Free French, originated with the British Exchequer. In June 1943, the British provided 80 million francs for the Resistance.[94] Meanwhile, SOE's air-liaison section allowed the unified national control of the Resistance, which was set up under de Gaulle, to get onto its feet. And it was SOE that provided the all-important arms and explosives. Moulin's initial request had been for light arms, and only 23 tons of stores were dropped into France in 1942. In 1943, by which time initial preparations for the D-Day landings were under way, the figure had risen to 586 tons.[95]

Yet, however much the BCRA and the Resistance depended on British aid, the relationship, along with that with the members of the French intelligence networks and the individual Frenchmen and women who sheltered British airmen, was ultimately one of interdependence. SOE agents would have been unable to operate in France without French aid.[96] The dangers this involved were stark. As one SOE circuit organiser later said,

> we had to recruit people who were living, well, managing to live, in their homes with their families and we were putting the whole lot in great danger. I remember many times when a man who was enthusiastic about joining would take me home, he'd have a pretty wife and a little girl, and he knew what the Germans did. We were shoving the whole lot into danger ... and not just them but a number of their friends.[97]

These risks were taken for the sake of what was seen as a common commitment against the Germans and represent one of the clearest manifestations of the way in which the Entente was gradually re-forming in the wake of the French defeat. Despite all the difficulties, by 1942 it was clear that the French borders were more permeable than the Germans, or indeed Vichy, might have hoped or expected. But the most important means of penetration was, paradoxically, not clandestine but very public. Radio was a weapon of war, one in the use of which the British excelled as much as they had done in radar, fighter design and signal's intelligence.

# 8

# 'Ici Londres'

Contrary to Hitler's hopes, the Armistice had not ended the battle for France. No sooner was it signed than a propaganda war broke out. The French began jamming the BBC on 27 June 1940, four days after the Armistice, and Vichy Radio began to broadcast on 5 July, under the personal authorisation of Hitler. Radio Paris, which was now under German control, was on the air by the end of July.[1] For the British, this was not just a very important war but also a peculiarly challenging one. In contrast to propaganda efforts directed at other occupied countries, such as Holland or Norway, French sympathies were uncertain, and the main task was to try and change minds.

In fighting this war of words and ideas, London had three main weapons at its disposal: radio, paper and rumours, hundreds of which were created for use in France. These had first to be approved through a committee system in Whitehall and were then spread by SIS and SOE through contacts with neutral travellers, journalists and diplomats. Their aim was to boost French and undermine German morale, as well as to undermine French confidence in Vichy and the German occupation. Thus a rumour was planted that the Germans wanted to dismantle the Eiffel Tower and use the metal for munitions. Pétain was said to be allowed to write only the beginning and the end of his speeches himself. Another rumour suggested that the Germans dropped bombs on French residential areas in towns immediately after the British had hit legitimate targets. According to Rex Leeper, Head of the Foreign Office's Political Warfare Executive (PWE), rumours spread quickly in Europe in 1942, but evidence of their impact is, perhaps inevitably, limited.[2]

The propaganda war took more tangible form in a paper bombardment of France. In addition to dropping bombs and supplies, the RAF also dropped magazines and leaflets. More than 676 million leaflets were dropped over France during the war, second only to the total dropped on Germany. (A single bomber carried up to 24,000 leaflets.) Over 500 titles were produced in French, including an illustrated magazine *Accord* and a regular *Courrier de l'Air*, which carried news, photographs, features and cartoons. Other material included war news from around the world as well as explanations and justifications of British policy. On the night of the invasion of Madagascar, some 2,484,000 leaflets were dropped on urban centres in unoccupied France explaining the British action. Leafleting was also used to explain, as well as to warn of bombing attacks, with endurance of the bombing portrayed as a form of resistance.[3]

Distribution was uneven, the bulk being dropped over the Occupied Zone, since this was within range of the RAF operational training units used for the deliveries. Leaflets supplemented broadcasts. The material was more graphic and was regarded by at least some people as having a greater permanence than the spoken word. Leaflets helped service the clandestine resistance press in France, as well as providing what a former *résistant* described as 'a sort of material bond with those who were working elsewhere for our liberation.'[4] Not all leaflets, however, could be overtly delivered by air. So-called 'black' leaflets, which purported to come from a source other than the one from which they actually emanated, had to be dropped in containers and then distributed so as to give the impression that they had been produced in France. Much smaller in number, they were also more precisely targeted.[5] German attempts to prevent people getting hold of the leaflets included sending out special squads of men with long strong-pronged sticks to pick them up before dawn. In Occupied France, the punishment for possessing a leaflet was prison or even execution.[6]

Much more effective than leafleting was radio. This was a remarkably flexible medium, at once, in the words of a BBC intelligence report, 'the most public thing in the world and the most private.'[7] Broadcasting to France came in two forms. Britain ran a series of 'black' radio stations, which purported to be broadcasting from France. Radio Catholique, aimed at parish priests, put over the message that if they were not prepared to support the Resistance they should at least not stand in the way of those of their parishioners who were. During his 1941 visit to London, Jean Moulin described the station as having great effect.[8] Radio Travail was aimed at industrial workers and union leaders, dissociating itself from the Free French and the Communists, while Radio Inconnu was aimed at the petit bourgeoisie. It was vulgarly abusive of the Germans, regularly attacked Pétain and Vichy and advocated the assassination of Darlan and

Laval. It was also successful at spreading rumours which were then taken up by the French press.[9]

Two other stations were linked with the Free French. Radio Gaulle was an unsuccessful joint venture between PWE and the Free French, intended to train certain kinds of resistance groups. Radio Honneur et Patrie only began broadcasting in 1943, when it became known as the official voice of the Resistance. Policy was determined at weekly meetings between PWE, the Free French, SOE and visiting members of the Resistance. According to one of the British participants, this was the only occasion he knew of when the French really let themselves go in front of the English, resulting, however, not in bad feelings but in friendship and understanding.[10]

By far the most important British station, however, was the BBC French Service, with its call sign 'Ici Londres': 'This is London.' A remarkably cost-effective operation – its staff in December 1941 was roughly the equivalent of a company of infantry – it added a completely new dimension to Anglo-French relations, helping Britain to mount what no less an authority on propaganda than Joseph Goebbels described as 'the intellectual invasion of the Continent.'[11] The BBC had begun broadcasting in French (along with German and Italian) at the time of the Munich Crisis in September 1938. Following the collapse of France, BBC transmissions, which now constituted Britain's only link to Metropolitan France, were immediately increased. By June 1943, the BBC was broadcasting for five and a half hours a day, half an hour more than the German transmission.[12] Although they had lost an ally, the British had gained an audience.

Unlike SOE, the BBC was, from the outset, a highly professional operation, which understood the critical importance of winning the trust of its listeners. There was an immense thirst for news in France, and the BBC quickly gained a reputation for accurate and unembroidered reporting, which its audience verified by cross-checking with other stations, notably Swiss radio.[13] During the difficult early years of the war, it was a point of principle that reverses and defeats would be fully reported. 'No harm can be done by admitting any military reverses,' a directive issued in summer 1942 by PWE emphasised. 'These will become evident to our listeners in a short time and it is better that we should tell the full extent of our defeat than leave it to the enemy.'[14] Besides, a radio station which had not hidden the truth when things were going badly would be more readily believed when it told good news. On more than one occasion in the early years listeners were told, 'This evening the news is bad.'[15]

The BBC was also careful to respect its audience. The listener was not regarded as an object of contempt who could be manipulated by propaganda but rather as somebody capable of judgement, who could be told the facts and convinced by reason.[16] Wounded French pride was taken into account. A 1941 Foreign Office paper stressed the need to flatter the French and to 'make them feel our equals.'[17] In a broadcast Eden made on 14 July 1942, he referred to France as a 'sister nation,' who was an ally as well as a friend.[18] At the same time, there was an appreciation that this was an audience whose primary concern was the day-to-day practical problem of keeping alive.[19] One of the worst-fed people in Occupied Europe, the French faced a daily battle with shortages and scarcity, with everything from clothes to food, wine, tobacco and petrol rationed. The BBC intelligence report for October 1943 quoted a French child (by then in foster care in Switzerland): 'pas beau la vie, pas beau ... pas manger chez maman, jamais dîner, jamais manger.'[20] In their hearts the French might, as one listener claimed, be anti-German, but in practice they were 'one hundred per cent food hunters.'[21]

A further, and important, requirement had been appreciated from the outset: the need to sound authentically French. 'Whatever directives are issued,' one official wrote in November 1940, 'must be put into practice by Frenchmen and intelligent Frenchmen.'[22] One of the most successful programmes was called *Les Français parlent aux Français*. Like the rest of the schedule, it was presented by a remarkably talented team, who became household names in France.[23] All this helps explain why the BBC quickly gained the trust of its French listeners, remaining largely untainted by the brush of 'perfidious Albion,' or any of the other main accusations on the Anglophobe charge sheet.

The objectives set for the BBC, which were in general similar to those of the leafleting operation, were highly ambitious, in part unrealistically so.[24] The primary aim was to rally France by restoring 'the self-respect of the French people by assuming that they had never accepted defeat' and morally rearming them for a renewal of the struggle by persuading them 'of the certainty of an Allied victory.'[25] From almost the moment of the Armistice the BBC sought to put across the same message which Churchill had tried to convey to Reynaud's government: that Britain would fight on and was the only hope of restoring French grandeur and liberty.

This argument began to gain credibility with the battle of Britain. It was the BBC that gave France the news that Britain was surviving the Blitz and defeating the Luftwaffe. The battle of Britain, one BBC broadcast pointed out, was as much a French as a British victory.[26] Coverage was given to the gradual widening of the war. Much was made of America's great industrial potential, which began to be made available to Britain with the introduction of Lend-Lease in 1941. Hitler's attack on the Soviet Union was described as a supreme folly. Hitler had broken his word to the Russians and would do the same to the French.[27] Much coverage was thereafter given to the Eastern Front. A feature programme broadcast in September 1941 portrayed Napoleon's 1812 Russian campaign, with the parallels clearly drawn. The day after Pearl Harbor the French were told that the war was now global and that it was clear that the Axis could not win.[28] When the RAF sent a thousand bombers to attack Cologne in 1942, the French Service publicised the news. 'Les Boches seront punis, battus et écrasés.' ('The Germans will be punished, beaten and squashed.') The French were also told of resistance movements elsewhere in Europe.[29]

Closely related to this primary objective was the discrediting of the German occupation and the encouragement of passive French resistance. Of these, the former task was relatively straightforward. Anxious to minimise civil resistance, at the beginning of the occupation the Germans had been instructed to behave very correctly. The harsh reality soon became evident. The virtual annexation of Alsace-Lorraine, the growing economic exploitation of the country and, from autumn 1941, the execution of French hostages in reprisal for Resistance activity, were all grist to the propaganda mill. By 1942, British objectives had become more ambitious, with the aim of demoralising the German forces of occupation, which had been identified as one of the soft spots of the German war machine, and getting the French to cooperate in this task.[30]

Encouraging French resistance was a more complex matter. British officials conceived one of their roles as expressing what they saw as the wishes of Occupied France to the people of the Unoccupied Zone. In doing so, they could help organise French national unity and stiffen the attitudes of the 'less combative' section of the nation by reminding them of what the more combative sections were doing.[31] At the same time, there was also consistent concern to prevent a premature revolt before Britain was in a position to restart the war in Europe, which could only provoke futile bloodshed.[32] Thus, the PWE directive for 12 September 1941 stressed the need to avoid anything that might be interpreted as applying to 'concerted sabotage activities' or violence of any kind, while encouraging the French to 'group themselves in whatever way is possible, and let them know that we are aware they are doing this.'[33]

The BBC's third main objective was to undermine Vichy and impede collaboration. Attacks were directed against both policy and personalities. The belief that a collaborating France might play an important part in a Germanic Europe was repeatedly attacked, as were the major Vichy initiatives in collaboration. 'Do you know where Hitler is leading you?' one BBC speaker asked in the wake of Pétain's meeting with the Führer at Montoire. 'To an open war with Britain. To an economic war with the United States. To a moral war with the rest of the civilized world.'[34] The arrival of German forces in Syria the following May led de Gaulle to warn in a broadcast that 'the men of Vichy' who had delivered Syria to Germany would tomorrow hand over North and West Africa.[35] Attention was paid to the French fleet. A PWE directive of 7 March 1941 underscored the message that if Germany was unable to seize the fleet at once it might still set about a process of infiltration. France can contribute greatly to Germany's defeat by preventing this. The directive of 4 July warned of the risk of Darlan, in a moment of desperation, using the fleet 'against France's allies and on Germany's behalf.'[36]

Of the Vichy leadership, Pétain escaped direct personal criticism by the BBC, an issue on which the Marshal was very sensitive. Rather, he was portrayed as a 'tired, ineffective, mistaken, yet honest old man': 'une tragique illusion.'[37] This was in the first place recognition of his popularity in France, which meant that attacks were likely to be counterproductive. But there was also a desire not to underscore differences with the Americans, who were anxious to retain their links with Vichy, as well as the vain hope that Pétain might yet decide to continue the war from North Africa.[38]

Laval, by contrast, was subject to quite uninhibited attack, which was stepped up on his return to power in April 1942. 'We did not mince our words in describing this 'excellent *serviteur de l'Allemagne,*' the BBC output report for 12–18 April noted.[39] Attacks on what were described as 'the smaller men' were no less vitriolic. Jacques Doriot, a strong proponent of collaboration, was described in a PWE directive of July 1942 as 'a thug,' Benoist-Méchin, who had negotiated the Paris Protocols, as 'the creature of the Germans and lackey of Laval. Treat with contempt.'[40] The banker Gabriel Le Roy Ladurie was referred to as 'a crooked financier who is tied up with a number of internal trusts.'[41] Darlan initially came in for relatively more lenient treatment. The PWE directive of 2 May 1941 noted that there was no occasion for personal attacks on his character as nothing detrimental was known about him. In the wake of the Paris Protocols, however, the tone changed. BBC attacks included a song to the tune of 'Frère Jacques': 'Qui trahit la France? / C'est Darlan, c'est Darlan' (Who betrays France? / It's Darlan, it's Darlan).[42]

A fourth aim was to explain and defend British policy, including of course the bombing, and to counter the Anglophobia fanned by German and Vichy propaganda. The breakdown of the Entente, seriously exacerbated by Mers-el-Kébir, had precipitated an outburst of anti-British sentiment on a scale not seen since the Fashoda Incident of 1898. The failure of its former ally to furnish more aid in May and June provided an obvious scapegoat for defeat, while condemning the British became a safety valve for pent-up emotions that could not be openly directed against the Germans.[43] The BBC sought to counter this mood, along with some of the more specific accusations, including the claim that at Dunkirk the British had run from France, leaving the French to cover their retreat. By autumn 1940, sentiment was beginning to change in Britain's favour. A letter from the British mission in Geneva quoted two Frenchmen who had recently arrived from France. 'Although my informants agree that feelings in France on the subject of Britain are mixed, even those who do not like us hope that we will win.'[44] The BBC's intelligence report for November suggested that while Anglophiles were now in the ascendancy, they lacked dynamism.[45]

It is impossible to generalise about French attitudes towards Britain across both the Occupied and Unoccupied Zones, as well as the complex of class and political groupings over the following years. But the view expressed by an officer of the Deuxième Bureau in 1941 that this was not simple or easily defined, was close to the mark. 'France for the French – not for the Boches – nor for the English,' seems to reflect a widespread view.[46] The Canadian diplomat Pierre Dupuy contrasted the difference between Anglophiles and Anglophobes at Vichy. Whereas the former said 'pourvue que les Anglais gagnent,' the latter said 'pourvue que ces cochons d'Anglais gagnent.'[47] Suspicion or hostility to England, however, was never far from the surface, particularly at the time of British military reverses. There was the old stereotype of 'perfidious Albion,' out only for its own interests at French expense – and constantly eyeing France's vulnerable empire. Anglophobia in some French circles, including certain types of senior officer, the haut bourgeoisie, left-wing pacifists and sections of Communist cadres, was acknowledged by PWE as probably irreducible. The BBC was instructed to makes these targets of mockery or dislike for reasons other than Anglophobia but to avoid sweeping attacks on any of them as a whole class.[48]

In seeking to put across these various messages, the BBC was in constant competition with Radio Paris and Radio Vichy, mostly notably with Philippe Henriot, who proved a skilled propagandist. The duel was stepped up in 1942, with the creation of a monitoring service that allowed immediate BBC responses to claims or statements made on French radio. By the following year, large quantities of documents and clandestine papers were being brought out from France for use in BBC transmissions.[49] While it is clear that the British got the better of their antagonists, the evidence on which any assessment of impact depends is inevitably impressionistic. Although the reports of the French *préfets,* as of the German army, paid attention to BBC listening, there could be no accurate statistical surveys of audiences. That said, a combination of wartime evidence, along with the later testimony of those in France, allows us to suggest the ways in which the French reacted to the BBC and the way it helped mould French opinion.

The number of radio sets in France has been variously estimated as between 4 and 6 million.[50] Although this means that many households did not have a set, a good deal of group listening was reported, with news also being passed on, if not always accurately, by word of mouth. Listenership, however, was by no means uniform. British reports in the summer of 1942 suggested that while an estimated 75 per cent of the population of Rennes were regular listeners, in Paris, where there was a constant fear of being caught listening, the figure was only estimated at 25–30 per cent. Contacts in Lyons did not listen very regularly.[51] Jamming was a constant problem that often made broadcasts very difficult to hear. Irène Némirovsky's wartime novel *Suite Française* describes a neighbour's radio sending out 'a series of piercing, plaintive, droning notes like Arab music or the screeching of crickets (it was the BBC of London distorted by interference).'[52] This was not always a disadvantage. According to one French journalist, jamming actually increased listening in rural areas, where the peasants believed the broadcasts would not be jammed if they did not contain important information. But it certainly worried the authorities in Britain, encouraging recourse to the less effective use of leaflets, some of which contained details of alternative wavelengths where reception was believed to be better.[53] Over time, audiences were also threatened as radio tubes and valves wore out and it became increasingly difficult to find spares, licensed repairers and replacement sets.[54]

Nevertheless, by the end of 1940, listening appears to have been widespread. A listener from Savoy wrote that even in the remotest farms in the mountains the peasants listened.[55] Vichy's own estimates put the number of listeners to de Gaulle's BBC broadcasts in 1941 at around 300,000 listeners, a figure which increased tenfold the following year.[56] According to one German military report from Brittany, the French population only believed what was said on the BBC, while the Propaganda Abteilung reported that all politically minded Frenchmen either listened to the French broadcasts of 'English radio' or asked their neighbours about it on a regular basis.[57] A September 1941 French Gendarmerie report from the Gard *département* in the south of France described the BBC as exercising a 'tremendous influence' over public opinion.[58] Listening in public places was banned in the Unoccupied Zone in late 1940, but the circumspection to which this gave rise did not last. Formerly, according to an official report of 1943, 'people sought to disguise the fact that they were listening and took precautions vis-à-vis neighbours. Today however people listen with windows open.'[59] The BBC even penetrated prisons. Agnès Humbert, who had been arrested as a member of the Resistance, records how when de Gaulle called for an hour's silence on 11 May 1941 this was observed, and then followed by a spirited rendering of 'La Marseillaise.'[60]

The BBC provided a lifeline to a country completely cut off from the rest of the world, whose population was metaphorically, as indeed at times literally, listening in the dark.[61] The timetable of the BBC broadcasts ruled everyday life, with the news orientating the conversations of the following day.[62] Asked to write a composition about what she did on Sundays, an eleven-year-old girl described a day that began with mass in the morning and ended with listening to the English radio.[63] Referring to a discussion programme entitled *Les Trois Amis,* a student wrote, 'as they chat they give us courage to go on waiting.'[64] Liliane Schroeder, a twenty-two-year-old girl living in Paris, described her feelings listening to a BBC music programme: 'And I am liable to prison, to the confiscation of the set, like innumerable other people who would not miss their news from the BBC for anything in the world and who gain patience, comfort, hope and a hint of gaiety from the English transmissions.'[65]

Most valued was the news: news of the war, including news of Italian reverses, which one *préfet* report from the Occupied Zone in April 1941 noted was being followed with some pleasure, and – no less important – of what was happening elsewhere in France and its empire. Much of this concerned developments which Vichy or the Germans did not want the French to know about, such as the arrival of German forces in Syria in May 1941. The BBC was for many the main source of news of the pastoral letter issued in August 1942 by the Bishop of Toulouse, Monsignor Saliège, condemning the persecution of the Jews.[66] But the radio also provided the opportunity to listen to discussion and debate, to hear French voices and, occasionally, to laugh. After the liberation, one listener recalled Churchill's broadcast in October 1940. 'We are waiting,' the Prime Minister had declared, 'for the long-promised invasion. So are the fishes.'[67] Listening to London, especially in groups, helped to create a sense of purpose while also, as the British intended, keeping the two zones in touch with one another. Above all, perhaps, it helped undermine the defeatism that had gripped the country in the summer of 1940.[68]

The BBC's most important political success was to put the Free French on the map. Indeed, de Gaulle's was the first modern political reputation to be made entirely by radio.[69] When de Gaulle arrived in London on 17 June 1940, his name was virtually unknown to the French public. With the exception of his brief spell as Under-Secretary of War in June 1940, his whole career had been spent within the relative anonymity of the French army. The General was to make a total of sixty-seven BBC broadcasts, ten of them between 18 June and 13 July.[70] Although caricatured by Vichy propaganda as *le général micro* (the microphone general), he was a superb broadcaster, speaking clearly and forcefully and with a voice capable of cutting through the jamming. He took his task very seriously. In his war memoirs he writes of speaking with the impression that he was accomplishing 'for the millions who were listening to me … a sort of priestly duty.'[71]

The Free French were quickly given their own daily five-minute slot within the main French transmission, and the French Service was under instructions constantly to emphasise the General's role and personality. The BBC was further instructed to publicise the military activities of the Free French forces, attaching them to the tradition of the French armed forces and fostering the idea that, through them, France was still fighting on.[72] One result was that de Gaulle and the British came to be closely associated, with the expression 'on prend les Anglais' being used to mean that people listened to Gaullist radio. More important, de Gaulle's name became increasingly well known in France, thereby helping ensure that when the mosaic of French resistance movements began to come together in autumn 1941, they looked to de Gaulle for leadership. A December 1942 article in the pro-Vichy journal *L'Alerte* complained that without radio Gaullism would not exist in France. It was through this 'methodical empoisonment, practised through six daily injections' that the General had been able to gain a preponderant role in public affairs to which his pre-war errors did not entitle him.[73]

At the same time, the BBC was helping to create a dissident atmosphere in France, thereby enabling the French to start to '*think* Resistance.'[74] This was an inherently gradual, cumulative business. Following the liberation, a visiting BBC correspondent reported how people told him that at first 'they had believed that Pétain was right, and that the only thing for France was to make the best of defeat. Slowly they began to listen regularly to London and to believe that France would one day be liberated. They began to hope and then work for liberation.'[75] But in a country whose state of mind was heavily influenced by events elsewhere, this process was hampered by the string of military reverses the British suffered in 1941 and 1942. 'Everyone hopes,' one listener wrote in summer 1942, 'but few act. Many fear "tacit understandings."'[76] Around the same time, a doctor at a Paris hospital reported open discussion of the news heard on the BBC. His colleagues were all anxious to be rid of the Germans but did nothing about it. For some, indeed, listening to the BBC was an alibi for inaction.[77]

Others, however, did react. The direct power of broadcasting is best illustrated by the response to calls over the BBC for various forms of demonstration. The first of these came at the end of December 1940, when de Gaulle called for the French people to remain indoors for an hour on New Year's Day. Despite German attempts to entice people out by announcing the sale of potatoes and other scarce commodities, there was a limited but noticeable response.[78] A graffiti outburst in 1941 of 'V' for victory signs and Free French crosses of Lorraine was largely prompted by radio campaigns. In the northern industrial town of Lille, 5,500 'V' signs were located and erased on 28 March, and Paris was flooded by them.[79] Radio calls for demonstrations on May Day 1942 brought 100,000 people onto the streets in Marseilles, with perhaps as many in Lyons and smaller events being held in most of the larger towns. This marked a new phase in French activism, since for the first time the initiative had come from Jean Moulin in France, with the campaign being jointly orchestrated by the Resistance press and the BBC.[80] The demonstrations on 14 July, which had been heavily publicised on the BBC, drew crowds in excess of 1.5 million. Descriptions of the events were quickly passed to London, to be broadcast back to the rest of France. When the police opened fire in Marseilles, killing four people, the BBC called for demonstrations at the cemetery.[81]

Another successful BBC campaign aimed at dissuading people from using nickel coins which the Germans wanted to take out of circulation for use in war industries.[82] Much more important was the sustained campaign that continued into 1944 against Laval's STO. British concern to prevent

French workers going to Germany stemmed both from the help which they would give to the German war effort and the debilitating impact of the STO on the Resistance, who were threatened with the loss of some of their most active members. To counter this, SOE printed some 20,000 forged ration cards and stepped up its payments to the Resistance to allow those in hiding to buy food. The BBC campaign was waged with the slogan 'Ne va pas en Allemagne' (Don't go to Germany) and was aimed both at French officials, who were discouraged from facilitating the process, as well as those being drafted. According to PWE's own later account, this had only limited success, although Aurélie Luneau's history of the BBC French Service suggests that it did have some impact.[83]

All of this was grist to the mill of the French Resistance. As Georges Bidault, the President of the CNR, later remarked, without the BBC everything would have been more precarious. Broadcasting helped reassure and strengthen opinion in both the Occupied and Unoccupied Zones.[84] The BBC brought people together as well as inspiring action. One of the first resistance networks had been started in response to an early de Gaulle broadcast, and the underground newspapers which had already begun to appear at the end of 1940 drew material from BBC broadcasts. The BBC acted as a powerful vector and amplifier of the Resistance.[85] By the very fact of talking about it, the BBC conferred a national reality on the Resistance, giving the impression, however misleading in the early days, of a coherent organisation.[86]

By 1941, BBC broadcasts were acquiring a more direct operational role, with the transmission of so-called 'personal messages,' which acted as communication codes with agents in the field. Thus:

> One man, hearing 'the dandelions do not like the sardine' would know that his radio-operator had reached London safe and sound; for another 'Father Christmas is dressed in pink' meant that Morandat or Bingen was on his way to a landing-ground in the neighbourhood of Valence; and a third, hearing 'Louis XIV greets Vercingetorix,' knew that a given network had been disrupted and that it was no longer to be relied upon.[87]

SOE was as much the beneficiary as the Resistance. The messages enhanced the prestige of SOE circuit operators, who would ask their French comrades to choose a phrase, which would later be broadcast over the French Service as a signal for an air drop. The operator would radio their message back to London, the French would listen, and it would come through on the BBC. It was, in the later words of one SOE agent, 'the first manifestation of power; you'd been able to give an order to tell the formidable British broadcasting company what to say.'[88] They could even save lives. In 1943, a Resistance leader, Lucie Aubrac, used a BBC personal message to convince a state prosecutor that he would be killed by the Resistance if he did not release her husband from a Vichy jail.[89]

The BBC French Service's role can be overstated. Its audience was not universal, it was certainly not immune to French criticism, and it was no silver bullet allowing Britain to compensate for the military weakness that delayed liberation. PWE's objectives were only partially achieved. But it did provide Britain with a means of outflanking and subverting the German occupation, as well as of subverting Vichy. Denied any kind of overt physical presence, Britain retained influence in France. It was able to engage with the French people to a unique degree, to the point of being regarded as a quasi-domestic broadcaster. This might not have been as dramatic an achievement as the German military victory of June 1940, but in its own way it was as striking.

# Part II

# 'Somewhat Difficult People'

# 9

# The Awkward General

If the BBC's audience in France constituted the public dimension of the new wartime Anglo-French entente, the political spearhead was de Gaulle's Free French movement. Although few in London in June 1940 foresaw it, de Gaulle was to prove the man of the future. By the end of 1943, the General was sole Chairman of the French Committee of National Liberation, France's de-facto government in exile. Following the liberation in 1944 he assumed the premiership. In the process, the entente entered into a new, uniquely personalised phase, which was to prove far more difficult than the Anglo-French relationship of the pre-war years. The burden of smouldering historic suspicions and rivalries, coming on top of the sensitivities of defeat as they affected an exceptionally proud and prickly French leader, made for constant friction. The consequent dramas, particularly the personal relationship between Churchill and de Gaulle, have few, if any, parallels in the history of modern diplomacy. Rarely has a British ally caused – or been caused – quite so much trouble.

De Gaulle was a man who polarised opinion, whether in France or in Britain, and from the outset British policy-makers were ambivalent about their new ally.[1] Was he the symbol of a France in temporary eclipse, or simply the troublesome leader of a small and quarrelsome group of exiles who sat around the restaurants of Soho intriguing?[2] His most important supporter was the Prime Minister, who had been quick to spot the adamantine will of a man who seemed to embody the spirit of the old France Churchill loved. Spears, who had shepherded the General to London from Bordeaux, quickly became a tireless, if not always tactful promoter of de Gaulle's cause. So too did Major Desmond Morton, who was charged by Churchill with liaison with exile movements and chaired the official Committee on Foreign Resistance that oversaw French policy. Among ministers, Anthony Eden was an important, although by no means an uncritical admirer.[3] Other supporters included the Francophile Minister of Information, Duff Cooper, and the Royal Family. The Free French were taken up by many of London society's leading hostesses. The public too, in so far as they were aware of de Gaulle, were supportive. News in the summer of 1940 that Vichy was condemning him to death and confiscating his property brought anonymous gifts of jewellery.[4]

Others, however, were considerably less impressed. There was suspicion of him on the political left. Hugh Dalton initially viewed de Gaulle with the same dislike that much of the French left held for generals in politics, while Clement Attlee, the Deputy Prime Minister, described de Gaulle and his entourage as practically fascist.[5] The latter charge, while frequently repeated on both sides of the Atlantic, appears to have derived from an authoritarian manner that belied the General's democratic convictions. British officials were unlikely to warm to so driven, imperious and unbending a figure, whose sense of mission and impression of self-importance often seemed to verge on the ridiculous. Charles Peake, who in 1942 became British Representative to the French National Committee, was a perceptive and sympathetic observer of the General. He described an occasion at a City lunch, where a comparison was drawn by a British speaker between de Gaulle and Joan of Arc. The General 'stiffened, his head gave a hardly perceptible jerk and he raised his eyes to the cornice at which he gazed for two or three seconds. When he rose to speak, I have little doubt that he was sensible of the Maid's presence at his elbow.'[6] It was all very un-British, and his frequent rudeness only made things even worse.

One of the more graphic, if unflattering, images of the General comes from Alan Lascelles, Assistant Private Secretary to the King. Carting potatoes, Lascelles recorded in his diary, 'I was continually struck by the resemblance the average large potato bears to General de Gaulle, though the potato is, of course, the more malleable of the two.'[7] The Foreign Office under Halifax and Cadogan was not much more sympathetic (although, according to Philippe de Gaulle, the Free French had an informant 'close to' the Foreign Office).[8] The army's attitude was at best stand-offish and at worst obstructive.[9] The Free French had inevitably been tarred by the French army's defeat and the Dakar fiasco, during which the Free French gained a reputation for poor security they were never able to shake off. Frenchmen, in the army's view, could not be trusted with secrets.[10] Nor could the army get over its professional dislike for the General's insubordination. For British officers, as for Vichy, de Gaulle was a rebel rather than a hero. That said, there was clearly an element of personal dislike, since the British military establishment got on with the much more helpful and emollient General Catroux, as they did with the commander of the Free French navy, Admiral Muselier. Few expressed this antipathy more clearly than General Sir Alan Brooke, who became Chief of the Imperial General Staff in 1941. In his diary he complained of de Gaulle's overbearing manner, 'megalomania' and lack of cooperative spirit.[11]

Army attitudes might perhaps have been different had the General had more troops at his command, but few had rallied to the Free French flag.[12] As of summer 1940, de Gaulle could boast no more than 4,000 soldiers and 1,000 sailors. Under Article 10 of the Armistice, which Vichy took measures to enforce, French soldiers were prevented from fleeing abroad or fighting on the side of another country. After Dakar, de Gaulle came to be seen as fighting Frenchmen and doing little against the Germans.[13]

The bulk of the 50,000 troops under de Gaulle's command in the second half of 1941 were, thus, colonial forces that had come over with the risings in Equatorial Africa. Their main area of operation was in the Western Desert, beginning in 1941 with raids against Italian forces in Libya.[14] In 1941, the Free French navy was manning forty-nine units, mostly small craft, a number of which were employed on Atlantic convoy duties. Free French merchant seamen also contributed to the Allied war effort. The first of four Free French squadrons to serve with the RAF was formed in 1941.[15] De Gaulle naturally tried to make the most of these slim resources. On 9 October 1940 he telegraphed Wavell that his arrival in French Africa and reorganisation of local bases allowed him to put at his disposal important reinforcements for the Middle East. The same day he telegraphed Churchill from 'French Africa, free of enemy control,' with a population of 14 million.[16]

If the territories of French Equatorial Africa – Chad, the Cameroons, French Congo and Gabon – appear relatively obscure, their location between Nigeria to the west, the Belgian Congo to the south and the Sudan to the east was of strategic significance. Chad had a border with Libya, one of the main war zones of the early war years. Free French control of Chad shortened air communications to the Middle East. Planes could be shipped to Takoradi in the Gold Coast (today's Ghana) where they were assembled and flown to Lagos, from there to Fort Lamy in Chad, then to Khartoum and finally on to Cairo. The route remained in operation until the Anglo-American landings in North Africa in November 1942, by which time some 5,000 British aircraft had reached the Middle East. Churchill credited it with making the difference between survival and defeat in Egypt in the dark days of 1941. According to Smuts, the rallying of Equatorial Africa had enabled him to overcome opposition within South Africa to joining Britain in the war.[17]

By 1942, the Free French territories, which now included the Levant, were described by William Strang as being of 'considerable value to the united war effort.'[18] The latter, however, was a concept in which de Gaulle often seemed to show little interest. Rather than concentrating on the war against Germany, the General gave the impression of pursuing his own agenda. While desperately anxious to get his soldiers into the field to validate his claim that France had never left the war, he was as much concerned with the restoration of France's pride and self-respect. De Gaulle, Eden complained, seemed to be conducting 'a private war against Vichy,' while cooperation with his allies was 'secondary in his mind.'[19] This led to resentment on the British side, while de Gaulle complained that Britain's struggle to the death against Germany was aggravating 'the greedy will to power which is the dominating trait of their race.'[20]

It was but one of a series of strains in a grossly unequal alliance, during a stage in the war when de Gaulle was under intense stress. He was condemned to death at home, living in exile in a foreign country – 'friendly, of course, but alien, where everyone pursued a goal and spoke a language not our own, and where everything made me feel that our prize was out of all proportion to our poor means of achieving it.'[21] Petts Wood, Shropshire, Berkhamsted and Hampstead, where he and his family successively lived, simply did not feel like home. An impatient man, he was naturally frustrated, first by the initial slow progress of his own movement and later by the way in which he found himself excluded from Allied councils. When challenged on this point by Charles Peake, de Gaulle remarked that patience was more specifically a British than a French virtue.[22] Acutely conscious of the humiliation and diminution of France, he overreacted to both real and imagined slights, which he suspected would not be permitted were France in full control of its destiny.[23]

The General was no less conscious of his well-nigh total dependence on his hosts, neatly summarised by a cartoon published in summer 1940 showing a sturdy Churchill wading ashore, carrying the dripping figure of de Gaulle in his arms.[24] The British afforded some of the political legitimacy he initially so patently lacked, along with the publicity to get him known internationally as well as in France. They provided him with offices. No. 4 Carlton Gardens, an elegant townhouse overlooking the Mall and St James's Park, was put at his disposal. (Characteristically, the Englishness of the surroundings left the General unaffected, and the visitor felt himself at once in France.)[25] They supplied him with various communications facilities. His overseas telegrams went through the Foreign Office network. SOE provided him with the radio facilities for communications with France, as well as training his agents and ferrying them in and out of the country. He needed an RAF aircraft if he was to travel abroad. As the General plaintively admitted in a telegram to Free French imperial leaders in June 1942, he did not have any means of his own for moving about without the agreement of the English. The Royal Navy protected the Free French colonies in Equatorial Africa; the army provided equipment for his soldiers.[26]

Above all, the British provided resources. De Gaulle had arrived in London with virtually no money. Britain made good the deficiency. The first transfer of £1,000 was authorised on 4 July.[27] Under a subsequent agreement, the French National Committee was required to submit an annual budget to the Treasury, which approved or disapproved each item following discussions with the relevant British ministry. Advances were then paid at the beginning of each month. In September 1941, British advances to the Free French – all money was subsequently repaid – were running at £8 million a year. By the end of 1942, the Free French debt stood at £24,476,000. Six months later, at which point the British payments ended, it had reached nearly £35 million, with monthly subventions now averaging £1.5 million pounds.[28] De Gaulle himself had originally been given a salary by the British but had subsequently replaced this from French sources. Britain also purchased products from French Equatorial Africa and facilitated the conversion of funds from these sales into sterling. The overall figures may not have been large. In absolute terms, the total Free French debt to the Treasury amounted to less than three weeks' worth of France's occupation indemnity payments to Germany under the terms of the Armistice.[29] But the Free French had nowhere else to raise such sums.

'The bloke who lends money,' Harold Mack commented in 1942, during one of the periodic debates in Whitehall about Britain's difficult guest, 'is never really popular with the person to whom he lends.'[30] Churchill made a not dissimilar point when he remarked that 'England's grievous offence in de Gaulle's eyes is that she has helped France. He cannot bear to think that she needed help.'[31] Over and above pride and resentment, de Gaulle was always on his guard against the dangers to the Free French position resulting from what looked very much like a client–patron relationship. As early as 24 June 1940, he was talking of the need to defend French interests against its allies 'until victory.'[32] In January 1941 he was complaining that 'the British yoke had become unbearable. I could not move in any sphere without clashing with the English.'[33] What to de Gaulle was a compulsive need to compensate for extreme weakness, compounded in the General's eyes by what he saw as a natural French propensity to 'yield to foreigners and become divided,' could easily look to his allies like sheer bloody-mindedness.[34]

In practice, as René Pleven acknowledged, the British rarely sought to make use of their economic leverage.[35] But there was inevitably some feeling that he who paid the piper should call the tune, which came to the fore when de Gaulle was behaving in what was seen as an unreasonable, if not downright ungrateful fashion. And he was at times subjected to strong political and psychological pressure. As he wrote in his war memoirs,

> to resist the British machine, when it set itself in motion to impose something, was a severe test. Without having experienced it oneself, it is impossible to imagine what a concentration of effort, what a variety of procedures, what insistence, by turns gracious, pressing and threatening, the English were capable of deploying in order to obtain satisfaction.[36]

His success in resisting is reflected in a letter Eden sent to Samuel Hoare in Madrid in 1942. 'I expect,' the Foreign Secretary wrote, 'that most of the Frenchmen you meet regard de Gaulle as being in our pocket and that everything he says or does has our prior approval. If you had to deal with him for a week you would know that this is far from being the truth.'[37]

Under all these circumstances it is perhaps surprising that for almost a year the relationship between Britain and the Free French had been good.[38] This was despite a series of incidents, mostly of British making, that created difficulties for the General. Mers-el-Kébir was a serious setback to de Gaulle's hopes of recruiting supporters. The General, who briefly considered retiring to Canada, had a furious interview with the First Lord of the Admiralty, A. V. Alexander. But he publicly supported the action, noting in his memoirs that the British government had been 'clever enough and elegant enough' to allow him to use the BBC microphone, however disagreeable for the British the terms of his statement might have been.[39] De Gaulle refrained from recriminations after Dakar, when the Free French received considerably more than their fair share of public blame. Nor did he react strongly against the British attempts to reach a modus vivendi with Vichy about which he was kept informed, although he had deliberately delayed responding to a request from Churchill in November to return to London.[40] After protests, he accepted embarrassed British apologies over an incident in January 1941, when the head of the Free French Navy, Admiral Muselier, was arrested over what were quickly shown to be false charges of treason. The English, he wrote at the time to his wife, are valiant and '*solide*' allies '*mais bien fatigant.*' And while occasionally allowing himself outbursts of temper in discussion with senior SOE officials over activities he regarded as outrageous, the General always took care afterwards to make clear there had been no personal animosity.[41]

De Gaulle's willingness to accept discretion as the better part of valour reflected a combination of weakness and prudence. The General may not have overlooked or forgotten these various incidents. According to Spears, the 'struggle with the British Authorities and the difficulties he encountered caused de Gaulle to become more solitary, more arbitrary and indeed more difficult to deal with as time went on.'[42] But in the early months, before he had built up any kind of reputation, he had no real option but to swallow his pride and capitalise on the friendly relations which he had established with Churchill. De Gaulle at this period was a frequent visitor at Chequers, the Prime Minister's official country house. There was, and would always remain, a genuine admiration between the two men. One of de Gaulle's aides-de-camp spoke of a complete and dazzling communion of thought and immense intellectual esteem. Philippe de Gaulle quotes his father as saying that with Churchill, 'I never found the time long.'[43]

The trouble began when de Gaulle left England for Africa and the Middle East in March 1941. A successful British campaign, supported by Free French units, was under way against Italian forces in Abyssinia and Italian Somaliland. No French territory had come over to the Free French since autumn 1940, and de Gaulle saw the opportunity of rallying the French port of Djibouti, capital of French Somaliland, with its garrison of some 10,000 troops. The General regarded blockade as the most effective means of bringing the French colony over, a view which did not, however, find favour with Wavell. According to Spears' subsequent account, the differences of opinion over how to treat the Vichy authorities underlined the British incapacity to understand the French. Wavell wanted to negotiate with the Vichy governor, allowing supplies to reach Djibouti in exchange for the right to send supplies to British troops and Italian civilians in Abyssinia. De Gaulle replied that the governor would refer the matter to Vichy, which could not act without Axis consent, and that once he realised that he had something in hand with which he could barter his demands would be endless. After a good deal of pressure, the War Cabinet's Defence Committee in London agreed to maintain the blockade. But British reluctance had aroused de Gaulle's suspicions of British imperial designs in an area where Britain, France and Italy had long been in competition.[44]

More serious was Wavell's unwillingness to contemplate a proposal put forward by de Gaulle, again backed by Spears, to rally the Levant to the Free French cause. Wavell, as already noted, was short of troops, as well as being sceptical about the practicality of Free French plans. British officers were offended by his criticisms and did not take well to doubts being voiced by a French general about their ability to conduct modern warfare. 'I understand that I can't do anything right as far as the Free French are concerned,' Wavell remarked to Spears on 12 May. 'They don't like me and I am pretty tired of them myself.'[45] Indeed, when, in July, Wavell was transferred to India, de Gaulle placed under arrest three senior French officers who had paid him a farewell visit.[46]

Having failed in his immediate purpose in Cairo, de Gaulle retired to French Equatorial Africa, in a mood of intense anti-British exasperation.[47] At Fort Lamy in Chad there was an incident when de Gaulle flared up at what Max Egremont, Spears's biographer, describes as British attempts to dominate him, threatening to close the airport to British aircraft, thereby disrupting the Takoradi air route. Exasperated in turn that the General's pique should be allowed to add an additional burden to the back-breaking war load Britain was already carrying, Spears threatened to call in British troops to take over the aerodrome.[48] In Brazzaville, de Gaulle called in the British Consul-General, Robert Parr, whom he had first met the previous autumn and who was to prove himself another of the Foreign Office's shrewd judges of the Free French leader.[49] What was striking about this visit was less de Gaulle's warning against any British accommodation with Vichy but more his personal comments. He was alone, there was nobody with whom he could consult, and sometimes he felt he could not go on much longer.[50] This was not entirely accurate: the problem was not that de Gaulle could not get advice but that he would not take it. The incident does, however, provide a useful reminder that despite appearances to the contrary, encouraged by the image he promoted, this austere French general was human.

The immediate impasse was broken by Darlan's decision to allow German aircraft to operate out of Syria. But Operation Exporter, the first successful Anglo-Free French military operation, far from improving Britain's relations with de Gaulle permanently undermined them. At the root of the ensuing conflict lay what in another context de Gaulle had referred to as the 'stale reek' of old rivalries.[51] De Gaulle saw himself as the trustee of France's vulnerable empire, which he once likened to 'a ripe cheese, a constant temptation to a hungry appetite.'[52] The General had unsuccessfully sought an unequivocal British commitment to restore the French empire after the war, during negotiations in summer 1940 aimed at putting Anglo-Free French relations on a legal footing. His war memoirs reveal suspicions of potential British designs not only on Djibouti but also Dakar.[53] As to the Levant, where he had served as a staff officer from 1929 to 1931, picking up the acute sense of Anglo-French rivalry shared by French officers and officials there, the memoirs are eloquent.[54] The English game, he wrote,

> settled in London by firmly established services, carried out on the spot by a team without scruples but not without resources, accepted by the Foreign Office, which sometimes sighed over it but never disowned it, and supported by the Prime Minister, whose ambiguous promises and calculated emotions camouflaged what was intended – aimed at establishing British 'leadership' in the whole Middle East. British policy would therefore endeavour, sometimes stealthily and sometimes harshly, to replace France at Damascus and at Beirut.[55]

This was, perhaps, not wholly wrong. The historian A. B. Gaunson writes of Britain's 'oblique political ambitions' in the Levant.[56] While the British had no desire to supplant the French there, they viewed events in the Levant within the larger framework of their own increasingly insecure position in the Arab world. They had no wish to reawaken the old Arab bitterness and suspicions associated with the 1916 Anglo-French Sykes–Picot agreement, which had sought to carve up parts of the old Ottoman Empire, and the subsequent abandonment of Syria to the French. They were therefore determined to ensure that they did not reap any of the odium of being seen to throw out Vichy, only to hand the two territories, held by France under League of Nations mandates, over to the Free French.[57] Britain's position was bluntly set out in a telegram on 7 July from Churchill to Oliver Lyttelton, the British Resident Minister in the Middle East.

> Our position is to give the Arabs independence. We are quite willing that the Free French should represent the interests of France and prove that among the nations of Europe France is the favoured and privileged power in Syria. Our only British interests except ordinary trade are to keep the Germans out and win the war.

From this point of view the Arabs bulk far more largely in our minds than the Free French and there can be no question of any lengthy delay in negotiating treaties which satisfy them that they have not merely exchanged one set of Frenchmen for another.[58]

Independence, however, inevitably both diminished France's position and raised French suspicions.[59] Since, as Harold Macmillan noted,

on the whole French policy towards native ambitions has been what we should now call reactionary but used to believe normal, they find it impossible to believe that we should honestly wish the French to hand over the government of any territory under their influence to its inhabitants except for the purpose of substituting our own influence for that of our Ally.[60]

All this contributed to de Gaulle's highly nervous state of mind in the run-up to Operation Exporter. 'Will these people not think I am making rather a clown of myself, a man who is not a government, with only a very small force, taking on himself to guarantee the independence of two very real nations?' Spears quotes him as asking.[61] De Gaulle also admitted to a sense of shame at the way his compatriots were behaving. And there was another, political factor. Precisely because Britain was again attacking the (Vichy) French, it was important to safeguard French interests and feelings.[62]

Under these circumstances there was indeed a premium on handling the Free French with tact and sensitivity. 'A word of affection and comprehension from you,' Spears telegraphed to the Prime Minister two days before the operation began, 'would do a world of good and tend to smooth over the many difficulties that, whatever happens, are bound to arise.'[63] Churchill obliged, while in Palestine the High Commissioner, Sir Harold MacMichael, gave Catroux a bust of Napoleon for luck, but most other officials seemed oblivious of Free French raw nerves.[64] The army certainly had little time for de Gaulle's concerns. Their immediate priority was to find the necessary forces and to produce a plan of attack, and if in the process de Gaulle was offended because the Free French were preceded by Indian troops, that was just too bad. The General, suspecting that the move masked Machiavellian British intent, was deeply upset.[65]

A major incident occurred on 21 June, following feelers put out by Dentz through the Americans for an armistice. De Gaulle had outlined his views to British officials in Cairo two days earlier, but the Foreign Office had subsequently telegraphed its own terms to Washington without reference to de Gaulle. This was in fact an oversight, but de Gaulle was, as Spears reported, 'cut to the quick' by the omission, which he saw as something much more sinister and was accordingly very, very angry.[66] It was on this occasion that he remarked,

> I do not think I shall ever get on with *les Anglais*. You are all the same, exclusively centred upon your own interests and business, quite insensitive to the requirements of others. You think I am interested in England winning the war? I am not. I am only interested in France's victory.[67]

When Spears objected that these were in fact one and the same thing, the General replied, 'Not at all.'[68] Yet in an earlier passage in his own account of the Lebanese affair Spears refers to de Gaulle being 'absorbed by calculations of how his own movement in France would be affected' if the Levant states rallied to his cause. Spears continues: 'I was interested only in the extent to which the British cause would be strengthened by their becoming involved on our side.'[69] Coincidence of interest, as de Gaulle well understood, was not the same as identity of cause.

Much worse was to follow when, on 14 July, General Wilson, styling himself Commander of British, rather than Allied forces, signed an armistice in which Free French interests were systematically disregarded.[70] De Gaulle had looked towards Dentz's army of the Levant as an important source of troops and equipment for the Free French. In the event, Vichy forces were allowed to keep their equipment, while the Free French were forbidden from trying to recruit. Behind this extraordinary set of concessions, which dismayed British officials in Cairo and London, lay a failure to coordinate the military and political dimensions of policy.[71] Negotiation of the armistice had been left to the military. 'Jumbo' Wilson has been described as one of the most consistently successful British generals of the Second World War, but the Acre Convention was not his finest hour.[72] While understandably anxious to end as quickly as possible a slow and distasteful campaign, which was diverting troops who might be much more profitably used against the Germans, he had neither the taste nor understanding for political questions. He had also, as Gaunson notes, come to look askance upon, 'the troublesome enigma of Free France. He disliked the whole experience of supporting Gaullist military rebels against [General] de Verdilac's loyal professionals, and seemed more at home with soldiers who "just did their duty."'[73]

De Gaulle's response to this humiliating and damaging agreement demonstrated a brutality that shocked his allies. Spears and Lyttelton were expecting trouble when they met the General in Cairo on 21 July, but not on the scale on which it came. What now ensued was the first of what was to be a series of set-piece confrontations between de Gaulle and the British. The General, who had a taste for political theatre, was a skilful practitioner of psychological warfare. But he also gave the impression of a man tormented by fury and injured pride, who looked as though he had not slept for a week.[74] After an hour's stormy discussion, de Gaulle presented Lyttelton with a note that announced that Free French forces would be withdrawn from British command in three days' time. General Catroux would take immediate authority over the whole of the Levant, and Free French forces were being ordered to enter contact with Vichy troops and to take control over their war *matériel*. Lyttelton refused to accept what he described as an ultimatum. And having noted that General de Larminat, who had accompanied de Gaulle, seemed thoroughly frightened by the General's behaviour, the British minister suggested an adjournment to allow de Larminat to work on his angry chief.[75]

The British contingent was now thoroughly alarmed. If de Gaulle began independently ordering his troops about in Syria, he would almost certainly find himself in conflict with the British command. Given the presence of large numbers of Vichy forces, who had still not been disarmed, this could create a highly dangerous situation. Preparations were therefore put in hand to deny de Gaulle wireless and telegraph facilities, and, if necessary, to depose him in favour of Catroux.[76] But having effected his point so dramatically in the morning, by the time of the late-afternoon session the atmosphere had completely changed. The following day, a new agreement was drawn up, much more to de Gaulle's satisfaction. The Free French would be allowed to try to recruit from Vichy forces, war *matériel* was recognised as French property, and the special troops of the Levant would be integrated into the Free French rather than the British forces. The General also received an official assurance that Britain had no designs on the Levant.[77] The British too were relieved. 'Considering this fish took out the entire line on Monday and looked likely to carry away the whole tackle,' Lyttelton telegraphed back to Churchill, 'I feel some relief that after playing it up and down the pool for three days it is now on the bank.'[78] The image would have made a gift to a cartoonist.

This should perhaps have been the point where de Gaulle stood back and sought to mend his diplomatic fences. But trouble continued on the ground in the Levant. In one incident at the end of July, Free French troops were sent to Soueida, the capital of the Jebel Druze in Lebanon, where they found the Union Jack flying over the Maison de France. When the British refused to leave, the Free French threatened to open fire. Noting that relations with the Free French were extremely strained, a SIS officer compared them to 'trying to live amicably with a jealous, touchy and domineering wife.'[79] That was scarcely de Gaulle's view. 'Meddling by England was leading to the gravest complications,' the Foreign Office was warned. A telegram from the General to the Free French in London spoke of being in the midst of a grave crisis.[80]

Some, like Diego Brosset, who was Catroux's chief of staff, were impressed. De Gaulle had 'joué gros jeu' (played a great game) and had won.[81] The General possessed that 'seed of recklessness, whether of folly or genius, without which it was impossible to do great things.'[82] That was not, however, a view shared by de Gaulle's colleagues in London. Militarily and financially, they warned,

> we cannot exist without the support of England. From the political point of view, a rupture between us and the British would disconcert the French people and would spread disarray in our ranks, to the greater delight of Germany and Vichy. At the same time, the British government would be freed from its commitments to restore France. Practically, the rupture would mean the end of Free France, that is to say the disappearance of the last hope of saving our unfortunate country.[83]

From Brazzaville, Robert Parr warned that if the General were allowed to continue in a frame of mind linking his own political perplexities

> first to British obtuseness, then to British policy, and finally to British perfidy, he will end by becoming so completely the victim of his own single-mindedness that he will never be able to rid himself of the burden of distrust and dislike of Great Britain which he is at present unconsciously binding on his shoulders.[84]

And that would have long-term repercussions for Anglo-French relations should events bring de Gaulle 'back to Paris as the recognised saviour of France.'[85]

These warnings, however, did little to temper the impending crisis. British impatience and indignation with the General was growing. Churchill was becoming worked up. On his way to the USA in pursuit of much bigger fish than de Gaulle, the Prime Minister made his feelings clear. The Free French, he minuted on 6 August,

> cannot be allowed to mess up our Syrian position and spoil our relations with the Arabs. Their pretensions require to be sternly corrected, even the use of force not being excluded. It is important to let them realize in good time that they will be made to obey. I don't see how they can resist.[86]

In Cairo, the new Commander-in-Chief, General Sir Claude Auchinleck, warned that if de Gaulle ceased to act as an ally Britain should look for an alternative Free French leader. (Suggestions by British officers at Middle East Headquarters in Cairo of detaining de Gaulle in a mental hospital were, however, stamped upon.)[87] Meanwhile, de Gaulle, who had by now moved back to Equatorial Africa, continued to give way to his exasperation with *les Anglais*. British soldiers and officials, he complained, either failed to appreciate the importance of the Free French or were using the movement. The General was said to have talked about moving Free French headquarters from Carlton Gardens to Brazzaville and even to have suggested that the Belgian government should move from London to Leopoldville in the Belgian Congo, in order to be free of English influence.[88]

Then de Gaulle did something untypical. For all his private criticism of the British, the General was normally careful to avoid public attacks. But, at the end of August, he gave a newspaper interview to the *Chicago Daily News*. De Gaulle was anxious to attract the attention of the Americans, who he believed would shortly enter the war and to whom he was now looking as an alternative source of support. In the interview, the General offered the Americans the use of Free French bases in Africa on the basis of a long-term lease, adding that he would not ask for any old American destroyers in return. This was an unkind, if not cheap dig at the 'destroyers for bases' deal Britain had been forced to make with the USA the previous August. More important was his response to the question as to why Britain did not close the door on Vichy and recognise his own government. The interviewer had touched on what for de Gaulle was a highly sensitive nerve, and he gave full vent to his frustrations. England, he replied, was afraid of the French fleet and was effectively carrying out a wartime deal with Hitler in which Vichy served as a go-between. Vichy served Germany by keeping the French people in subjugation and selling the French Empire piecemeal to Germany. It served Britain by keeping the fleet from Hitler. Britain was exploiting Vichy in the same way as Germany. The only difference was the purpose.[89]

As a piece of analysis, as Charles Williams, one of the General's English biographers comments, this 'had something to commend it. As a political gesture, if that is what it was, it was the sheerest idiocy.'[90] De Gaulle appears to have realised his mistake, trying unsuccessfully to stop the interview from being published. He returned to London in a furious temper, to a very frosty welcome. Churchill's initial reaction had been to talk of a complete change of policy, involving closer relations with Vichy, and to ask Morton to consider another leader. This was a typical Churchillian overreaction. Nevertheless, all cooperation with the Free French was halted, including the suspension of intelligence cooperation and Free French broadcasts on the BBC.[91] Hervé Alphand, who arrived at this point to join the Free French, found all the English people he met violently critical of the General and his collaborators. De Gaulle, he noted in his journal, irritated the British not because he was disloyal to them but because he represented French interests, which did not always coincide exactly with his allies, and because his manners were brusque 'and as distant as possible from classic diplomacy.'[92] Alphand also noted that some in the General's entourage detested England.[93]

This was true, but it failed to take into account the sense of outrage in London caused by the General's behaviour. In the words of one senior British officer, it seemed 'unbelievable' that all this should be coming from a man who owed his very political existence and that of his whole movement 'to this nation as a whole and HMG [His Majesty's Government] in particular.'[94] In the Prime Minister's eyes, de Gaulle was guilty of bad behaviour, ingratitude and, last and by no means least, Anglophobia. Here lay the source of a good deal of the trouble between the two men over the following years. There was an interesting exchange when they met on 12 September. When Churchill had complained that 'he was no longer dealing with a friend,' de Gaulle had not directly rebutted the charge, saying rather that 'it could not be seriously maintained that he was an enemy of Great Britain.'[95] The General never shared the Prime Minister's sentimental view of Anglo-French relations. In his opinion, as expressed privately a few days earlier, the English did not like the French any more than the French liked the English. The only thing that counted was interests. England for de Gaulle was simply 'an ally, a necessary ally.'[96] That curt phrase 'a necessary ally' encapsulates de Gaulle's view of *les Anglais*.

Elsewhere in Whitehall there was puzzlement over de Gaulle's behaviour. Was the General, as Parr believed, dead tired and close to a nervous breakdown?[97] Or was there rather method to the General's madness? In Morton's view, while de Gaulle might be no diplomat, there was a 'calculating brain behind that curious countenance ... If he rows like a lunatic with one man and attempts to charm another by quiet reasonableness, it is because he thinks that such an attitude is the one more likely to gain his ends with the person in question.'[98] This accorded with Spears' opinion. Spears, who had observed the General closely over the previous few months, believed that he had quickly discovered that educated Englishmen detested rows, which they considered vulgar and for which they were also too slow-witted, too unused to manipulating words to be a match for 'rapid-speaking foreigners.'[99] The General had therefore cultivated the practice of being intolerably rude on some occasions, leaving his English opponent able to think of nothing but how to answer at their next encounter.

> He mulls over de Gaulle's words and rehearses his own answers, and is therefore utterly nonplussed to be greeted by a completely changed de Gaulle, one who is now easy and polite. The Englishman is so relieved at not having to use the harsh expressions he has prepared that he concedes practically every one of the General's demands.[100]

This question about the General's motives and methods fed into a more practical question that went to the heart of Britain's relationship with the General, one which was never satisfactorily resolved. How much allowance should be made for the distressing circumstances that drove so much of de Gaulle's behaviour? Morton, while often sympathetic to the General, was uncompromising. 'An ordinary man may be permitted to exhibit nerves, impatience and bad temper in a way denied to one setting oneself up as the Head of an important Movement even of a State.'[101] The General himself, in seeking to explain his conduct, made the most of the argument. In discussion with Eden he claimed that while overwhelming military strength gave Britain the right to dictate, this in fact increased the importance of showing all possible consideration. It was realisation of their own helplessness that made the French so watchful of British behaviour in the Levant. Eden's response was that he understood all this, 'but good relations demanded reciprocity and there had been faults on both sides.'[102] In his earlier conversation with Churchill, de Gaulle had several times referred to French humiliations in Syria. Events there 'had added to the great difficulty of his personal position, to his isolation, and no doubt to the factor of his personal temperament.'[103] And in a masterly piece of understatement, he said, or he is at least quoted in the British record as having said, that the leaders and members of the Free French movement were 'necessarily *somewhat difficult people*: else they would not be where they were.'[104] This might be special pleading, but the General had a point.

Things were patched up. De Gaulle apologised to Churchill and promised to consider a suggestion by the Prime Minister for the formation of a French national committee. By the end of what had begun as a very frigid interview, the General had been offered one of Churchill's cigars. Afterwards, he sent Churchill a cigar box engraved with the Cross of Lorraine, which elicited the decidedly dubious reaction of, 'H'm, double cross of Lorraine, h'm very interesting.'[105] Morton subsequently reported to the Committee on Foreign Allied Resistance that 'relations would now return to normal, except that we would not in future go out of our way to do anything for him which was not in the best interests of our war effort.'[106] De Gaulle in turn reported to Catroux in Beirut that 'the serious difficulties to which the Syrian affair has given rise between our British allies and us seem on the way to being smoothed out.'[107]

The immediate sequel to the affair saw de Gaulle outwit Churchill. The Prime Minister's object in proposing the establishment of a national committee had been to create a body to keep the General in check. Britain could thus 'spread its recognition of de Gaulle over the Committee as a whole, while keeping de Gaulle as the figurehead.'[108] In doing so the British hoped to exploit growing impatience within the Free French movement with the General's authoritarian and undiplomatic style. The central figure in this intrigue was Admiral Emile Muselier, a colourful if controversial sailor, who, as already noted, had the advantage of getting on well with his British counterparts.

Major Morton and Lord Bessborough, a close friend of Churchill's, attended a lunch at the Savoy hotel, where Muselier outlined his plans to try to force through an executive council on de Gaulle, in which effective power would lie with the Admiral. If de Gaulle refused, Muselier would threaten to remove his ships from Free French control and to put them at British disposal. Churchill's reaction to news of this meeting, which had been lubricated by considerable quantities of brandy, illustrates a new, and by no means benevolent attitude to his former protégé. De Gaulle, the Prime Minister was reported by Major Morton as having said, would 'remain as a War Lord in control of the military aspect of the movement, and in this capacity we could easily control him.'[109] Of course if the dissidents went too far, he might have to intervene to knock heads together, though he hoped this would not be necessary. Once the crisis was resolved, Churchill would, after a decent interval,

> do something to show a special mark of favour to General de Gaulle, which would be of benefit to our war effort and improve personal relations between General de Gaulle and the Prime Minister. In other words if General de Gaulle shows that he has learned sense, the Prime Minister would make him a great man.[110]

Eden was not happy at this latter prospect, minuting that he hoped 'we shall go very slow about this. De Gaulle is best kept on a string for some time to come.'[111]

The plot misfired. By far the more skilful politician, de Gaulle easily outmanoeuvred Muselier. Morton, Eden, A. V. Alexander and Churchill all became involved in trying to smooth matters over. On the afternoon of 24 September, Muselier and de Gaulle were both summoned to the Foreign Office where de Gaulle sat in one room for hours with Eden and the Admiral in another with the First Lord of the Admiralty, while Cadogan plied between the two. When the crisis was eventually resolved, a national committee was formed, with de Gaulle very much in charge. Britain's first intervention into Free French affairs had failed.[112]

Seen against the background of the great battle now raging on the Eastern Front, where on 19 September the Germans had taken Kiev plus 210,000 prisoners, the Levant affair and the dramas to which it gave rise were a sideshow that only served to underscore France's marginality. To de Gaulle, faced with a combination of real and imagined British wrongs, it was everything, and he overreacted accordingly. Temperamentally no diplomat, the General lacked any sense of how to 'manage' his somewhat difficult allies, whom he seemed to treat more as swindling business partners than as comrades in arms.[113] The result was to alienate two powerful patrons – Spears and Churchill – which was to cause him a great deal of trouble.

# 10

# Mutual Frustration

On 25 November 1941, de Gaulle travelled to Oxford, where his elder daughter was studying, to talk to the University French Club. From the praise the General lavished on the Entente, none of his audience could have guessed at the quarrels in which he had recently been engaged. Despite the determined attempts by German propaganda, the General asserted, the confidence and affection felt in France for the people of Britain remained intact; indeed, the British were far more popular in France than they had ever been. Similar attitudes, he insisted, existed on the British part. He quoted Shakespeare's *Timon of Athens* to describe Britain's attitude to France: 'I am not of that feather, to shake off / My friend when he most needs me.'

The events of the war had demonstrated how the security of France depended on Britain, while it would be 'hard to imagine Britain's future if France, only a few minutes away by plane, ceased to be her ally.' This mutual interdependence would continue into the post-war era. Future Anglo-French collaboration was 'rendered imperative by excellent reasons of practical policy and the most valid arguments of sentiment, but it is above all made necessary by a duty common to our great and ancient nations – the need to preserve our civilisation.'[1]

This speech should be read as an expression of genuine conviction as much as an exercise in fence-mending and public relations; the Free French were at this time far from popular in Britain, where the view that France had 'let us down' and all Frenchmen were rotten retained currency.[2] De Gaulle, who understood France's dependence on alliances, believed in the Entente, whatever his feelings about *les Anglais*. Since his interview with Churchill he had proposed that French forces should participate in a forthcoming British offensive in Libya (Operation Crusader) and requested British help with the formation in France and North Africa of an organisation to coordinate Resistance groups.[3] Eleven days before his Oxford speech, the General had written privately to Catroux that while France's imperative duty was to maintain its position in the Levant, 'we also have the obligation to avoid everything which might increase England's difficulties and to neglect nothing in order to facilitate her task by a genuine collaboration.' Over and above a common interest in winning the war, France owed loyalty to a country committed to the restoration of French greatness and independence. And, in a striking formulation, de Gaulle referred to anxiety 'to see the mean rivalries of the past succeeded by the feeling of the solidarity of the two greatest Moslem powers in face of Islam.'[4]

Yet nothing de Gaulle could now say, nor indeed the evidence of the support he was gaining from the French Resistance, which Jean Moulin had underscored on his visit to London in October, could reverse the permanent loss of confidence and goodwill on Churchill's part. The year 1942 was to witness a succession of Anglo-Free French crises. While of themselves insignificant, when seen in the wider context of the war they were to absorb a great deal of British time and energy while subjecting de Gaulle to constant pressure. The result was a vicious circle of mutual frustration, which both the Free French and the Foreign Office would have much preferred to avoid.

De Gaulle's relations with his hosts were further complicated by America's entry into the war. On hearing the news of the attack on Pearl Harbor on 7 December, the General remarked that 'From now on, the British will do nothing without Roosevelt's agreement.'[5] Although he would only meet de Gaulle twice, Roosevelt had developed a visceral dislike and distrust of the Free French leader, whom he regarded as a divisive force, pretentious, unrepresentative and with potentially fascist tendencies. De Gaulle was altogether too independently minded and uncompliant for the President's taste. For a man who saw himself as France's liberator, de Gaulle was a competitor. The General was also an unashamed defender of the French Empire; in other words, like Churchill, he was an imperialist, a breed to which Roosevelt was firmly opposed.[6] Cordell Hull, the US Secretary of State, who was equally unsympathetic, had been known to describe the Free French as polecats. Hull was acutely sensitive to Free French attacks on America's policy of maintaining relations with Vichy in the hope of preventing Pétain's government from moving closer into the German orbit. In his memoirs, Hull wrote of de Gaulle's 'unhappy faculty of alienating most of those of any nationality with whom he came into contact, while at the same time undoubtedly inspiring millions of Frenchmen who were far removed from him.'[7]

The danger signs for de Gaulle soon made themselves felt. One was the creation of the Combined Chiefs of Staff Committee, based in Washington, designed to ensure smooth cooperation between the British and American high commands. When de Gaulle demanded French representation, General Ismay replied that if Canada, New Zealand, Australia, Holland, Belgium and Norway also had the right to be represented, 'the only place we could have a meeting is the Albert Hall.'[8] More dramatic, if also more absurd, was the crisis that broke over Christmas, concerning two small and obscure French islands off the coast of Newfoundland. The Free French had been expressing an interest in rallying Saint-Pierre and Miquelon to the Gaullist cause since the autumn of 1940. Originally opposed by the British because of Canadian objection, by the autumn of 1941 the idea was finding approval in London. The islands' governor was believed to be virulently anti-British, and there was concern that a powerful radio transmitter on Saint-Pierre might be used to provide Vichy, and by implication therefore the Germans, with information about the movement of Allied convoys. French trawlers from the island, operating off Newfoundland, were also suspected of reporting convoy movements from Halifax.[9]

This, however, was not a question which the British government could decide on its own. As Eden had written to de Gaulle in October 1941, the islands' geographical position 'prevents us from assenting to any operation involving a change in the *status quo* without express agreement of the Canadian and US Governments.'[10] When, in mid-December, less than a week after Pearl Harbor, the General made a formal request for British agreement, Churchill approved the operation, subject to a brief delay while the Americans were consulted. The Foreign Office, which omitted to consult the advice of its North America department, assumed that there would be no difficulty.[11] But the Americans did object, and de Gaulle was asked to cancel the operation; verbal assurances were given that he would do so. Then came news that the Canadian government was planning to land technicians on the island to supervise the radio station. De Gaulle regarded this as foreign intervention on French territory and ordered Admiral Muselier to take the islands. British liaison officers on the ships were kept in the dark; indeed, one of them noted that the Free French had 'made a great point of their independence in this operation, and will not I think, allow this precedent to be overlooked.' The islands were occupied on Christmas Eve.[12]

Cordell Hull was furious at a coup that threatened America's whole Vichy policy. The USA had recently concluded an agreement with Admiral Robert, Vichy's High Commissioner for the Antilles, Guiana and

Saint-Pierre, for the neutralisation of French territories and ships in the Western Hemisphere. On 13 December, Roosevelt had also reaffirmed to Pétain America's commitment to the 1940 Havana Convention, whereby all American republics had agreed to oppose the transfer of sovereignty, possession and control of any territory in the Western Hemisphere held by a European power. Behind all this lurked the old Monroe doctrine embodying American opposition to European intervention in what was regarded as an American sphere of influence. The British were wrongly suspected of complicity in the affair.[13] In a message to Muselier, de Gaulle claimed that his hosts were pleased with the French action both for reasons of maritime security and because of the danger of US encroachments on their American possessions but were concerned to have known nothing of the project. 'We shall not quibble with them on this point.'[14]

It was unfortunate from de Gaulle's point of view that Churchill was in Washington for a visit designed to cement the Anglo-American alliance created by Pearl Harbor. The Prime Minister initially ignored Hull's demands for a Free French withdrawal, as well as his complaints of Free French radio and press attacks on the American government made from London.[15] Indeed, Churchill went out of his way in a speech to the Canadian Parliament in Ottawa on 30 December to attack Vichy and praise the Free French. But with Hull standing his ground, Churchill began to change his mind. He now supported a compromise solution calling for a Free French withdrawal from the islands, with joint supervision by the USA, Canada and Britain. The Prime Minister was not disposed to have the new alliance, which he had worked so assiduously to cultivate since the fall of France, complicated by de Gaulle. The General in turn told Eden, who was charged with the thankless task of trying to get de Gaulle's agreement, that he found it troublesome that His Majesty's Govenment 'attached so much importance to giving satisfaction' to the USA. For a short while a breach with the General seemed on the cards.[16]

When de Gaulle saw Churchill on 22 January, following the latter's return to London, he found the Prime Minister extremely tense and preoccupied. The war was going badly for Britain. Kuala Lumpur had fallen to Japanese troops on 10 January. On the 16th, the Japanese had invaded Burma. In the Western Desert, Rommel, who had been on the defensive, had just launched a counter-attack against Auchinleck's forces. De Gaulle was subjected to a torrent of indignation, some of which the official British translator vainly tried to bowdlerise. As usual, on such occasions, de Gaulle stood his ground. No sooner was the door closed behind the General than Churchill turned round and said with sincere admiration, 'That was very well done. I couldn't have done it better myself.'[17]

De Gaulle had got away with his fait accompli, but only at a price. Treading on the toes of Great Powers is rarely wise, and de Gaulle's behaviour had deepened antipathy to him in Washington, where it now became received wisdom in the Roosevelt Administration that de Gaulle couldn't be trusted.[18] It also again exasperated officials in London. At one point during the affair the British had held up a ship intended to provide supplies for Muselier on Saint-Pierre and Miquelon. De Gaulle had responded by threatening to cancel an official visit to Liverpool, behaving, in the words of one senior British naval officer, 'like a naughty boy.'[19] Strang responded that the General's behaviour was 'just what one might have expected.'[20] A few days later, Eden, in equally schoolmasterly vein, referred to the General's behaviour being in many respects 'unsatisfactory.'[21] But the main charge against de Gaulle was that he had broken his word. 'Breach of faith,' 'deception' and 'dishonest' are all terms that appear in the files. It was another black mark.[22]

De Gaulle's most troublesome immediate critic, however, proved to be the man who had carried out the operation. On his return to London, Admiral Muselier attacked de Gaulle for withholding the truth to him about the undertakings given not to take Saint-Pierre and Miquelon. More important, he resigned from the French National Committee (FNC), while remaining Commander-in-Chief of the Free French navy. This was perhaps the most direct challenge de Gaulle faced to his authority during the war. British involvement was bound to be seen as intervention in French internal affairs, a consideration that neither deterred nor indeed worried ministers.[23] Britain had been instrumental in getting Muselier onto the FNC the previous September. The Admiralty, under whose operational command the Free French ships came, was unhappy with the way de Gaulle treated his navy. The General, one British admiral complained, knew nothing about ships and sailors.[24] The War Cabinet decided therefore that Muselier must retain his position as Commander-in-Chief, and that if de Gaulle did not concur action would have to be taken to enforce their demand.[25]

But how was this to be done? The only pressure the British could apply was to cut off his funds; the danger then was that he would threaten to go to Brazzaville or to Moscow. De Gaulle was known to be in contact with the Soviet ambassador in London, Ivan Maisky.[26] The alternative, which had only limited chance of success, was a combination of persuasion and pressure, a task which again fell to Eden. There was some very frank speaking when the Foreign Secretary saw de Gaulle on 5 March. The

General responded sharply to Eden's reminders of the importance of British help. All the British had done had been to lend the Free French money, and he had contributed a great deal more to the Allied cause than that money had been worth. De Gaulle returned to Carlton Gardens in a very excited state.[27]

Stalemate followed. Eden had two more difficult meetings with de Gaulle, who, despite threats, refused to budge.[28] On 10 March, there was an incident when Muselier sought to disrupt a meeting between de Gaulle and senior French naval officers. De Gaulle then asked the British government to place the Admiral under close arrest and retired to his home in Berkhamsted, leaving behind a sealed letter to be broadcast in the event of his deposition. Much of this consisted of an attack on British intervention in the affair, which he described as

a flagrant violation of the undertakings made to me by the British Government. To yield would be to destroy by my own act what sovereignty and honour is left to France. I will not do that.

The English intervention in the Muselier affair follows, moreover, a series of other pressures and abuses of the same sort – (example: what has happened in Syria) – which I have been able to repel only with great difficulty and which harass my confidence in the genuineness of the British as allies.[29]

In the event, the document was not required. A difference was emerging between the Foreign Office and the Admiralty. The former believed that the Admiralty was exaggerating the risk of trouble in the Free French navy if Muselier ceased to be commander-in-chief. And, while acknowledging that Britain would continue to quarrel with de Gaulle as long as he remained head of the Free French, the diplomats were reluctant to see the issue forced to the point where de Gaulle resigned or was removed. 'I do not suggest,' Strang minuted, 'that this would, in the long run, be an undesirable result, but it would create a large number of serious problems.'[30] Muselier effectively resolved the issue on 19 March when he called on the navy to go on strike. The British promptly withdrew their support.

If the Admiral had proved even more of a loose cannon than the General, the latter had gained little credit from the affair. A Foreign Office telegram sent to Washington on 24 April painted an unflattering picture. De Gaulle had been more tiresome than usual in recent months. He was dishonest over St Pierre. He almost created a schism in the Movement by his handling of Admiral Muselier ... In Syria he and his people are giving us great trouble ... He regards himself as the real France and likens himself to Joan of Arc. He tries to assert France's position using violent tactics, and he has no diplomat of sufficient standing or experience to induce him to use other methods. He is much incensed at having been told by the Prime Minister that he represents only one of several Frances.[31]

Small wonder, therefore, that when shortly afterwards the British launched Operation Ironclad against Vichy forces in Madagascar, Free French forces were excluded. Small wonder too that this left de Gaulle, who had been pressing unsuccessfully for such an operation since Pearl Harbor, feeling thoroughly aggrieved.[32] Madagascar was an issue on which the British and Free French seemed unable to agree. During a conversation with Charles Peake shortly after the fall of Singapore, de Gaulle had brushed aside the British diplomat's argument that there were a number of other higher strategic priorities, leaving Peake with the impression that the General was

dwelling in a world apart from that which most of us are called upon to inhabit, and that he is either unable or unwilling to see that the Free French force can play no greater role than is commensurate with their contribution to the allied cause and to the requirements of our strategy as a whole.[33]

For their part, the Joint Planning Staff regarded de Gaulle's plan as tactically unsound. They also expressed strong reservations over Free French participation, based on previous experience of joint operations at Dakar and in the Levant. 'The notorious lack of security' among the Free French was regarded as 'almost certain' to prevent the element of surprise essential to the operation. Second, Free French involvement was expected to lead to strong resistance by the defending Vichy forces.[34] 'The Free French are out of the business,' Churchill minuted ten days later, 'and should be kept out.'[35] By the end of the month he was calling for de Gaulle's people to be 'misled about Ironclad ... to ensure the security of the operation.'[36] Confidence in the Free French had fallen sharply since the heady days in summer 1940 when the Prime Minister was planning Operation Menace with de Gaulle.[37]

As a result, the first de Gaulle heard about the Madagascar landings came from a telephone call from a press agency on 5 May. This was a serious blow, a very visible expression of no confidence, undermining Free French prestige in France and the movement's very *raison d'être*. It was made no easier by the fact that de Gaulle had recently been seriously ill with malignant malaria, exacerbated by lack of exercise, excessive smoking and nervous exhaustion. Speaking to officers on his own staff in the wake of Ironclad, de Gaulle bluntly stated that the Free French were finished and that they should enlist with the Canadian army.[38]

He waited six days before accepting an invitation to see Eden, a delay that alarmed the Foreign Office sufficiently to temporarily hold up the despatch of de Gaulle's telegrams for fear that he might issue 'some ill-judged communiqué,' possibly through Brazzaville.[39] In making his complaints to Eden, whom he finally saw on 11 May, the General needed to be slightly cautious. He had after all taken unilateral action of his own over Saint-Pierre and Miquelon. But he made no attempt to hide his anxieties over the British action, which had revived all his suspicions of British designs on French imperial territory. Eden had no easy task to keep his temper, but, he recorded in his diary, 'I am sorry for any exile, so I just did.'[40]

De Gaulle, however, needed not sympathy but a public assurance that the Free French would participate in the administration of Madagascar. Two days later an agreed communiqué was issued stating that the Free France 'should play its due part' in the administration of liberated French territory.[41] Just what was meant by playing their 'due part,' or when they might be able to do so, was another question. Churchill was by no means enthusiastic, telling the local force commander that it would be several months before Free French representatives arrived, if ever.[42] This suited the military, who believed that Free French involvement would complicate negotiations with the Governor over a modus vivendi. Sir Alan Brooke's continuing hostility to the General is reflected in a diary entry for 2 June, in which he complained that Eden's support for de Gaulle 'will go near to losing the war for us if we do not watch it.'[43] Over at the Foreign Office, Eden's Private Secretary Oliver Harvey complained in his diary that the soldiers 'cannot get out of their stupid heads the idea that de Gaulle is a "rebel," whereas Vichyites are "loyalists."'[44] Eden's arguments with the soldiers over the Free French role on the island were to continue over the summer.[45]

Speaking to Charles Peake on 20 May, the General asked why émigré governments had such a melancholy record in history. The answer, he went on, was that they ended up by taking on the complexion of their hosts, and so becoming an embarrassment to them as well as an object of contempt to their own people ... He was only too well aware that if he could become a good Englishman, his popularity here would at once increase, and faces which now frowned on him would smile. But he had his duty to do, and it was unlikely, in any event to bring him any personal credit.[46]

No less striking was the way in which the General saw conspiracy against Free French interests across Syria, Somaliland, Madagascar and West Africa.[47] On 6 June he sent a telegram to senior French leaders in the Levant and Africa in which he claimed not only that the British had designs on Madagascar but that Britain and the USA, of which he was also becoming very suspicious, were planning a military operation against Dakar, from which Free French forces would be excluded. If this were to happen, the Free French would have to break with Britain and attempt to regroup in Africa. The same day he also asked Ivan Maisky whether, in such an event, the Free French could relocate to Soviet territory.[48]

It was Churchill who defused the situation. On 10 June he invited de Gaulle to Downing Street, where the Prime Minister went out of his way to be agreeable. He congratulated the General on the spectacular recent Free French success at Bir Hakeim in the Libyan desert. Under pressure from Rommel, the Commander of the British 8th Army had ordered a Free French division under General Joseph-Pierre Koenig, to hold his southern flank for a week. They had held out for sixteen days against an enemy force three times their number. This was a considerable psychological boost for the Free French, the first occasion a significant body of Free French troops had fought as an autonomous unit against the Axis. The British press was ecstatic, and the affair was heavily publicised by the BBC French Service.[49] Having been told by his visitor that there was 'no colony, however fine, that would be worth the friendship of France to Great Britain,' Churchill replied that Britain had 'no design on the French Empire. I want a great France with a great army. That is indispensable for peace, order and security in Europe.' At the end of the meeting, the Prime Minister accompanied the General to the Downing Street door, assuring his visitor that, 'I shall not desert you, you can rely on me.'[50]

It was a notable example of the effectiveness of personal diplomacy. Churchill's words had what the historian François Kersaudy describes as an 'anaesthetic effect' on the Free French leader, although in his private account of the conversation the General ascribed much of the new British

147

friendliness to a recent journey to London by the Soviet Foreign Minister, Vyacheslav Molotov.[51] Russian demands for a second front, de Gaulle wrongly claimed, 'have suspended other projects which were formerly being cherished.'[52] Whatever the cause, de Gaulle's mood had changed dramatically. When de Gaulle saw Eden on 30 June, nine days after the fall of Tobruk to the Germans, the General expressed sympathy and understanding about Britain's military difficulties in Libya. He spoke publicly in Edinburgh about the friendship between Scotland and France. An address to a meeting of MPs was so successful that his audience had broken out spontaneously into 'La Marseillaise.' At a dinner with two British generals, he had been at great pains to be courteous and friendly, while impressing his hosts with his knowledge of armoured warfare. Even General Sir Alan Brooke, who had been induced to stand de Gaulle lunch, found his guest in one of his better moods.[53]

Officials were anxious to reciprocate. The General's good mood was in any case too good an opportunity to miss, given the growing evidence of support for him in France, details of which Eden had circulated to the Cabinet on 1 June. According to informants belonging to left-wing circles in touch with the trade unions, Christian syndicalists and militant sections of the Socialist Party, resistance in France was synonymous with Gaullism, and de Gaulle was the accepted leader of the French resistance.[54] This did not mean that ministers were willing to take him into their military confidence. A request to be allowed to participate in planning for landings in France, which were currently being discussed in London, was turned down by the Chiefs of Staff, who continued to regard the Free French as a security risk.[55] Nor did anything come of Peake's suggestion that what the General really wanted was to be asked for his advice.[56] But de Gaulle was taken on various trips to see the British war effort, and, on 14 July, the British, in the General's words, 'enlarged the basis of the relationship with us' by agreeing that the Free French should henceforth be known as the 'Fighting French.'[57] De Gaulle had for some time been suggesting this term, which both he and the BBC were already using, to emphasise the point that France was still present in the war. Although this did not mean formal recognition of the National Committee, for the first time Britain was recognising the de Gaulle movement as the symbol of French resistance, both in France and elsewhere.[58]

Of more immediate practical importance, Churchill was finally induced to relax a travel ban imposed on de Gaulle at the time of the Saint-Pierre and Miquelon affair.[59] De Gaulle had been pressing to travel to Africa since

March. On 10 April Eden had minuted to Churchill that with the Muselier affair 'patched up,' it would not be wise to stand in the way of him visiting his own territories.[60] The Foreign Secretary had returned to the question on the 27th, warning that there was no adequate reason that could be given de Gaulle for the ban and that it would only increase his suspicion of Britain, making him even more difficult to handle than normal. Churchill remained unresponsive. 'There is nothing hostile to England this man may not do once he gets off the chain.' It is hardly surprising that in his memoirs Passy refers to Britain as de Gaulle's 'island prison.'[61] Not until July did the Prime Minister relent.

Prior to his departure from Britain, Eden reminded de Gaulle that he had made a number of unfriendly statements during his last trip abroad. The General, Eden reported, 'took this in quite good part and said I need have no fears on this score.'[62] It was a rash promise. Buoyed by the warm local receptions he received in Africa and the Middle East, and faced with British officials who were much easier to bully or browbeat than the Prime Minister or Foreign Secretary, de Gaulle had a tendency to throw his weight around and to give much freer vent to his feelings than he could in London.[63] Ominously, he was planning to visit Syria and Lebanon where relations with the British had remained seriously strained since the row that had followed the armistice negotiations the previous July.

At the core of the Anglo-Fighting French problem in Syria and Lebanon was a steady and irreversible erosion of the French position, which the French naturally resisted and the British did not fully understand. Local aspirations, which were for independence, could not be reconciled with French pre-eminence.[64] The British tried. On the one hand, they were anxious not to set a precedent for Arab nationalism elsewhere in the Middle East. As Churchill put it to Spears, 'What people might learn to do against the French in the Levant might be turned to account against us later. We should discourage the throwing of stones since we had greenhouses of our own – acres of them.'[65] Spears was thus under instructions to maintain the Fighting French 'shopfront' and back them 'wholeheartedly.'[66] At the same time, precisely because of their awareness of the threat Arab nationalism posed to their own interests, the British remained determined to ensure that the French implemented their promise of independence to Syria and Lebanon. This meant delegating real rather than nominal powers to the local authorities. It also meant elections, which the British wanted to be held at an early date, while the French insisted that they should be postponed until the end of the war.[67]

Under these circumstances it was, to say the least, unfortunate that the man who had been appointed British Minister to the Syrian and Lebanese republics, as well as the Head of the Anglo-French Liaison Mission in the Levant, was the former Francophile General Spears. Spears quickly became an ardent convert to the causes of Syrian and Lebanese independence. But the zeal with which he pursued this cause had perhaps less to do with the reactionary attitude of the local administration than with his own breach with de Gaulle and disillusion with France.[68]

Something of the flavour of Spear's new attitude to the country he had once loved can be gathered from his complaint, written in December 1940, that

> The refusal of the French to go on with the struggle in Africa was absolutely disgraceful and the fact that none of those in power were ashamed to break their undertaking to us to carry on the war to the end together was unpardonable ... The ease with which a greater part of the nation turned to detesting us can never be forgotten or forgiven. The feeling is made up of jealousy and atavistic delight.[69]

All that was left of the spirit of France, in Spears' eyes was de Gaulle, and the British General had behaved more like a patron saint to the Free French than a liaison officer. In return he had expected a complete personal loyalty which was entirely outside de Gaulle's character. The critical turning point for Spears was the big row with Lyttelton after the Acre Convention. Even more than Churchill, Spears had turned against him. A member of his Beirut mission remarked that he never knew what was meant by animals eating their young until he had seen Spears 'devouring' the Free French movement.[70]

Circumstances gave Spears every opportunity for pursuing his vendetta. The British had an important say on a variety of key administrative matters such as security, public order and communications. This created inevitable tensions with a relatively inefficient French administration, dependent on British subsidies. The fact that the Levant remained under British military command provided an additional source of irritation. There were good security reasons for this. In the summer of 1942, as Rommel was pushing into Egypt, German forces also launched an offensive into the Caucasus. The spectre of linking the Eastern Front with that in North Africa was not entirely far-fetched. The problem from the French perspective, however, was that the British army, in François Kersaudy's words, was 'conspicuous, ubiquitous,

Plate 1   Unwelcome tourist. Hitler in Paris, June 1940.

Plate 2   Would-be collaborators: Marshal Pétain and Hitler, Montoire, October 1940.

Plate 3    Happier days: the First Lord of the Admiralty, Winston Churchill, and Admiral
Darlan, Paris, November 1939.

Plate 4    Scuttled: aerial view of the French fleet at Toulon, 28 November 1942.

Plate 5    RAF bombers over the port of Brest, December 1941.

Plate 6   'An eagle with bad habits': General de Gaulle in London.

Plate 7   General Sir Edward Spears and General Catroux do not agree,
Beirut, November 1943.

Plate 8    Liberator and liberated: unenthusiastic French civilians
show ID cards to a British officer

Plate 9 'Some day we shall walk down the Champs-Elysées together.' 11 November 1944.

cumbersome and highly embarrassing' to the French administration. To make matters worse, the old British military prejudices against the Free French died hard. To quote Kersaudy again, for many officers from second lieutenant upwards 'F. F. did not necessarily mean Free French – or Fighting French.' 'In every domain, every day, everywhere,' de Gaulle claimed in his war memoirs, 'there were interferences on the part of our allies, multiplied by an army of uniformed agents.'[71]

It was against this background that a furious row broke out almost immediately after de Gaulle's arrival in Cairo. On 8 August de Gaulle met with the new resident minister, Richard Casey, whom the General found 'sympathetic but rather ill-informed.'[72] His host was rather less impressed, reporting that de Gaulle had come to see him 'uncompromising and intransigent ... He accused us of trying to oust the French from their position in Syria and Lebanon ... The discussion degenerated into an undignified shouting match, he in French and I in English.'[73] The catalyst for the argument was the question of elections, on which de Gaulle was adamant. 'As long as the Germans are advancing in the Caucasus and are almost up the Nile Delta,' he subsequently wrote to Pleven and Maurice Dejean, the FNC Commissioner on Foreign Affairs in London, 'and as long as Gandhi and Nehru are under arrest, we shall not hold elections.'[74] (Leading members of the Congress Party had just been arrested in India.)

De Gaulle had not actually said anything substantially different from what Catroux had been saying, but his very different style rebounded to his immediate disadvantage.[75] Churchill was currently in Cairo, making more changes to the British High Command. The Prime Minister had also been persuaded by Casey to recall Spears as a means of relaxing tensions in the Levant. But on hearing of the row with Casey, which can only have confirmed him in his view that it was unwise to allow de Gaulle to travel outside Britain, Churchill changed his mind.[76] De Gaulle had shot himself in the foot at the very outset of his mission.

Undeterred, the General proceeded to Lebanon and Syria, in an attempt to reinforce the links that bound the two territories to France. In the words of a French report from Beirut,

The political significance of the General's visit to the Levant will escape no one. The demonstrations of enthusiasm which greeted the Head of the Fighting French in the towns and villages of Syria and Lebanon, have signally demonstrated that despite its misfortunes, France has lost nothing of its prestige.[77]

At the same time, de Gaulle maintained his campaign against the British, writing to Churchill, being rude to the British representative in Aleppo and pleasant to the military commander, General Holmes. He demanded that the Levant command be handed over to France. He complained to the Americans and Russians. Casey was sent a forty-page indictment of British activity in the Levant.[78] Psychological warfare was, as ever, de Gaulle's *métier*, and he had become practised at dividing his critics and exploiting gaps between different British authorities. 'I play everybody against everybody,' he is reported as having said around this time, 'and win each time.'[79] Expressing himself in telegrams back to the National Committee in London as 'deeply uneasy about the future of Anglo-French relations,' de Gaulle justified his attitude as

> the only one that corresponds to our dignity and to responsibilities. The stupid greed of our allies here is checked by one thing alone, and that thing is the fear of pushing us too far. *We shall not increase in our importance by humbling ourselves.*[80]

It was the unfortunate members of the National Committee back in London rather than de Gaulle who bore the brunt of British displeasure. The British were determined that de Gaulle should come back to London, and, unusually, were prepared to use financial pressure to force their point. The Treasury was instructed not to pay the Fighting French the monthly subsidy for their operations in the Levant, amounting to £200,000–300,000, until the General returned. But there was also a carrot in the form of hints of British concessions over Madagascar.[81] De Gaulle took his time, suspecting that the British were not simply concerned with Madagascar but wanted him safely in London when Anglo-American forces landed in North Africa, an operation of which he was aware, despite not having been officially informed or consulted. He would return to London, but not before making a tour of Africa.

Before finally coming back to London, he told Catroux that he wanted to 'lance the abscess of Anglo-French relations,' an abscess which remained completely unknown to either the British and French public or to the Resistance.[82] His return on 25 September came as something of a shock. 'How distant,' he wrote in his war memoirs, 'were the loyal territories, the eager troops, the enthusiastic crowds … Here, once again, were what is known as power, stripped of the contacts and recognition that occasionally manage to sweeten it.'[83]

His interview three days later with Churchill and Eden was an occasion worthier of a playwright than an official note-taker. Cadogan described it as a 'pitched battle.'[84] Nothing new was said, whether on Syria, Madagascar or on the wider problems of de Gaulle's relations with Britain. Both sides rehearsed their grievances. In his war memoirs, de Gaulle accuses Churchill of attacking him in 'a bitter and highly emotional tone,' and Eden of losing his temper.[85] For his part, Eden later said that he had never seen anything like it by way of rudeness since Ribbentrop (former German Ambassador in Britain and now Foreign Minister). The interview concluded with Churchill accusing de Gaulle of waging war against England rather than Germany and being 'the main obstacle to effective collaboration with Britain and America.' The General responded that he would 'accept the consequences.' Discovering that the General was due to make a broadcast, the Prime Minister rang up the BBC to give instructions that the transmission should be immediately cut off if he departed from the script.[86]

The Fighting French were seriously alarmed. They had been particularly concerned by Churchill's remark that 'there were other parts and aspects of France which might become more prominent.'[87] Rumours circulated in Carlton Gardens that Churchill was planning to intern de Gaulle on the Isle of Man and that de Gaulle had ordered the internment of Britons in Equatorial Africa.[88] The former were not entirely unfounded. Fearing that the General might take what Eden referred to as 'rash steps against us,' a series of security measures were taken.[89] MI5 watched his movements in case he tried to slip away, his phone calls were monitored, and some of his outgoing telegrams were temporarily suspended.[90]

After a good deal of diplomatic agitation by members of the National Committee, who demonstrably closed ranks behind their leader, de Gaulle received Peake at Carlton Gardens.

He received me kindly, putting his arm through mine and sitting me down in his own armchair. He then began by referring to our friendship and saying that he wished to speak to me as a friend and that he hoped I would not think it necessary to repeat to the Foreign Office our conversation which would be quite informal.

Which Peake of course promptly did, including the General's offer to act as a bridge between Britain and the Russians, who, the General reported, were apt to be 'rather spiteful' about the British.[91]

De Gaulle continued to smoulder against *les Anglais*. Writing in his journal on 11 October, Hervé Alphand was struck by the General's Anglophobia:

> For him England, perfidious, egoistic, only thinks of despoiling our empire. She is incapable of conducting the war and does not even take account of the collapse of her power. He places his hopes in the United States and the Soviet Union.[92]

The General had sacked Maurice Dejean as Commissioner for Foreign Affairs for taking too soft a line with the Foreign Office over Syria. Charles Peake complained that de Gaulle had 'no conception of the most rudimentary basis of negotiation. I am in despair. I do not think that his quarrel with the Prime Minister will ever be patched up,' and it seemed de Gaulle had outlived his usefulness.[93]

In fact, the ground was shifting. The British were moving towards an agreement that would allow the Fighting French to take over the administration of Madagascar. Much more importantly, final preparations were being made for the landings in North Africa, which would allow de Gaulle to break out of the claustrophobic world in which his relations with *les Anglais* had become trapped. It was against this background that on 30 October Major Morton called on de Gaulle to deliver a message from Churchill congratulating him on the enterprise of the Fighting French submarine *Junon* in Norway and expressing regret over the heavy French casualties suffered during fighting in Egypt. Despite the difficulties, Morton assured the General, the Prime Minister had not forgotten the part played by de Gaulle after the defeat of France. De Gaulle responded in kind, recognising the immense burdens that the Prime Minister had to bear and admitting to being a man 'of quick spirit and temper.'[94] According to Pleven, the visit came at a time when de Gaulle was both depressed and doubtful and had lifted relations onto that 'sentimental and emotional plane which always drew a response from the General. This was the moment when we might find him anxious to cooperate.'[95] The next few weeks would subject this new spirit of goodwill to severe test.

# 11

# A Shabby but Inevitable Compromise

On the night of 7/8 November, the BBC broadcast the cryptic message, 'Hello Franklin, Robert is coming.'[1] This was the signal for the largest and most ambitious amphibious operation in history to date: the Anglo-American landings in North Africa. In conjunction with Montgomery's 8th Army to the east in Libya, Operation Torch was aimed at gaining complete control of North Africa from the Atlantic to the Red Sea. Its strategic consequences were to dominate the war for the next two years, generating a great deal of Allied controversy. For the defeat of the Germans in Tunisia in May 1943 ensured that the initial Allied re-entry point into the European continent would be through Italy rather than Metropolitan France.[2] Torch's impact on French politics was no less decisive. Under a highly controversial agreement negotiated by the American military, the figure who suddenly emerged as head of the French administration in North Africa was none other than Admiral Darlan. The Fighting French were outraged, and for the first time in the war French policy became a matter of political controversy in Britain. The result was a six-week-long crisis during which British ministers and officials scrabbled to regain control of French policy from Darlan and the Americans.

German interest in North Africa had been primarily defensive. Although the Germans had made demands for extensive base facilities there three weeks after the Armistice, these were never pressed. Hitler's main concern had been that North Africa might defect to de Gaulle or Britain, thereby exposing Italy and southern France to attack.[3] Churchill, by contrast, had been eyeing North Africa since the Armistice, and the Mediterranean played a central part in British strategy.[4] Defeat, in Douglas Porch's words, 'would probably not mean the defeat of Britain, while victory there would sustain morale, undermine Italy, encourage American aid, overextend Axis forces, protect Middle Eastern oilfields, draw the French back into the war, keep Spain on the sidelines, and contain the Arab penchant for creative anarchy.'[5] Control of North Africa would have an additional critical advantage; it would reopen the Mediterranean to Allied convoys, shortening supply lines to the Middle East by several thousand miles and saving a million tons of shipping.[6]

When in December 1941 Churchill had travelled to Washington in the wake of Pearl Harbor, he had advocated an Anglo-American landing in North Africa, either with or without Vichy consent. Roosevelt, who had for some time shown a lively interest in north-west Africa, was receptive. But the subsequent British and American reverses in the Far East, along with the British setback in the Western Desert and heavy shipping losses, pushed the operation into the background.[7]

By the time it returned to the front of the strategic agenda in spring 1942, the North African plan, known as Super-Gymnast, was faced with a serious rival in the form of Sledgehammer, a cross-Channel operation into France. This was partly in response to the need to try to take some of the pressure off the Soviet Union on the Eastern Front. A constant fear of both the British and the American high commands was that the Germans might move south-east into the Caucasus and Iraq at exactly the same time as Japanese forces managed to close the Persian Gulf and thus the southern exit of the Suez Canal.[8] In addition, the Americans were concerned to avoid a dispersion of military effort. The American Secretary of War, Henry Stimson, described the British strategy of fighting in North Africa as 'the stopping up of rat holes,' while the American Chief of Staff, General George Marshall, had a political dislike of a North African operation, which he regarded as serving British post-war interests.[9]

The British, who had much more experience in fighting the Germans in both the first and the current world wars, in turn felt that Marshall was being unrealistic about the problems of operating in France in 1942.[10] They believed that the Americans failed to take into account the discrepancy between battle-hardened German forces and the raw American divisions. Nor did the Americans appreciate that the shortages of shipping and tank landing craft meant that the Germans could reinforce the point of attack three to four times faster than could the Allies.[11] These considerations overrode any possible advantages of using a cross-Channel operation as a means of helping Stalin. As Churchill put it:

The fact that we had made a gallant but fruitless attempt to open a second front in this area would be no consolation to the Russians. An assault in this area would probably cause a patriot uprising in the north of France and failure on our part would result in terrible consequences to our French supporters.[12]

On 11 June, the War Cabinet decided that there would be no landings in France unless the forces were capable of staying on the Continent, which in effect meant until the Germans were demoralised by failure in Russia.[13] Since, however, both Churchill and Roosevelt were determined that there must be some action against German ground forces in 1942 (Roosevelt was particularly anxious that American soldiers should be engaged before the mid-term US elections in November), North Africa re-emerged as the only alternative. After a tense meeting in London with the American Chiefs of Staff, the decision for what became Operation Torch was finally taken on 25 July.

All this was high strategy. It had, however, political consequences, for Britain as well as France. Having gained their main point, the British felt it politic to concede command of the operation to the Americans.[14] This was not entirely wise. While in certain respects a closer, more informal and congenial affair than the Entente, the new Anglo-American alliance was by no means straightforward. Anglophobia was not a French monopoly. A visceral dislike of the British penetrated deep into the military and political elites in Washington, and on a number of issues London and Washington did not see eye to eye.[15] One of them was France. The British had for some time regarded the Americans as too sympathetic to Vichy. There was particular concern about Admiral Leahy, who after being withdrawn from Vichy in April 1942 had become Roosevelt's Chief of Staff, as well as about a State Department official, Robert Murphy, who was to play a crucial role in North Africa. For their part, the Americans mistakenly believed that de Gaulle was in British pockets.[16] British officials found it extraordinarily difficult to get across to the State Department Britain's sense of obligation to the man who had stood with them in the dark days of June 1940. 'We were down and out,' Halifax once told Hull, and 'de Gaulle had come out on our side with great courage and risked his life in doing it. When you had been tiger shooting with someone who had not run away, you felt differently towards him than to someone who had not happened to be in on it.' The Secretary of State, who did not like the implicit criticism of US policy in 1940, was not convinced.[17]

The British and Americans also disagreed about the future of France. For obvious geographical reasons, France was of much greater importance to the British than to their transatlantic allies. This did not prevent Roosevelt from having some clear views about France, which he regarded, correctly, as being finished as a Great Power. It was a prospect which the British, who looked to France as an essential part of the post-war European balance of power, could not afford to contemplate. Roosevelt spoke about France being disarmed after the war and the creation of a new state of Walloonia, comprising parts of north-east France and the Walloon-speaking parts of Belgium. Roosevelt also talked about the internationalisation of French territories overseas, including Indochina and the strategically important ports of Bizerta and Dakar, where the President was interested in establishing American bases. 'It seemed to me,' Eden wrote following discussions in Washington in March 1943, 'that Roosevelt wanted to hold the strings of France's future in his own hands ... I did not like this.'[18] This was not far off the mark. According to Robert Murphy, the President would discuss the replacement of French officials and changes to French law 'as if these were matters for Americans to decide.'[19]

Matters were further complicated by what Eden described as a 'Lafayette' problem, the American belief that for historical reasons going back to the American War of Independence they knew better how to handle France than the British did. This was reinforced by the series of recent hostile Anglo-French encounters starting with Mers-el-Kébir. Lurking behind all of this was a sense of Anglo-American rivalry in North Africa, which was to become evident in the wake of the Torch landings.[20]

Few of these problems were evident during the planning stage for Torch, which took place in London. The Force Commander, General Dwight Eisenhower, had weekly lunches with Churchill and went out of his way to make the newly established Allied Forces Headquarters (AFHQ) a genuinely integrated affair.[21] Harold Mack, Head of the Foreign Office's French Department, had been appointed Eisenhower's personal adviser on political matters. All Eisenhower's remarks on the politics of Torch 'seem full of good sense,' Strang minuted on 18 September. 'I suspect Mr Mack has been educating him.'[22] Since Britain was participating in the operation and had a close interest in what was done in North Africa following the landings, 'we naturally assume,' the Foreign Office had informed the Washington embassy three days earlier, 'that the US will work in close concert with us whatever they do, in the same way as the US authorities are collaborating with us here in the planning of the operation itself.'[23]

The British made no objections to US insistence that Torch should have the appearance of an all-American operation, in the hope that French forces would then be less likely to offer the resistance that British forces had met in Dakar, the Levant and Madagascar. At one point Churchill had even suggested that British troops might wear American uniform, and two of the British destroyers involved in the attack did in fact fly the American flag. The BBC European News directive of 8 November stressed that all language broadcasts must make clear that this was an American operation, although supported by the Royal Navy and the RAF.[24]

Nor did the British object to American insistence on the exclusion of de Gaulle. In May 1942, the Chiefs of Staff had issued a directive to SOE for the preparation of a negotiated agreement with French authorities of sufficient standing to ensure favourable entry of Allied forces in North Africa. SOE had been authorised to tell the French that should an agreement be reached they would be under no obligation to serve under de Gaulle or the French National Committee.[25] A paper produced by the Joint Planning Staff in August noted that the General had no substantial following in North Africa and was likely to stiffen resistance.[26] Indeed, Torch was seen as opening up the prospect, by no means unattractive to Churchill and some senior officials, of weakening de Gaulle. The landings, Churchill suggested, might 'alter the whole perspective,' attracting 'other and larger figures' from North Africa or Metropolitan France.[27] If the French in North Africa joined the war, a Foreign Office memo noted, de Gaulle's importance would diminish and he might coalesce with the larger body of dissident Frenchmen. 'We should encourage this.'[28]

The name which now came to the fore was that of General Henri Giraud. A dashing if somewhat old-fashioned cavalry officer, Giraud had been de Gaulle's commanding officer before the war at Metz, where he had once met Churchill. Captured in June 1940, he made a daring escape from the fortress of Königstein deep in Germany in April 1942. This infuriated Hitler, who described Giraud as a general of great ability and energy 'who might well join the opposition forces of de Gaulle and take command of them.'[29] The same idea seems to have occurred to Churchill and Eden. Having discussed the subject on 28 April, shortly after the Muselier crisis had been patched up, Eden minuted to Churchill:

I have been reflecting about what you just told me about Giraud's whereabouts. I do not believe there is any possibility of Pétain going to North Africa. He took his decision about that in 1940. The best we could hope for would be that Giraud would go himself with Pétain's connivance to North Africa, or that he should come here. I believe that the last would be the best solution of all, and I think that this is the one for which we should work. We should then have a real leader of the Free French movement, a man whose name and record inspires devotion among all sections of the French Army and people. Many possibilities would be open to us which are now closed.[30]

SIS was instructed to offer Giraud any help he might need, which they did via the Alliance network. Although Giraud showed no interest in coming to London, he expressed an ambition to coordinate resistance movements in Europe to be able to cooperate with an Anglo-American landing on the Continent in the spring of 1943. He requested arms and also asked that his name should not be mentioned on the BBC because of the suspicion with which he was regarded in Vichy. Shortly afterwards, he was in discussion with the Americans about North Africa.[31]

Under the code name 'Kingpin,' Giraud was assigned a key role in the political planning the Americans undertook for Torch. Shortly before the operation he was brought out of France to Gibraltar by a British submarine, operating under temporary American command. Sir Stewart Menzies, the head of SIS, had taken personal control of the operation.[32] On 7 November, Churchill sent him a message that made reference to the Prime Minister's own brief incarceration during the Boer war.

As a fellow escapee I am delighted that we are working together again. I remember all our talks at Metz. For thirty five years I have had faith in France and I rejoice that our two nations and the US are now going to strike the first great blow together for the recovery of Alsace-Lorraine.[33]

The following morning the great convoys, the one from Scotland, the other from the USA, comprising a total of 370 transport and 300 warships, reached their destinations, where they achieved complete surprise. Twenty thousand British and Americans landed at Algiers, 19,000 American troops at Oran and 25,000 Americans along the Atlantic coast of Morocco.[34] It was only now that de Gaulle was told. This was against the advice of the Foreign Office that 'it would pay us' to tell the General in advance.[35] It was important that de Gaulle should 'send out the right kind of messages to his representatives abroad and that he should, if possible, take the right kind of attitude here in London.'[36] Churchill had duly pressed this view to Roosevelt, pointing out that as far as the security of the operation was concerned, Britain controlled de Gaulle's outgoing telegrams, but Roosevelt had refused. The one *douceur* Britain had been able to offer was agreement on 5 November for the appointment of General Legentilhomme as Governor of Madagascar.[37]

This second exclusion within six months from a military operation on French soil was an affront de Gaulle did not forget; indeed, he regarded it as a sign that Britain had broken its contract with the Fighting French.[38] But when he arrived for lunch at No. 10 on 8 November, the General was in a surprisingly amicable mood. According to French accounts, Churchill did not attempt to hide the fact that he had been 'ulcéré' by the fact that the American communiqué had not mentioned Britain. The Prime Minister went out of his way to reassure de Gaulle that the Fighting French were not being superseded and to express 'his warm affection for General de Gaulle.' 'You see,' Churchill declared in French and with tears in his eyes, 'we will walk down the Champs-Elysées together.' At the more practical level there was an offer to send Gaullist emissaries to Algiers.[39] In the evening, the Prime Minister talked with John Winant, the American Ambassador in London, and General Walter Bedell Smith, Eisenhower's Chief of Staff. The Prime Minister described himself as honour-bound to support de Gaulle and expressed concern that Giraud could turn into a source of difficulty. Britain and the USA could not 'each have a pet Frenchman.'[40] It was a warning the British would have cause to repeat.

Pétain's reaction to the news of the landings was curious. Having given the order to resist, he received the American chargé d'affaires, Robert Tuck. At the end of the interview, Tuck reported, the Marshal took 'both my hands in his looking at me steadfastly and smiling. He accompanied me to the antechamber and turned briskly back to his office humming a little tune.'[41]

Yet the consequences for Vichy were disastrous. Hitler's initial instinct had been to press Vichy to declare war on Britain and the USA. But since Germany's primary concern was simply to gain access to air bases in Tunisia so that troops and equipment could be transported to North Africa, the point was not pressed. The first German planes began to arrive in Tunisia the following day. Laval meanwhile was summoned to see Hitler in Munich. It was a wasted journey. Even before his unfortunate guest's arrival, Hitler had decided to occupy the whole of France. German troops crossed the demarcation line on 11 November, the anniversary of the 1918 Armistice. French troops, which had by now little fighting value other than as a police force, were ordered not to resist.[42] Two weeks later, Hitler ordered the

Armistice army to be disbanded. Although Pétain's government survived, it ceased to have any claim to an independent existence, becoming in effect just another occupied country. Of the once substantial French Empire, only Martinique and the French West Indies maintained their allegiance to Vichy.

Vichy's fate had been sealed by developments in North Africa. Contrary to American expectations, Pétain's orders had, as usual, been obeyed. In three days of fighting, which was fiercest in Morocco, where only Americans were engaged, the French suffered 1,346 casualties, the Americans 1,225 and the British 662.[43] But already by the evening of 8 November a ceasefire had been ordered in Algiers. The man responsible was Darlan, who happened to be in Algiers visiting his son, who was seriously ill with polio. The Admiral was Commander-in-Chief of the French forces, and, unlike Giraud, had the political authority to speak in the name of the Marshal. This did not prevent five days of utter political confusion, as French commanders in Morocco, Algeria and Tunisia wrestled with their consciences or tried to work out which way to jump. Who was the enemy? Who should be obeyed? The chaotic result, in the words of a subsequent French enquiry, was that

> Political and military power in North Africa was exerted from the morning of the 8th to the evening of the 8th by Admiral Darlan; from the evening of the 8th to around noon on the 10th directly by the Vichy government whose representative continued to be Admiral Darlan at Algiers; from the evening of the 10th to 0800 on the 11th by the Vichy government; from 0800 on the 11th ... until 1530 on the 13th by General Noguès; and from 1530 on the 13th ... by Admiral Darlan.[44]

This uncertainty desperately frustrated the Americans, who at one stage feared that they might have a small French civil war on their hands.[45] Like General Wilson at Acre, the American commander, General Mark Clark, had no political advisers, and his priorities were purely military. He had come to North Africa to fight the Germans, not the French; his troops were untried; and this was unfamiliar territory. He badly needed to end the fighting as quickly as possible and secure his lines of communication through Morocco and Algeria to Tunisia, where the Germans were pouring in troops. Concern about possible Spanish intervention in the event of continued instability added to the list of American worries.[46]

Fortunately, the resistance proved short-lived. According to British intelligence sources, General Noguès's forces were nearly out of ammunition, while Darlan saw American recognition of French sovereignty as a means of putting a barrier against de Gaulle, Giraud or anybody else who might try to usurp Pétain's authority. A dramatic reversal of policy now brought the French army in North Africa back into the war on the Allied side. Saul, in George Mikes' ironic words, appeared to have become Paul.[47] His reward was to be recognised by the American commanders, in the name of both the American and British governments, which had not been consulted on the matter, as High Commissioner in North Africa. 'No one, least of all myself, like dealing with the skunk,' Admiral Cunningham, the naval commander of the operation, reported to the First Sea Lord, 'but above all we must have stability in North Africa.' Another British officer referred to 'this shabby but inevitable compromise.'[48]

The British had found themselves spectators at this drama, the most critical moment in French politics since the signature of the Armistice. Harold Mack had remained with Eisenhower in Gibraltar, and only one British naval liaison officer was present during Clark's negotiations with the French, although Cunningham accompanied Eisenhower on his first visit to Algiers on 13 November, to sign the agreement negotiated by Clark. Darlan's involvement had not come completely out of the blue. London was aware that the highly pragmatic admiral had for some time been putting out feelers to the Americans, and the possibility of working with him rather than with Giraud had been raised when Eisenhower met with the War Cabinet in London on 17 October. This had caused some unease. Darlan was distrusted in the Foreign Office, not unreasonably so given that only three days earlier he had said that French interests lay in seeing the protagonists in the conflict, above all the English, exhaust themselves. But the idea had not been ruled out, least of all by Churchill.[49]

Like Roosevelt and Darlan, the Prime Minister was a pragmatic realist who believed Britain was fighting Hitler rather than Evil.[50] However rude and abusive the Prime Minister might be about Darlan, Churchill's position had not changed since his positive response to the Admiral's secret approach of December 1941.[51] When on the day of the landings Eisenhower had first learned of Darlan's presence in Algiers and wondered how to react, Admiral Cunningham had reminded him of a remark by Churchill: 'Kiss Darlan's stern if you have to, but get the French navy.'[52] Churchill reiterated the point, if somewhat more delicately, in a minute he wrote on 12 November, while the negotiations between the Americans and Darlan in Algiers were still under way. If the Admiral could bring the French fleet out of Toulon, 'and help us decisively in gaining Tunis, he will of course have established a claim to a seat on the bandwagon.'[53] Otherwise his inclusion in the French administration would cause more trouble than it was worth. A telegram to this effect was duly despatched to Mack.[54]

Cadogan's diary has a somewhat different take on this telegram. 'Went to see [Eden] with draft telegram to Mack warning of danger of playing in too much with Darlan. If Darlan would give us fleet and Tunisia, I should be very grateful – and then throw him down a deep well.'[55] The problem, as the Foreign Office, unlike Churchill, was aware, was that that the political environment had changed since autumn 1940, when serious consideration had last been given in London to a modus vivendi with Vichy. The Paris Protocols, along with prolonged hostile propaganda in which Darlan had been billed as pro-German and pro-Nazi, meant that accommodation with one of Vichy's most senior figures was no longer politically possible.[56]

The reaction in Britain to the Darlan deal was indeed one of consternation. Ministers and officials variously likened Darlan to Judas, spoke of 'turncoats and traitors' and compared the deal with the 1935 Hoare–Laval pact.[57] The issue was not just the Admiral's Anglophobia, though this certainly did weigh in the Foreign Office, where Eden referred to his 'consistent' 'treachery towards us.' The main argument, however, was a moral one. In the words of a motion tabled in parliament, Britain's relations with 'Admiral Darlan and his kind are inconsistent with the ideals for which we entered and are fighting the war.' Or, to use the *Tribune*'s rather less parliamentary language, 'What kind of Europe have we in mind? One built by rats for rats?'[58]

This was a widely shared concern. The Darlan deal set a precedent that sent a shiver down the spines of the various other governments in exile – 'the lesser Allies,' as one Foreign Office minute described them. If the British and Americans were willing to deal with Darlan, which other 'Quislings' would they make use of?[59] Shoals of shocked and furious telegrams reached SOE from the field, and the head of SOE, Lord Selborne, warned Eden that the deal had produced violent reactions in all SOE subterranean operations in occupied countries, especially France. Eden in turn complained that propaganda to France was practically at a standstill. Almost the whole of the staff dealing with France in the BBC and PWE said they wanted to resign.[60]

Two other factors weighed at official level. Darlan was a noted anti-Communist, and there was concern about the deal's effect on the ever-suspicious Stalin.[61] More important, the deal threatened acute divisions in the French camp.[62] Catroux described Darlan as 'the worm in the fruit.'[63] In de Gaulle's eyes, Darlan was a traitor, as well as his principal rival.

Negotiations with the Admiral would undermine Fighting French credibility, not just in France but also within their own ranks. On the other hand, if a Vichy government was established in North Africa, the Resistance in France might fall into the hands of the Communists. Darlan's position in North Africa would also make it impossible to reunite the Empire and establish a united French war effort, with serious consequences for France's ability to protect its interests after the liberation.[64] When Charles Peake visited de Gaulle on 15 November, he found him under considerable tension. He had all the Sunday papers 'heavily scored in red and blue interspersed with telegram flimsies and cuttings from the tape machine spread out in front of him. Having no other occupation, he had spent the whole day poring over the contents and between times, listening to the wireless.' He then launched into a bitter tirade against American policy.[65]

Churchill's unease at this storm of protests is reflected in the series of telegrams he sent to the Americans. On 11 November he stressed to Roosevelt the importance of unifying all Frenchmen who were anti-German. Britain had obligations to de Gaulle and must make sure the Fighting French had a fair deal.[66] 'Anything for the battle,' the Prime Minister telegraphed to Eisenhower on the 14 November, 'but the politics will have to be sorted out later on.'[67] The next day Churchill again voiced his doubts to Roosevelt. 'We feel sure you will consult us on the long-term steps pursuing always the aim of uniting all Frenchmen who will fight Hitler.'[68] There was talk of sending Cadogan to Gibraltar to help 'sort out this tangle,' while Peake was instructed to get de Gaulle to hold his temper until he had met Churchill and Eden on 16 November.[69]

When the General saw the Prime Minister, the former was assured that his position was unassailable and advised not to batter himself against the Americans. 'Have patience and they will come to you, for there is no alternative.' 'You have nothing to worry about,' the Prime Minister also told his visitor. 'You aren't tainted like we are.' The General was invited to come and see him 'as often as he wished: every day if he liked.'[70] De Gaulle then made a personal appeal to the Prime Minister: 'You have been fighting this war since the first day,' he told his host,

In a manner of speaking you personally *are* this war. Your army is advancing in Libya. There would be no Americans in Africa if, on your side, you were not in the process of defeating Rommel. Up to this very moment, not a single one of Roosevelt's solders has met one of Hitler's soldiers ... Besides, in this African campaign it is Europe that is at stake, and England belongs to Europe. Yet you let America take charge of the conflict, though it is up to you to control it, at least in the moral realm. Do so! All of European public opinion will follow you.[71]

According to de Gaulle, the sally struck Churchill, and the two men parted having agreed that they must not allow the crisis to crack Franco-British solidarity.[72] The resolution did not last. De Gaulle was unwilling to take the Prime Minister's advice, while British policy, faced by a continuing choice between the Fighting French and the Americans, gravitated towards the more powerful ally.

# 12

# Death of an Admiral

The second week of November was a moment of celebration in London. Victories were suddenly being won. Torch had come just days after Montgomery had finally gained mastery in the North African desert war, defeating Rommel at El Alamein. Church bells were rung. Speaking at the Mansion House on 10 November, Churchill had referred to the two events as representing 'perhaps the end of the beginning' of the war. At the same time, Britain had unexpectedly lost control over French policy to the Americans. Hervé Alphand noted a feeling in London that the game was being played without it by a more powerful ally, which had contributed relatively little in the so-called common battle.[1]

If, for the time being at least, the British were saddled with Darlan, they could at least hope to gain some military advantages from him. The 120,000-strong North African army which now joined the battle in Tunisia was a prize that Churchill had been seeking since his attempts to lure Weygand over to the Allies in 1940.[2] Its relations with the British were strained. When Eisenhower had asked Giraud to place his forces under the command of General Kenneth Anderson, he met with bitter opposition. Aware that many French units still had vivid memories of Mers-el-Kébir and the Levant campaign, Giraud was concerned that troops would not obey his orders if under British command.[3]

The other great prize was the French fleet, the most modern half of which had been concentrated at Toulon, where Darlan had believed it would be safe from both the British and the Germans.[4] Clark had worked hard to try to bring the Toulon fleet over to the Allies. While willing to cooperate, Darlan baulked at directing it to sail for Gibraltar. He was also well aware that its commander, Admiral Laborde, was an old adversary. Virulently Anglophobe and fiercely loyal to Pétain, Laborde had initially wanted to sail to fight the British and the Americans rather than to join them.[5] In the event, he remained in port. But with Darlan having breached the terms of the Armistice, the Germans feared that the fleet would indeed go over to the Allies, and on the night of 26/27 November, an armoured SS corps arrived at Toulon to seize the ships. It was the scenario Churchill had feared in June 1940. Two weeks earlier in Tunisia French ships had been surrendered to the Germans. This time they scuttled. Only five submarines got away. Some seventy-five ships, including eight cruisers, twenty-nine destroyers and three capital ships (two of which, the *Strasbourg* and *Dunkerque,* had escaped at Mers-el-Kébir) were lost.[6]

There is a fierce irony in the fact that Darlan's repeated assurances to the British that the ships would never fall into German hands was vindicated at the very moment when the Admiral himself changed sides. The main losers were the Germans, who had counted on the cooperation of the French fleet to regain naval superiority in the Mediterranean, and of course the French.[7] The magnificent French fleet, Alphand recorded in his journal on 29 November,

which we wanted so much to see resume the war for the liberation of France was scuttled yesterday. It lies on the bottom of the Toulon roadstead, grandiose, tragic, nihilistic gesture of the French sailors and the end of the maritime grandeur of our country. How will it be possible in future to defend its empire? What will its future weight be in international negotiations?[8]

Despite Churchill's earlier anxiety to get hold of the ships, the British do not appear to have been unduly upset; indeed, the news relieved them of a serious anxiety. The BBC's European News Directive of 28 November described it as 'a major victory for the Allied cause.' Churchill and Eden were delighted at what they regarded as the first sign of spontaneous resistance to Germany by the French in France.[9] The Prime Minister telephoned de Gaulle to express what the General later described as the Prime Minister's 'nobly expressed but secretly complacent condolences.'[10] Passy complains in his memoirs of the 'vibrant halleluiah' with which the British press greeted the news.[11] But *The Times* wrote that 'even those who think that the French Fleet could have been more usefully employed in the reconquest of France, must nevertheless render deep homage to the way in which the Navy has honoured its solemn promises.'[12]

The remaining 130 French war ships now joined the Allies. They included the battleships *Jean Bart* and *Richelieu,* which was still at Dakar, where the governor, Pierre Boisson, along with some 80,000 men and seven territories in West Africa, rallied to Darlan.[13] Boisson, however, had not forgotten the Anglo-Free French attack of September 1940 and remained intensely suspicious of the British, complaining about overflights, raids by Free French forces and hostile Gaullist propaganda.[14] Much to British concern and irritation, negotiations with Boisson were carried out by the Americans. 'Every sort of flap about Eisenhower's "negotiations with Boisson,"' Cadogan complained in his diary on 5 December. 'These generally take the form of the Vichy French telling the Americans what they want, and the Americans giving it to them with both hands regardless of our interests or feelings.' The Americans were suspected by the British of regarding Dakar as a US sphere of influence and trying to keep them out. On Boisson's insistence, Britain agreed to stop Free French propaganda against him from British territories in West Africa. He also wanted the release of Vichy sympathisers in French Equatorial Africa. Here, in a sign of the Gaullophobia which was again afflicting the Prime Minister, Churchill wanted 'utmost pressure' put on the General to agree, warning that the Fighting French organisation would 'pay dearly if it finally antagonises the US.'[15]

It inevitably took time for the ice between the British and French officers who had remained loyal to Vichy to be broken. But by the end of the year, Giraud was admitting that the British forces had been most cooperative and that their actions were gradually eliminating the old animosities.[16] Relations with the French navy were helped by the fact that Darlan credited Cunningham with saving Force X; indeed, somewhat to the British admiral's embarrassment, Darlan had shaken him warmly by the hand at their first meeting, thanking him for Admiral Godfroy.[17] Cunningham quickly established harmonious relations with French admirals. At a military ceremony held in Algiers on 2 December, Darlan stood side by side with Cunningham and Eisenhower, and three weeks later the Admiral proposed a toast to British victory at a lunch party. Saul's conversion to Paul may not have been complete – his underlying hatred of the British remained – but a working relationship seemed to have been established.[18] Shortly afterwards, General Noguès, who was regarded by the British as a Vicar of Bray figure, told Cunningham that while there had been a time when Frenchmen were dead against the English, this was now over and very little was needed to help all pull together.[19]

While the military in Algiers were concerned with rebuilding broken Anglo-French bridges, the problem preoccupying London was how to ensure the Admiral's 'elimination,' a term which, in the light of subsequent events, has a somewhat sinister ring.[20] Some reassurance, at least initially, had been drawn from Roosevelt's public reference on 17 November to Darlan as a 'temporary expedient.' But three weeks later, when Halifax met the President, the latter showed little sign of wanting to dispense with the Admiral's services any time soon; indeed, he now had in mind the establishment of a joint American-Franco-British commission on which Darlan would sit, albeit with reduced status.[21] For his part, Eisenhower insisted that Darlan was being dealt with 'merely in his capacity as de facto head of the local administration,' and that the Admiral had been given no reason to believe that any additional recognition would be extended.[22] But the Commander-in-Chief was acutely sensitive of his continued need for French cooperation. The Germans had won the race for Tunisia, and Eisenhower feared that military reverses might lead to yet another switch of loyalty on Darlan's part, with very serious implications for the security of the Allied line of communications. Nobody, a British officer reported,

> trusts Darlan, but Darlan is invested with the extraordinary '*pouvoir légitime*' and his claims to be the mouthpiece of the Marshal do reassure many in a crumbling world where France is in German and Italian hands, the Marshal is a virtual and Weygand an actual prisoner, and Laval is openly pro-Boche.[23]

All this worried the Foreign Office, because the reports reaching London all suggested that Darlan was digging in and extending his authority.[24] While Eisenhower quoted him as saying that he would conduct affairs 'on a liberal and enlightened basis,' the evidence suggested that exactly the opposite was happening.[25] December witnessed a rapid deterioration in the political situation in North Africa. German sympathisers who had been ejected when the Allies first landed were reinstated, and French soldiers who had helped the Allies were being punished for desertion. A report of 7 December from the British consul in Tangier complained that the Americans had totally neglected the administrative side of affairs in Morocco and that this was causing much criticism both of the USA and Britain. SOE, which had immediately established a mission in Algiers to organise the infiltration of agents into southern Europe, was also highly critical. According to an SOE report of 18 December, Frenchmen hostile to Darlan and Vichy were turning to the British, who were powerless to help. The result was to divide the French against the collaborationists and the Americans against the British, while throwing confusion in the minds of 'all our supporters here.'[26]

One way of trying to reassert British influence was the appointment of a senior British figure in Algiers. Back on 17 November, the Foreign Office had proposed the appointment of somebody in Algiers comparable in status to the British Minister in Cairo, who, while working closely with the military authorities, would report directly to the War Cabinet in London.[27] Information from Algiers had been sparse. Mack was with Eisenhower in Gibraltar and did not arrive in Algiers until 25 November. And when he did get there his capacity for independent reporting was constrained by his role as Eisenhower's political adviser. Mack's reports to the Foreign Office thus came in the unusual form of handwritten letters addressed to William Strang. 'You probably do not realise how much in the dark we have hitherto been,' Strang replied. London had not been able to gain 'a clear idea of the forces at work and of the resulting political layout.'[28] What Strang didn't add was that Mack was now viewed in the Foreign Office as too sympathetic to Darlan as well as lacking the political weight to influence an American commander who was regarded as politically naive.[29]

Roosevelt, who had not been enamoured by the proposal for a more senior British figure, had countered with proposals for the appointment of both a British and American representative. The President wanted these to be on Eisenhower's staff, which, according to Oliver Harvey, would be an impossible position for a British minister and would 'stultify him from the start.'[30] The President, Eden's Private Secretary believed, was determined to keep Britain out of any effective say in North Africa. It was all 'disquieting for the future of Anglo-American co-operation.'[31] Not until Christmas was an agreement finally reached between London and Washington.

Meanwhile, tensions had emerged with the Fighting French over BBC broadcasts critical of Darlan. On 19 November, use of BBC facilities was denied for the broadcast of a message from French Resistance groups requesting that 'the destiny of liberated French North Africa be put under General de Gaulle's hands as soon as possible.'[32] When Peake saw the General the following day, the floodgates of the General's bitterness and frustration opened over the unfortunate British diplomat.[33] Two days later, a de Gaulle broadcast attacking Darlan was stopped. The news came as a considerable shock to the General. He was, he told Peake, obliged to accept the Prime Minister's decision, since he was not on his own territory and could be restrained. Darlan, the General bitterly remarked, could say what

171

he liked to the French people, but he, who had fought with Britain from the beginning, was prevented from making his own case.[34]

This cut little ice with the Prime Minister. In a message to Roosevelt enclosing the proposed text of de Gaulle's broadcast, Churchill showed how unresponsive he had in fact been to the appeal the General had made to him on 16 November, to assert a European policy. 'If your view was that broadcasts of this kind were undesirable at the moment,' the Prime Minister wrote, 'being your ardent and active lieutenant, I should bow to your decision without demur.'[35] The Fighting French reacted by suspending their daily BBC broadcasts, a development regarded by Eden as 'a real loss to us in France.'[36] The issue was raised in Parliament, and despite attempts to agree an amended text one sentence continued to create difficulty. When de Gaulle was told by Peake that this would have to go, 'there was a silence during which the General showed great emotion, but made no comment.' De Gaulle then said that he had no doubt that Mr Eden had more important things to do and showed Peake out very coldly.[37] In the event, the ban was eventually circumvented by the use of Radio Brazzaville. The text was also published in London in the paper *Les Marseillaises*, where over the weekend it escaped the censor.[38]

Contrary again to the tenor of de Gaulle's conversation with the Prime Minister on 16 November, de Gaulle's position in London does not seem to have been secure. 'We still continue to support de Gaulle as hitherto,' Strang wrote on 28 November, 'and shall do our best to see he gets a fair deal, though if anything like a respectable administration should be established in North Africa, we should do our best to persuade him to coalesce with it.'[39]

The Prime Minister's attitude was even more ambivalent. On 18 November, the day after Roosevelt had described the Admiral as a 'temporary expedient,' Churchill minuted that if Darlan rendered effective service against the Germans 'that would have to be set to his credit.'[40] When Darlan subsequently complained about being treated like a squeezed lemon, Churchill had directed that a most friendly reply should be made to him.[41] These sentiments seemed to go hand in hand with a recurrence of the Prime Minister's Gaullophobia, which Harvey attributed to the prickings of a bad conscience. Eden had a shouting match with Churchill on the evening of 28 November when the Prime Minister declared Darlan was not as bad as de Gaulle. 'That man hates us and would do anything to fight with Germans against us.'[42] This, as Cadogan noted in his diary, was 'just untrue. Tiresome he may be, but sound on essentials.'[43]

The Prime Minister made his views more widely known when he addressed a secret session of the House of Commons on 10 December. Public feeling on the Darlan affair was still running high, and the government found itself in the embarrassing position of having to answer for the actions of the Americans, for which they had no responsibility but from which they were unable to disassociate themselves.[44] Churchill performed the task with skill, managing to imply that the blame for the current situation lay with the Americans while arguing for an at least temporary continuation of the Algiers status quo.[45] No French figure came out particularly well from his account, least of all the man he sarcastically referred to as 'the venerable and illustrious marshal.'[46] Churchill's remarks on Darlan, however, scarcely reflected the widely felt abhorrence of the Admiral. A certain obligation, he told the House, had been contracted to Darlan. It was a matter of fair dealing. The priority was French unity. If Darlan proceeded to render important services, he would undoubtedly deserve consideration in spite of his record.

No less notable were the Prime Minister's words about de Gaulle. Churchill took the opportunity to rehearse to MPs at some length the General's misdeeds over the past eighteen months. While he continued to help him, the Prime Minister warned the House that he could not recommend that they base all their hopes and confidence on the General 'and still less to assume at this stage that it is our duty to place, so far as we have the power, the destiny of France in his hands.'[47]

Harold Nicolson thought that he had never heard Churchill 'more forceful, informative or convincing,' although by the Prime Minister's own subsequent admission an undercurrent of hostility and dismay remained.[48] Tempers were certainly frayed. Violet Bonham-Carter and Clemmie Churchill had a violent row on the subject, during which the latter, to Violet Bonham-Carter's amazement, 'completely lost her temper & nearly emptied a glass of champagne over her & me.'[49] An SOE minute written on 16 December referred to recent hints by some government departments and agencies that they were preparing for a possible 'sell-out' of de Gaulle. While this was by no means a definite policy, it had 'evidently crossed their minds that they may have to reinsure.'[50] Similar rumours may have reached de Gaulle, who two days later asked Peake what the government's attitude would be if he and the National Committee were to dissolve the Fighting French movement.[51] At the War Cabinet meeting on 21 December, the Prime Minister expressed doubts whether de Gaulle realised that the French administration in North Africa under Darlan could develop in a way that might overshadow the Fighting French.[52]

This was clearly an impossible situation. 'We must, I suggest,' Cunningham signalled from Algiers the next day, 'make up our minds whether or not we are backing Darlan. At present nobody knows exactly where we stand.'[53] In the event, the question was to be resolved abruptly and violently. Algiers was a midden of intrigue, and rumours ran like quicksand. As early as 19 November Cunningham had discovered a plot to replace Darlan with the French royalist pretender, the Comte de Paris. By the second half of December the rumours were taking a more murderous turn.[54] On Christmas Eve, a young gunman, Fernand Bonnier de la Chapelle, walked into the Admiral's office and shot him dead. Cunningham and other senior British officers attended the funeral, while detachments from the RAF, the army and the Royal Navy participated in the last honours of a man who over the span of two and a half years had moved from ally to enemy and back again to ally.

When news of the assassination reached Washington, the British Embassy expressed the hope that the press would be restrained.[55] PWE duly emphasised the need to avoid any kind of split with the Americans, while the lengthy News Directive issued by the BBC also stressed the need for neutrality. It was very important that announcers 'should not by their tone of voice show either pleasure or sorrow.' Translators, in choosing the word for the killer, 'should avoid one which has any condemnatory sense ... We do not prejudge the assailant even by our description of him.'[56]

In private, there was less constraint. Colonel Dewavrin was slightly taken aback when a senior member of SOE handed him a glass of champagne and proposed a toast to the death of the traitor Darlan. 'A sigh of relief and satisfaction will run through the country,' Harvey recorded in his diary, 'at the removal of this horrible quisling who deserted us in 1939 [sic] who fought us and denounced us while we were fighting alone and finally who fought even the Americans until they capitulated on his terms.'[57] Hugh Dalton expressed his delight, while Violet Bonham-Carter recorded in her diary that 'Fate has been kind for once!'[58] When Churchill phoned Eden at home to tell him of the news, the two agreed 'that the event could be turned to profit.'[59] Eden, as he recorded in his diary, had 'not felt so relieved by any event for years.'[60]

Fingers were immediately pointed. The Gaullists and the Comte de Paris, were, and at least in the former case, remain obvious suspects.[61] German and Italian radios blamed British intelligence. When the French then claimed to have discovered a plot to assassinate Giraud, it was felt necessary to issue a denial. 'Whatever French may have discovered,' the First Sea Lord, Sir Dudley Pound, indignantly telegraphed to Cunningham, 'it cannot incriminate any branch of the British Secret Services, who do not indulge in such activities.'[62]

The truth, however, appears somewhat murkier. The assassination, as Darlan's foremost French biographers remark, 'had been mounted and executed by the hand of a master,' and it remains one of the most significant mysteries of the war.[63] On Giraud's orders, Bonnier was executed within twenty-four hours and buried in an anonymous grave, his confession having been destroyed.[64] There is no other paper trail, and some of the British files dealing with the events immediately afterwards, along with Eisenhower's correspondence, appear singularly incurious about who was responsible. The explanation is not hard to find. There were too many beneficiaries from Darlan's death, and neither the British nor the Americans would have benefited from a rigorous enquiry. As late as 1995, M. R. D. Foot, the doyen of SOE historians, referred to the assassination as 'probably one of those questions into which historians will do well not to enquire too closely.'[65]

Certain facts, however, are by now clear. Bonnier was one of a small group of young Frenchmen who were being trained by SOE for operations in France. On hearing news of the Darlan deal, they had drawn lots for which of them was to have the 'honour' of assassinating the Admiral. According to Sir Brook Richards, who was with SOE in Algiers, nothing was said 'at the time' to any of the SOE officers, but Bonnier found reason for staying in Algiers, when the other members of the groups were moved to Bône on 16 November.[66] In the 2004 edition of his *SOE in France*, Foot was prepared to state that while there was no evidence to indicate that Bonnier was acting under SOE's orders, 'one or two of his superiors in SOE in Algiers may have turned a Nelsonian blind eye.'[67]

That may not be the whole of the story, for the plot only appears to have crystallised in the third week of December with the arrival in Algiers of General François d'Astier de La Vigerie. The General had been flown out of France by RAF Lysander the previous month and joined de Gaulle's staff. The RAF had subsequently flown him on to Algiers. This may simply have been part of the process of facilitating contacts between Giraud and de Gaulle, which SOE and SIS had been undertaking.[68] But de La Vigerie, who carried a large sum of money with him, clearly had other business. According to Richards again, Darlan's fate was sealed at a meeting on 19 December between the General, his brother Henri (a royalist and right-wing

Cagoulard who was Chief of Police in Algiers) and the Comte de Paris.[69] Bonnier had previously been introduced to Henri, and SOE had issued him with a pistol at the request of one of Henri's henchmen (although this was not used in the assassination).[70]

Perhaps SOE Headquarters had been unaware of his mission; perhaps they too preferred to turn a blind eye. What is certain is that a draft letter to Eden from Lord Selborne, dated 24 December, the day of the assassination, remains on the files. This complains that 'expedience treated as an expedient might have served our turn but entrenched and well watered, it has become a major problem to uproot.'[71] Selborne and his most senior officials were certainly embarrassed by the murder, which left them open to accusations in Whitehall – of irresponsibility, or worse. The fact that they were unable to provide answers to urgent questions from ministers and the Chiefs of Staff, cannot have helped.[72]

What is beyond doubt is the extreme embarrassment, if not worse, which would have been created by any revelation of British involvement in the assassination of an American appointee who had been responsible for bringing North and West Africa over to the Allies. Eisenhower had previously threatened to expel SOE if it provided support for pro-Gaullist and anti-Darlan elements, and was now reported to have threatened to resign if any British link to the killing were proven.[73] (In the event, he appears to have been dissuaded from expelling SOE's Massingham mission, by his British deputy chief of staff, who warned of the political consequences, although its commander and deputy did leave Algiers.)[74]

If there was a conspiracy, it almost certainly did not reach to the top. Ruthless as Churchill could be, it is difficult, if not impossible, to imagine the man who described himself as Roosevelt's 'ardent and active lieutenant,' and who had spoken sympathetically of the Admiral in the House of Commons a mere two weeks earlier, approving of his assassination. In his war memoirs, Churchill devotes more than a page to a far-from-unsympathetic survey of Darlan's relations with Britain, ending with the words, 'Let him rest in peace, and let us all be thankful that we have never had to face the trials under which he broke.'[75] The Prime Minister, as David Reynolds suggests, may well have had a guilty conscience about the Admiral, whose word he had doubted, in the event wrongly, in June 1940, and in whose assassination members of SOE had been at least indirectly complicit.[76] Darlan had become the symbol for what many Britons saw as France's betrayal in 1940 and 1941. But, as Cunningham privately noted, 'whatever he [Darlan] did in France, in the last few weeks he worked for us as best he could, and did a lot for us.'[77] Darlan's opportunism was as much a reflection of the rudderless nature of Vichy France's policy as it was of the character of a man who had at least as much reason to hate the English as they had to hate him.

# 13

# Kings of Brentford

On 2 January 1943, the new British Minister Resident, North Africa, arrived in Algiers. The forty-nine-year-old Harold Macmillan was an ambitious, independent-minded politician, who until now had had little opportunity to show his abilities. First elected to parliament in 1924, he had gained a reputation as something of a rebel, only achieving junior ministerial office in Churchill's 1940 administration. Attached to Eisenhower's staff, but not a member of it, his formal brief was to report to the government on the political situation and future plans for North Africa 'and represent to the Commander-in-Chief the views of His Majesty's Government on political matters.'[1] In fact, his main task, as far as London was concerned, was to regain influence with the Americans. This he did with conspicuous success, drawing on considerable natural diplomatic skills, which included making much of the fact that his mother hailed from Indiana. While not accredited to the local French authorities, with whom his relations were intended to be 'of an informal character,' much of his time in Algiers was to be spent dealing with French politics.[2] Macmillan thus found himself playing a key role in the new, much more fluid phase of Anglo-French relations as the war moved decisively in favour of the Allies and the prospect of France's liberation began to loom on the horizon.

'The Frenchman,' Eden minuted in early January, 'is a politically-minded animal, and we shall have no peace until one authority speaks for all, and not much then.'[3] The establishment of a single authority which could be recognised as a de-facto administration provisionally exercising sovereignty over certain departments of France and the whole of the French Empire (other than Indochina, which was still occupied by the Japanese), had several advantages. It would make for a more effective French contribution to the war effort and provide a body to which Frenchmen in France, including of course the Resistance, could look to as evidence that France was still in the war and would be present at the victory.[4] As, if not more, important, it would contain and defuse a potentially dangerous rivalry between Giraud and de Gaulle, which threatened Anglo-American relations as much as France's long-term political stability. 'We cannot,' as Harvey noted, 'afford to antagonise America, without whose help we cannot win the war, or the peace. We cannot allow her to become disgruntled and isolationist.'[5] The *New Statesman* described North Africa as a political cesspool whose stench threatened to poison Anglo-American relations.[6]

An opportunity for the British to press forward with this agenda was presented by a meeting in January between Churchill and Roosevelt at Anfa, a fashionable suburb of Casablanca. Variously described as a utility version of the field of the Cloth of Gold (the meeting in 1520 between Henry VIII and Francis I of France) and 'a mixture of a cruise, a summer school and a conference,' Anfa was in at least some respects very different in atmosphere from Anglo-French summits.[7] When news of the summit became public knowledge, the BBC French Service stressed the importance of the fact that Churchill and Roosevelt had chosen to meet on French territory. For the first time since June 1940, the BBC declared, French leaders were present at a meeting to discuss future strategy.[8] At issue was whether the Allies were to follow up on the North African landings by moving on to Sicily and Italy, as the British wanted, or, as the American Chiefs of Staff preferred, to resurrect plans for a 1943 cross-Channel operation. The answer, after some very hard bargaining, was the former. Eisenhower was again to command, while the cross-Channel operation would be left to whenever it was thought likely to succeed.

When it came to French affairs, which were brought up at the very end of the proceedings, the two Allied leaders showed none of the respect or understanding implied by the BBC. 'We'll call Giraud the bridegroom,' Roosevelt remarked to Churchill, 'and I'll produce him from Algiers; and you get the bride, de Gaulle, down from London, and we'll have a shot-gun wedding.'[9] The President's low opinion of the French could scarcely have been made more obvious, and it was hardly improved by what now transpired.

Giraud duly arrived on 17 January, but 'the bride' proved much less amenable to such peremptory summons. De Gaulle was already smarting from a series of previous unilateral American actions: his exclusion from Torch, the Clark–Darlan deal and the appointment of Giraud to succeed Darlan. Now he was being 'invited' by foreign leaders to a conference on French soil at which he could expect to find himself under heavy pressure to conform to Allied plans. The result was an extremely difficult interview with Eden and Cadogan. 'He is a species of mule,' Cadogan noted in his diary. 'He refuses to go, and nothing A[nthony] or I could say would move him.'[10] Eden's account to the War Cabinet of the meeting, if more diplomatic, was scarcely more flattering. De Gaulle seemed to have no consideration for the general advantage of the Allies, and it was difficult to escape the conclusion that they were looking towards a situation in which the General would be virtual dictator of France. In subsequent discussion it was argued that if de Gaulle adhered to his views it would be almost impossible to continue the present relationship with him.[11]

When told of de Gaulle's refusal, Roosevelt burst out laughing.[12] The Prime Minister was subjected to a series of jokes and jibes from the Americans, who suspected that Churchill was deliberately holding the General back. 'Who pays for de Gaulle's food?' Roosevelt asked Churchill, before himself answering the question, 'Well, the British do.' Behind this lay the President's belief that Britain and de Gaulle shared a common agenda in maintaining colonial empires, to which Roosevelt of course was strongly opposed.[13] In his telegrams back to London, the Prime Minister was incandescent with anger. 'The man must be mad to jeopardise the whole future of the relations of his Movement with the US.' If 'in his fantasy of egotism,' de Gaulle rejected the chance now offered, the Prime Minister would feel his removal from the headship of the Fighting French movement essential to its future support from His Majesty's Government.[14]

Tempers were now fully roused, and de Gaulle, not trusting himself to avoid saying things he would later regret, avoided seeing Eden. But though unimpressed by British threats, under pressure from his own French National Committee, he finally decided he had no alternative but to go to Anfa.[15] He arrived on 22 January, just as the conference was coming to an end. His bad mood was reinforced by the reception he got. A quarter century later the incident still rankled. 'A deliberate insult. French and American Guards of Honour for Roosevelt and Churchill. Not for me, even though it was the first time I had set foot on French soil since 1940 [sic]. Not even a car.'[16]

His first interview with Churchill was stony. The Prime Minister proposed Giraud and de Gaulle should become joint presidents of a governing committee which would also include Churchill's old friend General Alphonse Georges and a number of figures who had previously supported Vichy. Giraud, however, would exercise supreme military command. De Gaulle would have none of this. He strongly objected to the inclusion of anybody tainted with Vichy and had no intention of subordinating himself to Giraud.

The Allies had, as he scathingly put it in his war memoirs, 'without me, against me, instituted the system now in operation in Algiers. Apparently finding it of only middling satisfaction, they were now planning to swamp Fighting France in it too. But Fighting France would not play their game.'[17] At the end of the interview the General stalked out of the villa with his head high in the air.[18] Angry as he was, the Prime Minister once again could not hide his admiration. As de Gaulle left, Churchill remarked to his doctor, Sir Charles Wilson,

> 'His country has given up fighting, he himself is a refugee, and if we turn him down he's finished. Well, just look at him! Look at him!' he repeated. 'He might be Stalin with 200 divisions behind his words. I was pretty rough with him. I made it quite plain that if he could not be more helpful we were done with him.'
> 'How,' I asked, 'did he like that?'
> 'Oh,' the PM replied, 'he hardly seemed interested. My advances and my threats met with no response.'[19]

Over the next twenty-four hours, Macmillan, who had quickly registered that de Gaulle was the horse to back, along with a reluctant Murphy, sought to find a formula with which both generals could agree.[20] De Gaulle came under intense pressure. In a private message written on 23 January, the General complained of an atmosphere 'reminiscent of that of Berchtesgaden ... It is quite possible that the blindness and anger of the Americans and the English may put me in such a situation that our activity becomes impossible.'[21] Indeed, at a meeting between the British and the Americans later that evening, the possibility of breaking with the General, whom Murphy described as Frankenstein's monster of whom the British should welcome the opportunity of ridding themselves, was considered.[22]

The following morning, de Gaulle again saw Churchill for a meeting which is not mentioned in the Prime Minister's memoirs. De Gaulle later described this as the most ungracious of their wartime encounters, during which Churchill showered him 'with bitter reproaches in which I could see nothing but an alibi for his own embarrassment.'[23] In the end, all that this crude exercise in trying to bang French heads together achieved was a stage-managed handshake between the two generals for the sake of the press cameras, plus a brief joint communiqué. De Gaulle had successfully stood his ground, resisting formidable Anglo-American pressure. But it was the last wartime conference to which he was invited.

It was only after the conference that the British discovered that Roosevelt had signed several papers in the name of both the British and the American governments, without consultation with Churchill or the Combined Chiefs of Staff. Providing for the rearmament of the French army, the 'Anfa documents' recognised Giraud as the sole authority for the reunion of all Frenchmen fighting the Germans. Giraud was also recognised as having 'the right and duty of preserving all French interests' until the French people were 'able to designate their regular Government.'[24] These had been drawn up by one of Giraud's Algiers backers, Jacques Lemaigre-Dubreuil, in whom Murphy placed considerable confidence. The President's confidant, Harry Hopkins, had warned Murphy that the President would be ill advised to sign, but Roosevelt had nevertheless done so while in a particularly anti-Gaullist mood without, however, examining the papers' contents.[25]

The reaction in London was one of anger at what looked like an attempt to build up Giraud to restore a neo-Vichy regime in France, and Murphy was suspected of sharp practice. It was left to Churchill to sort out this very delicate matter on a visit to Algiers on 5 February. Macmillan describes the Prime Minister as handling the affair 'with some reticence but consummate skill.' But Murphy appears to have had an uncomfortable time, being told by the Prime Minister that he was sure the President would not approve of his being treated this way and threatened with a complaint to Roosevelt if the documents were not duly amended. 'He showed by his change of colour that he was alarmed,' Churchill reported back to Eden.[26] The modifications, duly haggled out by Murphy, Macmillan and Cadogan, ensured that facilities should be given not only to Giraud but also to 'the French National Committee under General de Gaulle.' The Prime Minister, the French historian Michèle Cointet notes, had once more saved de Gaulle.[27]

In Algiers, Churchill also saw three important former Vichy figures who had now come over to the Allied side: Pierre Boisson, Marcel Peyretoun (the Governor of Algeria) and General Noguès. The meeting cannot have been entirely easy. When Boisson said that he was pleased to meet the Prime Minister, the latter replied, 'I tried to meet you in 1940, but you did not want to meet me then.'[28] Later, however, Peyretoun and Noguès were told that if they marched with the Allies past differences would be overlooked. It was the same message as he had given to Darlan.[29] Speaking to the Cabinet after his return to London, Churchill defended Peyretoun, saying that his chief offence was that he had been Home Secretary in the Vichy government. Being Home Secretary might be a misfortune, Churchill (who had himself once occupied the same office in Britain) went on to say, but it was not a crime.[30]

While in North Africa Churchill also took the opportunity of trying to resolve the future of Force X, Admiral Godfroy's naval squadron at Alexandria. Following the Allied landings in North Africa, it had been hoped that Godfroy would rally to the Allies. This had not happened. Despite his willingness to bow to *force majeure* in July 1940, Godfroy remained loyal to the legitimate French government, which was still that of Marshal Pétain, and he would take no action which would in any way embarrass it or make life more difficult for the French people. He despised Darlan, whom he believed had no right to give orders, and argued that to hand his ships over to a foreign state constituted treason. Until the Allies had liberated Tunisia, they had not, in Godfroy's eyes, justified their claims to have liberated France.[31] The affair, as Macmillan later wrote, was an example of the difficulty of dealing with men who remained loyal to Vichy but were neither traitors nor time-servers.

> Godfroy was clearly a man of the highest moral standards. He was a tremendous snob ... But in a sense, his snobbery was based on old-fashioned concepts, on what he believed to be a gentleman's honour. He simply could not understand how anybody like our Prime Minister could expect him, or even ask him, to break his oath of loyalty. He hated the Germans and had a deep affection for the English ... however much he may have suffered from successive French governments in whom he placed no reliance – he even disapproved of many of Pétain's actions – he was tied by his oath.[32]

Although Churchill had been willing to await the outcome of the fighting in Tunisia, the slow military progress being made there meant that by the end of January the Prime Minister was becoming impatient. With the Toulon fleet scuttled and French ships in West Africa having come over to the Allies, Force X had become an anomaly. To Churchill it represented a waste of a valuable fighting resource at a time when all available forces were required in the Mediterranean, and he was therefore in no mood to continue indulging Godfroy's conscience.[33] A telegram from North Africa of 26 January invited his colleagues to consider whether the 'scandal' of Force X should not be brought to a head. The Prime Minister was anxious to stop paying the salaries of the French sailors as a means of bringing the Admiral and his 'fellow shirkers' to heel.[34]

Force X took up a quite disproportionate amount of British energy, particularly given the fact that, as Admiral Sir Henry Harwood who had succeeded Cunningham as Commander-in-Chief, Mediterranean, pointed out, the ships were actually of relatively little military value. British frustration is evident in telegram references to 'this ridiculous Godfroy' and the Admiral as a 'pathological case.'[35] A variety of different plans were mooted and failed, but by mid-March Macmillan felt able to advise the Foreign Office that he thought the fish in Alexandria harbour was on the line and, if played with patience, would be successfully landed.[36] Patience, of course, was no more one of Churchill's virtues than it was one of de Gaulle's, but with the aid of financial pressure on Godfroy it paid off. With the surrender of Axis troops in North Africa on 13 May, Godfroy finally came over. It was the end of the long-running French naval saga and of one of the oddest and most troublesome problems created for Britain by French division and defeat.[37]

It was also a sideshow. The real issue remained the need to try and build on the very fragile progress towards the achievement of French union made at Casablanca. The stakes were high. There was a genuine hatred between the Gaullist and Giraudist factions, both of which claimed to be sweeping away the vices of the pre-war Third Republic. On the political right, the heirs of Vichy felt they had buried a corrupt republic, seeing de Gaulle as a man who had betrayed his caste and now led a dangerous populist coalition. To Gaullists, Vichy was a Quisling regime that had forfeited all right to represent the French people. At the parade in May in Tunis to mark the surrender of Axis forces in North Africa, Fighting French troops marched with the British contingent rather than with their Giraudist compatriots.[38]

None of this boded well for the future, once the Germans had been expelled from Metropolitan France. On both French and British sides, there was concern about the possibility of civil war, which could benefit only the Communists and which would have serious repercussions for Europe. In Britain, opinion would probably be polarised in the same way as it had been during the Spanish Civil War.[39] Hence, as Macmillan argued, the need for 'a real Giraud–de Gaulle fusion now,' based on 'a broad and central political foundation,' seeking to rebuild French faith in liberal and democratic ideas.[40]

This very delicate diplomatic task was yet further complicated by the bad blood that had developed between Churchill and de Gaulle, each of whom felt he had been badly treated by the other at Anfa. The previous rows between the Prime Minister and the General had centred on de Gaulle's behaviour towards British ministers and officials. At Anfa, where Churchill had felt humiliated by de Gaulle's initial refusal to come, the dispute had become personal. From now on, precisely as the prospect of de Gaulle gaining power in France grew increasingly likely, Churchill seemed to be pursuing a constant, but futile rearguard action against the General, which caused as much trouble to British ministers and officials as it did to the General. It did not of course help that in a talk to French officers on his return from Anfa de Gaulle had referred to the British as France's hereditary enemies, a remark which had been picked up by Special Branch, or that Roosevelt had complained about de Gaulle's remarks about the Americans at a press conference the General gave in London on 9 February.[41]

The Prime Minister made his feelings clear the same day to René Massigli. Massigli was a former senior French diplomat who had just been brought out of France by the RAF. He was also very much an Anglophile who saw it as his role to smooth over the feathers ruffled by the prima donnas in this Anglo-French drama. His first meeting with Churchill provided a warning of how difficult this task might prove. While he continued to recognise British obligations, the Prime Minister told Massigli that he was no longer prepared to deal with de Gaulle personally so long as the General acted as if he possessed supreme authority over the Fighting French movement. It was up to the FNC to exercise control over de Gaulle. 'He would not have de Gaulle setting up as a dictator here.' Though on the whole favourably impressed by Massigli, Morton reported, Churchill found him too temperamental and not resolute enough.[42]

The latter was scarcely an accusation which could be levelled against the Prime Minister, who subsequently complained to George VI that de Gaulle,

is hostile to this country, and I put far more confidence in Giraud than in him. It is entirely his fault that a good arrangement was not made between the two French functions [sic]. The insolence with which he refused the President's invitation (and mine) to come and make a friendly settlement at Casablanca may be founded on stupidity rather than malice. Whatever the motive, the result has been the same, namely, to put him and his French National Committee practically out of court with the Americans. He now wishes to go on a tour round his dominions, *mes fiefs*, as he calls them. I have vetoed this, as he would simply make mischief and spread Anglophobia wherever he went.[43]

This new travel ban, which followed a Cabinet meeting on 3 March, where Churchill even threatened to have de Gaulle arrested, evoked a by now familiar set of reactions. Eden remonstrated, but was urged by Churchill to 'think of the Americans, who think us responsible for all de Gaulle's acts.'[44] De Gaulle was furious. Charles Peake had the unenviable job of telling the General.

> While I was speaking, I saw the unpropitious signs with which I have been only too familiar in the past. General de Gaulle's pallor increased and his eyes began to blaze. After an awkward pause, he said, that in other words I had come to announce that he was being held prisoner in this country.[45]

On another occasion, Churchill forbade Peake to allow 'the Monster of Hampstead' (where de Gaulle was currently living), to leave the country.[46] Strict security controls over his movements, involving the Foreign Office, the Home Office, the Security Services, the Admiralty and the Air Ministry, were imposed, and notes for press and BBC guidance in the event of a breach with the General issued. Although de Gaulle may have been unaware of these precautions, he certainly felt under pressure, complaining that most British and American press commentators seemed to believe that French unity must be constituted under Giraud.[47]

All this caused unease in the Foreign Office, where it was appreciated that de Gaulle was past breaking, particularly in France, where he now had a significant following. It would, in Harvey's words, be fatal to try and remove the General, a move he likened to 'burning Joan of Arc all over again.'[48] But it was also something of a prime-ministerial red herring. What mattered at this point was not what was said in Downing Street or Hampstead, but in Algiers, where Giraud remained very much in charge. On his visit to Algiers on 5 February, Churchill had asked Giraud to 'restore the laws of the Republic, particularly those affecting the Jews.' (Vicious Vichy anti-Semitic legislation was still in place.)[49] Giraud, however, was a difficult man to deal with. Macmillan likened him to the White Knight in *Through the Looking-Glass*, since he appeared to live only in the clouds. He professed, quite genuinely, to have no interest in politics; indeed, he had a complete ignorance of politics in any form. Roger Makins, Macmillan's deputy, complained to Strang of a lack of central direction and the absence of any single adviser to whom Giraud listened. 'I spend hours every day listening to the woes or ambitions of one faction or another. Nearly all my visitors are depressed, querulous and have bad colds. I often despair of the future of France.'[50] The best the British were able to achieve was to keep public opinion at home off the boil.

In fact, things were about to change for the better. In late February, a man arrived in Algiers who quickly gained Giraud's ear. Following his refusal to join the Free French in June 1940, Jean Monnet had asked Churchill for a job 'in order to serve the true interests of my country,' and had been sent to Washington on a British passport to join the British Purchasing Commission in North America.[51] Here he met with suspicion from the British military, perhaps, as his biographer, François Duchêne suggests, 'for no better reason than he was French and that they could not fathom how he operated.'[52] But he quickly gained the confidence of the Americans and established excellent contacts with the Roosevelt administration. On his arrival in Algiers, the British Embassy in Washington described his work as of 'the highest order,' adding that 'he knows all our secrets.'[53] Few, if any, Frenchmen could make a similar claim.

Monnet had been sent to Algiers by Roosevelt to act as Giraud's political adviser and to inject some democratic credentials into his regime. Working behind the scenes, eschewing drama, and without political allegiances, Monnet quickly gained influence over Giraud.[54] The result was a speech Giraud made on 14 March. In it he met almost all Allied demands, including the re-establishment of the democratic laws of the pre-war Third Republic, the ending of political censorship and the proclamation of elections by universal suffrage as the goal once France had been liberated. Various Vichy figures resigned from the government, though not General Noguès or Peyretoun, who, however, felt it prudent to visit Macmillan shortly afterwards to find out whether Britain would insist on his removal.[55]

The gulf between the two generals nevertheless remained wide. De Gaulle wanted a strong and independent French government in place at the time of liberation, without which, he feared, France would merely replace German with Anglo-Saxon domination. Giraud could not see the importance of this. All he believed necessary was a provisional central authority consisting of colonial governors and possibly other nominees of the two sides. Then there was the critical question of how power within the proposed new unified body was to be allocated. Giraud wished to combine a political role with that of Commander-in-Chief of French forces. De Gaulle, who thought that this arrangement would give Giraud too much power, insisted on the separation of political and military power. Giraud was happy to retain Noguès, Peyretoun and Boisson. De Gaulle demanded a clean break with the Vichy past, though his attitude may also have been coloured by more personal factors. Boisson had repelled Free French forces in Dakar in September 1940, while Peyretoun had signed de Gaulle's death warrant in Vichy.[56]

Last, but by no means least, was the conflict between two strong and prickly personalities, neither of whom played by the diplomatic rules. Both de Gaulle and Giraud spoke of themselves in the third person and were quite unwilling to subordinate themselves to the other. Giraud was a five- and de Gaulle a two-star general who was, in any case, fifteen years younger. As William Strang laconically put it, 'there are two kings of Brentford and neither will give way to the other.'[57] The activities of their respective supporters, the 'Tapers and tadpoles,' as Macmillan disparagingly referred to them, only served further to exacerbate matters.[58]

Three months of diplomacy lay ahead in which the British sought not just to broker a deal but also to mediate a French power struggle. Set against the larger military background of bitter fighting between German and Soviet troops in the Caucasus, the climax of the battle of the Atlantic, with twenty-seven Allied merchant ships lost to German U-boats in the second half of March, and the gradual success against the Germans in Tunisia, this Algiers diplomacy may appear something of a sideshow. But the stakes in this political battle, which sometimes led British diplomats to wish that all Frenchmen and France could go to the Devil, remained high.[59]

Macmillan approached the problem with sensitivity and detachment. He could facilitate contacts by social entertainment, cajole and, at times, apply pressure, but he also knew when it was necessary for the British to keep their distance and make the French face up to their responsibilities. 'We cannot go too fast,' he had minuted to Makins in late February. 'They must go through all the proper preliminaries of courtship before the wedding. It was the absence of these preliminaries which spoiled Anfa.'[60] Macmillan thus relied heavily on Monnet and Catroux, who had arrived in Algiers as de Gaulle's representative at the end of March. Catroux was another five-star general. He got on well with Giraud while also being willing to stand up to de Gaulle.[61] At the same time, Macmillan was careful to coordinate with the Americans, primarily Eisenhower's Chief of Staff, General Walter Bedell Smith, and Murphy, who had been reluctantly persuaded to back the union project.

Giraud's invitation to de Gaulle to come to Algiers was to give the Algiers team particular trouble. The latter was anxious to take up this offer. Giraud's difficulties, he believed, were increasing and the situation playing into his hands. In a talk with Peake at the end of February, de Gaulle reminded the

British diplomat 'of nothing so much as a tiger who, having feasted, has the taste of raw meat in his mouth and knows exactly where the next meal is coming from. I confess I do not much like him in this mood.'[62] Churchill, however, was now ready to allow de Gaulle to travel to Algiers, provided he did not go from there to Syria or Equatorial Africa, a condition which was easier stipulated than enforced.[63] Massigli was anxious for Churchill to see de Gaulle before he left and for him to say a kind word to him. One of the General's 'limitations,' he told Peake, was that he was apt to nurse a grievance and brood over fancied wrongs. It might be wise in the interests of Anglo-French relations to remove any pretext for doing so and to look only at the political factors of the situation while leaving personalities out of it.[64]

This, however, was a saga which still had a good way to run. Churchill did see de Gaulle, but kind words were not in evidence. Rather, the Prime Minister stressed the need for a prior entente with Giraud, on the basis of the terms de Gaulle had rejected at Anfa. According to de Gaulle's account, the Prime Minister

> conjured up the disagreeable consequences that, unless agreement could be achieved on this basis, my presence in North Africa would have from the point of view of public order and the military situation. The plane I requested was ready, the Prime Minister affirmed. But would it not be better to wait until Mr Eden, then on a trip to the United States had time to return, and until General Catroux, who had been in Algiers only a week, could exercise his influence?[65]

The General, Churchill informed Macmillan, 'was not in a bad mood and took what I said well.'[66]

Meanwhile, in Algiers, de Gaulle's arrival at this point was regarded as premature. Catroux was indignant at not being allowed to continue negotiations quietly and threatened to resign; the Americans wanted to issue a blank refusal. Macmillan sought to smooth things over by drafting a personal message from Eisenhower to de Gaulle as from one soldier to another, asking him to postpone the visit until after the outcome of military operations in Tunisia.[67] The ruse failed. Furious, de Gaulle issued a communiqué, which the BBC were asked not to put out, implying that he had been prevented from coming to North Africa to conduct negotiations for French union by the American Commander-in-Chief.[68] This prompted Eden to read de Gaulle a homily on his treatment of the USA and to try to make him see that his methods were the worst possible, but it made little impression. The result was a resurgence of anti-Gaullism among the Americans in Algiers, which Makins described as so violent to be almost pathological.[69]

Yet some progress was being made. For all his emphasis on the need for Frenchmen to sort their own differences, the fact was that de Gaulle was talking to the British about French internal affairs. More important, the negotiations between the two generals were continuing.[70] The French National Committee proposed that the two generals should be co-presidents of a united organisation but with Giraud giving up his position as Commander-in-Chief.[71] At this Giraud dug in his heels. He had just been visiting the battlefront in Tunisia. Here a rag-tag French army, which looked as though it had been equipped in a Moroccan flea market, and which was by no means well regarded by its American and British allies, had been fighting courageously.[72] Macmillan found Giraud in 'stubborn, egoistical and even defiant mood.'[73] 'He is a most difficult man to talk to,' he noted in his diary on 26 April, 'because he is really so nice and also so stately and stupid.'[74] The following day, however, Giraud had changed his mind. Now he was willing to accept the principle of a war cabinet with full collective responsibility and himself and de Gaulle as joint presidents. He was also ready to meet de Gaulle, though not in Algiers, where the prospect of large pro-Gaullist demonstrations continued to cause concern, but either at Biskra or the American airport at Marrakech. Macmillan immediately telegraphed to Churchill, asking him and Eden to put pressure on de Gaulle to accept the invitation without demur. This, he warned, might be

the last chance of accommodation between the two factions and that though French unity may be achieved in the future through a decline in fortunes of one or other general, or the rise of a third star, persistence of the division of the French camp at the present time is likely to throw a heavy strain on our relations with the United States, whose uncertain and equivocal French policy tends to diverge rather dangerously from our own.[75]

'All the cards,' Macmillan concluded, were in de Gaulle's hands. 'He has only to come in order to secure all he can reasonably demand. But if he hesitates, I think he is lost.'[76]

The Foreign Office called in René Massigli, who was now responsible for Foreign Affairs on the French National Committee. Churchill saw de Gaulle, but the General, however, was giving nothing away. Giraud had still not agreed to the subordination of the military to the civilian power, or to the exclusion from office of all ex-Vichy figures. And de Gaulle was intensely suspicious of Giraud's motives for specifying a meeting at two airports, where he feared that he would be subjected to the same kind of pressure he had come under at Anfa. The result was a barren meeting. According to the British record, de Gaulle 'was not in a bad mood; he was calmly mulish.' The Prime Minister observed that the outlook was bleak.[77]

Worse was to follow. The day he had seen Churchill, de Gaulle had also sent a passionate message to Catroux in which he angrily asserted that it was not up to Giraud 'to invite me, I say invite me, to come to North Africa. North Africa does not belong to him, any more than it belongs to me. Besides I have troops of my own.'[78] On 4 May, de Gaulle made a blistering attack on Giraud in a broadcast on Fighting French Radio from Brazzaville. This provoked a furious reaction. Monnet likened the General's methods to Hitler's and privately described him as an enemy of the French people. Giraud threatened to break off negotiations. Catroux was on the verge of resignation, while Massigli told the Foreign Office that he and others might also go. Macmillan therefore had to work hard to contain matters.

The Minister brought a quality previously conspicuously lacking in Anglo-French relations, namely a sense of humour. For a great country to remain divided because 'no one could decide whether the negotiations should take place in London or Brighton' was absurd.[79] In Britain it was almost a recognised procedure preliminary, he claimed, to forming a coalition government for one politician to make an offensive speech about another. One couldn't break off negotiations about such a thing. Murphy was shocked; Monnet amused. Macmillan now warned the Foreign Office that if negotiations were to be kept going, Britain would have to give 'rather positive advice,' which meant becoming increasingly involved in French affairs.[80]

Macmillan liked to say that he was no diplomat, and his diplomacy was at times highly unconventional. Its immediate focus was Monnet, with whom he went bathing – naked, as was the fashion with British troops in North Africa – in the relaxed atmosphere of the beautiful little Roman port of Tipasa, west of Algiers. There it was agreed that, together with Murphy, they would recommend a reply to de Gaulle from Giraud. Macmillan in turn agreed to advise his government that should de Gaulle refuse they would bring maximum pressure to the point of threatening to disown him. The letter was duly written and taken to London by Catroux. On the condition that de Gaulle accepted the principle of cabinet government and respected the terms of the French Constitution, Giraud proposed the formation of a six-man central committee, to be presided over alternately by himself and de Gaulle. The two generals would each appoint two members.[81]

De Gaulle was ready to accept, but it was now the turn of the Americans to put a spanner in the works. Murphy's lack of enthusiasm for the French union which the British were so assiduously promoting remained amply shared in Washington. Roosevelt had been angered by de Gaulle's continued attacks on Giraud, while Hull was much exercised over Gaullist propaganda and the British failure to support the American position. The Secretary of State had tried unsuccessfully to lobby Eden when the Foreign Secretary visited Washington in March.[82] In mid-May, however, Washington was entertaining a British guest who was rather more receptive to anti-Gaullist arguments.

Hull and Roosevelt worked hard on Churchill. The Secretary of State warned of serious friction in Anglo-American relations 'if this de Gaulle matter is allowed to go forward as it has been.'[83] Wherever any de Gaulle representative went, he kept everything in uproar. There was a 'universal belief' that Britain was behind de Gaulle with money, radio stations and 'other methods.'[84] Roosevelt subsequently presented the Prime Minister with a memorandum calling for the creation of a new French committee 'subject in its members to approval of you and me.'[85] A large amount of American documentary material, allegedly corroborating the General's misdeeds – described by Harvey as 'a miscellaneous collection of "dirt" which covers a number of minor cases of tiresomeness, none of them new, none of them of much importance' – was also provided, and forwarded on by Churchill to London. 'From anyone else,' Harvey recorded acidly, 'it would be the telegram of a cad.'[86] Establishment disapproval could scarcely be more explicit.

What most concerned the Foreign Office was the Prime Minister's proposal that the War Cabinet urgently consider whether it 'should not now eliminate de Gaulle as a political force.'[87] 'When we consider the absolutely vital interest which we have in preserving good relations with the US,' the Prime Minister argued, 'it seems to me most questionable that we should allow this marplot and mischief-maker to continue the harm that he is doing.'[88] But in a rare instance of the Cabinet not bowing to Churchill's will, a whole series of arguments were advanced against the Prime Minister's proposals for breaking with de Gaulle at the very moment he was about to meet Giraud.[89] Such action would look as though it had been undertaken under the pressure of the Americans, whose policy towards France, in the words of the War Cabinet minutes, 'had not met with success.'[90] De Gaulle's name was regarded as a symbol of the Republic, and the Gaullist movement 'stood for the Entente.'[91] To break with him would have 'an unfortunate effect on Allied governments resident in London and dependent upon us for financial support and other facilities. Might this not create the impression that such governments were within our power and could be broken at will?'[92] This was an argument which of course applied particularly to the French themselves.[93] As Attlee subsequently telegraphed to Washington, there was a risk of making a martyr out of de Gaulle and being accused of improper interference in French internal affairs and of treating the Fighting French movement like an Anglo-French protectorate.[94]

Faced with this formidable set of objections, Churchill was forced to drop the matter, at least for the time being, and the scene was therefore finally set for de Gaulle to depart for Algiers. Before he left the General wrote to George VI to thank him for British hospitality since June 1940. Unable to pay a farewell visit to Churchill, who, he was told, had just left for 'an unknown destination,' the General saw Eden. The man who had just been described as standing for the Entente emphasised the need for Britain and France to work together in the post-war world, where they would both find themselves uncomfortably situated between the Soviet Union and the USA. He, himself, intended to stay in North Africa, while leaving a strong delegation in London, which he would visit from time to time. There is a subtle difference between the British and de Gaulle's account of another part of the exchange. De Gaulle quotes Eden asking, 'What do you think of us?'[95] Harvey's version, which sounds more authentic, has Eden saying that he hoped that the General would not take away any too bitter memories, to which the General simply replied, 'Le peuple anglais a été merveilleux.' '(No compliments to HMG!)'[96] On 30 May, an RAF plane flew de Gaulle to Gibraltar. From there the General insisted on flying on to Algiers in a French machine.[97]

# 14

# 'C'est De Gaulle'

The creation in Algiers of the French Committee of National Liberation (FCNL) at the beginning of June 1943 marks a crucial milestone on the path of French recovery from defeat. Co-chaired by de Gaulle and Giraud, it was to direct the French war effort and to exercise sovereignty over all French territory not under enemy control. In fact, though not in name, it was a French provisional government. Although it was established on French soil, the British were still very much in attendance. Churchill had flown directly from Washington to Algiers, in part to oversee the forthcoming Allied invasion of Sicily, Operation Husky, but also of course to keep an eye on the French power struggle which was about to come to a head. As Charles Williams put it, the Prime Minister could not wait to be best man at this uniquely interesting wedding.[1] But Churchill, who was extremely tired, and who was not in the mood for more rows of the kind that had taken place at Anfa, had taken the precaution of sending for his more diplomatic foreign secretary to deal with the trouble he expected.[2]

The British had sought to bring new faces to the negotiating table. Eden had been keen to find a civilian of the stature of the former Prime Minister Edouard Herriot, who might be a useful keystone for any structure erected by the two generals. But it had proved impossible to make contact with him in France, and the SOE officer charged with the mission had therefore burnt Churchill's letter to Herriot.[3] Contact had successfully been made with Churchill's old friend General Georges. The original plan had been for Georges to act as Giraud's personal liaison officer to Churchill in London, but in the event he had been spirited out of France to Algiers by SIS. Writing to his wife from Algiers on 29 May, Churchill spoke of a lunch with Giraud and Georges, in whose company 'I recaptured some of my vanished illusions about France and her army.'[4] Nostalgia, however, was a bad guide to policy. Georges's reputation had been tainted by his involvement in the defeat of 1940. Lord Selborne noted that his name in France was mud.[5]

The initial formal meeting between the two French sides on 31 May went badly. Seven men were present: Georges and Monnet on Giraud's side of the table, Catroux and two members of the FNC on de Gaulle's. There was, however, no agenda or secretary. After an initial agreement that they should form themselves into a committee, de Gaulle put forward two familiar demands: that the military command should be subordinated to the political will as expressed by the committee, and that Noguès, Boisson and Peyretoun should be dismissed. This resulted in a heated discussion. De Gaulle was particularly angry at the presence of General Georges, an elderly general who had opposed the French army's modernisation before the war. Georges in turn was indignant at the attitude of the young upstart officer who had proved him wrong. In the end, de Gaulle walked out, slamming the door.[6]

Outside intervention seemed necessary. Macmillan explained to Monnet over dinner how he had muddled the whole affair, suggesting that he should call the next meeting and circulate an agenda. He even left him with the text of the proposed resolutions.[7] The following day he saw Giraud and pressed him to go ahead with the formation of the committee as soon as possible. Macmillan and Murphy also saw de Gaulle, who stressed France's need for 'new men for the new work that lay before her. She would not understand a government of old men associated with defeat. He had no intention of allowing himself to be imprisoned in an executive committee.' Macmillan's conclusion was that the negotiations would not be broken off and that de Gaulle would get his way as usual.[8]

This may have been premature since Peyretoun now sent in his resignation – to both Giraud and de Gaulle. De Gaulle accepted it without consulting an infuriated Giraud. Suddenly there were troop movements, and de Gaulle's old adversary, Admiral Muselier, who was in Algiers (in large part because the British had wanted to be rid of him) was appointed by Giraud to keep order against a possible putsch by de Gaulle.[9] Officers around Giraud meanwhile were considering arresting de Gaulle and his associates on the grounds that the unrest created by them and their supporters endangered Allied communications.[10]

Fortunately, Churchill was out of Algiers inspecting the battlefields in Tunisia, so it was left to Macmillan and Murphy to try and calm things down. They saw Giraud at lunchtime. In the afternoon, Macmillan met de Gaulle. The General, who found himself in a difficult position, told Macmillan that in spite of everything he would make another attempt to form the committee. The British Minister sensed this was the time to comfort the man who had taken so much on himself, and who recognised his mistakes. He thus put on a bravura performance, unlike anything any previous British politician or minister had tried with the General. He recalled his own service in France during the First World War and his opposition to Appeasement in the 1930s. He drew on his record as a radical MP, saying that he thought their views on social matters were very similar. Both countries had backward-looking old men. What was needed were new men with new minds.

> I told him that I had followed all that he had done with the greatest sympathy and admiration; that I realised his impatience on finding old men and old minds still in control; that I understood the difference between my country and his because we had not been subjected to great pressure; we had not suffered a great defeat and the sense of ignominy that followed that defeat. Nevertheless, I implored him to take courage; not to miss his opportunity to join honourably with Giraud in this national administration. I felt sure that as the weeks and months went by he could, without straining the law or acting in any way unconstitutionally, obtain for himself and those who were with him the reality of power.[11]

At the end of this harangue, the latter part of which would not have been approved by Churchill, de Gaulle promised to pay attention to what his visitor had said, but again expressed frustration at finding himself surrounded by 'such an antiquated point of view.' In somewhat headmasterly tone, Macmillan replied that disappointments were made to be borne and obstacles to be overcome and that he had every confidence the General would play his role in an honourable manner. The meeting ended on a very friendly note.[12] Macmillan's last conversation was with a thoroughly frustrated Catroux, who complained of finding himself 'between a madman and an ass.'[13] Macmillan and Murphy then held a press conference, designed to bring pressure on all sides.

By the following day, the crisis had abated, with the formation of the FCNL based on documents drawn up by de Gaulle. Once France had been liberated, it would hand over to a provisional government. Noguès and Boisson were summarily sacked.

Congratulations were now in order, and the British held a lunch party to celebrate, to which no Americans were invited. De Gaulle was not in the best of humour. He had not been best pleased to discover the Prime Minister lurking in the wings in Algiers. Only his personal respect for Churchill prevented him from declining the invitation, and Sir Alan Brooke, who sat next to the General at lunch, found him 'very sticky and stiff.'[14] In an exchange before the meal, Churchill had remarked that 'we should have had to take steps if too brutal a shock had occurred – if, for instance, you had devoured Giraud all at once,' while de Gaulle had remarked that he had had reason to fear some action against him over the past few days by the British Secret Service.[15]

When it came to the speeches, however, things seemed to have thawed out. Churchill, who felt a bit like the godfather of a re-emerging France, offered a toast to 'La Belle France, la France Victorieuse.' He spoke with tears in his eyes. De Gaulle paid tribute to the Prime Minister and the inspiration the British people had given the General. Eden spoke of the need for Britain and France to hold together after the war. Finally, photographs were taken.[16] As Makins privately wrote the next day, the whole affair had been 'nip and tuck.'[17] Had the negotiations failed, the British would have been faced with 'the disagreeable necessity of either supporting de Gaulle against American wishes or of throwing him over with all the lamentable consequences that would have had in France and in Europe.'[18]

Speaking to Parliament on 8 June, Churchill issued a scarcely coded warning to de Gaulle. The FCNL had

> only to work together in good faith and loyalty to each other, to set aside sectional or personal interests and keep all their hatreds for the enemy – they have only to do this to regain for France her inheritance, and in so doing to become themselves the inheritor of the gratitude of future generations of Frenchmen.[19]

Of much more practical importance, the Prime Minister went on to announce that the formation of the committee with collective responsibility superceded the situation created by the correspondence between himself and General de Gaulle in 1940. 'Our dealings, financial and otherwise, will henceforth be with the Committee as a whole.'[20] This, as far as Churchill was concerned, marked the end of the Fighting French movement. Three days later, what was intended as a last payment of £1.3 million was made to de Gaulle's account. A temporary ban was also imposed on the transmission of funds through the BCRA to resistance movements in France, so as to prevent de Gaulle using these for political ends rather than for the prosecution of the war effort.[21]

Churchill's private, and mistaken, assumption was that should he prove 'violent or unreasonable,' de Gaulle would be in a minority of five to two on the FCNL.[22] In fact, a decision had been taken on 5 June to expand the committee from seven to fourteen members, the choice of whom would make de Gaulle's position much more secure. Since it would take time for some of the new members to arrive from London, de Gaulle provoked a crisis at the next FCNL meeting. Giraud had nominated General Georges as Commissioner for Defence, a position de Gaulle, who saw control of the army as determining who would gain power in France at the time of liberation, wanted for himself. At the same time, de Gaulle also continued to insist on the need for Giraud to resign either as Commander-in-Chief of the French forces or as Co-President of the FCNL. When Giraud refused, de Gaulle declared he could no longer work with the committee in the form in which it was constituted and announced his resignation as co-president and member.[23]

This was a potentially dangerous manoeuvre. Giraud would have been perfectly entitled to accept de Gaulle's resignation. He had received an oral message of support from the American Under-Secretary of State, Sumner Welles, and was also pressed to do so by members of his own entourage. Once more there were troop movements. It was the British who again moved to calm things down.[24] Macmillan sought to dissuade Generals Georges and Giraud from taking this very welcome opportunity of accepting de Gaulle's resignation. When asked for his view, the British minister replied that he was afraid that his brain did not work as quickly as that of Frenchmen and that he would like to think about it. Nevertheless, he would venture to suggest that no action should be taken without careful consideration. De Gaulle's resignation at this point could lead to a complete break-up of the French Empire.[25] When he saw de Gaulle, the General complained about delays in the arrival from Britain of some of the new members of the FCNL. 'All the people who dislike me seem to get here,' he went on, 'Muselier, Georges and many others. Why do you bring them here?'[26] Macmillan again sought to preach patience to de Gaulle.

The Committee had only lasted a week. It would take a little time before the thing settled down, but that if he would work patiently and adopt a rather more friendly attitude towards his colleagues, I felt sure he would get his way on every point on which it was right that he should do so.[27]

If the French weren't enough of a problem, Macmillan's task was yet further complicated by Roosevelt. In a telegram to Eisenhower on 10 June, the President expressed concern at the possibility of de Gaulle gaining control over French forces in North and West Africa and suggested that it might be better to have de Gaulle resign now rather than later.[28] De Gaulle's domination of Dakar, the President telegraphed Churchill, was 'too serious for me to remain quiescent. Neither you nor I know where de Gaulle will end up.'[29] This brought Churchill readily back into the fray. Macmillan was instructed to do everything in his power to support the policy advocated by the President and also warned that were de Gaulle to gain control over the FCNL a situation of 'utmost difficulty' would immediately arise with the American government.[30] An official press circular was issued, parts of which appeared in the *Observer*, which was every bit as hostile as Churchill's 'secret speech' to the House of Commons six months earlier, warning that 'We can do our duty to the people of France in other ways.'[31] Oliver Harvey thoroughly disapproved. 'We must leave the French alone,' he noted in his diary, 'and let them fight out their quarrels now that they are united on French soil ... France is our nearest neighbour and we must continue to live with her and work with her whatever the Americans do.'[32]

Macmillan, however, was not a man to be intimidated by the Prime Minister's bullying, and it was now de Gaulle's turn to be taken bathing at Tipasa on 13 June. This time the occasion was slightly more formal. Macmillan again bathed naked, but de Gaulle sat in a dignified manner on a rock, with his military cap, uniform and belt. Afterwards, they dined at the local inn and, like the walrus and the carpenter, talked of many things – about politics, philosophy, religion, ancient and modern history, as well of course about the current political crisis.[33] De Gaulle, Macmillan recorded

recognised the responsibility of having made the union, which I kept pressing on him ... I formed the impression that he is still debating in his own mind what he would do. He said it would be more artistic to retire. He is obviously very disappointed that he cannot get complete control, and does not seem to be willing to go through the work of obtaining it gradually.

My policy was to try to discuss both possible lines quite objectively and quite calmly with him, of course hoping that he would play the game and accept any reasonable formula. But I did not try and overpersuade him because I thought it would probably have the opposite effect, and I wanted him to face the realities.[34]

Part of the urgency behind Macmillan's diplomacy is suggested by a letter from Makins to William Strang in the Foreign Office, warning that if de Gaulle walked out of the FCNL Giraud would turn into 'an amiable Quisling and I am quite sure that all the king's horses and all the king's men cannot put General Giraud and General Georges into France again.'[35] Makins was particularly critical of Georges, who made no secret of his special relationship with Churchill. Without him, Makins believed, there 'would have been very little trouble since Catroux would have been able to reach an acceptable arrangement.'[36] It was another private diplomatic rebuke of the Prime Minister's diplomacy.

Yet it remained the Americans as much as Georges, de Gaulle or even Churchill, who were stoking the current crisis. Murphy's reporting was persistently anti-Gaullist, and he now sent Washington a particularly inflammatory telegram. The immediate impetus had been a much delayed report by Murphy regarding the expansion of the FCNL. The American diplomat believed that Giraud had been done down and the Allies tricked.[37] This led the President to make another attempt to try to persuade the British to ditch de Gaulle, complaining to Churchill that he was 'fed up with de Gaulle and the secret personal and political machinations of that Committee in the last few days indicate that there is no possibility of our working with de Gaulle.' Or, as Cadogan noted in his diary,

> Roosevelt has lost his patience (and his head) about de Gaulle and is asking for the latter's head on a charger. P.M. of course disposed to agree with him. But of course it's most unwise. I don't know what case there was against St. John the Baptist, but public opinion was less formed – and less formidable in those days ... *We* shall be hard put to it to make a case against de G.[38]

It was left to Macmillan and Eisenhower, who did not share Murphy's hostility to de Gaulle, to resolve the situation. Asked by Eisenhower 'as a friend' what he thought he ought to do, Macmillan replied that they might interpret their instructions in their own way. Eisenhower then drafted a message for Washington, to which Macmillan was invited to offer amendments. In it the Commander-in-Chief advised the President that he considered the difficulties in Algiers had been exaggerated, an obvious criticism of Murphy, and that the question of the administration of French West Africa did not in fact arise. As to the French military command, he hoped to settle this by a personal meeting with de Gaulle and Giraud.[39]

By 22 June the immediate crisis had been resolved. Instead of a ministry of defence, a permanent military committee was established, with de Gaulle as Chairman and Giraud as a member. The FCNL would be responsible for the general direction of the French war effort and the overall command of the armed forces. The military command would be split, with Giraud in command of the North African and de Gaulle of all other forces in the French Empire. This was an unwieldy and at best a temporary solution, but it at least gained time in which the civilian members of the FCNL might become strong enough to stand up to the generals. Macmillan, Murphy and Eisenhower all recommended acceptance of the compromise to their governments. Any attempt to upset the agreement, Macmillan warned Churchill, 'will land us into very deep water indeed and may well compromise our future military plans' (for the invasion of Sicily).[40]

Outside observers saw the comic side. The *New York Times* referred to a 'French farce,' while the *New Statesman* published a nice piece of Shakespearian pastiche, which caused amusement in the Foreign Office.[41]

SCENE: A tent in Algiers. General de Gaulle discovered sulking. Enter General Giraud.
*Giraud:* General, I say that you have done me wrong.
*De Gaulle:* I only deal with written grievances.
*Giraud:* You do not answer letters; I will speak.
*De Gaulle:* If you speak softly we will give you audience.
*Giraud:* And who may 'we' be, General de Gaulle?
*De Gaulle:* We are the President. *'L'Etat c'est moi.'*
*Giraud:* We are co-Presidents. *L'Etat c'est nous.*[42]

With the FCNL now reasonably firmly established, diplomatic attention turned to the question of its recognition. This was supported by Macmillan and the Foreign Office but opposed by Churchill who wanted to see de Gaulle and 'his partisans' settling down to 'honest teamwork' with the FCNL first. 'I of course,' Churchill quipped in better mood, 'am exceedingly pro-French; unfortunately the French are exceedingly pro-voking.'[43] But there was a heated row at the Cabinet Defence Committee on 8 July, and a few days later prime minister and foreign secretary set out their respective positions in two papers for the Cabinet, which raised fundamental questions about the future orientation of British foreign policy.[44] Britain's main problem after the war, Eden argued, would be Germany, and the 1941 Anglo-Soviet treaty needed to be balanced with an understanding with a powerful France on Germany's western flank.

> In all our dealings, we should have due regard to French susceptibilities in matters of prestige and sovereignty. We should do everything to raise French morale and promote French self-confidence and bear patiently with manifestations of French sensitivities and excited and suspicious nationalism which are natural in the circumstances.[45]

Europe, he continued, in a clear jibe at the USA of which de Gaulle would have heartily approved, 'expects us to have a European policy of our own and to state it.'[46]

Churchill, on the other hand, put relations with the USA first and reserved his criticism for de Gaulle, which he expressed in highly intemperate terms. The General, the Prime Minister asserted, was

> animated by dictatorial instincts and consumed by personal ambition. All those who have worked with him know that he shows many of the symptoms of a budding Fuehrer. Although he has lately been quite ready to accept support from French Communists, or indeed from any quarter, it is a profound delusion to regard him as a liberal or democratic figure. He is inclined to set himself up as the supreme judge of the conduct of all Frenchmen at the time of and since the collapse of France. He seeks to appropriate for himself and his followers the title-deeds of France. There is no doubt in my mind that he would bring civil war into that country ... He would, I have no doubt, make anti-British alliances and combinations at any time when he thought it in his interests to do so, and he would do so with gusto.[47]

If over the next months it became clear that de Gaulle was now master of the FCNL, it might be possible to gain US recognition. To do so now would be to give offence to Washington and to draw onto the Administration the hostile criticism of those seeking to oust the President at the 1944 presidential election.[48]

This was Churchill at his worst. As Strang noted, the Prime Minister's policy towards France was governed too much by his personal relations with

Roosevelt and his personal antipathy to de Gaulle.[49] Moreover, in purely practical terms, the Prime Minister's position was untenable. The FCNL was a reality Britain had laboured hard to create. To refuse recognition was, in Macmillan's words, 'silly and ungracious.'[50] By undermining the concept of collective responsibility, non-recognition played into de Gaulle's hands and threatened lasting damage to Anglo-French relations.[51] By 21 July Churchill had been forced to relent. 'It seems to me,' he now wrote to Roosevelt,

> that something has got to be done about this. I am under considerable pressure from the Foreign Office, from my Cabinet Colleagues and also from force of circumstances to 'Recognise' the National Committee of Liberation in Algiers ... I am no more enamoured than you are of [de Gaulle] than you, but I would rather have him on the Committee than strutting about as a combination of Joan of Arc and Clemenceau.[52]

Roosevelt was unmoved. Although no final decisions had been made, planning for the D-Day landings in France was already under way. Their prospects were improved by the heavy casualties which the Germans were incurring on the Eastern Front. In July, the German army had suffered a shattering defeat in the battle of Kursk, which had involved some 4 million men on both sides and cost half a million lives. Against this background the President was determined not to give de Gaulle a white horse on which he could ride into France and make himself master of the government.[53] Despite parliamentary pressure and Foreign Office concern that Britain might be pre-empted by Soviet recognition, the matter had to be left until August, when Churchill and Roosevelt met in Quebec. Here the British found Hull thoroughly obstinate, and there were sharp exchanges with Eden.[54] In the end, there was an agreement to disagree, Britain and the USA issuing separate statements, the former notably more friendly than the latter. Hull nevertheless left 'distinctly sour,' though the very fact that there was an American formula and that it included the word 'recognition' could be considered a success for British diplomacy.[55] The French, Makins reported,

> really played up very well: they unanimously decided not to look a pair of gift horses in the mouth and, whatever was said in private (a member of the Committee is alleged to have remarked that the American formula was the sort of thing one says to a whipped dog), in public their attitude was cordial.[56]

De Gaulle had good reason to feel satisfied. Events were moving in his direction. He was back on French soil, amid familiar sounds, smells and foods. He had an agreeable house, to which his family had now moved, with enough of the East in its colours and forms to make the point that London had been left behind.[57] A French government was emerging, in which his position was unchallengeable. When some weeks later a Canadian diplomat raised the issue of collective responsibility with the General, the reply was that most members of the Committee had nothing behind them except personal prestige. In the final analysis, the responsibility – and here the General pointed at himself with an impressive gesture – 'c'est de Gaulle.'[58]

That did not of course mean that all was yet well. Algiers might be preferable to London, but it was not Paris. Macmillan's diary records a lunch party given by the French industrialist Charles Schneider and his wife.

Amusing conversation, a good display of jewellery, hairdressing and clothes, with a remarkable even touching outward vivacity covering deep wounds. Most of them have husbands or children whose present fate is unknown to them.

How they all *hate* North Africa and Algiers and *long* for France and Paris.[59]

Algiers also had more practical geographical disadvantages compared to London. De Gaulle no longer had access to the BBC, which meant that the personal contact radio had allowed him to make with the French people had slackened. Although Passy had remained in London, where his staff were in daily contact with the RAF and SOE, clandestine contact with France was also proving more difficult. As the General later put it,

It was from the London base that these had been organized. It was from there that our instructions and our missions had been sent. It was there that reports, agents, visitors and refugees arrived. In the use of planes, motorboats, telegrams, radio messages and couriers, a kind of gymnastics set to a rhythm from the English capital had become habitual to the valiant army of informants, transporters and purveyors. It was unthinkable to tear this web apart.[60]

It was impossible to recreate this system in North Africa because of the absence of technical facilities, as well as the much greater distances involved, which was a particular problem where air communication was concerned. The result was a series of retransmissions, delays and misunderstandings.[61]

There was another disadvantage of which the French may have been unaware. The British monitored a good deal of French diplomatic cable traffic between London and Algiers, although they did not necessarily learn a great deal in the process. Asked by Churchill in April 1944 about the reports being sent back to Algiers by Pierre Viénot, the FCNL's representative in London, Cadogan replied that they 'consist largely of records of his conversations, and, so far as we can judge, he reports these very accurately. We have not noticed him making any mischief or committing any indiscretions.'[62]

De Gaulle was, however, aware of being cut off from the diplomatic discussion taking place in London and Washington regarding the post-war future of the small and middle-sized states of Europe.[63] This in turn bore on the intractable problems of how, with the war now moving decisively against the Axis, France could gain a voice in the approaching peace settlements and re-establish its lost Great Power status. Washington and Moscow, which de Gaulle had repeatedly sought to court as a counter to the Anglo-Saxon powers, were unreceptive to the aspirations of a country which had done so little of the fighting in the war. Britain, de Gaulle acknowledged, did not proceed in so summary a fashion. The British, the General wrote, hoped that France would 'reappear in her avatar as yesterday's partner, tractable and familiar. But what was the good of hurrying matters?'[64] This was a typically Gaullist judgement, which says as much about the French sense of inferiority vis-à-vis their allies as about British policy. But on one point the General was right. London seemed in no hurry to bring about this resurrection. While publicly Churchill spoke of France taking its place as an equal partner of the three Great Powers, in private he noted that France could not 'masquerade as a Great Power for the purposes of the war.'[65] Eden too spoke of the need to restore France by stages.[66]

France's difficulties became evident with the Italian armistice of 8 September. The Allied invasion of Sicily had brought about the resignation of Mussolini. He was succeeded by Marshal Pietro Badoglio, who immediately began negotiations with the Allies. De Gaulle had been given to understand that he would be invited to send a representative. In the event, the French were only informed after the document had been signed.[67] A draft letter from Churchill to Stalin of 4 September stated that it would be unwise to allow French participation in discussions over the military occupation of Italy in view of the Italians' strong dislike of the French.[68] Makins privately likened the angry French reaction to that of a debutante who had not been invited to the ball of the season. But in a despatch to the Foreign Office he showed considerable empathy for French feelings. 'It is possible to imagine the bitterness of wounded pride [in the FCNL] which characterised the debate and the haunting fear that Italy was a prelude to France.'[69] The FCNL, Makins continued, smarted under a double sense of inferiority of being neither a government nor a Great Power. Anything which could be done to encourage the French to forget their wounded pride would assist post-war relations with France.[70]

This advice was not immediately taken. When a European Advisory Commission was established at the end of October by the American, British and Soviet Foreign Ministers meeting in Moscow, the French were again left out. This elicited some sharp protests. General de Lattre de Tassigny spoke of its deplorable effect on the Resistance groups who would regard it as 'a sort of public degradation.'[71] Surprisingly, in discussions with Macmillan on 5 November, the General made no mention of the matter. The talk was rather about social and economic change. De Gaulle had been reading the Beveridge Report and was impressed that such a document had been issued in wartime.[72] Eleven days later the French received a consolation prize: admission to the Advisory Commission on Italian affairs. But the French, as de Gaulle pointedly notes in his memoirs, were excluded from the Tehran summit between Churchill, Roosevelt and Stalin at the end of November, where the decision for the D-Day landings in France was taken.[73]

By then Anglo-French relations had weathered another Middle Eastern crisis. Under British pressure, the French had finally held elections in Lebanon and Syria, in which the British and French had both become deeply involved, backing rival candidates. The result was a defeat for the French, with the election of a government that began formulating a Bill for complete independence, thereby effectively unilaterally abrogating the French mandate. Whether or not Spears had directly encouraged this move is unclear, but he had certainly created the atmosphere in which the Lebanese ministers felt emboldened to throw down the gauntlet.[74] On 11 November, Jean Helleu, the French Delegate-General, responded to the passage of the requisite constitutional amendments through the Lebanese parliament by dissolving the assembly and arresting the ministers. Riots followed in Beirut, Tripoli and Saida, which were ruthlessly suppressed with some loss of life. The reaction elsewhere in the Middle East was strong.

Managing the ensuing crisis was peculiarly complex. Although the immediate focus was Beirut, the British Minister Resident in Cairo, Richard Casey, was also involved. Decisions were made by the War Cabinet in

London and the FCNL in Algiers. Churchill, meanwhile, was travelling to Teheran, but was kept informed. With the whole Arab world in furore, there was no dispute on the British side that Helleu's actions must be reversed. But there was a clear division between the hard-liners and those anxious to resolve the crisis with the least possible loss of French face. The former were of course led by Spears, who flew a team of journalists from Cairo to Beirut, through whom he sought to maintain a monopoly influence over public opinion in both Britain and the USA, while at the same time himself sending out a shower of frenzied telegrams to the Foreign Office.[75]

Churchill's response was coloured by the fact that shortly beforehand Giraud and General Georges had just been forced out the FCNL, giving de Gaulle the sole presidency he had long been seeking (although Giraud remained Commander-in-Chief of French forces). A telegram to Roosevelt dated 10 November expressed Churchill's discontent at these developments. Three days later, the Prime Minister was complaining to Roosevelt about 'the lamentable outrages committed by the French in Syria' which were 'a foretaste of what de Gaulle's leadership of France means.'[76] The Levant issues afforded 'full justification ... of bringing the issue with de Gaulle to a head.'[77]

When Macmillan met the Prime Minister aboard a warship in the Mediterranean on 15 November, he found Churchill incensed over Giraud's departure; the Prime Minister regarded the co-presidency as the basis on which Anglo-American recognition of the FCNL had been granted. But, Macmillan recorded in his diary, 'he knew in his heart that this was only a temporary expedient. I tried to explain my view of the new forces which were rising up, not in de Gaulle's hands and to some extent challenging his authority. This interested the P.M. enormously.'[78]

Lebanon, in Macmillan's eyes, was a test case. If the British played their hands tactfully, avoiding another Fashoda, which, he believed, Spears wanted, it would be possible to gain the support of Catroux, Massigli and half to two-thirds of the FCNL, putting de Gaulle in a minority.[79] This was shrewd. The FCNL was uneasily aware that Helleu had gone too far. Catroux was despatched to Beirut to re-establish a 'normal constitutional' situation there, which included the release of the Lebanese ministers. Although Helleu was not to be disavowed, once Catroux was in Beirut it would be possible to recall the Delegate-General 'for consultations.'[80]

The crisis still had some way to run, since the War Cabinet decided that they would also have to demand the reinstatement of the dismissed ministers as 'the absolute minimum required' to preserve Britain's good name in the

Middle East.[81] But Macmillan and Massigli conspired successfully to resolve the matter without undue humiliation for the French. By 24 November, Macmillan was able to explain to Churchill how de Gaulle's intransigence had been defused by the FCNL and why this method was more effective than direct British and American pressure, which simply played into de Gaulle's hands, allowing him to appeal to French pride.[82] Eden was anxious that the French should not be further humiliated, but once the dust settled the French were left hanging grimly on in an ugly state of mind. And, as Makins noted, another permanent grievance had been imprinted 'upon that sensitive film, the mind of de Gaulle.'[83]

Shortly before Christmas a new crisis erupted when a number of figures associated with Vichy were purged. This was arguably an internal French affair which had nothing to do with the Allies. Churchill did not see it that way. Among those arrested were Boisson and Peyretoun, to whom Churchill had given assurances earlier in the year, as well as Pierre Flandin, a pre-war friend. The Prime Minister, who was recuperating in Tunis from pneumonia, was incensed. Macmillan found himself subjected to a succession of violent telephone calls from Churchill who roared down the line like an excited bull. The Prime Minister again made his views known to Roosevelt in no uncertain terms. The President happily swung into action, instructing Eisenhower to release the three men and to discontinue their trial.[84]

The reaction in Algiers was one of dismay. Such direct interference in French affairs, Macmillan warned Eden, would create an extremely serious situation. The FCNL would refuse to release the prisoners, and the British and Americans would then have to use force. Eden too was alarmed. The Foreign Secretary feared that Eisenhower's action might force the resignation of the FCNL, which would have to be replaced by an administration led by Generals Giraud and Georges, with disastrous consequences on French morale, and which would make the prospects for further cooperation with the Resistance impossible. Behind these fears lurked the ultimate danger of civil war in France.[85] In the event, it was Roosevelt who backed down, while de Gaulle gave assurances that no trial would take place until after the liberation of France; meanwhile, the prisoners would be kept in their villas.[86]

Shortly afterwards, on 6 January 1944, Macmillan left Algiers. Although his tenure had been brief, his impact on Anglo-French relations was disproportionately great. With the possible exception of Eden, Macmillan can lay claim to having been more intimately and constructively involved in domestic French politics than any other modern British politician – to the point, indeed, where in his own judgement his involvement limited his future effectiveness. The Minister had been through 'too many "shy-making" experiences with these Frenchmen in their unregenerate "Balkan" days, to be of much more use to them.'[87] A tireless promoter of French union, he had done much to neutralise American hostility towards the project and to prevent France from remaining a cause of Anglo-American discord.[88] He had defused a succession of crises at a time when personal animosities had become dangerously enflamed, often acting as a kind of shock absorber 'à tous azimuts.' Or, as he noted in the privacy of his diary, 'what a lot of faces I spend my time saving – and not French faces only, by any means.' If Churchill showed some unsurprising irritation, most of his French contacts had been appreciative.[89]

Macmillan's responsibilities with the FCNL were taken over by another minister, Duff Cooper. The appointment had originally been offered to Oliver Harvey, but he had turned it down believing that in the light of the Prime Minister's involvement in French affairs and the level of Anglo-American tensions the job would be better done by a politician. Duff Cooper's ability to stand up to the Prime Minister was seen as an additional advantage.[90] Churchill wrote him two letters about de Gaulle, reflecting the Prime Minister's deeply ambivalent attitude to the General. The first expressed his by now well-rehearsed hostility. In the second the Prime Minister stated that he did 'not wish to overlook the good qualities of de Gaulle, and I certainly do not underrate the smouldering and explosive forces in his nature or that he is a figure of magnitude.'[91] Cooper was advised to 'win his confidence and cultivate friendly relations with him.'[92] In this Cooper had the advantage of being very much *persona grata* with the General, not least for the fact that he was very much a Francophile.[93] Like Eden and Macmillan, he was to prove what his wife, Lady Diana Cooper, dubbed one of the 'oil men,' pouring oil on troubled Anglo-French waters. But he had one advantage over his predecessor in that he was being appointed as an ambassador and could thus treat the FCNL as a French government in fact, if not in law.[94]

Cooper's immediate task was to sort out the last French problem to face Macmillan in Algiers: arranging a meeting between Churchill and de Gaulle. Macmillan had been anxious for the Prime Minister to see de Gaulle, whom he had not met for six months, and have a proper talk with him to try to reach some basis of understanding and agreement.[95] The war was moving towards its conclusion. Over Christmas, Soviet forces launched an offensive in the Ukraine. On 6 January, Soviet forces entered Poland. There was a crying need to try to break out of the vicious circle in which the relations between the two men had been trapped, preventing essentially minor issues being blown up out of all proportion.

De Gaulle, however, showed little enthusiasm for a meeting. The Prime Minister had arrived in North Africa on a British warship. He had made no sign to any official representative of the FCNL but had sent for General Georges. Now he was inviting de Gaulle to visit him in Marrakech as if he were in his own country.[96] Churchill's response was to claim he wanted to cancel the invitation. Macmillan had not been fooled.

> He only wanted to preserve his dignity and give vent to his feelings on the telephone (to which, of course, the French listen intently all day). He showed his disappointment when I agreed to cancel the invitation, and at the end of each of his calls (three today before dinner) ended up saying he would leave it to me.[97]

The next scene in this little comedy centred on an invitation by Churchill to General de Lattre de Tassigny. This was vetoed by de Gaulle. The news was greeted with the predictable prime-ministerial explosion, and Duff Cooper, who had by now taken over, had to work hard to smooth things out. Finally the two 'sacred monsters' met on 12 January.[98] Churchill spent much of the time remonstrating in bad French with the General – over the departure of Giraud, the recent arrests, the Levant and the failure to consult his allies. De Gaulle's attitude, as reported back to London by Duff Cooper, was that of one more sinned against than sinning. He had shot nobody, though many of his supporters had been shot; he had spoken ill of nobody, though many had spoken ill of him; and as to keeping his allies informed, well what about Torch?[99] On the subject of the Americans, the Prime Minister 'applied himself in the warmest and most picturesque terms' by describing the advantages his visitor would gain by coming round to Roosevelt's point of view.[100] 'Look here,' he at one point remarked,

> 'I am the leader of a strong, unbeaten nation. Yet every morning when I wake my first thought is, how can I please President Roosevelt, and my second is how I can conciliate Marshal Stalin. Your situation is very different. Why then should your first waking thought be how you can snap your fingers at the British and the Americans?'[101]

But the Prime Minister had answered his own question.

Churchill was once again impressed, repeating the remark he had first made at Anfa: 'There's no doubt about it! *C'est un grand animal*.'[102] De Gaulle described Churchill, who was after all still recovering from a serious illness, as 'going down hill.'[103] Emmanuel d'Astier de La Vigerie, to whom this remark was made, refrained from comment. 'I was dealing with the Gallic cock standing on tiptoe in front of Albion's bull, and in the end the two emblems hid the two countries.'[104] De Gaulle is also reported to have said after the meeting that he had come in the hope of effecting a reconciliation, and he believed he had succeeded.[105] Good will had certainly seemed in evidence when the next day de Gaulle and Churchill reviewed French troops. The message de Gaulle wanted to convey by this event, not just to the local crowds but to those who would see it on newsreel, was that the appearance of himself and Churchill side by side signified that the Allied armies would soon march together to victory.[106]

# 15

# Going Back

The prospect of an Allied invasion of France had been in the French public domain since spring 1942. A few months after the Americans had entered the war, the BBC had begun broadcasting a series of warnings that coastal areas were likely to become war zones and talking about the prospect of a 'Second Front.' It was raised again the following year through broadcasts and leafleting as part of a deception operation to draw attention away from the intended invasion of Sicily. But the advantages of diverting German attention were offset by the damage to French morale when the invasion, which Churchill had promised before the leaves fell, failed to materialise. At least one French broadcaster on the BBC in 1943 had called for patience, adding, 'I know very well that you do not much like it that one talks to you of patience.'[1]

Patience, however, was to be sorely needed. For a man who normally placed an exaggerated faith in boldness, Churchill showed an uncharacteristic caution when it came to the final and most difficult act in the drama which had opened with the German crossing of the Meuse back in May 1940 – namely, the liberation of France. He had good reason. Britain had already sent two expeditionary forces to France in less than thirty years. In 1914 and 1939, these had disembarked in orderly fashion at friendly ports. The next force would have to fight its way in across the beaches. The Channel, as the British knew to their advantage, and Hitler had understood in 1940, was a formidable barrier. Invasion in either direction faced the hazards of difficult tides and unpredictable weather. A sudden storm, such as the one that blew up on 19 June 1944, could wreck the operation. Beyond the sea lay an enemy who had built up powerful coastal defences and who had good communications and a large army in waiting. German troops were battle-hardened from the fighting on the Russian front. Tactical advantage would lie with the defender. Amphibious landings were notoriously the most difficult of all operations in war, and the Prime Minister talked of being haunted by the image of the Channel 'full of the corpses of defeated allies.'[2]

Behind this emotional language lurked the shadow of the casualties of Passchendaele and the Somme, as well as the Prime Minister's uncomfortable awareness of the British army's indifferent performance in the earlier part of the current war. Were the invasion to fail, Britain would not get a second chance. The country, which in 1944 was fighting concurrent campaigns in Italy and the Far East, simply would not have the *matériel* or manpower. Its army was shrinking; even before the liberation of Paris the first British division had to be broken up to provide replacements for others. And troops who had been fighting since the beginning of the war were quite simply tired. Nor, it should be noted, were concerns confined to the British. Most of the senior commanders of the D-Day landings, American as well as British, harboured doubts about the operation. On 12 May 1944, Bedell Smith, Eisenhower's Chief of Staff, put the chances of holding the beachheads at 'fifty-fifty.'[3]

Churchill therefore had pressed hard for a continuation of the Mediterranean strategy as a preliminary means of wearing down the Germans, prior to a cross-Channel assault that would deliver a final blow to a debilitated German army.[4] This was strongly opposed by both Stalin, who remained desperately anxious for a second front to take the pressure off his forces, and the Americans, who did not believe in peripheral strategies. A compromise had been reached in Washington in May 1943, whereby the Americans agreed to Allied landings in Sicily and the British grudgingly bowed to American determination to land in northern France around 1 May 1944.[5] General Marshall grumbled that British strategy was opportunistic and that the Mediterranean squandered scarce British resources on secondary, by which he meant British imperial, objectives. But the Americans had in fact little option, given the delays in defeating the Germans in Tunisia and the continued operations of German U-boats in the Atlantic. Moreover, as mistakes made during the landings at Salerno south of Naples in summer 1943 showed, the Allies were not yet ready for an amphibious operation on the scale of D-Day.[6]

There were further arguments at the next Anglo-American summit at Quebec in August 1943, where the British introduced two conditions: that Luftwaffe capabilities must be substantially diminished and that the number of German divisions in reserve to oppose the attacking forces should be reduced to fewer than a dozen. This task was implicitly allocated to the Red Army. Four out of every five Germans killed in the Second World

War died on the Eastern Front.[7] No sooner, however, was the ink dry on this agreement than the British began to chip away at it. It was only at the Tehran summit in November, under combined pressure from Roosevelt and Stalin, that the commitment to a cross-Channel landing became irreversible. According to Eisenhower's aide, Captain Butcher, once the British signed up to an agreement they were 100 per cent behind it. But Churchill continued to complain that this was a battle 'forced upon us by the Russians and the United States military authorities,' and the Prime Minister only came round to full support of the operation in early May 1944.[8]

That the command of the operation, which Churchill had originally offered to Sir Alan Brooke, should have gone to an American, said something about American suspicions that the British remained lukewarm towards the project and rather more about the way in which the balance of power in the war was shifting towards the USA. In 1943, American armaments production was worth some $37.5 billion (at 1944 prices), compared with $11.1 billion for Britain, while the USA was producing nearly three times the number of aircraft produced by Britain and the Commonwealth.[9] Hervé Alphand, arriving in London from New York in February 1944, noted how each time he found 'a more marked deterioration, a weary people, badly dressed, pale figures, a great tiredness,' which, he believed, found echoes in British diplomacy.[10]

Overlord, the code name which was given to the operation, underscores just how important the cross-Channel landings were. The directive to Eisenhower from the Combined Chiefs of Staff instructed him to 'enter the continent of Europe and, in conjunction with the other United Nations, undertake operations aimed at the heart of Germany and the destruction of her armed forces.'[11] Thus, while in 1940 France had represented Britain's forward line of defence, it now constituted the main gateway to the Continent and Germany, making it the focus of the detailed planning which was now carried out in London. When, in the run-up to the operation, the land commander General Bernard Montgomery gave a presentation of the operation, one of those present recalled him tracing the plan on a huge relief model of Normandy, tramping about 'like a giant though Lilliputian France.'[12]

The political aspects of proposed operations caused both heart-searching and controversy. A crucial part of Allied preparations focused on disrupting Germany's capacity to move reinforcements against the Allied beachhead. To this end, plans were drawn up for the extensive bombing of rail communications, focusing primarily on marshalling and repair yards in northern France and Belgium. They met heated opposition not just from the commanders of the British and American strategic bomber forces, who were strongly opposed to any diversion from their attacks on Germany, but also within the Cabinet. According to official estimates, the railway attacks might cause some 80,000–160,000 French and Belgian casualties, of which one quarter might be fatal. These, in the words of the official historians of the strategic bombing campaign, were regarded by the military as 'another of the regrettable necessities of war.'[13] It was not a view shared by Churchill or Eden. The Foreign Secretary was more than ever concerned about the political impact of bombing in France and the previous year had repeatedly expressed disquiet about the casualties caused by American high-altitude daylight attacks.[14]

The question was repeatedly and anxiously debated in the War Cabinet and its Defence Committee during April, while the offensive was in fact already under way. Always uneasy about the bombing of France, ministers regarded this massive bombardment of friendly countries with foreboding.[15] Over and above the obvious moral and humanitarian issues, there was great concern over the political repercussions, which was underscored by the fact that the bulk of the attacks were to be carried out by the RAF. In Churchill's words, addressed to Air Marshal Tedder, 'you are piling up an awful load of hatred.'[16] Eden pointed out the more specific risk of alienating French railwaymen, thereby hazarding the substantial help they currently provided by way of sabotage. With memories of Dakar and Mers-el-Kébir still alive, there was a natural reluctance to risk the goodwill believed to have been rebuilt over the past three years.[17]

The War Cabinet's concerns went beyond France. Opinion in friendly neutral countries, as indeed at home, might be adversely affected. The Minister of Information, Brendan Bracken, noted that Swiss radio and press, which had previously been friendly, now expressed horror at the impact of bombing on the civilian population. And Eden raised a longer-term concern. Post-war Eastern Europe and the Balkans would be largely dominated by the Russians, while the people of Western Europe would look to Britain. If present policy continued, 'we might find they regarded us with hatred.'[18]

During April and early May Churchill wrote a series of letters to Eisenhower. But while willing to make limited concessions, the General insisted that military necessity must take precedence over political concerns.[19] The Prime Minister then appealed to Roosevelt, pointing out that 'this slaughter is among a friendly people who have committed no crimes against us, and not among the German foe with all their record of cruelty and ruthlessness.'[20] But when Roosevelt turned him down, the Prime Minister dropped the matter.[21]

The BBC broadcast warnings, as well as taking considerable pains to explain the intensification of the campaign and assuring listeners that the attacks would only occur where other methods were ineffective or impractical. While special marking techniques were used to try to ensure the accuracy of the bombing, the marshalling yards at La Chapelle, Cambrai, Saint-Etienne and Rouen nevertheless all suffered heavy damage.[22] There was anger and disquiet within the FCNL. Harold Nicolson, who visited Algiers in late April, recorded that the Resistance leaders he spoke to objected bitterly to the bombardment of France, a view not, however, echoed by either de Gaulle or the commander of the French Forces of the Interior (FFI), General Joseph-Pierre Koenig, who remarked that in war 'it must be expected that people will be killed.'[23] French bishops made a public appeal to 'the Cardinals, Archbishops and Bishops of the British Empire and the USA.'[24] This was broadcast by Vichy radio, which was seeking to make the most of the raids to try and embitter French opinion.[25]

In the event, French casualties 'only' numbered some 10,000. But the military results of the campaign were mixed, since, while military traffic declined sharply, German mobile repair teams managed to maintain rail operations for military transport. Much more success was achieved by American P47 fighter bombers, which were able to destroy bridges with pinpoint accuracy.[26] By June, the issue had largely disappeared from the political agenda. Civilian casualties were presumed to be more acceptable once British and American troops were fighting in France, while reports from British agents on the ground indicated an absence of the hatred Churchill had feared. According to one former SOE officer who had worked in southern France, far more people were killed by Allied bombing than by the Germans. 'I tried to explain and alleviate the suffering by suggesting there were military reasons. But there weren't. They always bombed the wrong places.'[27]

A second, much longer-running and politically more explosive controversy concerned the civilian administration to be put into place in the wake of the Allied advance. This was not a problem with countries such as Holland or Norway, which had officially recognised governments who would automatically take on the role.[28] Nor would it necessarily have been a problem in the case of France, had not Roosevelt, abetted by Churchill, remained determined to try to impede de Gaulle from assuming power over a provisional French government. The result was a nine-month-long battle, not so much between Britain and the FCNL or indeed Britain and the Americans, but between Churchill and the Foreign Office. It would come to a head in highly undignified fashion on the eve of D-Day.

Anxious to avoid the Italian precedent of AMGOT (Allied Military Government of Occupied Territories), as early as 9 September 1943 the FCNL had sent the British and Americans a memorandum outlining the terms on which they would cooperate with the Allies in the forthcoming battle for France. It envisaged that outside the zones of active military operations administration would be left to French officials under a delegate of the FCNL.[29] This was strongly at variance with American proposals, which assumed the continuation of something like AMGOT until the French people had decided their future form of government by plebiscite. AMGOT was roundly condemned by Macmillan, who warned Eden 'very strongly, that if you try any of this nonsense in France, there will a bitter revolt against you.'[30] Macmillan, however, was preaching to the converted. In December, Pierre Viénot, the FCNL's representative in London, reporting to Algiers on a discussion at the Foreign Office on the civil-affairs question, concluded that 'they cannot do without us and they know it. We are on solid ground.'[31] Indeed, by the end of the year even the State Department had largely come round to the British view that a civil-affairs agreement should be negotiated with the FCNL.[32]

The State Department, however, had not converted Roosevelt to the idea. The President wanted military government because of his deep-seated antipathy to de Gaulle, a continued belief that the FCNL was not representative of the French people and his consequent fear of civil war in France which would threaten Allied communications.[33] Churchill was in full sympathy with these views. There was no guarantee, the Prime Minister wrote on 26 January, that de Gaulle would not

> hoist the Cross of Lorraine over every town hall, and that he and his vindictive crowd will not try to peg out their claims to be the sole judge for the time being of the conduct of all Frenchmen and the sole monopolists of official power. This is what the President dreads, and so do I.[34]

In two or three months, Churchill continued, a 'different atmosphere' might prevail in the FCNL.[35] Meanwhile, it would be 'most foolish for us to give ourselves over to them and thus throw away one of the few means of guiding them and making them "work their passage."'[36] Repeated objections by Eden, who was to write some forty-one minutes on the question of de

Gaulle between 1 March and 13 June, failed to shift the Prime Minister's position. Duff Cooper complained in his diary that 'it seemed intolerable that one obstinate old man,' by which he meant Roosevelt, 'should hold up everything in this way.'[37] Harvey's diary described Churchill as 'really as demented' as Roosevelt about France.[38]

In mid-March, Roosevelt finally issued a draft directive to Eisenhower giving him ultimate determination over how, when and where civil administration should be exercised by French citizens. He could consult the FCNL and authorise them to select and install the necessary personnel but was not limited to dealing exclusively with them. On the other hand, there could be no talks or relations with Vichy, 'except for the purpose of terminating its administration in toto.'[39] This latter exclusion may have come as something of a relief in London, where there had been some suspicion that key figures in Washington, notably Admiral Leahy, remained sympathetic to the Marshal.[40] But Duff Cooper thought that the Directive seemed intended as a deliberate insult to the FCNL, while Eden expressed concern over its lukewarm endorsement of the FCNL and the danger that this might reduce cooperation from Resistance groups. 'Surely we cannot make over the decision on our relations with France to an American general,' an impatient Foreign Secretary minuted to Churchill two weeks later on 6 April.[41]

Eden and Duff Cooper were not the only ones to complain. The Canadian Prime Minister, Mackenzie King, wanted the Directive modified to give greater prominence to the FCNL. There were growing calls in the British press for increased Allied cooperation with the FCNL; Eisenhower and the State Department were also pressing for a decision.[42]

Meanwhile, with less than two months to go before D-Day, planning was held up. Some progress appeared to be made when, on 19 April, General Bedell Smith invited General Koenig for informal talks and told him that Supreme Headquarters Allied Expeditionary Forces (SHAEF) wanted to open immediate discussions with the French military mission in London about collaboration – a term which now of course has a completely different meaning in French affairs – with the French civil and military authorities.[43] At this point, a new complication arose in the form of a ban on all outgoing telegrams from London, part of the stringent security measures surrounding Overlord. Allied embassies were only allowed to communicate with their governments on condition that they deposited copies of their codes with the British government and submitted all messages to them for review. This caused particular problems for the French, since it effectively cut London off from the FCNL in Algiers. In the words of Jacques Soustelle, the English 'completely closed their island.'[44]

Senior SOE officers took great trouble to try and explain that no insult was intended, but to little avail. Colonel Dewavrin had taken the matter calmly – so calmly indeed that one suspicious British official wondered whether the French had their own secret links to Algiers.[45] De Gaulle, who may not entirely have appreciated the risks of a major amphibious operation, took a very different view. In the General's eyes, the ban showed that France was being treated the same way as any other second-rate or neutral power. Worse still, the ban served notice on him of the Allies' decision, not previously expressed, to limit the role of the French in the liberation of their own country. Harold Nicolson, on his visit to Algiers, found the General bitter, and when told that he had a right to be furious but not to be 'blessé,' the response was a grunt. Viénot and Koenig were forbidden to settle any questions so long as the restrictions remained in place. Nevertheless, by late May, SIS and SOE were passing on messages, mostly of a routine nature, for the French to Algiers.[46]

At the beginning of May, Roosevelt had issued a modification to his March Directive, but this was still regarded as wholly unacceptable in the Foreign Office. Eden feared that, exasperated by the Anglo-Saxons, de Gaulle would turn to the Soviet Union. Harvey wrote about being 'in despair' about France.[47] On 18 May, Cadogan recorded another meeting: 'P.M. says, as usual, "Don't ask me to quarrel with Pres. over de G." No one asks him to but we do wish he would *reason* with Pres. He won't.'[48]

In fact, Churchill had finally written to Roosevelt six days earlier stressing the need to reach an understanding with the FCNL. He also proposed to invite de Gaulle to come to London for secret discussions, suggesting that the Americans should be represented either by Eisenhower or by a special representative from Washington. The timing of the invitation was a matter of some debate. The Chiefs of Staff were strongly against inviting de Gaulle before D-Day or giving the French any operational information. According to a Foreign Office minute to Cadogan, this reflected continuing military antipathy to the General: 'they all three dislike him intensely.'[49] But the arguments advanced concerned security. There was uncertainty as to the extent to which French underground operations had been penetrated by the Germans. There was also concern that his departure from Algiers, coupled with certain naval movements, would be read by the Germans as evidence that the invasion was imminent. Eden argued that the General would be greatly offended if not told in advance of D-Day and that the Allies would then lose the effective and valuable help of his voice on the BBC.[50]

In the event, an invitation was issued on 27 May, but without a date. Duff Cooper argued that this should be given, pointing out that while irritability was one of de Gaulle's weaknesses, indiscretion was not. When the matter was discussed in Cabinet on 30 May, Eden said that the issue was now Britain's future relations with France rather than the position of de Gaulle. Attlee warned that Roosevelt's attitude risked putting de Gaulle on a pinnacle and giving him the satisfaction of a grievance and the support of elements who might not otherwise be sympathetic towards him.[51] But when Churchill then sent a message asking de Gaulle to come 'at the earliest moment and in deepest secrecy,' the General bridled since it was clear that the Americans would not take part in discussions on civil administration.[52] Duff Cooper was forced to talk to him very frankly – to the point of rudeness. De Gaulle finally agreed, but on condition that he only came as a soldier to talk to Frenchmen taking part in the battle as well as to broadcast to the French people. He was flown in Churchill's personal plane to London, where he was met by a guard of honour and a large RAF band which gave an excellent rendering of 'La Marseillaise.' De Gaulle was pleased to find that Charles Peake had again been assigned to him for liaison.[53]

The island in which de Gaulle landed was by now so full of supplies and troops for the coming invasion that the joke was that only barrage balloons kept it sinking under their weight. There were some twenty American, fourteen British, three Canadian, one French and one Polish division, along with hundreds of thousands of special forces, corps troops, headquarter units and lines of communication personnel.[54] All of southern England, and much of the rest of the country, had become a vast military encampment. 'Transport centres like Cheltenham, Cirencester and Oxford became almost endless traffic jams, with long convoys of trucks halted or crawling along. The environs of Plymouth, Poole or Southampton were vast vehicle parks and quaysides such as Brixham in Devon disappeared under mounds of equipment ready for loading.'[55]

The only issues left unresolved for this meticulously planned operation were those involving the country about to be liberated. Churchill had made a further attempt on 28 May to persuade Roosevelt to send a senior American official to participate in discussions on civil affairs with the French. 'I see the growth of opinion very powerful here,' he wrote, and the feeling that France should be with us when we liberate France. Naturally, there is a great wave of sentiment for France on account of the bravery and success of French troops mainly African but well led by French officers in our Italian battle. There is also the sense that they should share in the work we have in hand. No one will understand their being cold-shouldered.[56]

Roosevelt, however, once more turned the Prime Minister down.

The President was also being obstructive on another issue: the currency to be issued by the Allied forces in France. Although the British were prepared to allow the FCNL to issue notes, the Americans had withheld their consent. In consequence, the British had agreed to allow 'supplemental francs' to be printed in the USA. These, however, were completely neutral in character. Although they carried 'Liberté, Egalité et Fraternité' on one side, Roosevelt vetoed 'République Française' on the other, on the grounds that it implied that the Allies wanted France to be a republic, when it might choose some other form of government. The American Secretary of the Treasury, Henry Morgenthau, had argued against this, but to no effect. De Gaulle was furious. A protest note from the FCNL described this as a step 'which has never been taken in the past by a friendly army.'[57]

'All good luck in your talks with prima donna,' Roosevelt had cabled to Churchill on 4 June.[58] This was cavalier in the extreme. It was the President who was responsible for the Anglo-French crisis which was about to erupt. General Antoine Béthouart, who accompanied de Gaulle to his meeting with Churchill at Portsmouth that day, described the General as strained and embittered. He was being invited at the very last moment as a spectator to events that vitally affected his country, without any previous discussion let alone agreement on the central question of the exercise of power in liberated France.[59] Matters were not helped by the presence of Smuts, who some six months earlier had publicly declared that France was no longer a Great Power. Small wonder that de Gaulle failed to respond to the Prime Minister's warm greeting.

The talks nevertheless proved relatively amicable until the point where Churchill pressed de Gaulle to visit Roosevelt, who, he pointed out, was likely to be re-elected for another four-year term in November. 'France would need his friendship, and it was the General's duty to gain it, just as it was the duty of a soldier to charge an enemy battery.'[60] This went down badly with de Gaulle, who asked why Churchill seemed to think that he needed to submit his candidacy for the authority in France to the President?

An angry Churchill now warned de Gaulle that if, after every effort had been exhausted, the President was on the one side and the FCNL was on the other, 'the Prime Minister would almost certainly side with the President, and that anyhow no quarrel would ever arise between Britain and the United States because of France.'[61] De Gaulle's account – the words do not appear in the official British record – quotes Churchill as saying

> We are going to liberate Europe, but it is because the Americans are in agreement with us to do so. This is something you ought to know: each time we must choose between Europe and the open sea, we shall always choose the open sea. Each time I must choose between you and Roosevelt, I shall always choose Roosevelt.[62]

There was another outburst when the Minister of Labour, Ernest Bevin, intervened to say that the Labour Party would be hurt if the General refused to enter into political talks. '*Blessés,*' said he. '*Vous dites vous serez blessés.* Had it not occurred to them that France was *blessée?* Had we no thoughts of French feelings?'[63] Bevin asked for a translation but was cut short by Churchill who wanted another go at the General. The Prime Minister was gracious and threatening in turn but without achieving the slightest effect.

Before lunch ended Churchill proposed a toast 'to de Gaulle who never accepted defeat.' De Gaulle replied, 'To England, to Victory, to Europe.' Churchill had expected de Gaulle to dine with him and go back to London on the Prime Minister's train. But the General 'drew himself up and stated that he preferred to motor with his French officers separately.' The French party returned to London, silent, anxious and preoccupied. Churchill showed no such reticence, privately, and quite unfairly, describing de Gaulle as 'this wicked man, this implacable foe of our country.'[64]

The following day, the eve of D-Day, with everybody under intense strain, there was a full-blown Anglo-French crisis. De Gaulle was refusing to allow French liaison officers, whose role was to identify to Allied commanders the people to be given responsibility for civil affairs, to embark for France. News of this came during a Cabinet meeting. 'Well, that puts the lid on,' Cadogan noted in his diary. 'We always start by putting ourselves in the wrong, and then de G puts himself *more* in the wrong.'[65] To make matters worse, the British also believed de Gaulle was refusing to broadcast. This was a misunderstanding. The General's objection was to the timing of his broadcast, which was scheduled to follow heads of the government in exile and then Eisenhower. As de Gaulle told Duff Cooper, if his broadcast followed directly after that of an American general, it would reduce him to the role of a puppet of the British and American governments who had put him up to say words put into his mouth and to rubber-stamp agreements arrived at without his knowledge or approval.[66]

The immediate result was that Cadogan had to sit through 'the usual passionate anti-de G harangue from P.M. On this subject, we get away from politics and diplomacy and even common sense. It's a girls' school. Roosevelt, P.M. and – it must be admitted de G. – all behave like girls approaching the age of puberty.'[67] When Churchill saw the unfortunate Pierre Viénot at 1 a.m. the following morning, there was an explosion. Viénot had just seen de Gaulle, who had launched into a violent diatribe against Churchill, Eden, Britain and the British, insulting Viénot in the process. Now Viénot was accused by a furious prime minister of being a blackmailer and told that his chief was an enemy.[68]

By this time the largest amphibious operation in history was under way. The pep talks given by British senior officers to their troops had often included snatches from the story of a previous British invasion of France, Shakespeare's *Henry V*, subject of a recent Laurence Olivier film. American airborne forces had begun dropping over France, and British glider troops had landed to seize bridges over the river Orne and the Caen canal. At 5.30 a.m., 2,000 Allied ships, supported by British and American heavy bombers, began a bombardment of the French coast. The first landings in an area west of Caen, between the rivers Orne and Vire, began an hour later, the Americans to the west at Utah and Omaha beaches, the British and Canadians immediately to the east at Gold, June and Sword beaches (see Map 2). The first announcement was made by the BBC in English at 9.30, followed by transmissions in French, Norwegian, Danish, Dutch and Flemish.[69] Churchill made a statement to the Commons at midday. 'He looked,' Harold Nicolson recorded in his diary,

as white as a sheet. The House noticed this at once, and we feared that he was about to announce some terrible disaster. He is called immediately, and places two separate fids of typescripts on the table. He begins with the first, which is about Rome ... He then picks up his other fid of notes and begins, 'I have also to announce to the House that during the night and early hours of this morning, the first of a series of landings in force upon the Continent of Europe has taken place ...' The House listens in hushed awe. He speaks for only seven minutes.[70]

By the end of the day, some six divisions, three American, two British and one Canadian, totalling some 156,000 troops, were ashore in France. Although the American landings at Omaha beach had come close to disaster, and casualties were not light, surprise had been achieved and the operation had been a stunning success.[71]

During the morning, some of the heat had been taken out of the Anglo-French crisis. De Gaulle was reluctantly persuaded to lift his ban on the French liaison officers, complaining as he did that while he was always making concessions, nobody made any to him.[72] The problem of his broadcast was also resolved. This had caused some anxiety. Eden had been unsure whether to announce that de Gaulle would speak, since if he failed to do so the Germans would make propaganda of the fact, and asked the head of PWE, Robert Bruce Lockhart, for advice. The latter declined, saying that the Foreign Secretary knew the General better than he did. 'The man is not sane,' Eden replied, 'but I suppose we must take the risk.'[73] In the event, all went well. As in the aftermath of the North African landings, de Gaulle made a fine speech, including a warm reference to Britain as 'the sole bastion of freedom and now the base of the liberating armies.' The one problem was a reference to 'the French government,' without the qualifying 'provisional,' although Eden let this through. (Three weeks earlier, the FCNL's Consultative Assembly had proposed changing its name to Gouvernement Provisoire de la République Française [GPRF].) Churchill appears not to have noticed the omission; indeed, the Prime Minister listened to the broadcast with tears rolling down his cheeks.[74]

The tension had not, however, been dispelled. It was glaringly obvious when, at a dinner the Foreign Secretary hosted for de Gaulle on the evening of 7 June, de Gaulle shouted at Eden that it was a scandal that the British should follow the American lead and accept their counterfeit money. A patient foreign secretary warned that it was fatal in national policy to have too much pride and argued on the lines of 'she stoops to conquer,' which proved somewhat difficult to translate into French. Eden went on to give a recent example where Britain had successfully taken this line with the USA. The story produced what the official record describes as 'a frosty smile which slowly developed into the nearest approach to a de Gaulle laugh.'[75]

On 9 June, Churchill began a message to Roosevelt, 'I want to know your wishes about the notes issued for the troops in France.' A subsequent message asked whether to let de Gaulle 'obtain new status as his price for backing these notes.' Roosevelt's reply was an unambiguous no. 'Provided it is clear that he acts entirely on his own responsibility and without our concurrence he can sign any statement on currency in whatever capacity he likes, even that of the King of Siam.'[76] On the civil-affairs question, the Foreign Office was trying to work out an agreement for talks in London between Viénot and British officials to agree a text that might subsequently be shown to the Americans. This at one point involved Eden in a shouting match with Churchill which went on until two in the morning.[77] In practice, the issue was resolved on the ground in France, where Fighting French officials simply took over from their Vichy predecessors. A final formal agreement on an administrative settlement was only reached on 25 August.

De Gaulle's immediate concern, however, was his desire to visit France. The Foreign Office were under instructions from Churchill to stall on the request in order to wait and see how the General behaved.[78] Perhaps too the Prime Minister wanted to get there first. On 12 June, Churchill, accompanied by Smuts and General Sir Alan Brooke, who had commanded the ill-fated BEF sent back to France after Dunkirk, crossed the Channel. 'It was a wonderful moment,' Brooke recorded in his diary,

> to find myself re-entering France almost exactly 4 years after being thrown out for the second time, at St Nazaire. Floods of memories came back of my last trip of despair, and those long four years of work and anxiety at last crowned by the success of a re-entry into France.[79]

De Gaulle's absence was critically remarked on by the British press. One cartoon showed Churchill and Smuts on the way to France with de Gaulle stranded on the English coast. It carried the caption, 'One of our liberators is missing.'[80]

The next day, the Prime Minister ungraciously gave way over de Gaulle's visit. 'Remember,' he minuted to Eden, 'that there is not a scrap of generosity about this man, who only wishes to pose as the saviour of France in this operation without a single French soldier at his back.'[81] (This latter statement was patently untrue. Some 74,000 French troops were fighting in Italy, a fact Churchill had himself referred to in an earlier message to Roosevelt.)[82] That evening, Eden again hosted a dinner for the General at which Churchill was conspicuously absent; the mood, Harvey recorded, 'was grim. I have never seen de Gaulle look so worn, *martyrisé*.'[83] But the General's first visit to France went well, his warm reception by the French obscuring his cool reception by the British authorities.

This brief excursion to France, along with the support he had received from Parliament and the press and de Gaulle's sense that events would now finally unfold in his favour, meant that his visit to London ended on a much happier note than it had begun. On 15 June, Eden visited the General at Carlton Gardens, the first time he had done so. He was received with some ceremony, a guard of honour having been drawn up outside, with officers posted at intervals up the stairs. This was in part a tribute to de Gaulle's high opinion of the Foreign Secretary who had done his best 'to make the clouds vanish.'[84] It may have also reflected the fact that, as Eden noted, de Gaulle was at his best as a host.[85] The following day, de Gaulle paid a formal farewell visit to Eden, who found his visitor in a more reasonable frame of mind than he had ever known him. De Gaulle stressed that despite the difficulties his intention was to work closely with Britain and the USA. To salve the wounds Churchill had inflicted on himself, as de Gaulle put it in his memoirs, he wrote the Prime Minister a warm letter, which elicited a markedly cooler response.[86] On his return to Algiers, the *Times* correspondent there reported French satisfaction with the visit. While no diplomatic agreement had been signed, the French had regained the conviction 'which events and the remoteness of the Algerian backwater had begun to efface, that the British are with them.'[87] It could have been very much worse.

# 16

# Down the Champs-Elysées Together

In his speech on the liberation of Paris on 26 August, de Gaulle claimed that the capital had liberated itself. Strictly speaking, this was correct. Liberation had been sparked by a rising, and the first forces to enter the capital were French. But the omission of reference to his Allies was part of a deliberate attempt, for which there were pressing political reasons, to disguise the fact that France had been liberated by foreign forces.[1] French participation in the D-Day landings had been limited to that of special forces and some ninety French warships and transports. The former were either already at sea or briefed and 'sealed' on a Gloucestershire airfield at the time de Gaulle was asked to give his consent for their involvement.[2] A rather more significant role had been allotted to French Resistance forces, notably those of the Maquis, in seeking to impede the Germans from bringing reinforcements against the Allied bridgeheads. The Maquis, a Corsican word for wild bushy country, had emerged in the wake of Laval's STO of February 1943, as young men quite literally took to the hills in areas such as the Massif Central and Savoie rather than go to Germany as conscript workers. According to Fighting French estimates, there were some 40,000 *maquisards* in the early part of 1943, and 100,000 a year later. To be effective as a guerrilla force, they needed arms in addition to the caches hidden by the French Armistice Army in 1940–1.[3]

De Gaulle, however, had received a very cautious reply when he had written to Churchill asking for support for the Maquis in March 1943. The British remained anxious about sparking a premature French uprising, and SOE had limited supply capabilities.[4] On the other hand, there were influential British figures who found the Maquis appealing.

One such was second in command of SOE's R/F-Section, Captain Yeo-Thomas, who in October 1943 visited the Maquis near Cahors and in the Ain and was sufficiently impressed to report that properly supported and armed they 'could provide us with formidable and efficient support on D-Day.'[5] Yeo-Thomas, paradoxically perhaps for a man who had been recruited from the Parisian fashion business, was, in Matthew Cobb's words, a natural Churchillian, 'turbulent, ungovernable, physically brave and naturally patriotic.'[6] He subsequently secured an audience with the Prime Minister, whom he entranced with his tales of men and women risking torture and death waiting for agents in the darkness of the windy wilderness of eastern France.[7]

Another man who influenced Churchill in favour of arming the Maquis was Emmanuel d'Astier de La Vigerie, the FCNL's Commissaire de l'Intérieur and brother of Henri and François, who had been involved in the Darlan assassination. Following a meeting at Marrakech in January 1944, the Prime Minister described d'Astier to Roosevelt as

> a remarkable man of the Scarlet Pimpernel type ... He says that in Haute Savoie, south of Geneva between Grenoble and the Italian frontier, he has over 20,000 men all desperate, but only one in five has any weapon. If more weapons were available, very large numbers more would take to the mountains. As you know, I am very anxious to see a guerrilla *à la Tito* up in the Savoie and in the Alpes Maritimes ... He is a fine fellow, very fierce and bitter but one of the best Frenchmen I have struck in these bleak times.[8]

D'Astier subsequently came to London where he assured the Prime Minister that increased arms supplies would not lead to an intensification of intra-French rivalries. The War Cabinet, having in one historian's words been 'hustled by the Prime Minister in his inimitable way,' decided to double supplies to the Maquis in the south-east, although groups in central and northern France, whose needs did not coincide with immediate Allied interests, got nothing extra.[9] The immediate results were disappointing. Increased supplies were hampered by bureaucratic infighting between SIS and SOE in London and low cloud and the failure of some reception committees at the dropping areas in France. But between February and April sufficient arms were provided for some 65,000 men. Some 1,665 sorties were flown by the RAF and the United States Army Air Force (USAAF) in the second quarter of 1944.[10] This generated considerable excitement among

Maquis units, who believed, this time correctly, that a spring *débarquement* was at hand. Assured of a supply of arms, H. R. Kedward notes

> it was feasible to mobilize more than the small companies of fifteen to forty who had survived the winter in varying states of discomfort and insecurity. Preparations for sites where over a hundred could be incorporated into something more akin to a regular army unit, were invariably backed by London, where the SOE command were responsive to assurances from trusted agents that the military credentials of the operation were soundly based.[11]

According to subsequent British assessments, these deliveries were well timed. Earlier they might have inflated the Resistance dangerously before the Allied armies were ready to support them. Deliveries continued during the summer; indeed, by September the Resistance was described by one Foreign Office official as 'pretty well saturated with arms.'[12] Churchill had lost interest in the Resistance once Overlord had succeeded. It had fulfilled its political purpose, and, like de Gaulle, he distrusted its political radicalism.[13]

In addition to providing arms, the Allies also provided direction in the form of three-men 'Jedburgh' teams, consisting of a Briton, an American and a Frenchman, who were chosen with a view to their political adaptability and tact, attributes not necessarily possessed by other British special forces now operating in France. Their formal role was to provide a general staff for the Resistance and to coordinate local efforts in the best interests of Allied strategy. In practice, they also found themselves involved in instilling good guerrilla doctrine, reporting back on what was often a very confused political situation and exerting discipline on Resistance leaders. Their ability to order arms from London allowed them to arbitrate local disputes, including those with the Francs-Tireurs et Partisans (FTP), a Communist paramilitary group, whose agenda was the subject of a good deal of Allied concern. In at least one instance, a Jedburgh leader cut off the supply arms to the FTP until they had recognised the GPRF nominee as *préfet* of the region. All in all they were estimated to have provided reinforcement to the Resistance out of proportion to their numbers as well as providing a further example of how intimately defeat involved outsiders in French affairs.[14]

With the D-Day landings, Resistance groups, together with SOE units already in France, began sabotage missions against German communications. These were particularly effective against the railways, notably in the more remote regions – Lyon, Dijon, Doubs, the east, the centre and the south-west – where 600 derailings took place during June and July. Sabotage immobilised some 1,800 locomotives and more than 6,000 railway cars, as well as telegraph communications. In his memoirs, Eisenhower paid particular tribute to the role of the FFI in Brittany, though his overall conclusion that the contribution of the Resistance to the Liberation was the equivalent of fifteen divisions may have been overgenerous. The contrast with June 1940, when, as the military historian Basil Liddell Hart noted, well-felled trees backed by snipers would have done much to have slowed the progress of the German *Blitzkrieg*, reflects how much had changed in France over the previous four years.[15]

The signal for these operations had been given by the BBC. The first series of messages to alert SOE circuits had gone out on 1 June. On 5 June the BBC broadcast some 200 messages in the 9.15 p.m. French transmission to Resistance groups. 'Bientôt tu voleras' instructed one circuit to attack a rail target; 'Vive l'heure des vacances' told another to move against telecommunications; 'J'ai une faim de loup' was an instruction to take control of a zone.[16] The BBC now became an arm of war in the true sense of the word. It broadcast despatches from French and British war correspondents and announced the successes of the FFI and the Resistance, as well as giving instructions from the GPRF, Conseil National de la Résistance and Allied Supreme Command. Police officers were urged to join the Resistance. Factories working for the Germans were urged to close and those doing essential work for the French to remain open. Railway and communication workers not specifically engaged in sabotage were encouraged to make life difficult for the Germans without going so far as to provoke open revolt.[17]

Striking a balance between calls for collective action and prudence was not easy. One effect of the broadcasts was to produce an influx of recruits for the Maquis, which lacked sufficient arms to go round. Much worse, the Germans put down local revolts with great brutality, notably at Tulle in the Corrèze on 9 May and Oradour-sur-Glane in the Haute-Vienne, where the following day the same SS Division killed 642 men, women and children before razing the town to the ground. News of these disasters was not reported for fear of creating panic and undermining civilian morale. Orders for a general uprising, to be conducted area by area, starting in Brittany, were only given over the BBC at the beginning of August, followed by Loire and Garonne on 12 and 13 August and all the major towns on the 17th.[18]

By mid-July the Allies had disembarked some thirty divisions, half British and Canadian and half American.[19] British troops had been issued with a guidebook, the sympathetic tone of which is reflected in the injunctions to remember that,

> We are helping to free France. Thousands of Frenchmen have been shot in France for keeping alive the spirit of freedom. Let the French know that you realize the great part Frenchmen have played, both in the last war, and in this war.
>
> The French are more polite than most of us. Remember to call them 'Monsieur, Madame, Mademoiselle,' not just 'Oy!'[20]

Among the list of don'ts were,

> Don't criticize the French army's defeat of 1940.
> If a Frenchman raises one of the points which have strained Anglo-French relations since 1940, drop the matter.
> Don't, even if food is offered to you, eat the French out of house and home. If you do, someone may starve.[21]

One uncertainty which had faced the planners in London had been French reaction to the Liberation.[22] The evidence reaching Britain from postal and telegraph censorship in May 1944 suggested that while most writers thought that invasion would result in victory and the end of French sufferings, others feared that 'the great blow would be terrible.'[23] Initial reports suggested that the Allied reception had been lukewarm. General Sir Alan Brooke noted that the French 'did not seem in any way pleased to see us arrive as a victorious country to liberate France.' It was a view shared by British press correspondents, as well as more junior soldiers. 'It was rather a shock,' one NCO noted, 'to find that we were not welcomed ecstatically as liberators by the local people, as we were told we should be ... They saw us as bringers of destruction and pain.' Normandy had suffered continually over the past four years. Liberation cost some 20,000 Normans their lives, and the area was chewed into what one historian describes as 'a bloody, unrecognisable mess.' Caen was particularly badly damaged. One British soldier wrote of it being left 'a waste of brick and stone, like a field of corn that has been ploughed. The people gazed at us without emotion of any kind; one could hardly look them in the face knowing who had done this.'[24] Away from the fighting the welcome was much warmer, with fruit and flowers thrown into the advancing Allied vehicles. Not all the British troops appear to have responded, however. A senior British officer noted a distrust and lack of sympathy for the French, amounting to marked dislike.[25]

Once ashore, the Americans had been allotted the task of striking west across the Cotentin peninsula to isolate and then seize the port of Cherbourg, which they finally succeeded in capturing on 30 June. The British, who were on the left flank, drew on themselves the majority of German armoured divisions and reinforcements by virtue of being on the edge of good open tank country. Acutely aware of the shortage of British and Canadian manpower, Montgomery moved with caution. There was a ten-week battle of attrition between the German and the British, supported by the Canadian and Poles, which cost some 65,000 British casualties.[26]

It was not until 20 August that Allied forces were able to break out of Normandy. By then the Allied forces had scored a considerable victory, destroying two powerful German armies in just seventy-six days. This allowed the Allies to overrun the V1 sites in northern France. The first of the so-called 'buzz-bombs' had hit London on the night of 12/13 June. Since they were aimed at the capital rather than at the British invasion ports, these were a nuisance rather than a serious threat, but they nevertheless had an effect on morale. This new air assault, which continued intermittently round the clock, was in some ways worse than the Blitz of 1940/1. Dawn, as Churchill later wrote, 'brought no relief, and cloud no comfort.' Some 6,184 people were killed and 17,981 seriously injured. It was the last German threat to Britain posed from French territory.[27]

On 15 August, a second Allied landing took place in France, on the Mediterranean coast near Saint-Tropez. News of this on the BBC domestic service was followed by 'La Marseillaise' and, according to Harold Nicolson, was met with great excitement.[28] Operation Dragoon, which had been agreed in principle at the Tehran summit in December 1943, was of vital political importance to the French, who were to provide half the troops.[29] But Churchill, supported by the Chiefs of Staff, had yet again proved himself reluctant to support a French landing. Indeed, the Prime Minister, this time for domestic and international political reasons, had fought a passionate rearguard action against the southern French landings, which would mean the withdrawal of troops from the Italian theatre where the British were still dominant. Victory in Italy would rebound to British credit in a way that victory in France would not. Churchill, moreover, was now looking towards the post-war world. He was anxious to exploit the Italian campaign to drive up through the Po valley, through the Ljubljana gap, into Austria and Hungary, to counter Russia's potentially predominant role in south-east Europe.[30]

The result was a series of tense Anglo-American arguments, which Churchill lost. This was partly due to military requirements: the Americans saw the new French landings as essential to support the struggling campaign in Normandy and to ease the shortage of French port facilities. More uncomfortably, it also reflected declining British influence in the final stage of the war.[31] The 150,000 strong Operation Dragoon was a primarily Franco-American landing, supported by the Royal Navy and the RAF. Both the Resistance and SOE were active in disrupting communications and clearing roads. One British agent emerged from two years' clandestine activity, struck a Union Jack on the bonnet of a powerful car and set about attacking German road transports with phosphorous grenades. Another directed the affairs of the Ain and Haute-Savoie, persuading both the FFI and FTP to follow his orders, which were veiled as suggestion, for getting rid of the German armies. General Wilson, by now Supreme Allied Commander in the Mediterranean, estimated that the existence of the FFI in southern France reduced the fighting efficiency of the Wehrmacht there to 40 per cent at the time of the Dragoon landings.[32]

Ten days later came the liberation of Paris. Mindful of the examples of Stalingrad and the Warsaw uprising, Eisenhower had wanted to bypass the capital, which was of little strategic importance in his planned advance towards the Rhine. There were also political considerations. Concern about the strength of the Communists had led the Foreign Office to oppose a request by General Koenig for 40,000 Sten guns to be dropped to the Resistance in the Paris area. In the words of Charles Peake, who was now with SHAEF, 'there will always be a temptation to put them to mischievous uses should political passions be enflamed when the war is over.'[33] But the Resistance already had weapons from SOE, and on 19 August the CNR and the Comité Parisien de Libération both called for immediate insurrection in the capital.[34] Three days later, Eisenhower authorised a French division commanded by General Leclerc, which had landed in Normandy on 1 August, to enter Paris.

One reason why this division had been chosen was because its troops were white. Despite, or perhaps because of, the presence of large numbers of black American troops in Britain, British officers had impressed on de Gaulle's chief of staff the difficulties of receiving black troops in the UK. The Free French in their turn had also been anxious to avoid the use of colonial troops in the liberation of their capital.[35] News of the liberation of Paris was deliberately announced prematurely by the Gaullist representative at the BBC in order to try to undermine the Communist FTP. The actual event was greeted with great enthusiasm in Britain. The bells of St Paul's were rung and a service of thanksgiving was held in the crypt. King George VI sent a warm message to de Gaulle, and Eden broadcast on the BBC. A cartoon published in the *Daily Mail* showed the gargoyles on Notre Dame smiling down on the city.[36]

Britons could now return to Paris. The historian John Wheeler-Bennett, who flew out immediately to SHAEF headquarters in Versailles, described the contrast he found between the two capitals. He had left London

> a battered, shattered city, pock-marked and scarred, war-weary and monstrously bored with the monotony of its wartime diet ... Yet, notwithstanding all this there was a spirit and a pride which was unshakeable and magnificent, a supreme faith in the ultimate victory in our test of endurance. Paris was anything but this. Plate glass windows gleamed in guilty splendour; the gravel paths in the Tuileries garden were raked with meticulous perfection and in the Bois sleek saddle-horses in splendid fettle flaunted their paces.[37]

The Ambassador, Duff Cooper, arrived on 13 September, escorted by some forty-eight Spitfires.

By the beginning of September, with most of France liberated, SIS began to wind up its business, while members of SOE's F-Section, de Gaulle's old bugbear, packed their bags and slipped out of the country. Not all went quietly. The south-west of France had, since the Liberation, been effectively under the control of a series of feudal lords whose power and influence was similar to that of their fifteenth-century Gascon counterparts.[38] The most influential of these was Lieutenant-Colonel George Starr, who effectively controlled Toulouse. Meeting him on 16 September, de Gaulle, who thoroughly disliked the idea of an Englishman exercising such power in France, accused him of being a mercenary and of interference in French affairs. Starr answered back bluntly and was ordered out of the country. But de Gaulle shook him by the hand saying, 'they told me you were fearless and knew how to say *merde*.' Starr received the *Croix de Guerre* and *Légion d'Honneur*.[39] The incident encapsulates much of the ambivalent sentiment associated at the highest French political level with the liberation.

Major Roger Landes was less fortunate. In the wake of D-Day, Landes had built a force of some 2,000 men, which launched massive sabotage on road and rail routes north out of Bordeaux to Normandy. This force had expanded to around 20,000 by the time de Gaulle established his provisional government. When de Gaulle visited Bordeaux in the autumn, Landes was introduced to him wearing British uniform. 'You are British,' de Gaulle declared, 'Your place is not here.' Landes was given two hours to leave the city. When the order to leave was repeated later at the *préfecture*, Landes' bodyguard drew a gun. A crowd of some 4,000 people demonstrated in front of the hotel where Landes was staying, in support of him and against de Gaulle. An official protest was lodged, and, on his return to England, Landes was duly summoned to the Foreign Office, where officials seemed unconcerned. 'You were not the only one to have trouble with de Gaulle at the end of the war,' he was told. 'Forget about it.'[40]

The Foreign Office was rather less forgiving to another of de Gaulle's adversaries: General Spears. Churchill had remained obdurate in the face of pressure from both Eden and Duff Cooper for Spears' removal from the Levant. Over and above the Prime Minister's instinctive loyalty to his friends, Churchill was loath to dismiss a man who stood up so bluntly to the French. The French have an intense dislike of Spears, he told Eden in March 1944, 'because he fights for British interests in French which is more French than theirs ... I have always sustained Spears and there is no doubt at all that he has shown great force of character in Syria.'[41] The most the Prime Minister was then willing to do was to tell Spears 'not to overegg the pudding,' advice Spears was unwise enough not to take.[42] When he was then recalled for consultations in London in July, the French greeted the news with immense satisfaction. The final dismissal came only on 23 November.[43]

These, however, were sideshows. The main issue facing the Foreign Office in the late summer and autumn of 1944 was de-jure recognition of the GPRF as France's provisional government. Here the British once again found themselves – or perhaps more accurately allowed themselves to be made – hostage to US policy. Opinion in Washington divided along similar lines to that in London. On the one hand there were the pragmatists who recognised that de Gaulle was the key figure in French politics and wished to deal with him accordingly. These included Harry Hopkins, the Secretary of State for War, Henry Stimson, as well as Eisenhower in France. On the other hand was a president who remained deeply distrustful of the General and could easily outdo Churchill when it came to stubbornness. Of Dutch descent, he had once described himself as 'a pig-headed Dutchman.'[44]

That did not mean to say that the President never changed his mind. Indeed, there was a disconcerting unpredictability to his policy that revealed itself in early July, when de Gaulle at last visited the American capital. The British Embassy noted the exceptional public cordiality with which

Roosevelt and Hull had received their guest, leading it to speculate that the White House might 'adopt' de Gaulle, leaving the British out on a limb.[45] This was unduly pessimistic. Although on his best behaviour, de Gaulle failed to impress Roosevelt.[46] But the British were taken aback when, in a major change of policy, of which they were given no prior notice, the Americans suddenly announced that they were recognising the GPRF as the de-facto authority in the civil administration in France.[47]

Nor was London best pleased to hear from de Gaulle that in outlining his ideas for the post-war world the President had talked about the 'authority' the USA would have to exercise in Dakar, India, the Dutch East Indies, Singapore and elsewhere. Churchill showed no appreciation for this unwelcome intelligence, telling Eden that it would be a good thing to let the President know 'the kind of way de Gaulle interprets friendliness. I have now had four years experience of him, and it is always the same.'[48] Eden demurred, arguing that de Gaulle had behaved towards them as an Ally should do in respect to the talks with Roosevelt.[49] But while Churchill had provided Roosevelt with a detailed account of de Gaulle's June visit to London, the President's account of the Washington visit amounted to no more than a single line.[50]

The Foreign Secretary continued to press the case for de-jure recognition while from Washington Halifax argued that 'we ought not to hesitate to take the lead in European questions because we have nothing to lose and perhaps something to gain with the Americans in forcing the pace somewhat over France.'[51] Churchill predictably disagreed, describing a serious divergence from the Americans at this stage as a serious mistake. The Prime Minister had not yet reconciled himself to formal recognition of de Gaulle as head of the French government. 'One does not know what may happen and it is as well to keep our hands free,' he minuted on 18 August. The liberation of southern and western France might create a large area from which 'a real Provisional Government might be drawn, instead of one being composed entirely of the FCNL whose interests in seizing the title deeds of France is obvious.'[52] Yet when he had spoken in parliament some two weeks earlier, Churchill's tone was very different. Despite all his difficulties with the General, the Prime Minister told the House,

'I have never forgotten and can never forget, that he stood forth as the first eminent Frenchman to face the common foe in what seemed to be the hour of ruin in his country, and, possibly, of ours, and it is only fair and becoming, that he should stand first and foremost on the day when

France shall again *be raised, and raise herself*, to her rightful place among the Great Powers of Europe and the world.'[53]

The logic of such a statement pointed to recognition, as did the pressure not only from the Foreign Office but also the press and Parliament, where one MP pointed out that it was humiliating to the French that Britain had recognised the Italian but not the French government. On 27 September, Churchill telegraphed Roosevelt that he proposed to tell Parliament, without committing the President, that the government was studying the question from week to week in the light of changing events. Roosevelt replied that he thought it wise to delay recognition until the Germans had been driven from the whole of France.[54] On 14 October, Churchill, who was now with Eden in Moscow, told Roosevelt that there was no doubt that the French had been cooperating with Supreme Headquarters and that the provisional government had the support of the majority of the French people. 'I suggest that we can now safely recognise General de Gaulle's administration as the Provisional Government of France.'[55]

Although this was in line with the advice he was receiving from the State Department, Roosevelt still prevaricated.[56] Cadogan 'let himself go' in a personal telegram to Eden, warning that

continuing withholding of recognition causes increasing bewilderment and criticism, not only in French circles. As cordial relations with a restored and liberated France is a vital British interest, I should have hoped that the President might have allowed our right to a preponderant voice in this matter.[57]

At this point, possibly with the forthcoming US elections in mind, Roosevelt again suddenly changed tack; the USA declared its willingness to recognise the French provisional government. 'God help us!,' Cadogan noted on 21 October. 'Is this simple inefficiency and crossing of wires or are the U.S. trying to do us down?'[58] The American Ambassador in Paris, Jefferson Caffery, promptly informed the French Foreign Minister, Georges Bidault, without the courtesy of telling Duff Cooper. Determined not to be left out on a limb, London instructed Duff Cooper to give formal recognition at the same time as the Americans. Finally, on 23 October, the Americans, British and Russians all recognised de Gaulle. 'At *last!*' Cadogan noted, 'What a fuss about nothing.'[59] That evening, Duff Cooper attended a dinner party which he found even drearier than the parties the de Gaulles normally gave. When the Ambassador said he hoped de Gaulle was glad that recognition was finally finished, the General shrugged his shoulders, saying it would never finish. But Cooper suspected that de Gaulle was in fact secretly pleased.[60] Thus, wrote Churchill in his memoirs, 'we completed the process begun in the dark and far-off days of 1940.'[61]

It was not in fact quite the end. On 5 October, the French writer François Mauriac had published an article in *Le Figaro* entitled 'Complaint,' which contained a glowing tribute to Britain. What, the writer than asked, did he complain about?

I hardly know. We never quite grow up. Even in old age we console ourselves sometimes with picture books. Perhaps I dreamed – don't laugh at me, seeing Mr Churchill and General de Gaulle visiting together the unknown soldier; and then we would have seen what the unconquerable England and her Old Pilot really mean to the people of France. He would have seen, he will see, please God.[62]

Churchill did indeed see, on Armistice Day, 11 November. They made a curious pair, one journalist noted, 'the one so rotund and merry, the other so tall and grave, like Mr Pickwick and Don Quixote.'[63] But the Prime Minister's welcome was every bit as warm as Mauriac had predicted. The reception, Duff Cooper recorded in his diary,

had to be seen to be believed. It was greater than anything I have ever known. There were crowds in every window, even in the top floors of the highest houses and on the roofs, and the cheering was the loudest and most spontaneous and most genuine.

We walked down from the Arc de Triomphe to the tribune, whence we watched the march-past, which lasted nearly an hour. Whenever there was a pause in the procession there were loud cries of CHURCHILL from all over the crowd.[64]

Churchill then went on to lay a wreath at the statue of Clemenceau, where, on de Gaulle's orders, the band played 'Le Père de la Victoire.' 'For you,' Churchill said to him in English.[65]

The following day, Churchill went to the Hôtel de Ville, where he was presented with the Freedom of the City of Paris, a quite exceptional honour. There he addressed a group of Resistance leaders hostile to de Gaulle, urging them to rally round their leader and to do their utmost to make France united and indivisible.[66] Churchill returned home impressed, his mood partly perhaps buoyed by Göring's gold bath which had been put at his disposal. He told Duff Cooper that much had been achieved and the Entente restored to full vigour. 'I re-established friendly private relations with de Gaulle,' he reported to Roosevelt, 'who is better since he lost a large part of his inferiority complex.'[67]

For Churchill it was a vindication. In June 1940, when deciding to turn down the French request for more British fighters, the Prime Minister had told the War Cabinet that if Britain were defeated 'the war would be lost for France no less than for ourselves, whereas, provided we were strong ourselves, we could win the war, and in so doing, restore France to her position.'[68] He had also made the latter pledge to Reynaud's government, many of whose members were incredulous, a few days later, on his last visit to France in 1940.[69] That promise was now being redeemed. But if the Entente had survived, its future was unclear. Churchill's memoirs make no reference to the political discussions during the Paris visit. De Gaulle's memoirs, by contrast, are revealing on the subject. Anxious to re-establish France's position as a Great Power, and no doubt mindful of his failure to make headway with either the USA or the Soviet Union, he had proposed a new and closer entente, an early version of the Grand European Design he would later pursue as French president in the late 1950s and 1960s.[70]

Britain, as well as France, the General warned Churchill, would emerge weakened from the war in the face of 'centrifugal forces at work within the Commonwealth, and, particularly, the rise of America and Russia, not to mention China.'[71] If Britain and France acted together they could ensure that they retained a determining voice in the coming peace settlements. They could thus maintain the equilibrium of Europe and the survival of Western civilisation. Britain and France should come to an agreement to uphold these interests together.

> Our two nations will follow us. America and Russian, hobbled by their rivalry, will not be able to raise any objections. Moreover we shall have the support of many states and of world-side public opinion, which instinctively shies away from giants. Thus England and France will together create peace, as twice in twenty years they confronted war.[72]

Churchill recognised the danger de Gaulle had outlined. A few weeks earlier he had told Violet Bonham-Carter that at the Tehran summit he realised for the first time 'what a really small country this is. On the one hand the big Russian bear with its paws outstretched – on the other the great American Elephant – & between them the poor little British donkey – who is the only one that knows the right way home.'[73] But while Churchill wanted an alliance with France, he did not want a special relationship. 'In politics, as in strategy,' he replied to de Gaulle,

> it is better to persuade the stronger than to pit yourself against him. That is what I am trying to do. The Americans have immense resources. They do not always use them to the best advantage. I am trying to enlighten them, without forgetting, of course, to benefit my country.[74]

As for the Russians, he was trying to restrain Stalin, who, if he had an enormous appetite, also had a great deal of common sense. Churchill was probably being more realistic than de Gaulle; the prospects of a European counterweight to the superpowers was in 1944 at best uncertain. But the message was clear. Although the Entente had survived, it had been permanently eclipsed by the 'special relationship' with Washington, and Britain was no longer interested in France as a privileged, or indeed equal, partner. The General took due note.[75]

# 17

# Rights and Wrongs

Seen in retrospect, the tangled Anglo-French stories of the years of the Occupation, when Britain was physically as well as politically divided from its nearest Continental neighbour, have something of the structure of the classic novel or epic. They begin with defeat and disaster. There follows a period of trial and tribulation, in which the patience, courage and resolution of all concerned are well and truly tested. Finally there is the return and restoration, celebrated by Churchill and de Gaulle's walk down the Champs-Elysées. As in any story, the focus is on the testing middle period, which here was also characterised by a deep-seated ambivalence. The years 1940–4 saw the development of closer bonds of friendship between the two countries than in any previous period, yet at the same time official relations degenerated to a point only just short of open warfare. For the French it was sometimes unclear whether Britain was friend or enemy, a point graphically illustrated by the Darlan story. To French leaders in Vichy, Britain was a threat. To the many French men and women who tuned in nightly, the BBC French Service provided a lifeline. De Gaulle argued consistently in favour of the Entente, but his suspicions of les Anglais became increasingly ingrained.

Viewed from Whitehall, France had presented an almost continuous succession of problems. The most intractable was Vichy, whose uncertain and at times downright hostile policy had complicated the early and most difficult years of Britain's war. British military deficiencies ensured that its policy, was inherently short-term veering between expediency and principle, as between unrealistic hope and excessive fears.[1] London had no leverage over a French government which inclined to collaboration with Britain's enemy rather than a modus vivendi with its former ally while continuing to command the loyalty of its officials and officers. It was only once US military power entered the equation that there was any prospect of bringing Vichy leaders back to the Alliance. Until then, neither the menaces nor promises had any effect.

That said, the weakness of the British position vis-à-vis Vichy should not be exaggerated. While Britain remained a fighting power, Vichy represented little more than a rump state with a neutered fleet and an almost indefensible empire, whose policy was founded on the two false premises that Germany had won the war and would be willing to collaborate with its defeated rival. Obsessed with expansion to the east, as well as understandably distrustful of the French, Hitler, however, was never prepared to pay the political price which would have made serious military collaboration worthwhile. The one time he appeared willing briefly to do so with the Paris Protocols, Darlan's policy of military concessions to Germany was vetoed by determination of Weygand and other ministers, to keep Germany out of France's empire, by which time in fact Hitler already appears to have lost interest.

Vichy thus proved to be a political cul de sac, squeezed within an Anglo-German vice and with neither the resources nor the diplomatic skills to negotiate its survival in a world war. By the end of 1941, by which time both the Soviet Union and the USA had entered the war, Vichy's days were numbered. After the occupation of the whole of France in November 1942, and the subsequent disappearance of Darlan from the North African scene, it could be more or less safely ignored. By holding out in 1940, through BBC French Service broadcasts and its part in Operation Torch, Britain played a significant role in its demise.

Moreover, despite Vichy and the Germans, contact with the French, as opposed to France, had never been lost. If the old Entente had foundered in part over strategic divisions created by the Channel, its post-Armistice successor was made possible by the way in which, after June 1940, the same waterway allowed Britain to continue the war. The French side of the new entente was made up of a more or less coordinated coalition consisting of the Free French in London, Africa and the Levant, Resistance elements in France willing to help SOE or to provide intelligence to SIS, plus the larger French public who came to regard the BBC as 'their' radio.

Welcome, indeed vital, as this new Entente was for the British, at the political level it was to prove even more troublesome than its predecessor. Although these tensions came to focus around de Gaulle, it is important to try to make some distinction between personality and circumstance. If there was a clash of personalities between Churchill and de Gaulle, the fundamental problem lay in the friction inherent in the inequalities in terms of pride and self-confidence, as well as sheer power, between a Britain which had chosen to fight on and the initially tiny Free French movement which was desperately seeking to shake off the stigma of French capitulation. The leaders of an organisation such as the Free French, as de Gaulle had pointed out to Churchill on the occasion of their first big row in 1941, were of necessity going to be 'somewhat difficult people.' The same would probably have been true if the situation had been reversed and Churchill had found himself leader of the 'Free British.'

When it came to main bones of contention, de Gaulle was by no means alone in his deep-seated suspicions of the British designs on the French Empire, the main cause of the original deterioration in his relations with *les Anglais*. In this the French might have been fighting old battles, but the circumstances of the current conflict inevitably made those suspicions more acute. The other centre of Anglo-Free French dispute is at first sight more personal, namely de Gaulle's fight to establish his right to act as sole representative of Fighting France. This was rejected by the Foreign Office which, until 1942–3, quite reasonably argued that there was insufficient evidence of French support for the General to justify his claims. It was rejected by SOE and SIS who needed to be able to work with non-Gaullist elements in France. While the element of personal ambition certainly cannot be discounted, any other Free French leader, certainly any other strong Free French leader, would have been similarly anxious to establish and legitimate his position. In the process they would have run up against the same kind of bureaucratic opposition in London.

The point at which de Gaulle's personality became important was in the way he chose to fight the Free French corner. As President of the Fifth Republic in the late 1950s and 1960s, de Gaulle proved himself to be a skilled and sophisticated diplomat. During the war, by contrast, there was a raw and angry quality to his behaviour. De Gaulle was not only too poor to bow, he was temperamentally incapable of doing so. A master of psychological warfare, the General had little diplomatic sense of how to manage his patrons. Unable to appreciate that it was possible to be both firm and tactful and that compromise need not be equated with appeasement, he repeatedly overstepped the bounds of acceptable behaviour. To the despair of other members of the Free French movement, he often seemed neither to realise nor care how much he risked alienating his friends.[2]

Much of this was understood, if not exactly appreciated, in Whitehall. As a Foreign Office telegram of January 1943 put it, the General has small use for the normal processes of international intercourse and has more than once brought our relations near to breaking point. For all that we have in the end always had patience with him, for the sake of France, whose resistance he worthily represents and because, whether or not he is Anglophobe, he sincerely believes that Germany is the enemy who must be destroyed.[3]

The best way of dealing with the General's outbursts was for ministers and officials to grit their teeth and respond with the combination of firmness, understanding and patience shown by Eden and Charles Peake. The smallest act of courtesy or special kindness, as Macmillan noted, touched de Gaulle deeply.[4] A sense of humour also helped. Anger and indignation were best confined to paper; they still crackle through the old files and diaries.

This, however, was not a method that commended itself to everybody, least of all to Churchill, whose personality and restless activism too often served to compound the difficulties of Anglo-French relations. Churchill had been at his best in May and June 1940, seeking to bolster the Reynaud government's will to fight on and instinctively backing de Gaulle in the face of official British caution the moment France collapsed. Yet in 1943 and 1944, at the point when his initial judgement of the General was being vindicated, the Prime Minister turned passionately and irrationally against him. If the original fault lay with de Gaulle who quarrelled with the British rather than Churchill, the blame after the Anfa conference lay squarely with Churchill, whose quarrel was with de Gaulle.

At one level it is perhaps surprising that one of the most Francophile of British prime ministers came to quarrel so violently with the dominant French leader of his generation. But Churchill was an Englishman first and foremost, just as the General was first – and exclusively – a Frenchman. This ensured that once new wartime problems made themselves felt, both men found themselves entrapped within the mould of old Anglo-French suspicions and rivalries. It did not help that, like Spears, Churchill had become partially disillusioned with France after the collapse of 1940. 'Je cherche la France que j'aime,' he had told Pierre Viénot in April 1944.[5] A few months later he spoke of his 'illusions about France' having been greatly corroded.[6]

Churchill's main problem with de Gaulle, however, lay in the fact that, again like Spears, the Prime Minister personalised Anglo-French relations. Having saved and befriended de Gaulle in 1940, Churchill felt betrayed by the way in which the General had rounded on British officials over their handling of Syria and Lebanon. He thus came to see in de Gaulle not the plucky ally of June 1940, with whom he shared a common language of defiance, but an inveterate troublemaker and unreconstructed Anglophobe, whose accession to power in post-war France would be seriously detrimental to British interests.

This latter view was strengthened by the deep-seated hostility to the General reigning in Washington. That hostility, the most important of a whole series of Anglo-American differences over France, could be resisted, as the War Cabinet's refusal to break with de Gaulle in May 1943 underlines. It could also, at least at the local level, be managed, as Harold Macmillan demonstrated in Algiers. Churchill, however, showed little interest in doing either. The deference revealed by his correspondence with Roosevelt is only partially to be explained by an unwillingness to allow de Gaulle to complicate the 'special relationship' with Washington he had so assiduously cultivated. The Prime Minister was perfectly capable of fighting his corner with the Americans when he wanted to. But changing Roosevelt's mind was a very difficult business, and Churchill had no intention of wasting political capital with the President in the defence of a French leader he would rather be rid of. On the contrary, Roosevelt was an ally against the General, who could provide a useful alibi in his constant arguments over de Gaulle with the Foreign Office and the War Cabinet. Prime minister and president reinforced each other's annoyance over the General's failure, as the American historian Warren Kimball puts it, 'to accede docilely to their wishes.'[7]

Yet however foolish or ill judged Churchill's behaviour often seems, its influence, beyond making life difficult for everybody, was remarkably limited. Faced with determined Foreign Office or Cabinet opposition, the Prime Minister eventually always backed down. Emotional as he could be about the prospect of a de Gaulle government, Churchill was nothing if not ultimately a political realist. Nor did he ever lose his personal admiration for the General. As Macmillan shrewdly observed, the Prime Minister felt about his former protégé, 'like a man who has quarrelled with his son. He will cut him off with a shilling. But (in his heart) he would kill the fatted calf if only the prodigal would confess his faults and take his orders obediently in future.'[8] Churchill's later attitude to de Gaulle was a mixture of amusement and indignation.[9] To a later generation it all reads like great political drama, laced with comedy and a certain amount of downright pettiness. But that should not obscure the fact that this tempestuous relationship was part of the stress of the war, of its emotional history, which is every bit as real as the politics and strategy.

More important than the rights and wrongs of these highly personalised rows is the power and influence Britain exercised over the affairs of occupied France. Over and above its early weakness vis-à-vis Vichy, there were important things Britain could not do. It could not save French Jews. It could not on its own liberate France – for this it needed the prior attrition of the German army on the Eastern Front, plus substantial American support. France's Great Power status was beyond saving. Churchill had talked of restoring French greatness, but the best Britain could do was ensure that in 1945 France gained a seat on the United Nations Security Council, as well as an occupation zone in Germany.

What the British could do, in line with de Gaulle's prediction in his first broadcast of 18 June 1940, was to exploit their natural defensive advantages to ensure that the French defeat did not mean the end of the war and indefinite German hegemony over Europe, with all the evil consequences which this would have entailed for France. Far from enjoying the privileged position Vichy leaders sought within the new German empire, France would have been exposed and vulnerable, its democracy and self-respect crushed. Britain's continuation of the war after June 1940 bought time for resistance to emerge in France. The BBC helped sustain French morale and create a climate of dissidence in France. British resources, not least the BBC French Service, allowed de Gaulle to put himself on the French political map and then, via SOE's organisation and communications, to link his name with the Resistance movement.[10] In the wake of the political chaos brought about by the North Africa landings, British diplomacy helped mediate the emergence of a legitimate French authority, capable of taking over in the wake of liberation and preventing disorder and potential civil war in France. The following year Britain provided nearly half the troops landed in Normandy as well as the all-important logistic base for the operation.

The repercussions of Britain's wartime actions were to be felt well into the post-war era. In 1958 it was de Gaulle who prevented an army takeover in the face of the disastrous Algerian war and who established the Fifth Republic, which has provided the stability which both the pre-war Third and short-lived post-war Fourth Republics conspicuously lacked. Britain, in other words, had gone a long way towards redeeming the failures of policy that had culminated in the great Anglo-French defeat of 1940.

With the exception of a statue of de Gaulle outside his former Carlton Gardens headquarters, London bears little evidence of its status as a wartime

French capital in exile.[11] Indeed, the extent to which Britain succeeded in moulding the mid-century history of one of the most important countries of Continental Europe has never been fully registered on the English side of the Channel. The story of the wartime ententes has been submerged within the larger and more dramatic British narrative of the war, which concentrates on the military campaigns as well as the political relationship between the 'Big Three.' France thus appears intermittently as the country from which British forces withdrew in glorious disarray in May 1940, returning four years later en route to Germany. De Gaulle is known for his political rows with Churchill rather than as the vital ally who ensured the stable post-war France Britain needed. While much has been written in English about SOE, with its stories of clandestine deeds, personal bravery and betrayal, far less attention has been devoted to SIS, which remains largely inaccessible to historians, or the BBC French Service.

There is of course also a more political reason why the British role as a power in French affairs has remained largely obscured. In 1945, the Anglophile French journalist, Pierre Bourdan, who had been one of the earliest recruits of the BBC French Service, wrote that in the summer of 1940, 'England was more European than she has ever been, and she has ever been since, because she identified her own defence with the liberation of Europe.'[12] Yet what was remembered of the war was not the extraordinarily close engagement with the Continent that ensued but the moment when, following the defeat of France, Britain stood alone in its 'finest hour.' At the same time, the French defeat had fundamentally reorientated British strategic thinking from the Channel to the Atlantic, while leaving a certain disdain and contempt for the French in official British circles.[13] With France thus downgraded in terms of both priorities and regard, there was little incentive to dwell on what Britain had done for its cross-Channel neighbour.

In France Britain's help in first providing moral support during and then shortening the 'dark years,' which some Frenchmen in 1940 had feared might last a century, was much more widely acknowledged. Churchill's reception in Paris on 11 November 1944 had been spontaneous and genuine, and accorded with the sentiments of many BBC French Service listeners. In his last broadcast, Jacques Duchêne thanked Englishmen at the BBC 'because they knew not only to respect our freedom but how to organise it.'[14] The General too thanked the staff of the BBC, who, on their return to France in 1944, were treated as popular heroes. The BBC has a place in the French mythology of the war, which remains largely unknown in Britain.[15]

247

There is a rue Winston Churchill in Paris, as well as a full-sized statue of the wartime British prime minister, which stands close to that of General de Gaulle on the Champs-Elysées. Outside of Paris there are a number of memorials to members of British special forces, including a spectacular memorial inaugurated in 1991 in the small town of Valençay in the Loire Valley, to members of SOE's F-Section who died during the war. A number of officers were decorated by the French, and the daughter of one of them, Richard Pinder of F-Section, was given a signed photograph by de Gaulle, which the General is recalled as handing over with the words, 'La France est reconnaissante.'[16] A British diplomat, Sir Stephen Wall, was taken aback when in a major speech in the USA in 1982, President François Mitterrand turned to the British representative to pay tribute to the country which had stood alone against tyranny in 1940. At the sixty-fifth anniversary ceremonies in Normandy in 2009 to mark the D-Day landings, one British veteran remarked how French schoolchildren had come up to him to say thank you.[17] The seventieth anniversary of de Gaulle's first broadcast in 2011 was marked by a visit to the BBC studios in London by President Nicolas Sarkozy.

Yet, contrary to Louis Marin's prediction of August 1944, general French appreciation of Britain's role in the liberation did not ensure the closest Anglo-French relations for a generation; indeed, there was an inevitable ambivalence in French attitudes to their rescuers.[18] Not everybody was happy to acknowledge the extent of British help, whether for fear of having to acknowledge a consequent debt or of undermining the French role in their own liberation. A review published in the *Times Literary Supplement* in 1963 of four French books about the Resistance complained that all omitted the British role. Parachute deliveries of supplies were treated 'like rainstorms – things that just happen,' while Foot's 1966 *SOE in France*, intended to provide an authoritative account of British aid to the Resistance, failed to find a French publisher.[19] Some continued to nurse a grievance for Britain having fought on in 1940. As one French general told General Ismay in November 1944, 'there will be Frenchmen who will not forgive you for two generations. You made our shame so great by fighting on.'[20] Then there was the view reflected in a letter written from France to English friends in 1943. 'We are grateful to you for giving us the possibility of delivering our unhappy country from the German yoke, but we reproach you very, very much for your behaviour towards us at different times.'[21]

Paradoxically, this is probably least true of the group who suffered most: the friends and relatives of the victims of Allied wartime bombing operations. Between June 1940 and May 1945, some 600,000 tons of bombs were dropped on France, some 22 per cent of the total dropped by the RAF and USAAF in Europe. They cost some 67,078 French lives, out of the total of 470,000 French civilians who died in the war. Such attacks inevitably created anger. An eyewitness described how men and women emerged from the rubble of an attack on Lille on the night of 9/10 April 1944 in which 456 died, shouting 'Bastards, bastards.' It was partly to atone for this, as well as to say thank you for the French help to British aircrew, that the head of Bomber Command, Air Chief Marshall Sir Arthur Harris, established a small fund, financed from subscriptions from Bomber Command's members, for French children who had suffered from the bombing.[22] Overall, however, these casualties seem to have been accepted as the inevitable price France had to pay for the occupation and ultimate liberation.

The French also suffered some 10,000 killed and injured in the five hostile encounters between British and French forces between July 1940 and November 1942. The British casualties in the same encounters numbered some 4,370.[23] The most controversial of these remains Mers-el-Kébir. In Britain, the attack on the French fleet is more or less forgotten (though the story was included in 2006 in a BBC radio series entitled 'The Things We Forgot to Remember'). On the other side of the Channel it remains a taboo subject, approached, as one French historian wrote in 2007, 'with reticence and mistrust.'[24] Perhaps the fairest verdict is that of the American naval historian, Arthur Marder, that it was 'a case of right against right,' a point which de Gaulle had conceded publicly but privately sometimes denied.[25] The French lost far fewer ships, though not of course men, as a result of the British bombardment, than it did when the German attempt to seize the French fleet led to the mass scuttling in Toulon harbour in November 1942, but for the French navy the British attack was an act of betrayal, and Churchill received hate mail from France on the anniversary of the action.[26]

Vichy naturally also felt aggrieved by the British blockade, its repeated incursions into the French Empire and support for de Gaulle. Not much credit was given for the way in which continued British resistance to Hitler, together with the threat of secession in parts of the empire by Gaullist elements, allowed Vichy a certain latitude of diplomatic manoeuvre, deterring until November 1942 much more dangerous German and Italian encroachments on French territory. In the end, Britain had helped ensure that Vichy found itself on the wrong side of history, and that, apart from Mers-el-Kébir, its grievances would not outlast the war.

Much more pertinent for the international politics of the post-war era was that de Gaulle's attitude towards the country which had done much more to help than hinder him was deeply ambivalent. In a conversation after his Marrakech meeting with Churchill in January 1944, de Gaulle is reported to have said that Britain had been in a bad hole in the summer of 1940 and wondered 'whether we would have done as much for them had our positions been reversed.'[27] The General acknowledged his debts. His war memoirs include a particularly warm tribute to Eden, whom he described as having the art of 'creating and maintaining around the negotiation a sympathetic attitude which favoured agreement when that was possible and avoided wounds when it was not.'[28] As for Churchill, the General stressed that 'the harsh and painful incidents' that often arose between them had influenced his attitude to the Prime Minister but had not influenced his judgement.[29] 'Winston Churchill appeared to me, from one end of the drama to the other, as the great champion of a great enterprise, and the great artist of a great history.'[30]

On his return to power in 1958 (de Gaulle had resigned as Prime Minister in 1946), the General bestowed the Order of Liberation on Churchill. Although he himself set little store by such decorations, he was aware that Churchill did, and he personally decorated the former prime minister. Despite the General's sharp tongue, his son Philippe writes that he never heard his father denigrate Churchill.[31] In January 1965, during Churchill's last illness, de Gaulle talked about the former prime minister with the then British Ambassador, Sir Pierson Dixon. 'The impression he gave me,' Dixon noted in his diary, 'was a strange one. It was that in Winston he recognised perhaps one human being whose claim to greatness was stronger than his own. His attitude was if anything humble, and I have never noticed a trace of humility in the General before.'[32] De Gaulle subsequently wrote to Lady Churchill every year on the anniversary of her husband's death, until his own death in 1970.[33]

At the same time, of course, de Gaulle had a substantial charge sheet against his allies. It included, and the list is by no means complete, British negotiations with Vichy in 1940, interventions in Free French affairs on behalf of Admiral Muselier in 1941 and 1942, and Free French exclusion from the Madagascar North African and D-Day operations. There was the running sore of the Levant, which culminated in a crisis in May 1945, with the entry of British troops into Beirut after the the French opened artillery fire. Then there were the occasional restrictions on Free French broadcasts, repeated travel bans in 1942 and 1943 and hostile press and parliamentary briefings. At Anfa, Churchill had sought to subordinate de Gaulle to General Giraud. The Prime Minister subsequently tried to get rid of de Gaulle, and then allowed British policy regarding the recognition of the FCNL in 1943, its right to administer liberated France in 1944 and the GPRF's subsequent recognition as the legitimate government of France to be determined by American hostility towards the General.

This is not to suggest that the wrongs were exclusively on one side. On the contrary, the General was frequently the author of his own difficulties. British policy in Syria and Lebanon, while ambivalent and frequently insensitive, was never as Machiavellian as de Gaulle believed. But the General was not a man to forget a grievance, whether real or imagined. Harold Macmillan was to become only too well aware of this fact as Prime Minister in the late 1950s and early 1960s, when he again had dealings with de Gaulle. Their talks frequently began with complaints about British and American wartime policy, including Syria, the rows around D-Day and the French exclusion from the 1945 Yalta conference. 'Things,' Macmillan noted in his diary for 29 November 1961, 'would have been easier if Southern England had been occupied by the Nazis – if we'd had Lloyd George for Pétain, then we would have been equal.'[34]

Macmillan was not the only man to discover that the General had a long memory. In the wake of de Gaulle's 1963 veto of Britain's first application to join the Common Market, Paul Reynaud sent de Gaulle a letter of remonstrance, reminding him of Britain's role in saving France in the two world wars. The reply came in the form of an empty envelope, addressed in the General's hand, on the back of which was written, 'In case of absence please forward to Agincourt (Somme) or to Waterloo (Belgium).' When news of this reached the Foreign Office, the Permanent Under-Secretary, Sir Harold Caccia, who had been on Macmillan's staff in Algiers, minuted that 'de Gaulle will never forget or forgive us for the war.'[35]

That, however, seems too narrow a verdict. Certainly, the press conference in which the General had outlined his reasons for the veto suggests a settling of historic scores in the age-old rivalry between the cross-Channel neighbours, which in de Gaulle's eyes had continued during the war.[36] Churchill may have exaggerated, but he had been right to worry that a French government led by de Gaulle would be damaging to British interests. But what counted most with the General in 1963 was Britain's 'special relationship' with Washington. De Gaulle had been scarred by his wartime treatment by the

Americans, becoming obsessed with what he saw as the threat posed by post-war American hegemony to both France and Europe. Eden, who kept in touch with him after 1945, believed that the General's mindset had been fixed since November 1942, the month of Torch and the Darlan deal.[37] De Gaulle certainly never forgot Churchill's alleged declaration on the eve of D-Day that each time he had to choose between him and Roosevelt he would choose the latter; indeed, he repeated it to Macmillan shortly before the EEC veto.[38] Nor is it surprising that, having had his offer of a privileged partnership with Britain rejected by Churchill in November 1944, de Gaulle should have chosen instead to look in 1958 to Konrad Adenauer in West Germany.

Unlike Churchill, however, de Gaulle was capable of separating politics and personalities. His admiration for the British people and institutions, notably the British administrative machine's devotion to public service and its sense of cohesion, as also for the rule of law and freedom of a press which had done much to champion his wartime cause, remained. He paid a moving tribute on this theme in an address to the joint Houses of Parliament during a state visit to Britain in 1960. 'In a strange and complex way,' the British Embassy in Paris noted following the General's death in 1970, de Gaulle had a 'special relationship' with Britain. 'On him, as on all those European leaders who spent the war in London, an indelible mark was left.'[39] And it seems fitting that the General's last visit to the country where he had spent the three critical years of wartime exile and which had launched his own remarkable political career, was to attend the funeral of his great patron and adversary, Winston Churchill. France's recent history, as the General well knew, would have been very different without Churchill and the administration and country which he had led.

# Notes

## 1 'L'Entente Est Morte. Vive L'Entente!'

1.   Mark Pottle (ed.), *Champion Redoubtable* (London, 1998), p. 225.
2.   Charles de Gaulle, *The Complete War Memoirs* (New York, 1972), p. 39.
3.   Albert Speer, *Inside the Third Reich* (New York, 1970), pp. 170–1.
4.   David Garnett, *The Secret History of PWE* (London, 2002), p. 48; Alan Bullock, *Stalin and Hitler* (London, 1991), p. 743.
5.   David Reynolds, '1940: Fulcrum of the Twentieth Century,' *International Affairs*, April 1990, p. 329.
6.   William Langer, *Our Vichy Gamble* (New York, 1947), p. 3; Theodore Fontane, *Before the Storm* (Oxford, 1985), p. 256.
7.   Reynolds, '1940,' p. 328.
8.   Andrew Shennan, *The Fall of France* (Harlow, 2000), pp. 165–6.
9.   Robert Marjolin, *Memoirs* (London, 1989), p. 100.
10.  Robert Murphy, *Diplomat among Warriors* (London, 1964), p. 70; Julian Jackson, *France: The Dark Years* (Oxford, 2001), p. 142.
11.  Admiral Leahy, *I Was There* (London, 1950), pp. 53, 81.
12.  Jackson, *France*, p. 1; Jacques Crémieux-Brilhac, *Ici Londres: Les Voix de la liberté, 1940–44*, 5 vols. (Paris, 1975), vol. I, p. x; Shennan, *The Fall of France*, p. 126.
13.  Carmen Callil, *Bad Faith* (London, 2005), p. 214.
14.  Frederic Spotts, *The Shameful Peace* (New Haven, Conn., 2009), p. 4.
15.  Ian Buruma, 'Who Did Not Collaborate?,' *New York Review of Books*, 24 February 2011.
16.  Jackson, *France*, p. 185.
17.  Alex Danchev and Daniel Todman (eds.), *War Diaries, 1939–45: Field Marshall Lord Alanbrooke* (London, 2001), p. 105.
18.  *The Times*, 20 June 1940.
19.  Richard Overy, *The Battle* (London, 2000), pp. 108–9; *Fuehrer Conferences on Naval Affairs* (London, 1990), p. 119.
20.  Peter Unwin, *The Narrow Sea* (London, 2003), p. 258.
21.  Robert Mackay, *Half the Battle* (Manchester, 2002), p. 144; Général Catroux, *Dans la bataille de Méditerranée* (Paris, 1949), p. 29; David Reynolds, *In Command of History* (London, 2004), p. 204.
22.  J. R. M. Butler, *Grand Strategy* (London, 1957), vol. II, p. 209; Winston Churchill, *The Hinge of Fate* (London, 1951), pp. 388–90; Douglas Porch, *Hitler's Mediterranean Gamble* (London, 2004), p. 47.

23. Ashley Jackson, *The British Empire in the Second World War* (London, 2006), p. 173; Porch, *Hitler's Mediterranean Gamble*, p. 98; Martin Gilbert, *Finest Hour* (London, 1983), p. 1273.
24. Charles Williams, *The Last Great Frenchman* (London, 1993), p. 115.
25. Janet Teissier du Cros, *Divided Loyalties* (London, 1992), p. 95.
26. Andrew Roberts, *The Holy Fox* (London, 1991), p. 203.
27. De Gaulle, *Complete War Memoirs*, p. 57.
28. Danchev and Todman, *Alanbrooke War Diaries*, p. 200; Charles de Gaulle, *War Memoirs: Documents*, 3 vols. (London, 1959), vol. II, pp. 73–4; Elizabeth Barker, *Churchill and Eden* (London, 1978), p. 15.
29. Douglas Johnson, 'Churchill and France,' in Robert Blake and William Roger Louis (eds.), *Churchill* (Oxford, 1994), p. 43; Roy Jenkins, 'Churchill and France,' in Richard Mayne, Douglas Johnson, and Robert Tombs, *Cross Channel Currents* (London, 2004), p. 91.
30. Duff Hart-Davis, *King's Counsellor* (London, 2006), p. 231.
31. François Kersaudy, *Churchill and de Gaulle* (London, 1981), p. 30.
32. Paul Addison, cited by Vernon Bogdanor, 'In Churchill's Subterranean War Rooms,' *Financial Times*, 6/7 June 2009.
33. Jean Lacouture, *De Gaulle*, vol. I (London, 1993), p. 81.
34. Lacouture, *De Gaulle*, p. 146.
35. Lacouture, *De Gaulle*, pp. 144–5, 146.
36. Lacouture, *De Gaulle*, p. 186.
37. Nigel Nicolson (ed.), *Harold Nicolson, Letters and Diaries, 1939–45* (London, 1967), p. 289.
38. Peter Mangold, *The Almost Impossible Ally* (London, 2006), p. 27; M. R. D. Foot, *SOE in France* (London, 1966), p. 136; Lacouture, *De Gaulle*, p. 5; Leonard Miall, letter to the *Independent*, 28 June 1990.
39. Anthony Beevor and Artemis Cooper, *Paris after the Liberation* (London, 1994), p. 123.
40. PREM3/182/6, Despatch Algiers, 3 January 1944.
41. Institut Charles de Gaulle, *La France Libre* (Paris, 2005), p. 182.
42. Lacouture, *De Gaulle*, p. 220; Kersaudy, *Churchill and de Gaulle*, pp. 33–5; Eric Roussel, *Charles de Gaulle* (Paris, 2002), p. 951; Alain Peyrefitte, *C'était de Gaulle*, vol. I (Paris, 1994), p. 153.
43. Reynolds, '1940,' p. 332 (emphasis in original).
44. Paul Baudouin, *The Private Diaries of Paul Baudouin* (London, 1948), p. 161.
45. BBC Written Archives Centre (WAC), E2/193/5; BBC Intelligence Report, 18 December 1942.
46. FO371/36327, Despatch Makins, 13 September 1943; FO371/24312, tel., Beirut, 30 August 1940; Gloria Maguire, *Anglo-American Policy towards the Free French* (Basingstoke, 1995), p. 137.
47. Charles Dickens, *A Tale of Two Cities* (London, 2006), p. 5.
48. Matthew Cobb, *The Resistance* (London, 2009), pp. 291–2.
49. Martin Gilbert, *Churchill War Papers* (London, 1994), vol. II, pp. 690–1.

## 2   Historical Baggage

1. Peter Unwin, *The Narrow Sea* (London, 2004), pp. 1–3; William Shakespeare, *Richard II*, Act II, scene 1.

2. A. S. Byatt, *The Children's Book* (London, 2010), pp. 178–9.
3. Robert Tombs and Isabelle Tombs, *That Sweet Enemy* (London, 2006), pp. 99, 447.
4. Philip Bell, *France and Britain*, vol. I (Harlow, 1996), p. 105.
5. Sir John Glubb, *Story of the Arab Legion* (London, 1948), p. 342.
6. Tombs and Tombs, *That Sweet Enemy*, p. 425; Bell, *France and Britain*, p. 105.
7. Edward Spears, *Assignment to Catastrophe*, 2 vols. (London, 1954), vol. II, p. 21.
8. J. V. Keiger, *France and the World since 1870* (London, 2001), pp. 162–3; Bell, *France and Britain*, p. 11; François Kersaudy, *Churchill and de Gaulle* (London, 1981), p. 33.
9. Tombs and Tombs, *That Sweet Enemy*, p. 378.
10. Bell, *France and Britain*, p. 103; Robert Gibson, *Best of Enemies* (London, 1996), pp. 195–8, 278.
11. Gibson, *Best of Enemies*, pp. 38–9.
12. Gibson, *Best of Enemies*, pp. 38–9; Robert Gildea, *Marianne in Chains* (London, 2002), pp. 311–12.
13. Tombs and Tombs, *That Sweet Enemy*, p. 45.
14. Tombs and Tombs, *That Sweet Enemy*, pp. 245–8.
15. Linda Colley, *Britons: Forging the Nation* (London, 1992), pp. 24–5, 366–8.
16. Tombs and Tombs, *That Sweet Enemy*, pp. 340, 443.
17. Henri Brunschwig, 'Anglophobia and French African Policy,' in Prosser Gifford and William Roger Louis (eds.), *France and Britain in Africa* (New Haven, Conn., 1971), p. 28.
18. Bell, *France and Britain*, p. 10; Tombs and Tombs, *That Sweet Enemy*, pp. 453–4.
19. John Ramsden, *Don't Mention the War* (London, 2001), p. 47.
20. Bell, *France and Britain*, p. 49; Keith Wilson, *The Policy of the Entente* (Cambridge, 1965), p. 114.
21. Tombs and Tombs, *That Sweet Enemy*, p. 466.
22. Bell, *France and Britain*, p. 93.
23. Bell, *France and Britain*, pp. 63, 77–82.
24. Bell, *France and Britain*, p. 96.
25. Bell, *France and Britain*, pp. 72–3; Julian Jackson, *The Fall of France* (Oxford, 2003), p. 66.
26. Tombs and Tombs, *That Sweet Enemy*, p. 473; Bell, *France and Britain*, p. 100.
27. Tombs and Tombs, *That Sweet Enemy*, p. 498; FO371/28351, 'The Fulfilment of Our Military Obligations to France in the Present War.'
28. Paul Kennedy, *The Rise and Fall of Great Powers* (London, 1989), pp. 426, 430.
29. Tombs and Tombs, *That Sweet Enemy*, p. 483; Bell, *France and Britain*, pp. 226–7.
30. Keiger, *France and the World*, pp. 171–2; Anthony Adamthwaite, *Grandeur and Misery* (London, 1995), p. 98; George Melton, *Darlan* (Westport, Conn., 1998), p. 17.
31. Aviel Roshwald, *Estranged Bedfellows* (Oxford, 1990), p. 11.
32. Tombs and Tombs, *That Sweet Enemy*, pp. 514–15; Bell, *France and Britain*, pp. 126–7.
33. Richard Davis, 'Mesentente Cordiale: The Failure of Anglo-French Relations during the Ethiopian and Rhineland Crisis, 1934–36,' *European History*, October 1993, pp. 518, 523; Jackson, *The Fall of France*, p. 68.
34. Michael Dockrill, *British Establishment Perspectives on France, 1936–40* (Basingstoke, 1999), p. 53; Davis, 'Mesentente Cordiale,' p. 517; Bell, *France and Britain*, p. 220.
35. Dockrill, *British Establishment Perspectives*, p. 86; Peter Mangold, *Success and Failure in British Foreign Policy* (Basingstoke, 2001), p. 77.
36. Bell, *France and Britain*, p. 188.
37. Bell, *France and Britain*, pp. 201–3; Martyn Cornick '"*Faut-il réduire l'Angleterre en*

*esclavage?"* A Case Study of British Anglophobia,' *Franco-British Studies*, autumn 1992.

38. Tombs and Tombs, *That Sweet Enemy*, p. 533; Bell, *France and Britain*, pp. 215, 217; Anthony Adamthwaite, *France and the Coming of the Second World War* (London, 1977), p. 246.

39. Dockrill, *British Establishment Perspectives*, p. 114.

40. Bell, *France and Britain*, pp. 220–3.

41. Bell, *France and Britain*, pp. 226–7.

42. Bell, *France and Britain*, pp. 228–9.

43. Tombs and Tombs, *That Sweet Enemy*, p. 542; David Reynolds, '1940: Fulcrum of the Twentieth Century,' *International Affairs*, April 1990, p. 328.

44. Ernest May, *Strange Victory* (New York, 2000), pp. 277–8.

45. CAB66 (40) 145, 'Review of the Strategic Situation on the Assumption That Germany Has Decided to Seek a Decision in 1940,' 4 May 1940.

46. Martin Alexander, 'Fighting to the Last Frenchman,' in Joel Blatt (ed.), *The French Defeat of 1940* (Providence, RI, 1998), p. 315; Dockrill, *British Establishment Perspectives*, pp. 147–9.

47. Jackson, *The Fall of France*, p. 2.

48. J. Noakes and G. Pridham, *Nazism* (Exeter, 1988), vol. III, p. 762; May, *Strange Victory*, pp. 456–60.

49. Paul Baudouin, *The Private Diaries of Paul Baudouin* (London, 1948), p. 32.

50. John Harvey (ed.), *The Diplomatic Diaries of Oliver Harvey* (London, 1979), p. 370.

51. Spears, *Assignment to Catastrophe*, vol. I, p. 262; John Lukacs, *Five Days in London* (New Haven, Conn., 1999), pp. 87–9.

52. Lukacs, *Five Days in London*, pp. 17, 126; Bell, *France and Britain*, p. 222.

53. Winston Churchill, *Their Finest Hour* (London, 1949), p. 79; Reynolds, '1940,' p. 332.

54. Ian Kershaw, *Fateful Choices* (London, 2007), pp. 33–46.

55. Kershaw, *Fateful Choices*, p. 46; Martin Gilbert, *Finest Hour* (London, 1983), p. 468.

56. Martin Gilbert (ed.) *Winston Churchill War Papers*, vol. II (London, 1994), p. 252.

57. Warren F. Kimball (ed.), *Churchill and Roosevelt: The Complete Correspondence*, 3 vols. (Princeton, NJ, 1984), vol. I, p. 43.

58. Alex Danchev and Daniel Todman (eds.), *War Diaries, 1939–45: Field Marshall Lord Alanbrooke* (London, 2001), pp. 75, 87; Spears, *Assignment to Catastrophe*, vol. I, p. 52.

59. Gilbert, *Finest Hour*, p. 560.

60. Gilbert, *Finest Hour*, pp. 482–4, 560; Churchill, *Their Finest Hour*, pp. 127, 138; Lukacs, *Five Days in London*, p. 148.

61. Spears, *Assignment to Catastrophe*, vol. II, pp. 58, 158.

62. Eleanor Gates, *End of the Affair* (London, 1981), p. 112.

63. Gates, *End of the Affair*, p. 117; Nicholas Herman, *Dunkirk* (London, 1990), p. 50.

64. Baudouin, *Private Diaries*, p. 82; Harvey, *Diplomatic Diaries*, p. 373; Jackson, *The Fall of France*, p. 98.

65. Marc Ferro, *Pétain* (Paris, 1987), p. 50.

66. Gilbert, *Churchill War Papers*, vol. II, p. 281.

67. Spears, *Assignment to Catastrophe*, vol. I, p. 163.

68. Hanna Diamond, *Fleeing Hitler* (Oxford, 2007), pp. 7–10.

69. Antoine de Saint-Exupéry, *Flight to Arras* (Harmondsworth, 1961), p. 74.

70. Robert Paxton, *Vichy France* (New York, 2001), p. 15; Jackson, *The Fall of France*, pp. 174–7; Rod Kedward, *La Vie en bleu* (London, 2005), p. 246.

71. Churchill, *Their Finest Hour*, p. 137.
72. Gilbert, *Finest Hour*, p. 555.
73. PREM3/176, Salter memo, 'Anglo-French Unity', June 1940.
74. PREM3/176, Salter memo, 'Anglo-French Unity', June 1940.
75. PREM3/176, Amery to Churchill, 14 June 1940.
76. Maurice Druon, 'Franco-British Union:A Personal View,' in Robert Mayne, Douglas Johnson and Robert Tombs (eds.), *Cross Channel Currents: 100 Years of the Entente Cordiale* (London, 2004), p. 107; Churchill, *Their Finest Hour*, pp. 180, 182–4.
77. Sir John Colville, *The Fringes of Power* (London, 1985), pp. 159–60.
78. Avi Shlaim, 'Prelude to Downfall: The British Offer of Union to France, June 1940,' *Journal of Contemporary History*, July 1974, p. 56.
79. Shlaim, 'Prelude to Downfall,' p. 58; Léon Noel, 'Le Project d'union franco-britannique de juin 1940,' *Revue de l'Histoire de la Deuxième Guerre Mondiale*, January 1951, p. 31; Ferro, *Pétain*, p. 84; Jean Lacouture, *De Gaulle*, vol. I (London, 1993), p. 204.
80. Lacouture, *De Gaulle*, p. 204.
81. Baudouin, *Diaries*, p. 69; François Charles-Roux, *Cinq mois tragiques aux affaires étrangères* (Paris, 1949), p. 53.
82. David Ziman, *Instructions for British Servicemen in France* (1944, reprinted Oxford, 2005), p. 30.

### 3   A Ruthlessly Aggressive Act

1. FO371/24327, Foreign Office circular telegram, 15 June 1940.
2. FO371/24327, undated minute on tel., 15 June 1940.
3. Malcolm Muggeridge (ed.), *Ciano Diaries* (London, 1947), p. 267.
4. Maxime Weygand, *Recalled to Service* (London, 1952), p. 147.
5. Muggeridge, *Ciano Diaries*, p. 266.
6. *Documents on German Foreign Policy, 1918–45*, Series D (London, 1956–), vol. IX, p. 608.
7. Robert Paxton, *Parades and Politics at Vichy* (Princeton, NJ, 1966), p. 9.
8. Paul Baudouin, *The Private Diaries of Paul Baudouin* (London, 1948), p. 130; Arthur Marder, *From the Dardanelles to Oran* (Oxford, 1974), p. 193; Philip Bell, *France and Britain*, vol. II (Harlow, 1997), p. 13.
9. William Langer, *Our Vichy Gamble* (New York, 1947), pp. 48–9.
10. Marder, *From the Dardanelles*, p. 196.
11. Dominique Lormier, *Mers-el-Kébir* (Paris, 2007), pp. 116–17; *Documents on German Foreign Policy*, vol. X, p. 149.
12. David Brown, *The Road to Oran* (London, 2004), p. 116.
13. Ruth Ginio, *French Colonialism Unmasked* (Lincoln, Nebr., 2000), p. 12; Robert Aron, *The Vichy Regime* (London, 1958), p. 181; *Foreign Relations of the United States, 1940* (Washington, DC, 1957), vol. II, pp. 430–1.
14. FO371/28351, 'Relations with Vichy,' 20 December 1941.
15. Brown, *The Road to Oran*, p. 79.
16. CAB65/7, WM (40) 24 June 1940.
17. CAB65/7, WM (40), 24 June 1940, 178th; Llewellyn Woodward, *British Foreign Policy in the Second World War* (London, 1970), vol. I, pp. 313–14; Martin Mickelson, 'Operation Susan,' *Military Affairs*, October 1988, p. 193.
18. Andrew Cunningham, *A Sailor's Odyssey* (London, 1951), p. 244; Martin Gilbert, *Finest Hour* (London, 1983), p. 630; Bell, *France and Britain*, p. 13.

19. Marder, *From the Dardanelles*, p. 189.
20. George Melton, *Darlan* (Westport, Conn., 1998), pp. 25–6, 31, 62, 71; Winston Churchill, *Their Finest Hour* (London, 1948), p. 202.
21. Churchill, *Their Finest Hour*, pp. 202–3.
22. Marder, *From the Dardanelles*, p. 189; Edward Spears, *Assignment to Catastrophe*, vol. II (London, 1954), p. 306; Général Catroux, *Dans la bataille de la Méditerranée* (Paris, 1949), pp. 309–10.
23. Marder, *From the Dardanelles*, p. 199.
24. Brown, *The Road to Oran*, p. 161.
25. CAB65/13; WM (40), 22 June 1940, 176th; 24 June 1940, 180th.
26. Marder, *From the Dardanelles*, p. 213.
27. Marder, *From the Dardanelles*, pp. 212, 215.
28. Anthony Verrier, *Assassination in Algiers* (London, 1990), p. 40.
29. Churchill, *Their Finest Hour*, p. 207; Lormier, *Mers-el-Kébir*, p. 143; Edward Spears, *Two Men Who Saved France* (London, 1966), pp. 167–70.
30. Cunningham, *A Sailor's Odyssey*, p. 244.
31. Stephen Roskill, *Churchill and the Admirals* (London, 2004), pp. 151–2.
32. Warren Tute, *Reluctant Enemies* (London, 1990), p. 31; Marder, *From the Dardanelles*, p. 261; Hervé Coutau-Bégarie and Claude Huan, *Darlan* (Paris, 1989), pp. 122, 123, 129.
33. Harold Macmillan, *The Blast of War* (London, 1967), p. 265; PREM3/179/7: Alexander to Churchill, 26 December 1940; *La Délégation française auprès de la Commission Allemagne de l'Armistice*, vol. I (Paris, 1947) 17 July 1940.
34. John Winton, *Cunningham* (London, 1998), p. 89; Roskill, *Churchill and the Admirals*, pp. 154–6.
35. Philippe Lasterie, 'Could Admiral Gensoul Have Averted the Tragedy of Mers-el-Kébir?,' *Journal of Military History*, July 2004, p. 840.
36. Churchill, *Their Finest Hour*, pp. 208–9.
37. Churchill, *Their Finest Hour*, pp. 208–9.
38. Marder, *From the Dardanelles*, p. 246; Douglas Porch, *Hitler's Mediterranean Gamble* (London, 2004), p. 64.
39. Colin Smith, *England's Last War against France* (London, 2009), pp. 60, 65.
40. Lasterie, 'Gensoul,' p. 843; Gilbert, *Finest Hour*, pp. 636–7; Geoffrey Best, *Churchill* (London, 2001), p. 246; Roskill, *Churchill and the Admirals*, pp. 157–8.
41. Lormier, *Mers-el-Kébir*, p. 186. Lord Hastings Ismay, *Memoirs* (London, 1960), p. 149.
42. Gilbert, *Finest Hour*, p. 643; Marder, *From the Dardanelles*, p. 268.
43. Martin Gilbert, *Churchill's Darkest Decision*, Channel 4, May 2009; Best, *Churchill*, p. 246; Churchill, *Their Finest Hour*, p. 206.
44. Smith, *England's Last War*, p. 86.
45. Lormier, *Mers-el-Kébir*, p. 169.
46. Marder, *From the Dardanelles*, p. 271; Smith, *England's Last War*, p. 95; Gilbert, *Finest Hour*, pp. 642–3.
47. Paul Addison and James Crang (eds.), *Listening to Britain* (London, 2010), pp. 189, 192, 193, 203.
48. Muggeridge, *Ciano Diaries*, p. 274.
49. James Leutze (ed.), *The London Observer* (London, 1971), p. 11; Marder, *From the Dardanelles*, p. 217; Ian Kershaw, *Fateful Choices* (London, 2007), p. 213; David Reynolds, *The Creation of the Anglo-American Alliance* (London, 1981), pp. 112–13, 119.

50. François Charles-Roux, *Cinq mois tragiques aux affaires étrangères* (Paris, 1949), p. 144; Porch, *Hitler's Mediterranean Gamble*, p. 67; Gilbert, *Finest Hour*, p. 643.
51. *Documents on German Foreign Policy*, vol. X, p. 149.
52. Porch, *Hitler's Mediterranean Gamble*, pp. 68–9; Eberhard Jaeckel, *Frankreich in Hitler's Europa* (Stuttgart, 1966), p. 56.
53. André Gide, *Journals* (Harmondsworth, 1967), p. 648.
54. 'Anglo-French Policy towards Darlan and the Vichy Administration,' *Franco-British Studies*, spring 1989, p. 59.
55. Albert Kammerer, *La Passion de la flotte française* (Paris, 1951), p. 210.
56. Paul Auphan and Jacques Mordal, *La Marine française pendant la seconde guerre mondiale* (Paris, 1958), pp. 172–3; Charles-Roux, *Cinq mois*, p. 124.
57. Adrienne Doris Hytier, *Two Years of French Foreign Policy* (Paris, 1958), p. 61.
58. Yves Bouthillier, *Le Drame de Vichy* (Paris, 1950), pp. 151–2; Baudouin, *Diaries*, pp. 157, 161.
59. Kammerer, *Passion*, pp. 182, 199, 206–9; Paxton, *Parades and Politics*, pp. 72–5; Desmond Dinan, *The Politics of Persuasion* (Lanham, Md., 1988), pp. 26–7; FO371/24349, Vansittart Committee, 15 July 1940.
60. Baudouin, *Diaries*, p. 193.
61. Richard Minear, *Dr. Seuss Goes to War* (New York, 1999), pp. 158–60.
62. Baudouin, *Diaries*, p. 139.
63. Ian Ousby, *Occupation* (London, 1999), p. 77.
64. Charles Williams, *Pétain* (London, 2005), pp. 338–9.
65. *Foreign Relations of the United States, 1940*, vol. II, p. 379; Charles-Roux, *Cinq mois*, pp. 301, 303.
66. CAB65/7, WM (40) 19 June 1940; Philip Bell, *A Certain Eventuality* (Farnborough, 1974), pp. 89–90.
67. Marc Ferro, *Pétain* (Paris, 1987), pp. 90–5; Weygand, *Recalled to Service*, pp. 216–18; Robert Paxton, *Vichy France* (New York, 2001), p. 16.
68. Andrew Shennan, *The Fall of France* (Harlow, 2000), p. 16.
69. CAB65/7, WM (40), 24 June 1940, 180th; Churchill, *Their Finest Hour*, pp. 193–4.
70. Ben Pimlott, *The Second World War Diaries of Hugh Dalton* (London, 1986), p. 480.

## 4   Rebel and Empire

1. Laurence Hartwell, 'De Gaulle's Free French Army,' *Newlyn Fishing News*, 24 February 2010.
2. Hanna Diamond, *Fleeing Hitler* (Oxford, 2007), pp. 126–9; Nicholas Atkin, *The Forgotten French* (Manchester, 2003), p. ix.
3. Atkin, *The Forgotten French*, pp. ix, 122; Charles de Gaulle, *The Complete War Memoirs* (New York, 1972), pp. 89–90; Philip Bell, *A Certain Eventuality* (Farnborough, 1974), pp. 196–7.
4. Atkin, *The Forgotten French*, p. 129.
5. *The Times*, 9 June 1940.
6. John Colville, *The Fringes of Power* (London, 1985), p. 159.
7. Colville, *The Fringes of Power*, p. 160.
8. Philip Bell, 'La Grande Bretagne, de Gaulle et les françaises libres,' *Espoir*, June 1996, p. 33.
9. Philippe de Gaulle, *De Gaulle mon père* (Paris, 2003), p. 143.
10. De Gaulle, *The Complete War Memoirs*, p. 81.

11. De Gaulle, *The Complete War Memoirs*, p. 81.
12. Philippe de Gaulle, *Mon père*, p. 147; Robert Marjolin, *Memoirs* (London, 1989), p. 98.
13. CAB65/7, WM (40), 18 June 1940, 171st.
14. FO371/24348, Strang minute, 19 June 1940.
15. Bell, *A Certain Eventuality*, p. 94.
16. CAB65/7, WM (40), 23 June 1940, 177th.
17. Nigel Nicolson (ed.), *Harold Nicolson, Letters and Diaries, 1939–45* (London, 1967), pp. 98–9; François Duchêne, *Jean Monnet* (New York, 1994), p. 81.
18. CAB65/7, WM (40), 27 June 1940, 184th.
19. *The Times*, 28 June 1940; David Dilks (ed.), *The Diaries of Sir Alexander Cadogan, 1938–45* (London, 1971), p. 302.
20. Jean Lacouture, *De Gaulle* (London, 1984), vol. I, p. 243.
21. *Spears Papers*, Box 9, draft book on de Gaulle, p. 83.
22. FO371/24349, Ismay to Sargent, 29 June 1940, FO tel., 3 July 1940.
23. Bell, *A Certain Eventuality*, pp. 102–3.
24. Martin Gilbert, *Churchill War Papers* (London, 1994), vol. II, p. 508.
25. Atkin, *The Forgotten French*, p. 10.
26. Richard Mayne, Douglas Johnson and Robert Tombs (eds.), *Cross Channel Currents* (London, 2004), p. 119; *The Times*, 24 June 1940; G. H. Bennett, 'The RAF's Free French Fighter Squadrons,' *Global War Studies*, 7 (2) (2010): 73–4.
27. FO892/15, FO to High Commissioners, Western Pacific, 14 August 1940.
28. William Hitchcock, 'Pierre Boisson, French West Africa and the Postwar *Epuration*,' *French Historical Studies*, spring 2001, p. 312.
29. François Charles-Roux, *Cinq mois tragiques aux affaires étrangères* (Paris, 1949), p. 68; Hervé Coutau-Bégarie and Claude Huan, *Dakar* (Paris, 2004), p. 21.
30. FO371/284311, circular telegram, 17 June 1940; FO371/24327, circular instructions to authorities in French Empire, 23 June 1940.
31. *Foreign Relations of the United States* (Washington, DC, 1957), 1940, vol. II, p. 571; Aviel Roshwald, *Estranged Bedfellows* (Oxford, 1990), p. 13; Marjolin, *Memoirs*, p. 99.
32. FO371/24327, tel. no. 8, Military Mission, 25 June 1940; FO371/34328, tels. Algiers, 27 June 1940, and Rabat, 29 June 1940.
33. Hitchcock, 'Pierre Boisson,' p. 313; Gerhard Weinberg, *A World at Arms* (London, 1994), p. 160.
34. Alexander Kirkbride, *A Crackle of Thorns* (London, 1956), p. 145.
35. Lacouture, *De Gaulle*, vol. I, p. 212.
36. Harold Macmillan, *The Blast of War* (London, 1967), pp. 282–3; Dinan, *Persuasion*, p. 22; Robert Paxton *Parades and Politics at Vichy* (Princeton, NJ, 1966), p. 345.
37. Gilbert, *Finest*, pp. 630–1; Mickelson, 'Operation Susan,' *Military Affairs*, October 1988, p. 195; PREM3/416; War Cabinet, Chiefs of Staff Committee, 'Operation Catapult: Revised Draft Report,' 1 July 1940; FO371/24349, Committee on French Resistance, 29 June 1940.
38. Roshwald, *Estranged Bedfellows*, p. 16; Hitchcock, 'Pierre Boisson,' pp. 316–17.
39. Dinan, *Persuasion*, p. 45; CAB65/14, WM (40), 5 August 1940, 219th.
40. Winston Churchill, *Their Finest Hour* (London, 1949), p. 421.
41. Coutau-Bégarie and Huan, *Dakar*, pp. 8–9; Dinan, *Persuasion*, p. 51.
42. Dinan, *Persuasion*, p. 51; Churchill, *Their Finest Hour*, p. 422; Arthur Marder, *Operation Menace* (Oxford, 1971), p. 10.
43. Maxime Weygand, *Recalled to Service* (London, 1952), p. 257; Doris Hytier, *Two Years of French Foreign Policy* (Paris, 1958), pp. 85–6.
44. Dinan, *Persuasion*, p. 51.

45.  De Gaulle, *Complete War Memoirs*, pp. 115–16.
46.  De Gaulle, *Complete War Memoirs*, pp. 105–6; de Gaulle, *Mon père*, p. 201; Dinan, *Persuasion*, p. 50.
47.  Marder, *Operation Menace*, pp. 26, 27, 56–7; Churchill, *Their Finest Hour*, p. 422.
48.  CAB65/14, WM (40), 5 August 1940, 219th; 13 August 1940, 225th; Selina Hastings, *Evelyn Waugh* (London, 1994), p. 405.
49.  Coutau-Bégarie and Huan, *Dakar*, p. 92.
50.  Bell, *A Certain Eventuality*, p. 200.
51.  *Fuehrer Conferences on Naval Affairs* (London, 2005), p. 135.
52.  Paxton, *Parades and Politics*, pp. 79, 92.
53.  Churchill, *Their Finest Hour*, pp. 293–6.
54.  Warren Tute, *Reluctant Enemies* (London, 1990), p. 111; CAB65/15, WM (40), 16 September 1940, 250th; 17 September 1940, 252nd; Martin Gilbert, *Finest Hour* (London, 1983), pp. 787–90; Churchill, *Their Finest Hour*, pp. 427–8.
55.  Churchill, *Their Finest Hour*, p. 437.
56.  Marder, *Operation Menace*, pp. 129–30.
57.  André Béziat, *Franklin Roosevelt et la France* (Paris, 1997), pp. 111–12; CAB65/15, WM (40), 258th; Minute 2, 25 September 1940.
58.  Marder, *Operation Menace*, p. 158.
59.  Jacques Crémieux-Brilhac, *Ici Londres: les voix de la liberté*, 5 vols. (Paris, 1975), vol. I, p. 97; Churchill, *Their Finest Hour*, p. 436.
60.  Paul Auphan and Jacques Mordal, *La Marine française pendant la seconde guerre mondiale* (Paris, 1958), p. 238; Yves Bouthillier, *Le Drame de Vichy* (Paris, 1950), pp. 183–4; François-Georges Dreyfus, *Histoire de Vichy* (Paris, 1990), pp. 321–2.
61.  Martyn Cornick, 'Fighting Myth with Reality,' in Valerie Holman and Debra Kelly (eds.), *France at War* (Oxford, 2000), p. 73; Hitchcock, 'Pierre Boisson,' p. 319; Hytier, *Two Years*, p. 94.
62.  Tute, *Reluctant Enemies*, pp. 123–4.
63.  Eric Roussel, *Charles de Gaulle* (Paris, 2002), pp. 182–3.
64.  Colonel Passy, *Souvenirs* (Monte Carlo, 1947), vol. I, p. 95.
65.  François Kersaudy, *Churchill and de Gaulle* (London, 1981), p. 103.
66.  David Reynolds, *In Command of History* (London, 2004), p. 197.
67.  Bouthillier, *Le Drame de Vichy*, p. 163.

### 5 Modus Vivendi or Collaboration?

1.  *Foreign Relations of the United States*, 1940, vol. II, pp. 465–6; François Charles-Roux, *Cinq mois tragiques aux affaires étrangères* (Paris, 1949), p. 81.
2.  Charles-Roux, *Cinq mois*, p. 299; Paul Baudouin, *The Private Diaries of Paul Baudouin* (London, 1948), p. 185; Yves Bouthillier, *Le Drame de Vichy* (Paris, 1950), pp. 155–6; Hervé Coutau-Bégarie and Claude Huan, *Lettres et notes de l'Amiral Darlan* (Paris, 1992), p. 246.
3.  Baudouin, *Diaries*, pp. 185, 207–8; Charles-Roux, *Cinq mois*, p. 323; Doris Hytier, *Two Years of French Foreign Policy* (Paris, 1958), pp. 90–3; J. B. Duroselle, *L'Abîme* (Paris, 1982), p. 274.
4.  Charles-Roux, *Cinq mois*, p. 302; Philip Bell, *A Certain Eventuality* (Farnborough, 1974), p. 200.
5.  Geoffrey Warner, *Pierre Laval and the Eclipse of France* (London, 1968), p. 223; FO371/28346, tels. 3 and 13 September 1940; Baudouin, *Diaries*, pp. 198, 239.

6. Claude Huan, 'Les Négociations Franco-Britanniques de l'automne 1940,' *Guerres Mondiales et Conflits Contemporains*, October 1994; p. 142; ADM223/487, tel. naval attaché Madrid, 5 September 1940; naval attaché to Hoare, 5 September 1940.

7. Martin Thomas, *The French Empire at War* (Manchester, 1998), p. 75; CAB66/12, WP (40) 376, 'Position Towards the Vichy Government,' Admiralty memo, 29 September 1940; ADM223/487, minute, 28 September 1940.

8. PREM3/186A/1, Churchill to First Sea Lord, undated.

9. Andrew Roberts, *The Holy Fox* (London, 1991), p. 263; David Dilks (ed.), *The Diaries of Sir Alexander Cadogan, 1938–45* (London, 1971), p. 327.

10. CAB66/12, memo, 27 September 1940.

11. CAB65/15, WM (40), 1 October 1940, 263rd.

12. Samuel Hoare, *Ambassador on Special Mission* (London, 1946), p. 83; Charles-Roux, *Cinq mois*, p. 216.

13. CAB65/9, WM (40), 2 September 1940, 239th; Winston Churchill, *Their Finest Hour* (London, 1949), p. 460; Hoare, *Ambassador on Special Mission*, p. 86.

14. Hoare, *Ambassador on Special Mission*, pp. 87–8; FO371/28346, tel., 3 September 1940.

15. FO371/28346, Foreign Office to Madrid, 3 October 1940; Bell, *A Certain Eventuality*, pp. 222–4.

16. Martin Gilbert (ed.), *Churchill War Papers* (London, 1994), vol. II, p. 969.

17. Churchill, *Their Finest Hour*, pp. 451–3.

18. Robert Frank, 'Vichy et les Britanniques, 1940–41: Double jeu ou double language?' in J. P. Azema and François Béderida (eds.), *Le régime de Vichy et les Français* (Paris, 1992), pp. 145–6; Charles-Roux, *Cinq mois*, pp. 343, 345, 347, 349; Hoare, *Ambassador on Special Mission*, p. 88.

19. François Delpla, 'Du nouveau sur la mission Rougier,' *Guerres Mondiales et Conflits Contemporains*, April 1995, p. 112; Churchill, *Their Finest Hour*, p. 450; FO371/42044, Morton to 'C,' 27 April 1944; FO371/24361, Strang memo, 25 October 1940.

20. FO371/42044, Morton to Churchill, 25 October 1940.

21. Frank, 'Vichy et les Britanniques,' pp. 148–9; Thomas, *French Empire*, p. 90.

22. Baudouin, *Diaries*, pp. 274–5; Bouthillier, *Le Drame de Vichy*, p. 219; Delpla, 'Du nouveau sur la mission Rougier,' p. 112; Huan, 'Les Négociations,' p. 145; François-George Dreyfus, *Histoire de Vichy* (Paris, 1990), p. 326.

23. Hytier, *Two Years of French Foreign Policy*, p. 138.

24. Hytier, *Two Years of French Foreign Policy*, pp. 139–40; FO371/24348, Interview Laval and American journalist, undated November? December 1941; *Documents on German Foreign Policy*, vol. XI, p. 253.

25. *Documents on German Foreign Policy*, vol. XI, p. 253.

26. Eberhard Jaeckel, *Frankreich in Hitler's Europa* (Stuttgart, 1966), pp. 103–4; Ian Kershaw, *Fateful Choices* (London, 2007), pp. 76–7.

27. Kershaw, *Fateful Choices*, p. 79; Michael Salewski, *Die Deutsche Seekriegsleitung, 1935–45* (Frankfurt, 1970), vol. I, p. 305.

28. *Documents on German Foreign Policy*, vol. XI, p. 212–13.

29. Ian Kershaw, *Hitler* (London, 2000), vol. II, p. 328.

30. *Documents on German Foreign Policy*, vol. XI, p. 213; Kershaw, *Decisions*, p. 82.

31. Marc Ferro, *Pétain* (Paris, 1987), p. 177; Hans-Adolf Jacobsen, *Kriegestagebuch der Oberkammandos der Wehrmacht* (Frankfurt, 1965), vol. I, p. 135; *Documents on German Foreign Policy*, vol. XI, p. 416.

32. *Documents on German Foreign Policy*, vol. XI, pp. 401–2; Philippe Burrin, *Living with Defeat* (London, 1991), p. 100.

33. Jaeckel, *Frankreich*, p. 114; Charles Burchik and Hans-Adolf Jacobsen, *The Halder War Diaries* (London, 1988), pp. 273, 284.
34. *Documents on German Foreign Policy*, vol. XI, pp. 412–16.
35. *Documents on German Foreign Policy*, vol. XI, p. 416.
36. *Documents on German Foreign Policy*, vol. XI, p. 528.
37. Robert Paxton, *Parades and Politics at Vichy* (Princeton, NJ, 1966), pp. 87–91; Jacobsen, *Kriegestagebuch*, pp. 984–94.
38. Maxime Weygand, *Recalled to Service* (London, 1952), pp. 351–2; Thomas, *French Empire*, p. 82; Charles-Roux, *Cinq mois*, p. 185; Hervé Coutau-Bégarie and Claude Huan, *Darlan* (Paris, 1989), p. 342; Burrin, *Defeat*, p. 109; Salewski, *Seekriegsleitung*, vol. I, pp. 243–4.
39. FO371/24361, War Cabinet, 28 November 1940; FO371/28346, Halifax to Hoare, 1 November 1940.
40. FO371/28346, tel., Madrid, 4 November 1940; Halifax to Hoare, 7 November 1940.
41. Warren F. Kimball (ed.), *Churchill and Roosevelt: The Complete Correspondence*, 3 vols. (Princeton, NJ, 1984), vol. I, pp. 79, 91.
42. William Langer, *Our Vichy Gamble* (New York, 1947), p. 97.
43. FO371/28346, George VI to Pétain, 25 October 1940.
44. Martin Gilbert, *Finest Hour* (London, 1983), p. 866.
45. John Kent, *The Internationalisation of Colonialism* (Oxford, 1992), pp. 52–3.
46. John Colville, *The Fringes of Power* (London, 1985), p. 288.
47. CAB65/10, WM (40), 6 November 1940, 283rd; Llewellyn Woodward, *British Foreign Policy in the Second World War* (London, 1970), vol. I, p. 424; Bell, *A Certain Eventuality*, pp. 232–4; Martin Thomas, 'The Anglo-French Divorce and the Limitations of Strategic Planning over West Africa,' *Diplomacy and Statecraft*, (1) (1995), p. 271; Dilks, *Cadogan Diaries*, p. 334.
48. Churchill, *Their Finest Hour*, pp. 466–7.
49. Churchill, *Their Finest Hour*, pp. 466–7.
50. Roberts, *Holy Fox*, p. 263; CAB66/13, 'Relations with Vichy,' memo by the Foreign Secretary, 13 November 1940; FO371/28346, Halifax to Hoare, 7 November 1940.
51. FO37128346, Halifax to Hoare, 7 November 1940.
52. Woodward, *British Foreign Policy*, vol. I, p. 426.
53. FO371/28361, Cadogan minute, 12 December 1940.
54. CAB66/14, WP (40), 488, 'Contacts with the Vichy Government,' memo by the Foreign Secretary, 19 December 1940; FO371/42044, Mack to Morton, 19 July 1944.
55. Dilks, *Cadogan Diaries*, p. 339; R. T. Thomas, *Britain and Vichy* (London, 1979), p. 75.
56. Churchill, *Their Finest Hour*, p. 467; Burchik and Jacobsen, *Halder Diaries*, p. 307.
57. Huan, 'Les Négociations,' p. 148.
58. *Fuehrer Conferences on Naval Affairs* (London, 2005), pp. 165, 171.
59. Woodward, *British Foreign Policy*, vol. I, pp. 427–8.
60. FO371/32043, Cadogan minute, 4 April 1942; Thomas, *Britain and Vichy*, pp. 77, 81.
61. Gilbert, *Finest Hour*, pp. 957–8; Gaston Schmitt, *Les Accords secrets Franco-Britanniques de novembre–décembre 1940* (Paris, 1957), p. 101.
62. Thomas, *Britain and Vichy*, p. 57; *Documents on German Foreign Policy*, vol. XI, p. 416; FO371/28234, 'Dupuy Report: Visit to Vichy'; Huan, 'Les Négociations,' p. 154.
63. *Fuehrer Conferences*, p. 160.
64. Churchill, *Their Finest Hour*, pp. 550–1.

65. Churchill, *Their Finest Hour*, pp. 550–1; Bouthillier, *Le Drame de Vichy*, p. 282; Gilbert, *Churchill War Papers*, vol. III, pp. 41–2.

66. *Fuehrer Conferences*, p. 171.

67. PREM3186/A 5, draft message to Weygand, 23 July 1940.

68. J. R. M. Butler, *Grand Strategy* (London, 1957), vol. II; Gilbert, *Finest Hour*, p. 867; ADM223/487, Mittelman interviews at Weygand's headquarters.

69. Albert Kammerer, *La Passion de la flotte française* (Paris, 1951), pp. 313, 315; Thomas, *Britain and Vichy*, pp. 84–5; Schmitt, *Accords secrets*, pp. 118–19.

70. ADM223/487, Mittelman interviews at Weygand's headquarters.

71. Desmond Dinan, *The Politics of Persuasion* (Lanham, Md., 1988), p. 80.

72. Robert Aron, *The Vichy Regime* (London, 1958), p. 185; Thomas, *Britain and Vichy*, p. 83; W0193/182, 'Attitude of Gen. Weygand,' 8 November 1940; FO371/28464, minute on Weygand speech, Dakar, 29 October 1940.

73. Weygand, *Recalled to Service*, pp. 292, 360.

74. Langer, *Vichy Gamble*, p. 121; Thomas, *Britain and Vichy*, p. 85; FO892/105, message for Catroux, 28 January 1941; CAB65/16, WM (40), 311th; ADM223/487, Mittelman interviews at Weygand's headquarters; Robert Paxton, 'Le Régime de Vichy était-il neutre?' *Guerres Mondiales et Conflits Contemporains*, December 1994, pp. 160–1.

75. W. N. Medlicott, *The Economic Blockade* (London, 1952), vol. I, p. 562.

76. Frank, 'Vichy et les Britanniques,' p. 115.

77. Gilbert, *Churchill War Papers*, vol. III, p. 208.

78. Gilbert, *Churchill War Papers*, vol. III, p. 240.

79. Thomas, *Britain and Vichy*, pp. 88–9.

80. ADM199/1279, 'France, French Colonies and the Free French,' 31 October 1941; Coutau-Bégarie and Huan, *Darlan*, p. 479.

81. Gilbert, *Churchill War Papers*, vol. III, pp. 220, 358.

82. PREM3/186a/7, Churchill to Lampson, 3 April 1941; Nigel Nicolson, *Harold Nicolson, Letters and Diaries, 1939–45* (London, 1967), p. 156.

83. Langer, *Vichy Gamble*, p. 117.

84. Thomas, *Britain and Vichy*, pp. 102–3; Dinan, *Persuasion*, pp. 176–80; *Foreign Relations of the United States, 1941* (Washington, DC, 1959), vol. II, p. 169.

85. Gilbert, *Churchill War Papers*, vol. III, pp. 442–4.

86. Churchill, *Their Finest Hour*, pp. 456–7; Winston Churchill, *The Grand Alliance* (London, 1950), pp. 113–16.

87. Kammerer, *La Passion*, pp. 369–72.

88. Hytier, *Two Years of French Foreign Policy*, p. 247; Coutau-Bégarie and Huan, *Darlan*, pp. 296, 326; Salewski, *Seekriegsleitung*, vol. I, pp. 346–7; *Fuehrer Conferences*, pp. 188–9.

89. FO371/28217, Interview Pétain-Leahy, 3 May 1941; FO371/28348, Foreign Office to Washington, 29 April 1941.

90. FO/37128218, Mack minute, 7 May 1941; FO371/28215, 22 January 1941, tel., Washington, 17 January 1941; FO371/28215, 'Developments at Vichy,' 6 February 1941, memo circulated to Cabinet.

91. FO371/28218, tel., Washington, 15 May 1941, and minuting.

92. Dilks, *Cadogan Diaries*, p. 375.

93. *Documents on German Foreign Policy*, vol. XIII, p. 34.

94. Michel-Christian Davet, *La Double Affaire de Syrie* (Paris, 1967), p. 72; Jacques Benoist-Méchin, *De la défaite au désastre* (Paris, 1984), p. 70.

95. Coutau-Bégarie and Huan, *Darlan*, p. 327.

96. Coutau-Bégarie and Huan, *Darlan*, pp. 341–6.

97. Coutau-Bégarie and Huan, *Darlan*, pp. 341–6.

98. Davet, *La Double Affaire*, pp. 73–5; Julian Jackson, *France: The Dark Years* (Oxford, 2001), p. 179.
99. Jackson, *France*, p. 179; Duroselle, *L'Abîme*, p. 286; Dreyfus, *Histoire de Vichy*, p. 425.
100. Jaeckel, *Frankreich*, p. 168.
101. Davet, *La Double Affaire*, p. 114.
102. *Documents on German Foreign Policy*, vol. XII, p. 782.
103. Benoist-Méchin, *Désastre*, pp. 116–17; I. S. O. Playfair, *The Mediterranean and Middle East* (London, 1952), vol. I, p. 53; Coutau-Bégarie and Huan, *Darlan*, p. 433; Duroselle, *L'Abîme*, p. 286.
104. Jaeckel, *Frankreich*, pp. 169–71; George Melton, *Darlan* (Westport, Conn., 1998), p. 113; Stephen Roskill, *The War at Sea* (London, 1954), vol. I, p. 479; Kent, *Internationalisation*, p. 58.
105. Hytier, *Two Years of French Foreign Policy*, p. 263; Benoist-Méchin, *Désastre*, pp. 125–6.
106. Langer, *Vichy Gamble*, pp. 158–9; Duroselle, *L'Abîme*, p. 288; Weygand, *Recalled to Service*, p. 327; Dreyfus, *Histoire de Vichy*, p. 438; Jaeckel, *Frankreich*, p. 174.
107. Jaeckel, *Frankreich*, p. 173; Dreyfus, *Histoire de Vichy*, p. 434; *Documents on German Foreign Policy*, vol. XII, pp. 802–3, 943 and vol. XIII, p. 34; Robert Melka, 'Darlan between Britain and Germany,' *Journal of Contemporary History*, April 1973, p. 71.

## 6 Unfriendly States

1. Jacques Benoist-Méchin, *De la défaite au désastre* (Paris, 1984), pp. 68–9, 87–8.
2. Geoffrey Warner, *Iraq and Syria* (London, 1974), p. 34.
3. Aviel Roshwald, *Estranged Bedfellows* (Oxford, 1990), pp. 44–5; Max Egremont, *Under Two Flags* (London, 1997), pp. 221–2.
4. Adrienne Hytier, *Two Years of French Foreign Policy* (Paris, 1958), pp. 278–9; André Laffargue, *Le Général Dentz* (Paris, 1954), p. 36; Howard Sachar, *Europe Leaves the Middle East* (New York, 1972), pp. 183–4.
5. FO371/27322, tel., Beirut, 4 May 1941; FO371/27290, Wavell to Chief of the Imperial General Staff, 28 April 1941; Laffargue, *Dentz*, pp. 51–3.
6. Anthony Eden, *The Reckoning* (London, 1965), p. 249.
7. Winston Churchill, *Grand Alliance* (London, 1950), pp. 288, 291; PREM3/422/6, Churchill to Ismay, 8 May 1941; Warner, *Iraq and Syria*, p. 132; FO371/27291, Chiefs of Staff Committee Aide Mémoire, 15 April 1941.
8. FO371/27323, Cairo to Foreign Office, 19 May 1941; PREM3/422/6, Spears, 7 May 1941; Sachar, *Europe Leaves the Middle East*, p. 175; Eden, *The Reckoning*, pp. 240–7.
9. FO371/37323, Spears to Morton, 18 May 1941.
10. Martin Gilbert, *Churchill War Papers* (London, 1994), vol. III, p. 768; W0193/182, tels. to Commanders-in-Chief, South Atlantic and GOC-in-C West Africa, 7 June 1941; John Kennedy, *The Business of War* (London, 1958), p. 131.
11. Hervé Coutau-Bégarie and Claude Huan, *Darlan* (Paris, 1989), p. 428; Laffargue, *Dentz*, p. 190; Michel-Christian Davet, *La Double Affaire de Syrie* (Paris, 1967), p. 127; Roshwald, *Estranged Bedfellows*, pp. 76–7.
12. Colin Smith, *England's Last War Against France* (London, 2009), p. 260; Alan Moorhead, *African Trilogy* (London, 1998), p. 165.
13. Moorhead, *African Trilogy*, p. 165.
14. Benoist-Méchin, *Défaite*, p. 228; Henri de Wailly, *Syrie* (Paris, 2006), p. 337; Coutau-Bégarie and Huan, *Darlan*, pp. 430–1.

15. Laffargue, *Dentz*, p. 132; Hytier, *Two Years of French Foreign Policy*, p. 282.
16. Hytier, *Two Years of French Foreign Policy*, p. 282; Hervé Coutau-Bégarie and Claude Huan, *Lettres, Notes et carnets de l'amiral Darlan* (Paris, 1992), p. 387; Warner, *Iraq and Syria*, p. 145; Davet, *La Double Affaire*, p. 151; Edward Spears, *Fulfilment of a Mission* (London, 1977), p. 81; Benoist-Méchin, *Défaite*, p. 229; Wailly, *Syrie*, pp. 244–6.
17. Wailly, *Syrie*, pp. 224–5.
18. Robert Paxton, *Parades and Politics at Vichy* (Princeton, NJ, 1966), p. 237; Benoist-Méchin, *Défaite*, pp. 229–32.
19. Paul Auphan and Jacques Mordal, *La Marine française pendant la seconde guerre mondiale* (Paris, 1958), p. 248; Laffargue, *Dentz*, p. 172.
20. Davet, *La Double Affaire*, p. 163.
21. Davet, *La Double Affaire*, p. 176; Christopher Buckley, *Five Ventures* (London, 1954), p. 134; Anthony Mockler, *Our Enemies the French* (London, 1976), p. 194; J. R. M. Butler, *Grand Strategy* (London, 1957), vol. II, p. 522.
22. Butler, *Grand Strategy*, p. 233.
23. Sachar, *Europe Leaves the Middle East*, pp. 210–11.
24. Churchill, *Grand Alliance*, p. 296; Charles de Gaulle, *The Complete War Memoirs* (New York, 1972), p. 206.
25. Smith, *England's Last War*, pp. 188–9; François-Georges Dreyfus, *Histoire de Vichy* (Paris, 1990), p. 424.
26. Dreyfus, *Histoire de Vichy*, p. 444; I. S. O. Playfair, *The Mediterranean and the Middle East* (London, 1951), vol. II, p. 222.
27. Dreyfus, *Histoire de Vichy*, p. 444; Paxton, *Parades and Politics*, p. 327.
28. *Documents on German Foreign Policy*, vol. XIII, p. 673.
29. Charles Burchik and Hans-Adolf Jacobsen (eds.), *The Halder War Diaries* (London, 1988), p. 585.
30. Robert Paxton, *Vichy France* (New York, 2001), p. 123; J. B. Duroselle, *L'Abîme* (Paris, 1982), p. 300.
31. Philippe Burrin, *Living with Defeat* (London, 1991), pp. 125–7; Julian Jackson, *France: The Dark Years* (Oxford, 2003), pp. 183–4.
32. Coutau-Bégarie and Huan, *Darlan*, p. 472.
33. Warner, *Iraq and Syria*, p. 296.
34. Paxton, *Parades and Politics*, pp. 100–1.
35. Paxton, *Parades and Politics*, p. 312.
36. Hervé Alphand, *L'Etonnement d'être* (Paris, 1977), p. 104.
37. Alex Danchev and Daniel Todman (eds.), *War Diaries, 1939–45: Field Marshall Lord Alanbrooke* (London, 2001), p. 248.
38. J. Noakes and G. Pridham, *Nazism* (Exeter, 1988), vol. III, p. 852.
39. Admiral Leahy, *I Was There* (London, 1950), p. 551; FO371/31940, Mack minute, 28 May 1942; Hytier, *Two Years of French Foreign Policy*, p. 334.
40. PREM3/442/12, Churchill Secret Speech, 10 December 1942.
41. François Piétri, *Mes années d'Espagne* (Paris, 1954), pp. 121–2; FO371/28351, Hoare to Foreign Office, 21 November 1941.
42. FO371/28222, tel., Berne, 3 November 1941; FO371/28223, tel., Berne, 21 December 1941; ADM223/487, Director of Naval Intelligence memo, 4 April 1941.
43. Sébastien Albertelli, *Les Services secrets du général de Gaulle* (Paris, 2009), pp. 106–8; Georges Groussard, *Service Secret* (Paris, 1964), p. 148; R. T. Thomas, *Britain and Vichy* (London, 1979), p. 89; Anthony Cave-Brown, *The Secret Servant* (London, 1988), p. 427.

44. FO371/28566, Strang minute, 23 June 1941.

45. CAB84/32, 'Visit of Col. Groussard to this Country,' 9 July 1941.

46. Coutau-Bégarie and Huan, *Darlan*, p. 392; Thomas, *Britain and Vichy*, p. 90; Matthew Cobb, *The Resistance* (London, 2009), p. 330.

47. 'If only the English could see the bottom of my thoughts.' Nigel Nicolson (ed.), *Harold Nicolson, Letters and Diaries, 1939–45* (London, 1967), p. 192.

48. FO371/32040, Hoare to Eden, 26 January 1942; FO371/32040, Eden to Hoare, 10 February 1942.

49. W. J. M. Mackenzie, *The Secret History of SOE* (London, 2000), pp. 282, 287; HS6/311, Chief of the Imperial General Staff, minute, 6 May 1942; FO371/32081, 'France and the Fighting French,' 12 August 1942; Gustave Bertrand, *Enigma* (Paris, 1973), p. 128.

50. Coutau-Bégarie and Huan, *Darlan*, p. 422.

51. Michael Howard, *Grand Strategy* (London, 1970), vol. IV, p. 152; Thomas, *Britain and Vichy*, p. 144.

52. Thomas, *Britain and Vichy*, p. 120; PREM3/442/12, secret speech, 10 December 1942; CAB121/365, Minute Sargent, 21 December 1941; Gilbert, *Churchill War Papers*, vol. II, pp. 694, 1093–4, 1204.

53. Gilbert, *Churchill War Papers*, p. 1713.

54. Winston Churchill, *Their Finest Hour* (London, 1949), p. 450; PREM186/A/7, Churchill to Eden, 5 June 1942.

55. Thomas, *Britain and Vichy*, p. 117.

56. Howard, *Grand Strategy*, vol. IV, p. 145; FO371/31940, Mack memo, 21 April 1942.

57. René-Emile Godfroy, *L'Aventure de la Force X à Alexandre* (Paris, 1953), p. 41; Martin Thomas, 'After Mers-el-Kébir,' *English Historical Review*, June 1997, pp. 658–9.

58. *Franco-British Studies*, special edition, 'Operation Torch and Its Political Aftermath,' spring 1989, p. 34; Hytier, *Two Years of French Foreign Policy*, p. 285.

59. FO371/28351, FO meeting, 15 December 1941; Mack, 17 December 1941; ADM199/1279, Joint Planning Staff, 3 April 1942.

60. Warren Tute, *Reluctant Enemies* (London, 1990), p. 146; CAB121/357, Chiefs of Staff to Commander-in-Chief, Gibraltar, 5 May 1942.

61. Thomas, *French Empire*, p. 104; Spears, *Fulfilment of a Mission*, p. 24.

62. Gilbert, *Churchill War Papers*, vol. III, p. 703.

63. Gilbert, *Churchill War Papers*, vol. III, pp. 733–6, 757.

64. CAB66/23, 'Vichy Squadron at Alexandria,' 30 March 1942; Godfroy, *L'Aventure de la Force X*, p. 221.

65. ADM205/168, Churchill to First Sea Lord, 15 March 1942.

66. CAB66/23, 'Vichy Squadron.'

67. Godfroy, *L'Aventure de la Force X*, pp. 289, 297.

68. FO/371/31893, Cadogan minute, 9 July 1942.

69. FO371/31893, Strang minute, 29 June 1942; FO371/31894, Churchill to Smuts, 13 July 1942.

70. Albert Kammerer, *La Passion de la flotte française* (Paris, 1951), p. 339; Maxime Weygand, *Recalled to Service* (London, 1952), pp. 336–43.

71. *Documents on German Foreign Policy*, vol. XIII, pp. 934–5.

72. Eberhard Jaeckel, *Frankreich in Hitler's Europa* (Stuttgart, 1966), pp. 210–1; Kammerer, *Passion*, pp. 350–5.

73. Kammerer, *Passion*, p. 359; Coutau-Bégarie and Huan, *Darlan*, pp. 474–5.

74. Gilbert, *Churchill War Papers*, vol. III, p. 1253.

75. FO371/228223, Mack minutes, 11 and 16 December 1941, and whole file.

76. David Low, *The World at War* (Harmondsworth, 1942), p. 68; Christopher Bayly and Tim Harper, *Forgotten Armies* (London, 2004), p. 117; Gerhard Weinberg, *A World at War* (London, 1994), pp. 316–17.

77. Buckley, *Five Ventures*, p. 166; Martin Thomas, *The French Empire at War* (Manchester, 1998), pp. 140–1.

78. Weinberg, *A World at War*, p. 327; PREM3/265/11, Dominion's Office to Australian Government, 26 March 1942; Paxton, *Parades and Politics*, p. 313.

79. Desmond Dinan, *The Politics of Persuasion* (Lanham, Md., 1988), pp. 215–16; Smith, *England's Last War*, p. 288.

80. Winston Churchill, *The Hinge of Fate* (London, 1951), p. 200.

81. CAB121/623, 22 April 1942; Danchev and Todman, *Alanbrooke War Diaries*, p. 252.

82. CAB121/623, COS (42), 5 May 1942.

83. Paul Auphan, *L'Honneur de servir* (Paris, 1978), p. 342; Paxton, *Parades and Politics*, p. 325.

84. CAB121/624, Eden to Harlech, 8 June 1942.

85. CAB121/623, Makins to Hollis, 8 May 1942; Churchill, *Hinge of Fate*, p. 199.

86. Martin Thomas, 'Imperial Backwater or Strategic Outpost? The British Takeover of Vichy Madagascar,' *Historical Journal*, December 1996, p. 1052; PREM3/265/2, Churchill to Smuts, 16 May 1942.

87. PREM3/265/7, Harlech to FO, 6 June 1942.

88. FO371/31901, 'Political Objections to Negotiations with Vichy Authorities in Madagascar'; PREM3/265/7, Eden to Churchill, 2 June 1942; CAB121/624, Committee on Foreign Resistance, draft report, 'Madagascar,' 5 May 1942.

89. Martin Thomas, *The French Empire at War, 1940–45* (Manchester, 1998), p. 145; Buckley, *Five Ventures*, p. 189.

90. CAB121/624, Churchill to Chiefs of Staff, 19 July 1942; tel., Durban, 16 July 1942; 'Madagascar: Future Policy' Joint Planning Staff, 25 July 1942.

91. Thomas, *African Empire*, p. 145; Hytier, *Two Years of French Foreign Policy*, p. 350; Robert Aron, *The Vichy Regime* (London, 1958), p. 389; Paxton, *Parades and Politics*, pp. 324–5.

92. Smith, *England's Last War*, p. 354; Dinan, *The Politics of Persuasion*, p. 229.

## 7  Enemy-Controlled Territory

1. Lord Ismay, *Memoirs* (London, 1960), p. 140; Williamson Murray, *Luftwaffe* (London, 1988), p. 86.

2. *Fuehrer Conferences on Naval Affairs* (London, 2005), pp. 124, 129.

3. *The Rise and Fall of the German Air Force* (London, 2001), p. 96.

4. BBC, WAC, E1/703, French Service Directive, 4 July 1941.

5. Winston Churchill, *The Grand Alliance* (London, 1950), p. 106.

6. Thomas Wilson, *Churchill and the Prof* (London, 1995), pp. 118, 120; F. H. Hinsley, *British Intelligence in the Second World War* (London, 1979), vol. I, p. 335.

7. Gerhard Weinberg, *A World at Arms* (Cambridge, 1994), p. 176; Stephen Roskill, *The War at Sea* (London, 1954), vol. I, pp. 346, 349; ADM199/2467, 'The Importance of the Biscay Ports to the Axis,' 9 October 1942; *German Air Force*, pp. 104–6.

8. *German Air Force*, pp. 104–6.

9. Rod Kedward, *La Vie en bleu* (London, 2005), p. 249; Julian Jackson, *The Dark Years* (Oxford, 2003), pp. 187–8; Matthew Cobb, *The Resistance* (London, 2009), p. 41; Richard Evans, *The Third Reich at War* (London, 2008), p. 334.

10. J. Noakes and G. Pridham, *Nazism* (Exeter, 1988), vol. III, p. 909; Kedward, *La Vie en bleu*, p. 249.

11. M. R. D. Foot, *Resistance* (London, 1976), p. 24; Winston Churchill, *Their Finest Hour* (London, 1949), p. 578; Anthony Reed and David Fisher, *Colonel Z* (London, 1984), p. 286; Colonel Passy, *Souvenirs* (Monte Carlo, 1947), vol. I, pp. 54–8; Hinsley, *British Intelligence*, vol. I, p. 187; Keith Jeffery, *MI6* (London, 2010), p. 391; ADM199/2467, 'The Importance of the Biscay Ports to the Axis,' 9 October 1942.

12. Jeffery, *MI6*, p. 391.

13. Sébastien Albertelli, *Les Services secrets du général de Gaulle* (Paris, 2009), p. 159.

14. Albertelli, *Les Services secrets*, pp. 212, 213, 216; David de Young de la Marck, 'De Gaulle, Colonel Passy and British Intelligence,' *Intelligence and National Security*, spring 2003, pp. 36–7.

15. Jeffery, *MI6*, p. 529.

16. Jeffery, *MI6*, p. 393.

17. Gilbert Renault-Roulier, *On m'appelait Rémy* (Paris, 1954), pp. 102–4.

18. Jeffery, *MI6*, p. 392.

19. Cobb, *Resistance*, pp. 100–1.

20. Foot, *Resistance*, p. 242; Michèle Cointet, *Marie-Madeleine Fourcade* (Paris, 2006), p. 132.

21. Cointet, *Fourcade*, pp. 143, 217.

22. Cointet, *Fourcade*, pp. 99, 111, 121, 153–4, 215; Renault-Roulier, *Rémy*, pp. 240–2; Hinsley, *British Intelligence*, vol. I, p. 332.

23. R. V. Jones, *Most Secret War* (London, 1978), pp. 450–1; Jeffery, *MI6*, p. 534; 'French Fighter Who Located Doodlebug Launch Sites,' *Financial Times*, 18/19 April 2009.

24. Foot, *Resistance*, p. 242; Reed and Fisher, *Colonel Z*, p. 305.

25. Martin Thomas, 'Signals Intelligence and Vichy France,' *Intelligence and National Security*, 14 (1) (1999), p. 194; Gustave Bertrand, *Enigma* (Paris, 1973), pp. 117–20; Anthony Cave-Brown, *The Secret Servant* (London, 1988), p. 289; Jeffery, *MI6*, p. 529.

26. Jeffery, *MI6*, p. 390.

27. Cave-Brown, *Secret Servant*, p. 290; Bertrand, *Enigma*, p. 110; Thomas, 'Signals Intelligence,' p. 182.

28. Thomas, 'Signals Intelligence,' p. 183; Paul Paillole, *Services spéciaux* (Paris, 1975), pp. 251–2, 384; Simon Kitson, *The Hunt for Nazi Spies* (Chicago, Ill., 2008), p. xv.

29. Kitson, *The Hunt for Nazi Spies*, p. 161; Cointet, *Fourcade*, pp. 206, 136.

30. Cave-Brown, *Secret Servant*, p. 290.

31. Thomas, 'France in Britain's Signal's Intelligence,' *French History*, March 2000, p. 66; Kitson, *The Hunt for Nazi Spies*, p. 169.

32. FO371/42044, Dansey to Morton, 27 July 1944; Jeffery, *MI6*, pp. 434–5.

33. Thomas, 'France in Britain's Signals Intelligence,' pp. 61–3.

34. François-Georges Dreyfus, *Histoire de Vichy* (Paris, 1990), pp. 325–6; ADM223/487, History of NID 20.

35. Isabelle Tombs, 'Scrutinizing France,' *Intelligence and National Security*, 17 (2002): 105–26.

36. Martyn Cornick, 'The BBC and the Propaganda War against Occupied France,' *French History*, September 1994, pp. 321–2.

37. M. R. D. Foot and J. M. Langley, *MI9* (London, 1980), pp. 63–4; Rod Kedward, 'Britain and the French Resistance,' in Richard Mayne, Douglas Johnson and Robert Tombs (eds.), *Cross Channel Currents* (London, 2004), p. 125; Barbara Bertram, *French Resistance in Sussex* (Pulburough, 1995), p. 24.

38. 'Mitterrand's Secret War Record Reveals Narrow Escape from Gestapo,' *Financial Times*, 17/18 November 2007.

39. M. R. D. Foot, *SOE in France* (London, 1966), p. 488.
40. Philip Bell, *Britain and France* (Harlow, 1997), vol. II, p. 60.
41. PREM3/184/9, Eden to Churchill, 2 March 1942; Churchill to Eden, 3 March 1942; Eden to Churchill, 22 July 1942.
42. Charles William, *Pétain* (London, 2005), pp. 447–54.
43. Jones, *Secret War*, pp. 302–21; Churchill, *Grand Alliance*, p. 690; Cobb, *Resistance*, p. 54.
44. FO892/129, Torch Directive; PREM3/184/9, Mack to Kayser, 15 July 1943.
45. Jacques Crémieux-Brilhac, *Ici Londres: Les Voix de la liberté, 1940–44*, 5 vols. (Paris, 1975), vol. II, p. 221.
46. FO371/31999, War Cabinet, 8 January 1942.
47. AIR19/217, Bottomley to Bomber Command, 4 March 1942.
48. AIR19/217, Bottomley to Bomber Command, 20 July 1942.
49. FO371/32000, Strang, 24 April 1942.
50. F. H. Hinsley, *British Intelligence in the Second World War* (London, 1981), vol. II, p. 267; Martin Middlebrook and Chris Everill, *The Bomber Command War Diaries* (Leicester, 1996), p. 245.
51. AIR19/217, Letter Matthews, 13 March 1942; William Leahy, *I Was There* (London, 1950), pp. 103, 554.
52. *The Times*, 9 March 1942; Crémieux-Brilhac, *Ici Londres*, vol. II, pp. 67–9; BBC, WAC, E2/209/1; BBC Output report, 1–7 March 1942.
53. John Sweets, *Choices in Vichy France* (Oxford, 1986), p. 162.
54. AIR19/217, Eden to Sinclair, 16 March 1942.
55. FO371/31982, Mack, 22 June 1942; FO371/31939, Letter Viple, 8 March 1942; Roderick Bailey, *Forgotten Voices of the Second World War* (London, 2008), p. 182; Robert Gildea, *Marianne in Chains* (London, 2002), p. 185.
56. AIR19/217, Bottomley to CAS, 22 May 1942.
57. G. H. Bennett, 'The RAF's Free French Fighter Squadrons,' *Global War Studies*, 7 (2) (2010).
58. AIR19/217, Sinclair to Churchill, 25 July 1942; Eden to Sinclair, 1 October 1942; FO371/32000, Sinclair to Eden, 3 October 1942; W. J. M. Mackenzie, *The Secret History of SOE* (London, 2000), pp. 599–600.
59. AIR19/217, Sinclair, 12 June 1942.
60. AIR19/217, Eden to Sinclair, 18 December 1942.
61. Weinberg, *World at Arms*, p. 374.
62. AIR19/217, Bottomley to Bomber Command, 14 January 1943.
63. Roskill, *War at Sea*, p. 352; Hinsley, *British Intelligence*, vol. II, p. 754; Gildea, *Marianne*, p. 306; Lindsey Dodd and Andrew Knapp, 'How Many Frenchmen Did You Kill?,' *French History*, December 2008, pp. 479–80.
64. Robert Tombs and Isabelle Tombs, *That Sweet Enemy* (London, 2006), p. 586; Brook Richards, *Secret Flotillas* (London, 1996), vol. I, p. 657; Bailey, *Forgotten Voices*, pp. 65–7; Mackenzie, *Secret History*, p. 236; Foot, *SOE*, p. 67.
65. Foot, *SOE*, pp. 83–4; Mackenzie, *Secret History*, p. 237; AIR20/8450, 'Historical Record of Bomber Command Aircraft Engaged in Clandestine Operations.'
66. Foot, *SOE*, pp. 11–12; Mackenzie, *Secret History*, p. 222.
67. Mackenzie, *Secret History*, pp. 284–5; Foot, *SOE*, p. 231.
68. HS6/311, SOE to Strang, 28 May 1942 (date unclear on microfilm); Tombs and Tombs, *Sweet Enemy*, p. 586; Albertelli, *Les Services secrets*, pp. 71–2.
69. Mackenzie, *Secret History*, p. 257.
70. Foot, *SOE*, pp. 24–5.
71. Foot, *SOE*, p. 389.

72. Foot, *SOE*, p. 389.
73. Tombs and Tombs, *Sweet Enemy*, p. 585.
74. Tombs and Tombs, *Sweet Enemy*, p. 585; Foot, *SOE*, pp. 49–53.
75. Foot, *SOE*, pp. 74–5, 224; CAB103/571, Wilkinson to Trend, 12 December 1963.
76. Foot, *SOE*, pp. 298–306; Sarah Helms, *A Life in Secrets* (London, 2005), pp. 289–93, 339–40.
77. Matthew Cobb, 'French Fraud,' *Times Literary Supplement*, 26 June 2009; Foot, *SOE*, pp. 204–11.
78. Bailey, *Forgotten Voices*, pp. 98, 107; Foot, *SOE*, p. 53.
79. Foot, *SOE*, pp. 53, 119–20.
80. Foot, *SOE*, pp. 161–2.
81. David Stafford, *Britain and European Resistance* (London, 1980), pp. 70–1; Mackenzie, *Secret History*, p. 256.
82. Mackenzie, *Secret History*, p. 256; E. H. Cookridge, *Inside SOE* (London, 1966), p. 121.
83. Foot, *SOE*, p. 233.
84. Cookridge, *Inside SOE*, p. 313; Foot, *SOE*, pp. 233, 248–9; Jackson, *Dark Years*, p. 556; Albertelli, *Les Services secrets*, p. 76.
85. Mackenzie, *Secret History*, p. 601.
86. Martin Gilbert (ed.), *Churchill War Papers* (London, 1994), vol. II, p. 534.
87. Rod Kedward, *Resistance in Vichy France* (Oxford, 1978), pp. 80, 229; Cobb, *Resistance*, p. 61.
88. Cobb, *Resistance*, p. 3.
89. Kedward, 'Britain and the French Resistence,' p. 125; Albertelli, *Services secrets*, p. 76.
90. Foot, *SOE*, p. 180.
91. Foot, *SOE*, pp. 180–2, 491–2.
92. Mackenzie, *Secret History*, pp. 273–4; PREM3/184/6, Morton to Mack, 30 October 1941.
93. Jackson, *France*, pp. 431–2; Foot, *SOE*, p. 238.
94. Foot, *SOE*, pp. 31, 473, 498.
95. Foot, *SOE*, p. 473; PREM3/184/6, Selborne to Churchill, 24 June 1943.
96. Kedward, 'Britain and the French Resistence,' p. 127.
97. Bailey, *Forgotten Voices*, p. 107.

## 8 'Ici Londres'

1. Jacques Crémieux-Brilhac, *Ici Londres: Les Voix de la liberté, 1940–44*, 5 vols. (Paris, 1975), vol. I, pp. 6–11.
2. Tim Brooks, *British Propaganda to France* (Edinburgh, 2007), pp. 149–54.
3. Brooks, *British Propaganda*, pp. 42, 82–6; Robert Tombs and Isabelle Tombs, *That Sweet Enemy* (London, 2006), p. 583; Charles Cruickshank, *The Fourth Arm* (London, 1977), p. 96; David Garnett, *The Secret History of PWE* (London, 2002), p. 237.
4. Brooks, *British Propaganda*, pp. 130–42.
5. Brooks, *British Propaganda*, pp. 130–42.
6. Brooks, *British Propaganda*, pp. 39, 43, 44, 115–16.
7. BBC, WAC, E2/186/3, 23 December 1940; Garnett, *Secret History of PWE*, p. 50.
8. Cruickshank, *Fourth Arm*, p. 85; FO898/198, Moulin and Sutton, 11 November 1941.
9. Garnett, *Secret History of PWE*, p. 55.

10. Garnett, *Secret History of PWE*, pp. 269–70; FO898/420, Lieut.-Col. Fairlie, 'PWE White Propaganda to France: Summary of Results,' April 1945.
11. Crémieux-Brilhac, *Ici Londres*, vol. I, p. xix.
12. Hélène Eck (ed.), *La Guerre des ondes* (Paris, 1985), p. 61; Jacques Crémieux-Brilhac, 'Les Emissions françaises de la BBC pendant la guerre,' *Revue d'Histoire de la Deuxième Guerre Mondiale*, November, p. 79; BBC, WAC, E2/186/2, Monthly Intelligence Report, 8 July 1940.
13. FO894/420, 'PWE White Propaganda,' April 1945.
14. FO371/31798, French Service Directive, 26 July to 9 August 1942.
15. Crémieux-Brilhac, *Ici Londres*, vol. I, p. xvi.
16. Crémieux-Brilhac, *Ici Londres*, vol. I, p. xvi.
17. FO371/28428, 'Propaganda to France,' 28 February 1941.
18. Crémieux-Brilhac, *Ici Londres*, vol. II, p. 166.
19. FO371/31976, French Service Directive, 15 March 1942.
20. 'Life is not good, not good . . . mummy has nothing to eat, never have dinner, never eat.' BBC, WAC, E2/193/6, 6 October 1943.
21. Carmen Callil, *Bad Faith* (London, 2006), pp. 210–11; John Sweets, *Choices in Vichy France* (Oxford, 2006), p. 14; BBC, WAC, E2/193/2A, European Intelligence Report, 4 March 1942; E2/193/6, European Intelligence Report, 6 October 1943.
22. Michael Stenton, *Radio London and Resistance in Occupied Europe* (Oxford, 2000), p. 130.
23. BBC, WAC, E1/702/2, 13 May 1941; E2/193/6, European Intelligence Report, 2 October 1944; Eck, *Guerres des ondes*, pp. 67–8; Asa Briggs, *The War of Words* (London, 1970), p. 387.
24. Emile Delavenay, *Témoignage d'un village Savoyard au village mondial* (Aix-en-Provence, 1992), p. 208.
25. Briggs, *War of Words*, p. 404.
26. Eck, *Guerre des ondes*, pp. 63–4; Crémieux-Brilhac, *Ici Londres*, vol. I, pp. 118–19.
27. Crémieux-Brilhac, *Ici Londres*, vol. I, pp. 248–9.
28. Crémieux-Brilhac, *Ici Londres*, vol. II, pp. 2–3, 5.
29. Crémieux-Brilhac, *Ici Londres*, vol. I, p. 300.
30. FO371/31976, French Service Directives, 11–18 January 1942; CAB84/36, JP (41) 936 (S), 'Political Warfare Plan for France,' 7 November 1941.
31. BBC, WAC, E1/703, French Service Directive, 30 May 1941.
32. FO371/38230, Mack, 1 September 1941; Stenton, *Radio London*, pp. 170, 186, 191.
33. BBC, WAC, E1/703, French Service Directive, 12 September 1941.
34. Crémieux-Brilhac, *Ici Londres*, vol. I, pp. 130–1, 131–6, 140–1.
35. Crémieux-Brilhac, *Ici Londres*, vol. I, pp. 239–42.
36. BBC, WAC, E1/703, French Service Directives, 7 March 1941 and 4 July 1941.
37. BBC, WAC, E209/1, Output Report, 13–19 December 1942.
38. Garnett, *Secret History of PWE*, p. 53.
39. Crémieux-Brilhac, *Ici Londres*, vol. II, p. 90; BBC, WAC, E/209/1, Output Report, 12–18 April 1942.
40. FO371/31798, French Service Directive, 12–26 July 1942.
41. FO371/31798, French Service Directive, 12–26 July 1942.
42. Aurélie Luneau, *Radio Londres* (Paris, 2005), p. 170.
43. Philip Bell, *France and Britain* (Harlow, 1997), vol. II, p. 25.
44. FO371/25314, Letter Geneva, 24 November 1940; Delavenay, *Témoignage*, p. 212.
45. Paul Baudouin, *The Private Diaries of Paul Baudouin* (London, 1948), p. 218; Marie-Thérèse Viaud, 'La Dordogne,' in J. P. Azema and Frederic Bédarida (eds.), *Le Régime de Vichy et les Français* (Paris, 1992), p. 546.

46. Delavenay, *Témoignage*, p. 215; FO371/28230, Report by Father Dickinson of conversation with officer in command, Deuxième Bureau, 9 August 1941.
47. FO371/28230, Report by Father Dickinson, 'Let's hope the English win,' and 'Let's hope the English pigs win.'
48. BBC, WAC, E1/703, French Service Directive, 7 March 1941.
49. Luneau, *Radio Londres*, pp. 141–2; Eck, *Guerre des ondes*, p. 112.
50. Martyn Cornick, 'Fraternity among Listeners,' in Hanna Diamond and Simon Kitson (eds.), *Vichy, Occupation, Liberation* (Oxford, 2005), p. 102; Stenton, *Radio London*, p. 133; Brooks, *British Propaganda*, pp. 54–5.
51. ADM199/2484, MI19 RPS Report, 1 October 1942, p. 914.
52. Irène Némirovsky, *Suite Française*, trans. Sandra Smith (London, 2007), p. 244.
53. Brooks, *British Propaganda*, pp. 121–5; Cornick, 'Fraternity among Listeners,' pp. 106–7; Delavenay, *Témoignage*, p. 330; Henri Amouroux, *La Grande Histoire des Français sous l'Occupation* (Paris, 1979), vol. IV, p. 233; FO371/28432, z8266; FO371/31977, z3948, 17 April 1942.
54. Brooks, *British Propaganda*, pp. 55–7.
55. Brooks, *British Propaganda*, pp. 53–4; Briggs, *War of Words*, p. 232; Crémieux-Brilhac, *Ici Londres*, vol. I, p. 184.
56. Jean Lacouture, *De Gaulle*, vol. I (London, 1983), p. 375.
57. Christian Bougeard, 'La Bretagne,' in J. P. Azema and Frederic Bédarida (eds.), *Le Régime de Vichy et les français* (Paris, 1992), p. 538; Stenton, *Radio London*, p. 133.
58. Robert Zaretsky, *Nîmes at War* (Pennsylvania, Pa., 1995), p. 173.
59. Eck, *Guerre des ondes*, p. 191.
60. Agnès Humbert, *Resistance* (London, 2008), pp. 67–8.
61. E. Tangye Lean, *Voices in the Dark* (London, 1943).
62. Amouroux, *La Grande Histoire*, pp. 239–40; Lean, *Voices in the Dark*, p. 141; FO371/24314, Despatch Barcelona, 18 November 1940; Crémieux-Brilhac, *Ici Londres*, vol. I, p. xii.
63. Luneau, *Radio Londres*, p. 177.
64. BBC, WAC, E2/193/6, European Intelligence Report, 6 October 1943.
65. Liliane Schroeder, *Journal d'occupation* (Paris, 2000), p. 111.
66. *La Délégation Française auprès de la Commission Allemande de l'Armistice*, vol. IV, p. 598; Jacques Crémieux-Brilhac, *La France libre* (Paris, 1996), p. 215.
67. BBC, WAC, E2/193/6, European Intelligence Reports, 2 February 1944 and 2 October 1944; Winston Churchill, *Their Finest Hour* (London, 1949), p. 451.
68. Cornick, 'Fraternity among Listeners,' p. 110; FO371/24314, Postal Censorship Report, Occupied France, 25 October 1940.
69. Jean-Paul Cointet, *La France à Londres* (Brussels, 1990), p. 79; Rob Kedward, *La Vie en bleu* (London, 2005), p. 278.
70. Delavenay, *Témoignage*, p. 185; Luneau, *Radio Londres*, p. 61.
71. Luneau, *Radio Londres*, pp. 35, 55, 80; Charles de Gaulle, *The Complete War Memoirs* (New York, 1972), p. 154.
72. Rob Kedward, *Resistance in Vichy France* (Oxford, 1978) p. 212; FO371/28432, French Service Directive, 29 September 1941.
73. Luneau, *Radio Londres*, p. 176.
74. Tombs and Tombs, *Sweet Enemy*, p. 578; Aurélie Luneau, in Institut Charles de Gaulle, *La France Libre* (Paris, 2005), p. 120; Ian Buruma, 'Who Did Not Collaborate?,' *New York Review of Books*, 24 February 2011.
75. BBC, WAC, E2/193/2, European Intelligence Report, 31 July 1941; E2/193/2A, 27 August 1941.

76. BBC, WAC, E2/193/4, European Intelligence Report, 1 July 1942.
77. ADM199/2484, MI19 RPS Report, 20 August 1942; Eck, *Guerre des ondes*, p. 148.
78. Luneau, *Radio Londres*, pp. 94–5.
79. Luneau, *Radio Londres*, pp. 101–3.
80. Stenton, *Radio London*, p. 130; Crémieux-Brilhac, *La France Libre*, pp. 222–3.
81. Crémieux-Brilhac, *Ici Londres*, vol. II, p. 169; Stenton, *Radio London*, p. 206.
82. Luneau, *Radio Londres*, pp. 95–6.
83. Luneau, *Radio Londres*, pp. 145, 188–9; FO892/420, 'Summary of Results,' April 1945; PREM3/184/6, Churchill to Selborne, 18 June 1943.
84. Amouroux, *La Grande Histoire*, p. 223.
85. Brooks, *British Propaganda*, p. 127; Luneau, *La France Libre*, pp. 120–1; Kedward, *Resistance in Vichy France*, pp. 66–7; Kedward *La Vie en bleu*, p. 275; Matthew Cobb, *The Resistance* (London, 2009), p. 99.
86. Eck, *Guerre des ondes*, p. 78; Stenton, *Radio London*, p. 196; Cornick, 'Fraternity among Listeners,' p. 110.
87. Lacouture, *De Gaulle*, vol. I, p. 374.
88. Roderick Bailey, *Forgotten Voices of the Second World War* (London, 2008), p. 107.
89. M. R. D. Foot, *SOE in France* (London, 1966), p. 110; Cobb, *The Resistance*, p. 100.

## 9   The Awkward General

1. Jean Lacouture, *De Gaulle* (London, 1984), vol. I, p. 265.
2. John Harvey (ed.), *The War Diaries of Oliver Harvey* (London, 1978), p. 107.
3. Robert Rhodes-James, *Anthony Eden* (London, 1986), pp. 235–6; Anthony Eden, *The Reckoning* (London, 1965), pp. 249–50.
4. Charles de Gaulle, *The Complete War Memoirs* (New York, 1972), p. 102; Lacouture, *De Gaulle*, vol. I, pp. 250–1, 263–4; Charles Williams, *The Last Great Frenchman* (London, 1993), pp. 120–1; Jacques Crémieux-Brilhac, *La France Libre* (Paris, 1996), p. 74; Paul Addison and Jeremy Crang, *Listening to Britain* (London, 2010), pp. 272, 381.
5. David Stafford, *Britain and European Resistance* (London, 1980), p. 91.
6. Michael Stenton, *Radio London and Resistance in Occupied Europe* (Oxford, 2000), p. 181; PREM3/182/6, Macmillan despatch, 3 January 1944.
7. Duff Hart-Davis (ed.), *King's Counsellor* (London, 2006), p. 56.
8. Philippe de Gaulle, *De Gaulle mon père* (Paris, 2003), pp. 168, 172.
9. FO371/28545, Hankey minute, 7 August 1941.
10. Alex Danchev and Daniel Todman (eds.), *War Diaries, 1939–45: Field Marshall Lord Alanbrooke* (London, 2001), p. 101.
11. Danchev and Todman, *Alanbrooke War Diaries*, p. 101.
12. FO371/28213, Morton to Mack, 22 July 1941; PREM3/186/1/7, Morton to Churchill, 11 February 1941.
13. Robert Paxton, *Parades and Politics at Vichy* (Princeton, NJ, 1965), pp. 130–2, 135; Hanna Diamond, *Fleeing Hitler* (Oxford, 2007), pp. 128–9.
14. Spears Papers, Box 2, 'The Free French Movement,' Foreign Office print; Jacques Soustelle, *Envers et contre tout* (Paris, 1948), vol. I, pp. 287–9.
15. Philip Bell, *France and Britain* (Harlow, 1997), vol. II, p. 53; Paul Auphan and Jacques Mordal, *La Marine française pendant la seconde guerre mondiale* (Paris, 1958), pp. 198–205; Spears Papers, Box 2, 'The Free French Movement'; G. H. Bennett, 'The RAF's Free French Fighter Squadrons: The Rebirth of French Airpower, 1940–44,' *Global War Studies*, 7 (2) (2010), p. 80.

16. Charles de Gaulle, *Lettres, notes et carnets, juin 1940–juillet 1941* (Paris, 1981), p. 136.
17. Douglas Porch, *Hitler's Mediterranean Gamble* (London, 2004), pp. 111–12; de Gaulle, *Complete War Memoirs*, p. 323.
18. FO371/32028, Strang minute, 23 May 1942.
19. FO371/31872, Eden to Churchill, 20 January 1942.
20. De Gaulle, *Complete War Memoirs*, pp. 305–6; Eric Roussel, *Charles de Gaulle* (Paris, 2002), p. 305.
21. De Gaulle, *Complete War Memoirs*, p. 340.
22. FO371/32027, Mack to Morton, 22 July 1942; ADM199/616A, Peake, 2 July 1942.
23. FO371/32028, tel., Rooker, 3 October 1942; Keith Sainsbury in Neville Waites (ed.), *Troubled Neighbours* (London, 1981), p. 230.
24. *La France à travers de Gaulle* (Paris, 1969), p. 13.
25. M. R. D. Foot, *SOE in France* (London, 1966), p. 130.
26. Crémieux-Brilhac, *La France Libre*, p. 132; W. J. M. Mackenzie, *The Secret History of SOE* (London, 2000), p. 257; Charles de Gaulle, *War Memoirs: Documents*, 3 vols. (London, 1959), vol. I, p. 354; Bell, *France and Britain*, vol. II, p. 34.
27. Crémieux-Brilhac, *La France Libre*, p. 81.
28. Crémieux-Brilhac, *La France Libre*, pp. 184–7; Elizabeth Barker, *Churchill and Eden at War* (London, 1978), p. 36; PREM3/181/7, Chancellor of the Exchequer to Churchill, 12 June 1943; Gloria Maguire, *Anglo-American Policy towards the Free French* (Basingstoke, 1995), p. 117.
29. Maguire, *Anglo-American Policy*, p. 118.
30. FO371/32027, Mack to Morton, 22 July 1943.
31. Martin Gilbert, *The Road to Victory* (London, 1986), p. 305.
32. Roussel, *De Gaulle*, p. 148.
33. Bell, *France and Britain*, vol. II, p. 34.
34. De Gaulle, *Complete War Memoirs*, p. 163; Soustelle, *Envers et contre tout*, vol. I, p. 91; Aviel Roshwald, *Estranged Bedfellows* (Oxford, 1990), p. 121.
35. Crémieux-Brilhac, *La France Libre*, p. 197; Maguire, *Anglo-American Policy*, p. 117.
36. De Gaulle, *Complete War Memoirs*, p. 163.
37. FO371/32040, Eden to Hoare, 10 February 1942.
38. CAB66/39/41, Foreign Office memo outlining relations with de Gaulle, June 1940–June 1943.
39. Roussel, *De Gaulle*, p. 152; de Gaulle, *Complete War Memoirs*, pp. 92–3; Max Egremont, *Under Two Flags* (London, 1997), p. 198; François Kersaudy, *Churchill and de Gaulle* (London, 1981), pp. 85–6.
40. De Gaulle, *War Memoirs, Documents*, vol. I, pp. 42, 52–3; Crémieux-Brilhac, *La France Libre*, p. 138; De Gaulle, *Complete War Memoirs*.
41. De Gaulle, *Lettres, notes et carnets*, pp. 218–19; Foot, *SOE in France*, p. 136.
42. Spears Papers, Box 2, memo, 14 April 1954, 'French Forces in the Levant'; Sir Edward Spears, *Two Men Who Saved France* (London, 1966), p. 149.
43. Crémieux-Brilhac, *La France Libre*, p. 65; Kersaudy, *Churchill and de Gaulle*, pp. 87–9; Roussel, *De Gaulle*, p. 154; de Gaulle, *Mon père*, p. 178.
44. De Gaulle, *Complete War Memoirs*, pp. 168–9; De Gaulle, *War Memoirs, Documents*, vol. I, pp. 120–30, 132–4, 150, 157.
45. Adrian Fort, *Wavell* (London, 2009), pp. 224, 231.
46. I. S. O. Playfair, *The Mediterranean and the Middle East* (London, 1951), vol. II, p. 203; Meir Zamir, 'De Gaulle and the Question of Syria and Lebanon in the Second World War, Part 1,' *Middle Eastern Studies*, September 2007, p. 681.

47. Williams, *The Last Great Frenchman*, p. 145.
48. Egremont, *Under Two Flags*, p. 223; Edward Spears, *Fulfilment of a Mission: The Spears Mission to Syria and Lebanon, 1941–44* (London, 1977), pp. 49–50.
49. Spears, *Fulfilment of a Mission*, pp. 44–5; De Gaulle, *Complete War Memoirs*, p. 178.
50. FO371/28545, Letter from Parr, 2 September 1941; Kersaudy, *Churchill and de Gaulle*, p. 128; de Gaulle, *War Memoirs, Documents*, vol. I, p. 143.
51. De Gaulle, *Complete War Memoirs*, p. 91.
52. ADM199/616A, Peake to Foreign Office, 17 June 1941.
53. De Gaulle, *Complete War Memoirs*, pp. 95, 116, 196.
54. Bernard Ledwidge, *De Gaulle* (London, 1982), p. 36.
55. De Gaulle, *Complete War Memoirs*, p. 183; De Gaulle, *War Memoirs, Documents*, vol. I, p. 177.
56. A. B. Gaunson, *The Anglo-French Clash in Lebanon and Syria, 1940–45* (London, 1987), p. 76.
57. Roshwald, *Estranged Bedfellows*, pp. 69–70.
58. CAB65/19, Churchill to Lyttelton, 7 July 1941.
59. Gaunson, *The Anglo-French Clash*, p. 48.
60. PREM3/182/6, Macmillan despatch, 3 January 1944.
61. Spears, *Fulfilment of a Mission*, p. 97; A. B. Gaunson, 'Churchill, de Gaulle, Spears and the Levant Affair, 1941,' *Historical Journal*, 3 (1984), p. 705.
62. PREM3/442/6, Spears to Churchill, 5 June 1941.
63. PREM3/442/6, Spears to Churchill, 5 June 1941.
64. Général Catroux, *Dans la bataille de la Méditerranée* (Paris, 1949), p. 46.
65. PREM3/442/6, Spears to Churchill, 5 June 1941.
66. De Gaulle, *War Memoirs, Documents*, vol. I, pp. 172–3; PREM3/442/6, Spears to Churchill, 21 June 1941; Spears Papers, Box 2, Letter Somerville-Smith to Spears, 5 July 1941.
67. Spears, *Fulfilment of a Mission*, p. 121.
68. Spears, *Fulfilment of a Mission*, p. 121.
69. Spears, *Fulfilment of a Mission*, p. 30.
70. Gaunson, 'Churchill, de Gaulle, Spears', p. 707.
71. Roshwald, *Estranged Bedfellows*, p. 85.
72. Danchev and Todman, *Alanbrooke War Diaries*, p. xliii.
73. Gaunson, *The Anglo-French Clash*, p. 58.
74. Egremont, *Under Two Flags*, p. 229; de Gaulle, *Complete War Memoirs*, p. 191.
75. De Gaulle, *Complete War Memoirs*, p. 193; de Gaulle, *War Memoirs, Documents*, vol. I, p. 192; Spears, *Fulfilment of a Mission*, p. 134.
76. Spears, *Fulfilment of a Mission*, pp. 137–8.
77. De Gaulle, *War Memoirs, Documents*, vol. I, pp. 196–9, 201, 210–11.
78. CAB121/409, Lampson to Churchill, 25 July 1941.
79. Keith Jeffery, *MI6* (London, 2010), p. 434.
80. De Gaulle, *Complete War Memoirs*, pp. 198–9; de Gaulle, *War Memoirs, Documents*, vol. I, p. 210; Williams, *The Last Great Frenchman*, p. 153.
81. Guillaume Piketty (ed.), *Français en résistance* (Paris, 2009), p. 213.
82. Piketty, *Français en résistance*, p. 213.
83. De Gaulle, *War Memoirs, Documents*, vol. I, pp. 212, 227.
84. FO892/78, Parr to Eden, 26 July 1941.
85. FO892/78, Parr to Eden, 26 July 1941.
86. Martin Gilbert (ed.), *The Churchill War Papers* (London, 2000), vol. III, p. 1036.
87. Henry Colpyton, *Occasion, Chance and Change* (London, 1993), p. 196; Simon

Berthon, *Allies at War* (London, 2001), p. 131; Colonel Passy, *Souvenirs* (Monte Carlo, 1947), vol. I, p. 216.

88. FO371/28545, Letter Parr, 2 September 1941; Kersaudy, *Churchill and de Gaulle*, pp. 149–50.
89. Kersaudy, *Churchill and de Gaulle*, p. 146.
90. Williams, *The Last Great Frenchman*, p. 154.
91. Williams, *The Last Great Frenchman*, p. 154; FO371/28363, Mack minute, 28 August 1941.
92. Hervé Alphand, *L'Etonnement d'être* (Paris, 1977), p. 89.
93. Alphand, *L'Etonnement d'être*, p. 89.
94. W0106/5416A, Lieut.-Col. Myrtle, 28 July 1941.
95. Kersaudy, *Churchill and de Gaulle*, p. 156.
96. Roussel, *De Gaulle*, p. 228.
97. FO371/28545, Letter Parr, 2 September 1941.
98. FO371/28545, Morton to Cadogan, 3 September 1941.
99. Spears, *Fulfilment of a Mission*, p. 138.
100. FO371/31959, 'Admiral Muselier's Resignation,' Appendix C.
101. FO371/28545, Morton to Cadogan, 3 September 1941.
102. Spears Papers, Box 2, Eden to de Gaulle, 19 September 1941.
103. Kersaudy, *Churchill and de Gaulle*, pp. 158–60.
104. Kersaudy, *Churchill and de Gaulle*, pp. 158–60 (emphasis added).
105. Williams, *The Last Great Frenchman*, p. 156; Kenneth Young (ed.), *The Diaries of Sir Robert Bruce-Lockhart* (London, 1980), 7 October 1941.
106. Spears Papers, Box 2, 17 September 1941.
107. De Gaulle, *War Memoirs, Documents*, vol. I, p. 303.
108. Harvey, *War Diaries*, p. 47; CAB120/539, Churchill to Eden, 23 September 1941.
109. FO371/28545, Mack minute, 20 September 1942, Churchill minute, 23 September 1941.
110. FO371/28545, Mack minute, 20 September 1941.
111. FO371/28545, Eden minute, 20 September 1941.
112. Kersaudy, *Churchill and de Gaulle*, pp. 164–7; Harvey, *War Diaries*, pp. 45–7.
113. FO371/28545, Letter Parr, 2 September 1941.

## 10  Mutual Frustration

1. Charles de Gaulle, *War Memoirs: Documents*, 3 vols. (London, 1959), vol. I, pp. 313–20.
2. CAB21/1456, Report on Anglo-French Relations, 8 December 1941.
3. FO371/41880, 'General de Gaulle's Foreign Policy,' 6 July 1944; de Gaulle, *War Memoirs, Documents*, vol. I, pp. 376–7, 384–5.
4. De Gaulle, *War Memoirs, Documents*, vol. I, p. 312.
5. François Kersaudy, *Churchill and de Gaulle* (London, 1981), pp. 169–70.
6. Robert Murphy, *Diplomat among Warriors* (London, 1964), p. 104; Douglas Porch, *Hitler's Mediterranean Gamble* (London, 2004), p. 569.
7. Kersaudy, *Churchill and de Gaulle*, p. 295; Peter Mangold, *The Almost Impossible Ally* (London, 2006), p. 32; Cordell Hull, *Memoirs* (London, 1948), vol. II, p. 1159.
8. Andrew Roberts, *Masters and Commanders* (London, 2008), p. 76.
9. ADM199/872, Memo for First Sea Lord; Dominions Office to Canadian Government, 15 December 1941.

10. ADM199/872, Eden to de Gaulle, 20 October 1941.

11. FO371/31872, Minute, 19 January 1941.

12. Charles de Gaulle, *The Complete War Memoirs* (New York, 1972), pp. 214–15; Martin Thomas, *The French Empire at War* (Manchester, 1998), p. 135; Kersaudy, *Churchill and de Gaulle*, pp. 171–2; Jacques Crémieux-Brilhac, *La France Libre* (Paris, 1996), p. 280; Emile Muselier, *De Gaulle contre le Gaullisme* (Paris, 1946), p. 267; FO371/31873, British Liaison Officer on *Surcouf*, 1 January 1942.

13. Hull, *Memoirs*, p. 1130; Charles Williams, *The Last Great Frenchman* (London, 1993), pp. 167–8; Gloria Maguire, *Anglo-American Policy towards the Free French* (Basingstoke, 1995), p. 76; Thomas, *French Empire*, p. 176.

14. De Gaulle, *War Memoirs, Documents*, vol. I, p. 250.

15. Hull, *Memoirs*, vol. II, pp. 1134–5.

16. FO371/31873, Eden to de Gaulle, 14 January 1942; Eden to Churchill, 20 January 1942.

17. Sir Frank Roberts, *Facing the Dictators* (London, 1991), p. 54; Kersaudy, *Churchill and de Gaulle*, pp. 178–9.

18. Thomas, *French Empire*, p. 139.

19. FO371/31872, Admiral Dickens, 9 January 1942.

20. FO371/31872, Strang minute, 15 January 1942.

21. FO371/31873, Eden to Churchill, 20 January 1942.

22. FO371/31873, 'Diary of Events,' FO371/31874, z1260.

23. Williams, *The Last Great Frenchman*, p. 171; FO371/31959, De Gaulle to Peake, 4 March 1942; Eden to de Gaulle, 5 March 1942; Philippe de Gaulle, *De Gaulle mon père* (Paris, 2003), p. 241.

24. FO371/31959, Admiral Dickens, 9 December 1941.

25. FO371/31959, Letter to Strang, 22 December 1941; Eden to de Gaulle, 5 March 1942; Kersaudy, *Churchill and de Gaulle*, p. 180.

26. Kenneth Young (ed.), *The Diaries of Sir Robert Bruce-Lockhart* (London, 1980), p. 149.

27. FO371/31959, Eden to de Gaulle, 5 March 1942; Peake, tel., 6 March 1942.

28. FO371/31959, Eden to de Gaulle, 6 and 10 March 1942.

29. De Gaulle, *War Memoirs, Documents*, vol. I, pp. 410–1.

30. FO371/31959, Strang memo, 14 March 1942; FO371/31960, Strang minute, 14 March 1942; Kersaudy, *Churchill and de Gaulle*, pp. 181–2.

31. HS6/311, Foreign Office to Washington, 25 April 1942.

32. De Gaulle, *Complete War Memoirs*, p. 237.

33. PREM3/265/1, Peake to de Gaulle, 19 February 1942.

34. CAB121/622, 'Madagascar: Rallying by the Free French,' Joint Planning Staff, 25 February 1942.

35. PREM3/265/1, Churchill, 5 March 1942.

36. PREM3/265/1, Churchill, 5 March 1942.

37. PREM3/265/1, Churchill to Ismay, 30 March 1942; Martin Thomas, 'Imperial Backwater or Strategic Outpost? The British Takeover of Madagascar,' *Historical Journal*, December 1996, pp. 1055–6.

38. Williams, *The Last Great Frenchman*, pp. 180–1; ADM199/616A, Peake to de Gaulle, 17 June 1942; FO371/31899, Eden to de Gaulle, 11 May 1942; De Gaulle, *War Memoirs, Documents*, vol. I, pp. 344–8; Crémieux-Brilhac, *La France Libre*, p. 307.

39. FO371/31899, Strang to Cadogan, z3813.

40. De Gaulle, *Complete War Memoirs*, pp. 238–9.

41. FO371/31900, Foreign Office to Dominions, 13 May 1942.

42. John Harvey (ed.), *The War Diaries of Oliver Harvey* (London, 1978), p. 125.

43. FO371/31899, z3923; Alex Danchev and Daniel Todman (eds.), *War Diaries, 1939–45: Field Marshall Lord Alanbrooke* (London, 2001), pp. 262–3.

44. Harvey, *Harvey War Diaries*, p. 133.

45. FO371/31903, Eden minute, 5 July 1942.

46. ADM199/616A, de Gaulle to Peake, 20 May 1942.

47. De Gaulle, *Complete War Memoirs*, pp. 231, 240–1.

48. De Gaulle, *War Memoirs, Documents*, vol. I, pp. 353–4; de Gaulle, *Complete War Memoirs*, pp. 241–2; Crémieux-Brilhac, *La France Libre*, pp. 309–12; FO371/32028, Mack minute, 13 June 1942; ADM199/616A, Peake to de Gaulle, 17 June 1942.

49. Williams, *The Last Great Frenchman*, pp. 181–2; de Gaulle, *Mon père*, pp. 246–8; Henri Amouroux, *La Grande Histoire de la France sous l'occupation*, vol. IV (Paris, 1979), pp. 265–7.

50. De Gaulle, *War Memoirs, Documents*, vol. I, pp. 355–8, 417; Kersaudy, *Churchill and de Gaulle*, pp. 187–90.

51. Kersaudy, *Churchill and de Gaulle*, p. 190.

52. De Gaulle, *Complete War Memoirs*, p. 243; De Gaulle, *War Memoirs, Documents*, vol. I, p. 359.

53. CAB121/624, Foreign Office to Washington, 30 June 1942; De Gaulle, *War Memoirs, Documents*, vol. I, pp. 361–2; FO371/32027, Morton to Mack, 16 July 1942; Danchev and Todman, *Alanbrooke War Diaries*, p. 278; Harvey, *Harvey War Diaries*, p. 140.

54. FO371/32027, 'General de Gaulle and French Opinion,' Note by Secretary of State, 1 June 1942.

55. Elizabeth Barker, *Churchill and Eden at War* (London, 1978), pp. 61–2.

56. FO371/32027, Eden to Churchill, 9 July 1942.

57. De Gaulle, *Complete War Memoirs*, p. 311.

58. ADM199/616A, Foreign Office to Washington 3 July 1942; FO371/31951, 'Policy of HMG towards France,' West African War Council Paper 48, 27 October 1942; Jacques Soustelle, *Envers et contre tout* (Paris, 1947), vol. I, p. 324; Michael Stenton, *Radio London and Resistance in Occupied Europe* (Oxford, 2000) p. 203; De Gaulle, *Complete War Memoirs*, p. 311.

59. PREM3/192/7, Eden to Churchill, 10 April 1942.

60. PREM3/192/7, Eden to Churchill, 10 April 1942.

61. PREM3/192/7, Eden to Churchill, 27 April 1942; Churchill to Eden; Colonel Passy, *Souvenirs* (Monte Carlo, 1951), vol. II, p. 216.

62. PREM3/120/6, Eden to Peake, 28 July 1942.

63. FO371/32027, Strang to Dejean, 2 September 1942.

64. Aviel Roshwald, *Estranged Bedfellows* (Oxford, 1990), p. 120; A. B. Gaunson, *The Anglo-French Clash in Lebanon and Syria* (London, 1987), pp. 186–7.

65. Gaunson, *The Anglo-French Clash*, p. 147.

66. Kersaudy, *Churchill and de Gaulle*, p. 195.

67. De Gaulle, *Complete War Memoirs*, pp. 235–6; Gaunson, *Anglo-French Clash*, p. 86.

68. Gaunson, *Anglo-French Clash*, p. 69.

69. Max Egremont, *Under Two Flags* (London, 1997), p. 217.

70. Roshwald, *Estranged Bedfellows*, pp. 86–7, 107; Gaunson, *Anglo-French Clash*, pp. 66–7.

71. Gaunson, *Anglo-French Clash*, pp. 88–91; Kersaudy, *Churchill and de Gaulle*, pp. 195–6; de Gaulle, *Complete War Memoirs*, p. 327.

72. Gaunson, *Anglo-French Clash*, p. 95.

73. Gaunson, *Anglo-French Clash*, p. 95.

74. De Gaulle, *War Memoirs, Documents*, vol. II, p. 35.
75. Georges Catroux, *Dans la bataille de la Méditerranée* (Paris, 1949), p. 282.
76. Kersaudy, *Churchill and de Gaulle*, p. 199.
77. Pierre-Jean Rémy (ed.), *Diplomates en guerre* (Paris, 2007), p. 619.
78. De Gaulle, *War Memoirs, Documents*, vol. II, pp. 37–8, 41–3; Crémieux-Brilhac, *La France Libre*, pp. 398–9.
79. FO371/31950, Rooker to Foreign Office, 28 September 1942.
80. Jean Lacouture, *De Gaulle*, vol. I (London, 1993), p. 364.
81. Gaunson, *Anglo-French Clash*, pp. 100, 207; PREM3/120/6, Eden to Dejean, 10 September 1942; de Gaulle, *War Memoirs, Documents*, vol. II, pp. 49–51.
82. De Gaulle, *War Memoirs, Documents*, vol. II, p. 55; Catroux, *Bataille*, p. 287; Henri Frenay, *La Nuit finira* (Paris, 1973), p. 232.
83. Lacouture, *De Gaulle*, vol. I, p. 368.
84. David Dilks (ed.), *The Diaries of Sir Alexander Cadogan, 1938–45* (London, 1971), p. 479.
85. De Gaulle, *Complete War Memoirs*, pp. 341–2.
86. Kersaudy, *Churchill and de Gaulle*, pp. 202–9; Soustelle, *Envers et contre*, vol. I, pp. 360–2; Danchev and Todman, *Alanbrooke War Diaries*, p. 326.
87. Kersaudy, *Churchill and de Gaulle*, p. 206.
88. Crémieux-Brilhac, *La France Libre*, p. 415.
89. PREM3/120/6, Eden to Churchill, 1 October 1942.
90. FO371/32028, Morton to Churchill, 30 September 1942; Soustelle, *Envers et contre tout*, vol. I, p. 366.
91. Kersaudy, *Churchill and de Gaulle*, pp. 209–10; FO371/31950, Peake to de Gaulle, 6 October 1942.
92. Hervé Alphand, *L'Etonnement d'être* (Paris, 1977), pp. 104, 125.
93. Nigel Nicolson (ed.), *Harold Nicolson, Letters and Diaries, 1939–45* (London, 1967), p. 252.
94. FO371/31950, Morton to Churchill, 30 October 1942.
95. FO371/31950, Peake to Pleven, 31 October 1942.

## 11  A Shabby but Inevitable Compromise

1. Aurélie Luneau, *Radio Londres* (Paris, 2005), p. 168.
2. Winston Churchill, *The Hinge of Fate* (London, 1951), p. 390.
3. *Documents on German Foreign Policy*, vol. XI, pp. 1127–8, 213; vol. XII, p. 943; vol. XIII, pp. 934–5.
4. Douglas Porch, *Hitler's Mediterranean Gamble* (London, 2004), p. 326.
5. Porch, *Hitler's Mediterranean Gamble*, pp. 7–8.
6. Alex Danchev and Daniel Todman (eds.), *War Diaries, 1939–45: Field Marshall Lord Alanbrooke* (London, 2001), pp. 281–2; Keith Sainsbury, *The North African Landings* (London, 1976), pp. 43–4.
7. Sainsbury, *North African Landings*, pp. 34, 74; Robert Murphy, *Diplomat among Warriors* (London, 1964), pp. 126–7.
8. Andrew Roberts, *Masters and Commanders* (London, 2008), p. 127.
9. Warren F. Kimball (ed.), *Churchill and Roosevelt: The Complete Correspondence*, 3 vols. (Princeton, NJ, 1984), vol. I, p. 577.
10. Harry Butcher, *Three Years with Eisenhower* (London, 1946), pp. 8–9.
11. Danchev and Todman, *Alanbrooke War Diaries*, p. 281.

12. Martin Gilbert, *Road to Victory* (London, 1986), pp. 113–14.
13. Churchill, *Hinge of Fate*, p. 391.
14. Churchill, *Hinge of Fate*, p. 478; Danchev and Todman, *Alanbrooke War Diaries*, p. 285; Sainsbury, *North African Landings*, pp. 123–4.
15. Michael Howard, 'Soldier of Fortune,' *Times Literary Supplement*, 17 July 2009.
16. Kimball, *Churchill and Roosevelt*, vol. II, p. 104.
17. FO371/32155, tel., Washington, 22 December 1942; Cordell Hull, *Memoirs* (London, 1948), vol. II, p. 1232.
18. Anthony Eden, *The Reckoning* (London, 1965), p. 372.
19. Murphy, *Diplomat among Warriors*, pp. 211–12.
20. Eden, *The Reckoning*, p. 357; Peter Mangold, *The Almost Impossible Ally* (London, 2006), p. 33; Admiral Leahy, *I Was There* (London, 1950), p. 170.
21. Churchill, *Hinge of Fate*, p. 472.
22. Desmond Dinan, *The Politics of Persuasion* (Lanham, Md., 1988), p. 254.
23. FO371/32134, Foreign Office to Washington, 15 September 1942.
24. Warren Tute, *Reluctant Enemies* (London, 1990), p. 244; BBC, WAC, E2/131/8, European News Directive, 8 November 1942.
25. David Stafford, *Britain and European Resistance* (London, 1980), p. 89.
26. FO371/32133, JP (42) 748, Report by the Joint Planning Staff, 16 August 1942; Kimball, *Churchill and Roosevelt*, vol. I, p. 595; Llewellyn Woodward, *British Foreign Policy in the Second World War* (London, 1971), vol. II, p. 355.
27. PREM3/265/11, Churchill to Eden, 22 September 1942.
28. FO371/32027, Cadogan minute, 14 September 1942; FO371/32028, Sinclair minute, 14 September 1942; PREM3/120/6, Eden to Churchill, 22 September 1942.
29. Matthew Cobb, *The Resistance* (London, 2009), p. 141; Geoffrey Warner, *Pierre Laval and the Eclipse of France* (London, 1968), p. 297.
30. FO954/8, Eden to Churchill, 28 April 1942.
31. FO954/8, Churchill to Eden, 28 April 1942; PREM3/184/9, Morton to Churchill, 15 July 1942; Cobb, *Resistance*, p. 142.
32. Sir Patrick Reilly, unpublished memoir (Bodleian Library, Oxford), c. 6918, p. 222.
33. Churchill, *Hinge of Fate*, p. 547.
34. Porch, *Hitler's Mediterranean Gamble*, p. 343.
35. FO371/32135, Strang, 2 November 1942.
36. FO371/32135, Strang, 2 November 1942.
37. Kimball, *Churchill and Roosevelt*, vol. I, pp. 660–1.
38. Jacques Crémieux-Brilhac, *Ici Londres: Les Voix de la liberté, 1940–44*, 5 vols. (Paris, 1975), vol. I, p. xxiv; John Harvey (ed.), *The Diplomatic Diaries of Oliver Harvey* (London, 1979), p. 177.
39. Harvey, *Harvey War Diaries*, p. 179; Charles de Gaulle, *War Memoirs: Documents*, 3 vols. (London, 1959), vol. II, pp. 76–8; Jacques Soustelle, *Envers et contre tout* (Paris, 1947), vol. I, pp. 453–4; François Kersaudy, *Churchill and de Gaulle* (London, 1981), p. 220.
40. Porch, *Hitler's Mediterranean Gamble*, p. 343.
41. *Foreign Relations of the United States, 1942* (Washington, DC, 1962), vol. II, p. 432.
42. PREM3/184/4, Ismay to Churchill, 20 October 1942.
43. Porch, *Hitler's Mediterranean Gamble*, p. 352.
44. Porch, *Hitler's Mediterranean Gamble*, p. 359; Paul Auphan and Jacques Mordal, *La Marine française pendant la seconde guerre mondiale* (Paris, 1958), p. 312; Robert Paxton, *Parades and Politics at Vichy* (Princeton, NJ, 1966), p. 360.
45. W0204/4665, General Mark Clark, Record of Events, 11 November 1942.

46. Charles Williams, *The Last Great Frenchman* (London, 1993), p. 197.
47. Harvey, *Harvey War Diaries*, p. 187; George Mikes, *Darlan* (London, 1943), Chapter 7; Arthur Funk, *The Politics of Torch* (Lawrence, Ks., 1974), p. 238.
48. PREM3/442/9, Cunningham to First Sea Lord, 19 November 1942; Murphy, *Diplomat among Warriors*, pp. 154, 159; FO898/131, Lieut.-Col. Johnson to Brigadier Brook, 25 November 1942; CAB65/28, 30 November 1942.
49. Arthur Funk, 'Negotiating the "Deal with Darlan,"' *Journal of Contemporary History*, April 1973, p. 96; Murphy, *Diplomat among Warriors*, pp. 146–8; Butcher, *Three Years with Eisenhower*, p. 165; Harvey, *Harvey War Diaries*, p. 170; Danchev and Todman, *Alanbrooke War Diaries*, pp. 330–1.
50. Mark Pottle (ed.), *Champion Redoubtable* (London, 1998), pp. 252–3; Sainsbury, *North African Landings*, p. 45; Winston Churchill, *Their Finest Hour* (London, 1949), p. 550.
51. Arthur Funk, 'The US and Torch,' *Franco-British Studies*, spring 1989, p. 20; Murphy, *Diplomat among Warriors*, p. 152.
52. Butcher, *Three Years with Eisenhower*, p. 151.
53. FO371/32138, Churchill minute, 12 November 1942.
54. PREM3/442/9, Eden to Mack, 12 November 1942.
55. David Dilks (ed.), *The Diaries of Sir Alexander Cadogan, 1938–45* (London, 1971), pp. 491–2.
56. Butcher, *Three Years with Eisenhower*, p. 173; R. T. Thomas, *Britain and Vichy* (London, 1979), p. 119.
57. Harvey, *Harvey War Diaries*, pp. 184–6; FO371/32145, Eden to Churchill, 26 November 1942; Michael Stenton, *Radio London and Resistance in Occupied Europe* (Oxford, 2000), p. 214; Dilks, *Cadogan Diaries*, p. 493.
58. FO371/32143, Eden to Maisky, 20 November 1942; Philip Bell, 'British Public Opinion and the Darlan Deal,' *Franco-British Studies*, spring 1989, pp. 73–4.
59. Bell, 'British Public Opinion and the Darlan Deal,' pp. 74–5, 78–9; FO371/31954, Speaight, 15 November 1942; David Garnett, *The Secret History of PWE* (London, 2002), p. 259; Soustelle, *Envers et contre tout*, vol. II, p. 29.
60. FO371/32145, Eden to Churchill, 26 November 1942; M. R. D. Foot, *SOE in France* (London, 1966), p. 221.
61. Harvey, *Harvey War Diaries*, p. 184; FO371/32139, Jebb minute, 16 November 1942; FO371/ 32143, Eden to Maisky, 20 November 1942.
62. FO371/32138, Foreign Office to Washington, 13 November 1942; Eden, *The Reckoning*, p. 348.
63. Georges Catroux, *Dans la bataille de la Méditerranée* (Paris, 1949), pp. 302–4.
64. Eric Roussel, *Charles de Gaulle* (Paris, 2002), p. 318; De Gaulle, *War Memoirs, Documents*, vol. II, pp. 112–13; Colonel Passy, *Souvenirs* (Monte Carlo, 1951), vol. II, p. 359.
65. FO371/31951, Peake to de Gaulle, 15 November 1942.
66. Kimball, *Churchill and Roosevelt*, vol. I, p. 667.
67. PREM3/442/9, Churchill to Eisenhower, 14 November 1942.
68. Kimball, *Churchill and Roosevelt*, vol. II, p. 4.
69. Dilks, *Cadogan Diaries*, p. 493.
70. PREM3/442/9, War Cabinet, 16 November 1942; Harvey, *Harvey War Diaries*, p. 186; De Gaulle, *War Memoirs, Documents*, vol. II, pp. 90–1.
71. Charles de Gaulle, *The Complete War Memoirs* (New York, 1972), p. 362.
72. De Gaulle, *Complete War Memoirs*, pp. 361–2.

## 12 Death of an Admiral

1. Hervé Alphand, *L'Etonnement d'être* (Paris, 1977), p. 129.
2. Douglas Porch, *Hitler's Mediterranean Gamble* (London, 2004), p. 384.
3. FO371/31250, Anderson to Chief of the Imperial General Staff, 29 December 1942; *The Papers of Dwight D. Eisenhower: The War Years*, vol. II, p. 872.
4. Paul Auphan and Jacques Mordal, *La Marine française pendant la seconde guerre mondiale* (Paris, 1958), p. 312; Albert Kammerer, *La Passion de la flotte française* (Paris, 1951), p. 414.
5. W0204/4665, Record of Events, 10 November–24 December 1942; Paul Auphan, *L'Honneur de servir* (Paris, 1978), p. 239; Robert Paxton, *Parades and Politics at Vichy* (Princeton, NJ, 1966), p. 383; Kammerer, *La Passion*, p. 427.
6. Auphan and Mordal, *La Marine*, p. 324; Winston Churchill, *The Hinge of Fate* (London, 1951), p. 561; Warren Tute, *Reluctant Enemies* (London, 1990), pp. 290–2.
7. Porch, *Hitler's Mediterranean Gamble*, p. 365.
8. Alphand, *L'Etonnement*, pp. 129–30.
9. Harry Butcher, *Three Years with Eisenhower* (London, 1946), p. 175; John Harvey (ed.), *The Diplomatic Diaries of Oliver Harvey* (London, 1979), p. 193; BBC, WAC, E2/131/8, European News Directive, 28 November 1942; Churchill, *Hinge of Fate*, p. 563; Stephen Roskill, *The War at Sea* (London, 1954), vol. I, p. 338.
10. Charles de Gaulle, *The Complete War Memoirs* (New York, 1972), p. 359.
11. Colonel Passy, *Souvenirs* (Monte Carlo, 1951), vol. II, p. 265.
12. Tute, *Reluctant Enemies*, p. 294.
13. Jean Lacouture, *De Gaulle* (London, 1984), vol. I, p. 407; Arthur Funk, 'The US and Torch,' *Franco-British Studies*, spring 1989, p. 26.
14. *The Papers of Dwight D. Eisenhower*, pp. 788–9.
15. CAB120/530, Churchill to Eden, 1 December 1942; Churchill to Eden, 4 December 1942; Foreign Office to Washington, 1 December 1942; Eisenhower to Marshall, 4 December 1942; David Dilks (ed.), *The Diaries of Sir Alexander Cadogan, 1938–45* (London, 1971), p. 498.
16. *The Papers of Dwight D. Eisenhower*, p. 872.
17. PREM3/442/9, Cunningham to First Sea Lord, 14 November 1942.
18. Michael Simpson, *A Life of Admiral of the Fleet Andrew Cunningham* (London, 2004), p. 145; Robert Murphy, *Diplomat among Warriors* (London, 1964), p. 181; Hervé Coutau-Bégarie and Claude Huan, *Darlan* (Paris, 1989), p. 284.
19. FO371/32150, Cunningham to First Sea Lord, 28 December 1942; Harold Macmillan, *War Diaries: The Mediterranean, 1939–45* (London, 1984), p. 45.
20. FO371/32143, Strang minute on Mack, tel., 27 November 1942.
21. Llewellyn Woodward, *British Foreign Policy during the Second World War* (London, 1971), vol. II, p. 378.
22. WO204/303, Eisenhower to Combined Chiefs of Staff, 4 December 1942; CAB120/530, Eisenhower to Churchill, 5 December 1942.
23. FO892/131, Lieut.-Col. Johnston, 25 November 1942; WO204/300, Eisenhower to Combined Chiefs of Staff, 21 December 1942; Anthony Verrier, *Assassination in Algiers* (London, 1990), p. 221; *The Papers of Dwight D. Eisenhower*, p. 803.
24. Woodward, *British Foreign Policy*, vol. II, p. 369; FO371/32142, Letter Mack, 25 November 1942; FO371/32144, Foreign Office to Halifax, 5 December 1942; FO371/32148, Foreign Office to Washington, 18 December 1942; Eric Roussel, *Charles De Gaulle* (Paris, 2002), p. 325.
25. *The Papers of Dwight D. Eisenhower*, p. 663.

26. HS3/47, Colonel Keswick, 18 December 1942; CAB/120/530, tel., Tangiers, 7 December 1942; Tute, *Reluctant Enemies*, pp. 296–7.
27. Peter Mangold, *The Almost Impossible Ally* (London, 2006), p. 34.
28. Brook Richards, *Secret Flotillas* (London, 2001), vol. II, p. 251; FO371/32144, Mack to Strang, 27 November 1942; Strang to Mack, 28 November 1942.
29. Kenneth Young (ed.), *The Diaries of Sir Robert Bruce-Lockhart* (London, 1980), 25 December 1942; FO371/32144, Strang minute, 1 December 1942.
30. Harvey, *Harvey War Diaries*, p. 202.
31. Warren F. Kimball (ed.), *Churchill and Roosevelt: The Complete Correspondence*, 3 vols. (Princeton, NJ, 1984), vol. II, pp. 75, 77; CAB65/28, 23 December 1942; FO371/32150, Foreign Office to Moscow, 17 December 1942.
32. De Gaulle, *Complete War Memoirs*, p. 363.
33. W0106/5233, Peake to de Gaulle, 20 November 1942.
34. FO371/31952, Peake to de Gaulle, 21 November 1942.
35. Kimball, *Churchill and Roosevelt*, vol. II, pp. 29–30.
36. FO371/31952, Eden to Churchill, 26 November 1942; Asa Briggs, *The War of Words* (London, 1970), pp. 411–12; Harvey, *Harvey War Diaries*, p. 191.
37. PREM3/120/8, Cadogan to Churchill.
38. Jacques Soustelle, *Envers et contre tout* (Paris, 1947), vol. I, pp. 49–50.
39. FO371/32144, Strang to Mack, 28 November 1942.
40. CAB120/530, Churchill to Eden, 18 November 1942.
41. FO371/32145, Mack to Strang, 29 November 1942.
42. D. R. Thorpe, *Eden* (London, 2003), p. 275.
43. Dilks, *Cadogan Diaries*, p. 496; Butcher, *Three Years with Eisenhower*, pp. 177–8; Harvey, *Harvey War Diaries*, pp. 191, 192–3.
44. FO371/32144, Strang to Mack, 28 November 1942.
45. Geoffrey Best, *Churchill and War* (London, 2005), p. 141.
46. PREM3/442/12, secret speech, 10 December 1942.
47. PREM3/442/12, secret speech, 10 December 1942.
48. Nigel Nicolson (ed.), *Harold Nicolson, Letters and Diaries, 1939–45* (London, 1967), p. 266; Harold Macmillan, *The Blast of War* (London, 1967), pp. 216–17.
49. Mark Pottle (ed.), *Champion Redoubtable* (London, 1998), p. 248.
50. HS6/312, 16 December 1942.
51. Woodward, *British Foreign Policy*, vol. II, p. 397.
52. CAB65/28, WM (42), 21 December 1942, 171st.
53. CAB120/530, tel., Cunningham, 22 December 1942.
54. Richards, *Secret Flotillas*, vol. II, p. 251; Tute, *Reluctant Enemies*, p. 303; Charles Williams, *The Last Great Frenchman* (London, 1993), p. 203.
55. FO371/32148, Washington to Foreign Office, 24 December 1942.
56. BBC, WAC, E2/131/8, General Directive, 25 December 1942.
57. Harvey, *Harvey War Diaries*, p. 203.
58. Pottle, *Champion*, pp. 249–50.
59. Thorpe, *Eden*, p. 278.
60. Passy, *Souvenirs*, vol. II, p. 371; Ben Pimlott (ed.), *The Second World Diaries of Hugh Dalton* (London, 1986), p. 540.
61. Coutau-Bégarie and Huan, *Darlan*, pp. 705–8; Williams, *The Last Great Frenchman*, p. 202.
62. CAB120/530, First Sea Lord to Admiral Cunningham, 30 December 1942.
63. Coutau-Bégarie and Huan, *Darlan*, p. 328; Max Hastings, *Finest Years* (London, 2009), p. 349.

64. Williams, *The Last Great Frenchman*, p. 204; Richards, *Secret Flotillas*, vol. II, p. 253.
65. M. R. D. Foot, 'Eisenhower and the British,' in Guenther Bischof and Stephen Ambrose (eds.), *Eisenhower: A Centenary Reassessment* (Baton Rouge, La., 1995), pp. 44–5.
66. Richards, *Secret Flotillas*, vol. II, p. 228.
67. M. R. D. Foot, *SOE in France* (London, 2004), p. 199.
68. HS3/47, Col. Keswick, 18 December 1942.
69. The Cagoulards were an extreme right-wing group whose aim was to fight Communism by any means.
70. Richards, *Secret Flotilla*, vol. II, p. 251; Williams, *The Last Great Frenchman*, pp. 202–3.
71. HS3/47, Selborne draft letter to Eden, 24 December 1942.
72. Peter Wilkinson and Jean Bright Astley, *Gubbins and SOE* (London, 1993), p. 118.
73. HS3/46, SOE to Cadogan, 19 December 1942; Peter Tompkins, *The Murder of Admiral Darlan* (London, 1965), p. 225.
74. Richards, *Secret Flotillas*, vol. II, p. 254.
75. Churchill, *Hinge of Fate*, pp. 579–80.
76. David Reynolds, *In Command of History* (London, 2004), p. 330.
77. John Winton, *Cunningham* (London, 1998), pp. 290–1.

### 13   Kings of Brentford

1. Peter Mangold, *The Almost Impossible Ally* (London, 2006), pp. 35–6.
2. Mangold, *The Almost Impossible Ally*, pp. 35–6.
3. PREM3/442/21, Eden minute, 5 January 1943.
4. PREM3/181/8, Foreign Office to Washington, 2 January 1943; Strang to Welles, 23 March 1943; FO371/36036, Eden to Macmillan, 6 May 1943.
5. John Harvey (ed.), *The Diplomatic Diaries of Oliver Harvey* (London, 1979), vol. II, p. 209.
6. William Langer, *Our Vichy Gamble* (New York, 1947), p. 380; André Béziat, *Franklin Roosevelt et la France* (Paris, 1997), pp. 309–10.
7. Lord Egremont, *Wyndham and Children First* (London, 1968), p. 80; Harold Macmillan, *War Diaries: The Mediterranean, 1939–45* (London, 1984), p. 9.
8. Jacques Crémieux-Brilhac, *Ici Londres: Les Voix de la liberté, 1940–44*, 5 vols. (Paris, 1975), vol. III, pp. 84–5.
9. François Kersaudy, *Churchill and de Gaulle* (London, 1981), p. 238.
10. David Dilks (ed.), *The Diaries of Sir Alexander Cadogan, 1938–48* (London, 1971); Kersaudy, *Churchill and de Gaulle*, p. 238; Michael Howard, *Grand Strategy* (London, 1970), vol. IV, p. 280; FO660/86, Eden to Churchill, 17 January 1943; Jean Lacouture, *De Gaulle* (London, 1984), vol. I, p. 417; Eric Roussel, *De Gaulle* (Paris, 2002), p. 343.
11. CAB65/37, WM (43), 18 January 1943, 9th; Dilks, *Cadogan Diaries*, p. 504.
12. FO660/85, Dixon, 'Impressions of the Anfa Conference: The French Question.'
13. Lacouture, *De Gaulle*, vol. I, p. 418; Harold Macmillan, *The Blast of War* (London, 1967), p. 251; Elliot Roosevelt, *As He Saw It* (New York, 1946), pp. 115–16.
14. FO660/86, Churchill to Eden, 18 January 1943.
15. Harvey, *Harvey War Diaries*, p. 211.
16. Sir Dodds Parker, *Setting Europe Ablaze* (London, 1983), p. 122.
17. Charles de Gaulle, *The Complete War Memoirs* (New York, 1972), pp. 390–1.
18. Winston Churchill, *The Hinge of Fate* (London, 1951), p. 611.
19. Martin Gilbert, *Road to Victory* (London, 1986), p. 305.

20. Macmillan, *The Blast of War*, p. 249.
21. Lacouture, *De Gaulle*, vol. I, p. 425.
22. FO660/88, Dixon memo, 27 January 1943.
23. De Gaulle, *Complete War Memoirs*, p. 398; Lacouture, *De Gaulle*, vol. I, p. 427.
24. Arthur Funk, 'The "Anfa" Memorandum,' *Journal of Modern History*, September 1954, p. 251.
25. FO660/86, Anfa Diary; Michèle Cointet, *De Gaulle et Giraud* (Paris, 2005), pp. 281–2.
26. Harvey, *Harvey War Diaries*, pp. 215–16; Macmillan, *The Blast of War*, pp. 257–8; PREM3/182/8, Eden to Churchill, telescope 349; Churchill to Eden, 6 February 1943.
27. Macmillan, *The Blast of War*, pp. 256–8; Lacouture, *De Gaulle*, vol. I, p. 424; Cointet, *De Gaulle et Giraud*, p. 283.
28. Sherfield Papers (Bodleian Library, Oxford), unpublished memoirs, c953, p. 61.
29. Macmillan, *The Blast of War*, pp. 247, 251; Churchill, *Hinge of Fate*, p. 648.
30. Sir John Kennedy, *The Business of War* (London, 1958), p. 289.
31. PREM3/179/5, Commander-in-Chief, Mediterranean, 23 and 26 November 1942, 13 December 1942.
32. Macmillan, *The Blast of War*, p. 282.
33. Lord Casey, *Personal Experiences* (London, 1962), p. 133.
34. PREM3/179/5, Churchill to Eden, 26 January 1943; Sydney Zebel, 'Churchill, Macmillan and the Reactivation of Force X,' *Albion*, winter 1976, p. 363.
35. Casey, *Personal Experiences*, p. 133; PREM3/179/5, Discussion Cairo, 27 January 1943; Casey to Attlee, 1 February 1943; Cairo to Foreign Office, 28 February 1943; Churchill to Eden, 4 March 1943.
36. PREM3/179/5, Macmillan to Foreign Office, 13 March 1942.
37. Zebel, 'Churchill, Macmillan and the Reactivation of Force X,' p. 360.
38. François Duchêne, *Jean Monnet* (New York, 1994), pp. 99, 100.
39. Jean Monnet, *Memoirs* (London, 1978), p. 191; Harvey, *Harvey War Diaries*, pp. 216–17; Kennedy, *The Business of War*, p. 287.
40. Macmillan, *The Blast of War*, p. 296.
41. FO371/36047, Peake to Strang, 16 February 1943; Kersaudy, *Churchill and de Gaulle*, p. 261; De Gaulle, *Complete War Memoirs*, pp. 399–40.
42. FO371/36047, Strang memo, 10 February 1943.
43. Gilbert, *Road to Victory*, p. 346.
44. Andrew Roberts, *Masters and Commanders* (London, 2008), pp. 352–3.
45. FO371/36013, Peake tel., 2 March 1943.
46. Eden to Churchill, 2 March 1943; Harvey, *Harvey War Diaries*, p. 225; Kersaudy, *Churchill and de Gaulle*, p. 261.
47. PREM3/442/18, Churchill to Macmillan, 22 March 1943; PREM 3/442/21, Morton to Churchill, 10 March 1943.
48. Harvey, *Harvey War Diaries*, pp. 218–19, 227.
49. Gilbert, *The Road to Victory*, p. 333.
50. Sherfield Papers, c520; Makins to Strang, 2 March 1943, c953; unpublished memoirs, p. 94.
51. Duchêne, *Monnet*, pp. 83–94.
52. Duchêne, *Monnet*, pp. 83–94.
53. W0106/5233, Washington to Macmillan, 24 February 1943; Macmillan, *The Blast of War*, p. 297.
54. Mangold, *The Almost Impossible Ally*, p. 43.
55. Macmillan, *War Diaries*, p. 46.

56. Macmillan, *The Blast of War*, pp. 311–12; Simon Berthon, *Allies at War* (London, 2001), p. 242.
57. FO371/36119, Strang minute, 20 February 1943.
58. Cointet, *De Gaulle et Giraud*, p. 357.
59. Sherfield Papers, c953, unpublished memoir, p. 122.
60. FO660/18, Macmillan to Makins, 27 February 1943.
61. Macmillan, *War Diaries*, p. 53; Cointet, *De Gaulle et Giraud*, p. 241.
62. Charles de Gaulle, *Lettres, notes et carnets* (Paris, 1982), vol. IV, 19 March 1943; FO371/36047, Peake to de Gaulle, 24 February 1943.
63. PREM3/442/18, Churchill to Foreign Office, 16 March 1943.
64. FO371/36047, Peake memo, 23 March 1943.
65. De Gaulle, *Complete War Memoirs*, pp. 410–11.
66. PREM3/442/18, Churchill to Macmillan, 2 April 1943; Cointet, *De Gaulle et Giraud*, pp. 342–4.
67. Macmillan, *The Blast of War*, pp. 312–13; Macmillan, *War Diaries*, p. 57.
68. Hervé Alphand, *L'Etonnement d'être* (Paris, 1977), pp. 149–50; de Gaulle, *Complete War Memoirs*, p. 411.
69. FO954/9, Eden to de Gaulle, 6 April 1943; PREM 3/442/6, Despatch, 'The Weeks Between'; Sherfield Papers, c520, Makins to Strang, 7 April 1943.
70. W0106/5233, De Gaulle to Peake, 25 December 1942.
71. De Gaulle, *Complete War Memoirs*, p. 413.
72. Douglas Porch, *Hitler's Mediterranean Gamble* (London, 2004), pp. 384, 394–5.
73. Macmillan, *War Diaries*, pp. 68–72.
74. Macmillan, *War Diaries*, pp. 68–72.
75. FO371/ 36173, Macmillan to Churchill, 29 April 1943.
76. FO371/ 36173, Macmillan to Churchill, 29 April 1943.
77. PREM3/442/21, Churchill to de Gaulle, 30 April 1943.
78. Cointet, *De Gaulle et Giraud*, pp. 347–8.
79. Macmillan, *War Diaries*, p. 80.
80. FO660/48, Macmillan to Foreign Office, 6 May 1943.
81. Macmillan, *War Diaries*, pp. 82–3, 84–6; FO660/48, Macmillan to Makins, 13 May 1943; Duchêne, *Monnet*, p. 119.
82. Cordell Hull, *Memoirs* (London, 1948), vol. II, p. 1213.
83. Hull, *Memoirs*, vol. II, p. 1219.
84. Hull, *Memoirs*, vol. II, p. 1219.
85. Warren F. Kimball (ed.), *Churchill and Roosevelt: The Complete Correspondence*, 3 vols. (Princeton, NJ, 1984), vol. II, p. 210.
86. Kimball, *Churchill and Roosevelt*, vol. II, p. 223; Harvey, *Harvey War Diaries*, p. 260; *Foreign Relations of the United States, 1943* (Washington, DC, 1964), vol. II, pp. 111–12.
87. Kersaudy, *Churchill and de Gaulle*, pp. 274–5.
88. Kersaudy, *Churchill and de Gaulle*, pp. 274–5.
89. Duff Hart-Davis (ed.), *King's Counsellor* (London, 2006), p. 132.
90. CAB65/38, WM (43), 23 May 1943, 75th.
91. CAB65/38, WM (43), 23 May 1943, 75th.
92. CAB65/38, WM (43), 23 May 1943, 75th.
93. CAB65/38, WM (43), 23 May 1943, 75th.
94. CAB65/38, Attlee and Eden to Churchill, 23 May 1943.
95. De Gaulle, *Complete War Memoirs*, p. 418.
96. 'The English people have been marvellous', Harvey, *Harvey War Diaries*, p. 262.
97. Cointet, *De Gaulle et Giraud*, p. 375.

## 14 'C'est De Gaulle'

1. Charles Williams, *The Last Great Frenchman* (London, 1995), pp. 224–5.
2. John Harvey (ed.), *The Diplomatic Diaries of Oliver Harvey* (London, 1979), p. 263.
3. PREM3/184/7, Eden to Churchill, 18 April 1943.
4. Mary Soames, *Speaking for Themselves* (London, 1998), p. 484.
5. PREM3/184/5, Morton to 'C,' 30 April 1943; PREM3/184/6, Selborne to Churchill, 24 June 1943.
6. Williams, *The Last Great Frenchman*, pp. 225–6; Harold Macmillan, *The Blast of War* (London, 1967), p. 329; Michèle Cointet, *De Gaulle et Giraud* (Paris, 2005), p. 377.
7. Harold Macmillan, *War Diaries: The Mediterranean, 1935–45* (London, 1984), p. 98; FO660/49, Macmillan memo, 1 June 1943.
8. FO660/49, Macmillan to de Gaulle, 1 June 1943.
9. Sherfield Papers, c953, unpublished memoirs, p. 121.
10. Jean Lacouture, *De Gaulle* (London, 1984), vol. I, p. 447.
11. FO660/49, Macmillan to de Gaulle, 2 June 1943.
12. FO660/49, Macmillan to de Gaulle, 2 June 1943.
13. Cointet, *De Gaulle et Giraud*, p. 400; Macmillan, *War Diaries*, p. 107.
14. Alex Danchev and Daniel Todman (eds.), *War Diaries, 1939–45: Field Marshall Lord Alanbrooke* (London, 2001), p. 418.
15. Charles de Gaulle, *The Complete War Memoirs* (New York, 1972), p. 427; Cointet, *De Gaulle et Giraud*, p. 405.
16. Macmillan, *War Diaries*, pp. 109–10; François Kersaudy, *Churchill and de Gaulle* (London, 1981), p. 285.
17. Sherfield Papers, c.520, letter, 6 June 1943.
18. Sherfield Papers, c.953, unpublished memoirs, p. 136.
19. *Hansard Parliamentary Debates*, 1942–3, vol. 390, cols. 568–9, 8 June 1943.
20. *Hansard Parliamentary Debates*, 1942–3, vol. 390, cols. 568–9, 8 June 1943.
21. FO371/36031, Foreign Office to Algiers, 15 June 1943; FO371/36032, Morton to Mack, 26 June 1943.
22. Warren F. Kimball (ed.), *Churchill and Roosevelt: The Complete Correspondence*, 3 vols. (Princeton, NJ, 1984), vol. II, pp. 231–2; Eric Roussel, *De Gaulle* (Paris, 2002), p. 366.
23. De Gaulle, *Complete War Memoirs*, p. 430; Williams, *The Last Great Frenchman*, p. 228; Peter Mangold, *The Almost Impossible Ally* (London, 2006), p. 56; Cointet, *De Gaulle et Giraud*, pp. 406–7.
24. Cointet, *De Gaulle et Giraud*, pp. 411–12.
25. Macmillan, *War Diaries*, pp. 113–17.
26. Macmillan, *War Diaries*, pp. 113–17.
27. Macmillan, *War Diaries*, pp. 113–17.
28. FO660/50, Roosevelt to Eisenhower, 10 June 1943.
29. Kimball, *Churchill and Roosevelt*, vol. II, p. 237.
30. FO660/50, Churchill to Macmillan, 12 June 1943; FO954/8, Churchill to Macmillan, 13 June 1943.
31. Kersaudy, *Churchill and de Gaulle*, p. 287; Simon Berthon, *Allies at War* (London, 2001), pp. 277–8; David Dilks (ed.), *The Diaries of Sir Alexander Cadogan, 1938–45* (London, 1971), p. 536.
32. Harvey, *Harvey War Diaries*, pp. 266–7.
33. Reilly Papers, unpublished memoir, Ms. Eng., c6919, p. 11.
34. FO660/15, Macmillan memo, 14 June 1943.

35. Sherfield Papers, c.520, Makins to Strang, 15 June 1943.
36. Sherfield Papers, c.520, Makins to Strang, 15 June 1943.
37. PREM3/181/7, Macmillan to Foreign Office, 22 June 1943; Strang to Makins, 21 June 1943; FO371/36128, Mack minute, 22 June 1943; *Foreign Relations of the United States, 1943*, vol. II, pp. 152–3; Arthur Funk, *Charles de Gaulle* (Norman, Okla., 1959), p. 134.
38. Dilks, *Cadogan Diaries*, p. 537 (emphasis in original); Harvey, *Harvey War Diaries*, p. 270.
39. Mangold, *The Almost Impossible Ally*, pp. 59–60.
40. Mangold, *The Almost Impossible Ally*, p. 60.
41. Lacouture, *De Gaulle*, vol. I, p. 449.
42. *New Statesman*, 26 June 1943.
43. Duff Hart-Davis (ed.), *King's Counsellor* (London, 2006), p. 138.
44. FO371/36299, Churchill to Eden, 12 June 1943; Kersaudy, *Churchill and de Gaulle*, p. 290.
45. FO371/36301, Eden draft memo to Cabinet, 12 July 1943.
46. FO371/36301, Eden draft memo to Cabinet, 12 July 1943; Harvey, *Harvey War Diaries*, p. 274.
47. FO371/36301, 'US Policy towards France,' note by the Prime Minister, 13 July 1943.
48. FO371/36301, 'US Policy towards France.'
49. FO371/36301, Strang minute, 15 July 1943.
50. Macmillan, *War Diaries*, p. 150.
51. Sherfield Papers, c520, Makins to Mack, 2 August 1943; c953, unpublished memoirs, p. 141.
52. Kimball, *Churchill and Roosevelt*, vol. II, pp. 334–5.
53. Cordell Hull, *Memoirs* (London, 1948), vol. II, pp. 1242–3; Kersaudy, *Churchill and de Gaulle*, pp. 293–4; Harvey, *Harvey War Diaries*, pp. 280–1.
54. Cordell Hull, *Memoirs*, vol. II, p. 1132.
55. PREM3/181/9, Eden to Sargent, 25 August 1943; Kersaudy, *Churchill and de Gaulle*, p. 297.
56. Sherfield Papers, c.520, Makins to Strang, 2 September 1943; Macmillan, *War Diaries*, pp. 193–4.
57. Williams, *The Last Great Frenchman*, p. 237; Lacouture, *De Gaulle*, vol. I, pp. 491–2.
58. FO371/36036, De Gaulle to Stone, 16 October 1943.
59. Macmillan, *War Diaries*, p. 277 (emphasis in original).
60. De Gaulle, *Complete War Memoirs*, pp. 491–2.
61. De Gaulle, *Complete War Memoirs*, pp. 491–2.
62. Martin Thomas, 'France in Britain's Signals Intelligence,' *French History*, March 2000, p. 64.
63. De Gaulle, *Complete War Memoirs*, p. 529.
64. De Gaulle, *Complete War Memoirs*, p. 516
65. Kersaudy, *Churchill and de Gaulle*, p. 298.
66. Llewellyn Woodward, *British Foreign Policy in the Second World War* (London, 1971), vol. III, p. 11; Martin Gilbert, *The Road to Victory* (London, 1986), p. 1155; FO660/140, Eden to Foreign Office, 2 November 1943; FO371/36036, Cadogan minute, 3 November 1943.
67. De Gaulle, *Complete War Memoirs*, pp. 458–9; Charles de Gaulle, *War Memoirs, Documents*, 3 vols. (London, 1959), vol. II, pp. 212, 216–19.
68. Kimball, *Churchill and Roosevelt*, vol. II, p. 439.
69. FO371/36327, Despatch, 13 September 1943.

70. Sherfield Papers, c520, Letter to Sir E. Makins, 10 September 1943.
71. FO371/36036, Mack minute, 2 November 1943; FO660/140, Algiers to Foreign Office, 3 November 1943; Macmillan, *War Diaries*, p. 279.
72. Macmillan, *War Diaries*, pp. 281–2.
73. De Gaulle, *Complete War Memoirs*, p. 531; Hart-Davis, *King's Counsellor*, p. 184.
74. Meir Zamin, 'An Intimate Alliance,' *Middle Eastern Studies*, November 2005, pp. 819–21.
75. Aviel Roshwald, *Estranged Bedfellows* (Oxford, 1990), pp. 156–7; Sherfield Papers, c520, Makins to Caccia, 17 November 1943.
76. Kimball, *Churchill and Roosevelt*, vol. II, pp. 599–600.
77. Kimball, *Churchill and Roosevelt*, vol. II, pp. 599–600.
78. Macmillan, *War Diaries*, p. 294.
79. Macmillan, *War Diaries*, p. 297.
80. De Gaulle, *Complete War Memoirs*, pp. 527–8.
81. Roshwald, *Estranged Bedfellows*, pp. 162–3.
82. Macmillan, *War Diaries*, pp. 299–300.
83. A. B. Gaunson, *The Anglo-French Clash in Lebanon and Syria* (London, 1987), pp. 139–40; Edward Spears, *Fulfilment of a Mission* (London, 1977), p. 280; Sherfield Papers, c.520, Makins to Strang, 26 November 1943.
84. Mangold, *The Almost Impossible Ally*, p. 67.
85. Woodward, *British Foreign Policy*, vol. III, p. 6.
86. Macmillan, *Blast of War*, p. 445.
87. Mangold, *The Almost Impossible Ally*, p. 66.
88. Mangold, *The Almost Impossible Ally*, p. 72.
89. Mangold, *The Almost Impossible Ally*, p. 73; Sherfield Papers, c953, unpublished memoir, p. 139; Macmillan, *War Diaries*, p. 135.
90. Harvey, *Harvey War Diaries*, pp. 302–4.
91. John Charmley, *Duff Cooper* (London, 1986), pp. 169–70.
92. Charmley, *Duff Cooper*, pp. 169–70.
93. De Gaulle, *Complete War Memoirs*, p. 541.
94. Charmley, *Duff Cooper*, p. 173.
95. Macmillan, *War Diaries*, pp. 347–8; HS6/308, Macmillan to Eden, 20 December 1943.
96. Julian Norwich (ed.), *The Duff Cooper Diaries* (London, 2005), p. 283; de Gaulle, *Complete War Memoirs*, p. 546.
97. Macmillan, *War Diaries*, p. 350.
98. Norwich, *Duff Cooper Diaries*, pp. 288–9.
99. FO660/113, Cooper to Eden, 17 January 1944.
100. De Gaulle, *Complete War Memoirs*, p. 546.
101. Gilbert, *Road to Victory*, p. 646.
102. Gilbert, *Road to Victory*, p. 646.
103. Lacouture, *De Gaulle*, vol. I, p. 500.
104. Lacouture, *De Gaulle*, vol. I, p. 500.
105. Kersaudy, *Churchill and de Gaulle*, p. 314.
106. Norwich, *Duff Cooper Diaries*, p. 290; de Gaulle, *Complete War Memoirs*, pp. 547–8.

## 15 Going Back

1. Tim Brooks, *British Propaganda to France* (Edinburgh, 2007), pp. 89, 96; Aurélie Luneau, *Radio Londres* (Paris, 2005), pp. 190, 192.
2. Max Hastings, 'Man of War,' *Financial Times*, 5/6 September 2009; Max Hastings, 'Up and Against "the Finest Soldiers in the World,"' *New York Review of Books*, 3 April 2008, p. 19; Richard Overy, *Why the Allies Won* (London, 1995), p. 137; N. A. M. Rogers, *The Command of the Ocean* (London, 2004), p. 288.
3. Winston Churchill, *Closing the Ring* (London, 1952), pp. 514–15; Gerhard Weinberg, 'D Day after Fifty Years,' in Gerhard Weinberg, *Hitler, Germany and World War Two* (Cambridge, 1995), p. 263; Nigel Hamilton, *Monty* (London, 1983), vol. II, p. 562; David Reynolds, *Rich Relations* (London, 1996), pp. 360–1.
4. Douglas Porch, *Hitler's Mediterranean Gamble* (London, 2004), p. 453.
5. Hastings, 'Up and Against,' p. 19.
6. Hastings, 'Up and Against,' p. 19; Porch, *Hitler's Mediterranean Gamble*, p. 415.
7. Andrew Roberts, *Masters and Commanders* (London, 2008), p. 276.
8. Roberts, *Masters and Commanders*, p. 479; Overy, *Why the Allies Won*, pp. 142–3; Harry Butcher, *Three Years with Eisenhower* (London, 1946), p. 409; Weinberg, 'D Day after Fifty Years,' p. 262.
9. Roberts, *Masters and Commanders*, pp. 394, 397, 398, 432; Paul Kennedy, *The Rise and Fall of Great Powers* (London, 1989), pp. 455, 458.
10. Hervé Alphand, *L'Etonnement d'être* (Paris, 1977), p. 175.
11. Olivier Wiéviorka, *Normandy* (Cambridge, Mass., 2008), p. 88.
12. Reynolds, *Rich Relations*, p. 361.
13. Charles Webster and Noble Frankland, *The Strategic Air Offensive against Germany* (London, 1961), vol. III, p. 34; John Ehrman, *Grand Strategy* (London, 1956), vol. V, p. 297.
14. AIR19/218, Massigli to Eden, 16 April 1943; Eden to Sinclair, 30 September 1943; Eden to Sinclair, 11 June 1943.
15. Ehrman, *Grand Strategy*, p. 299.
16. Martin Gilbert, *The Road to Victory* (London, 1986), p. 748.
17. Ehrman, *Grand Strategy*, p. 298.
18. CAB65/46, WM (44), 3 April 1944, 43rd; 27 April 1944, 57th; 2 May 1944, 61st.
19. Webster and Frankland, *Strategic Air Offensive*, pp. 35–8.
20. Warren F. Kimball (ed.), *Churchill and Roosevelt: The Complete Correspondence*, 3 vols. (Princeton, NJ, 1984), vol. III, pp. 122–3.
21. Ehrman, *Grand Strategy*, p. 304.
22. Jacques Crémieux-Brilhac, *Ici Londres: Les Voix de la liberté, 1940–44*, 5 vols. (Paris, 1975), vol. V, pp. 24–5, 30; BBC, WAC, E2/209/3, Output Report, 7–20 April 1944; AIR19/218, Bottomley to Harris, 19 April 1944.
23. Nigel Nicolson (ed.), *Harold Nicolson, Letters and Diaries, 1939–45* (London, 1967), p. 303; Kimball, *Churchill and Roosevelt*, vol. III, pp. 123–4.
24. FO371/41984, French bishops appeal, 15 May 1944.
25. FO371/41984, French News Survey, 28–31 May 1944; tel., Algiers, 9 June 1944.
26. Wiéviorka, *Normandy*, p. 131; Overy, *Why the Allies Won*, pp. 149–50.
27. Lindsey Dodd and Andrew Knapp, 'How Many Frenchmen Did You Kill?' *French History*, December 2008, p. 486; H. R. Kedward, *In Search of the Maquis* (Oxford, 1993), p. 279.
28. Sir Frederick Morgan, *Overture to Overlord* (London, 1957), pp. 234–5.
29. David Dilks (ed.), *The Diaries of Sir Alexander Cadogan, 1938–45* (London, 1971),

p. 548; Wiéviorka, *Normandy*, p. 303; Llewellyn Woodward, *British Foreign Policy in the Second World War* (London, 1971), vol. III, p. 12; Charles de Gaulle, *The Complete War Memoirs* (New York, 1972), pp. 455, 543.

30.    Jean Lacouture, *De Gaulle* (London, 1984), vol. I, p. 502; FO371/35238, Macmillan to Eden, 4 October 1943.

31.    Charles de Gaulle, *War Memoirs: Documents*, 3 vols. (London, 1959), vol. II, p. 303.

32.    Woodward, *British Foreign Policy*, vol. III, p. 13.

33.    Arthur Funk, *Charles de Gaulle* (Norman, Okla., 1959), p. 198; François Kersaudy, *Churchill and de Gaulle* (London, 1981), p. 318.

34.    Woodward, *British Foreign Policy*, vol. III, p. 14.

35.    Woodward, *British Foreign Policy*, vol. III, p. 14.

36.    Woodward, *British Foreign Policy*, vol. III, p. 14.

37.    Julian Norwich, *The Duff Cooper Diaries* (London, 2005), p. 294.

38.    Wiéviorka, *Normandy*, p. 304.

39.    Kimball, *Churchill and Roosevelt*, vol. III, pp. 63–4.

40.    Woodward, *British Foreign Policy*, vol. III, pp. 19–21.

41.    Woodward, *British Foreign Policy*, vol. III, p. 33; FO371/41878, Eden to Churchill, 6 April 1944.

42.    Kersaudy, *Churchill and de Gaulle*, p. 322; Woodward, *British Foreign Policy*, vol. III, p. 33.

43.    Woodward, *British Foreign Policy*, vol. III, pp. 34–5.

44.    Jacques Soustelle, *Envers et contre tout* (Paris, 1947), vol. I, p. 389.

45.    M. R. D. Foot, *SOE in France* (London, 1966), pp. 364–5.

46.    FO371/41980, Mack minute, 8 May 1944; Woodward, *British Foreign Policy*, vol. III, pp. 42, 45, 46; Wiéviorka, *Normandy*, p. 167; Ehrman, *Grand Strategy*, pp. 317–18; de Gaulle, *Complete War Memoirs*, p. 553; Norwich, *Duff Cooper Diaries*, p. 304; Nicolson, *Nicolson Letters and Diaries*, p. 361.

47.    Woodward, *British Foreign Policy*, vol. III, p. 39; Eric Roussel, *Charles de Gaulle* (Paris, 2002), p. 422; John Harvey (ed.), *The Diplomatic Diaries of Oliver Harvey* (London, 1979), pp. 339–40; Dilks, *Cadogan Diaries*, pp. 627–8; Max Hastings, *Overlord* (London, 1984) p. 46.

48.    Dilks, *Cadogan Diaries*, p. 629 (emphasis in original).

49.    FO371/41993, Memo to Cadogan, 31 May 1944.

50.    CAB65/46, WM (44), 31 May 1944, 70th.

51.    FO660/128, Cooper to Churchill, 29 May 1944; CAB65/46, WM (44), 30 May 1944, 69th.

52.    FO660/128, Cooper to Churchill, 29 May 1944; Churchill to Cooper, 1 June 1944.

53.    Norwich, *Duff Cooper Diaries*, p. 307; Roussel, *De Gaulle*, p. 424.

54.    Weinberg, 'D Day after Fifty Years,' p. 255.

55.    Reynolds, *Rich Relations*, p. 368.

56.    Kimball, *Churchill and Roosevelt*, vol. III, p. 149.

57.    Woodward, *British Foreign Policy*, vol. III, p. 38; de Gaulle, *War Memoirs, Documents*, vol. II, p. 338; Hilary Footitt and John Symonds, *France* (Leicester, 1988), pp. 61–2.

58.    Kimball, *Churchill and Roosevelt*, vol. III, p. 167.

59.    Antoine Béthouart, *Cinq années d'esperance* (Paris, 1968), p. 242.

60.    Kersaudy, *Churchill and de Gaulle*, pp. 341–3.

61.    Kersaudy, *Churchill and de Gaulle*, pp. 341–3.

62.    De Gaulle, *Complete War Memoirs*, p. 557.

63.    Piers Dixon, *Double Diploma* (London, 1968), p. 91.

64. Kersaudy, *Churchill and de Gaulle*, p. 343; Churchill, *Closing the Ring*, p. 566; Béthouart, *Cinq années*, p. 244; John Charmley, *Duff Cooper* (London, 1986), p. 178.
65. Dilks, *Cadogan Diaries*, p. 635.
66. FO371/41993, Cooper to de Gaulle, 6 June 1944; de Gaulle, *Complete War Memoirs*, p. 560.
67. Dilks, *Cadogan Diaries*, pp. 634–5.
68. Kersaudy, *Churchill and de Gaulle*, p. 347; Norwich, *Duff Cooper Diaries*, p. 309; Footitt and Symonds, *France*, p. 68.
69. Reynolds, *Rich Relations*, p. 371; Crémieux-Brilhac, *Ici Londres*, vol. V, p. 45.
70. Nicolson, *Nicolson Letters and Diaries*, p. 267.
71. Wiéviorka, *Normandy*, p. 200.
72. FO371/41993, Cooper to de Gaulle, 6 June 1944.
73. Kenneth Young (ed.), *The Diaries of Robert Bruce-Lockhart* (London, 1980), vol. II, pp. 318–19.
74. FO371/41993, Cooper to de Gaulle, 6 June 1944; Kimball, *Churchill and Roosevelt*, vol. III, p. 170; Crémieux-Brilhac, *Ici Londres*, vol. V, pp. 47–8; Kersaudy, *Churchill and de Gaulle*, pp. 348–9.
75. Kersaudy, *Churchill and de Gaulle*, pp. 350–1; Norwich, *Duff Cooper Diaries*, p. 310; FO371/41879, Eden to Churchill, 7 June 1944.
76. Kimball, *Churchill and Roosevelt*, vol. III, pp. 174–5, 181.
77. Woodward, *British Foreign Policy*, vol. III, pp. 60–1; Footitt and Symonds, *France*, pp. 69–70.
78. Harvey, *Harvey War Diaries*, p. 344.
79. Alex Danchev and Daniel Todman (eds.), *War Diaries, 1939–45: Field Marshall Lord Alanbrooke* (London, 2001), p. 557.
80. Kersaudy, *Churchill and de Gaulle*, p. 353.
81. Woodward, *British Foreign Policy*, vol. III, p. 62; Harvey, *Harvey War Diaries*, p. 344.
82. Kimball, *Churchill and Roosevelt*, vol. III, pp. 146, 149.
83. Harvey, *Harvey War Diaries*, p. 345.
84. De Gaulle, *Complete War Memoirs*, p. 561.
85. Anthony Eden, *The Reckoning* (London, 1965), p. 437.
86. De Gaulle, *Complete War Memoirs*, pp. 565–6.
87. *The Times*, 21 June 1944; FO660/128, tel., Algiers, 19 June 1944; Harvey, *Harvey War Diaries*, p. 346; Kersaudy, *Churchill and de Gaulle*, pp. 352–4.

## 16  Down the Champs-Elysées Together

1. M. R. D. Foot, *SOE in France* (London, 1966), p. 386; Charles de Gaulle, *The Complete War Memoirs* (New York, 1972), p. 515.
2. De Gaulle, *Complete War Memoirs*, pp. 588, 589.
3. David Stafford, *Britain and the European Resistance* (London, 1980), pp. 129–30.
4. David Stafford, *Churchill and the Secret Service* (London, 1997), p. 236; Matthew Cobb, *The Resistance* (London, 2009), p. 236.
5. Cobb, *The Resistance*, p. 237.
6. Cobb, *The Resistance*, p. 237; Robert Tombs and Isabelle Tombs, *That Sweet Enemy* (London, 2006), p. 585.
7. Cobb, *The Resistance*, p.237
8. Cobb, *The Resistance*, p. 238; PREM3/185/1, War Cabinet, 27 January 1944; W. J. M. Mackenzie, *The Secret History of SOE* (London, 2000), p. 612.

9. PREM3/185/1, Lord Selborne, 25 April 1944; John Ehrman, *Grand Strategy* (London, 1956), vol. V, p. 326.

10. Hilary Foottit and John Symonds, *France, 1943–45* (Leicester, 1988), pp. 85–6; Julian Jackson, *The Dark Years* (Oxford, 2001), p. 548.

11. H. R. Kedward, *In Search of the Maquis* (Oxford, 1993), p. 182.

12. FO371/41907, Harvey to Peake, 19 September 1944.

13. Mackenzie, *Secret History of SOE*, pp. 603–8; Stafford, *Churchill*, p. 278.

14. Jackson, *The Dark Years*, pp. 556–7; de Gaulle, *Complete War Memoirs*, pp. 620–1; Mackenzie, *Secret History of SOE*, pp. 618–20.

15. De Gaulle, *Complete War Memoirs*, p. 620; Jackson, *Dark Years*, pp. 556–7; Foot, *SOE in France*, pp. 396–9.

16. Jacques Crémieux-Brilhac, *Ici Londres: Les Voix de la liberté, 1940–44*, 5 vols. (Paris, 1975), vol. V, pp. 41–4.

17. Tim Brooks, *British Propaganda to France* (London, 2007), p.101; Aurélie Luneau, *Radio Londres* (Paris, 2005), pp. 269, 271–2.

18. Luneau, *Radio Londres*, p. 273; Crémieux-Brilhac, *Ici Londres*, vol. I, p. xxxii; Jackson, *Dark Years*, pp. 645–6.

19. Winston Churchill, *Triumph and Tragedy* (London, 1954), p. 16.

20. David Ziman, *Instructions for British Servicemen in France* (Oxford, 2005), p. 43.

21. Ziman, *Instructions*, p. 44.

22. Olivier Wiéviorka, *Normandy* (Cambridge, Mass., 2008), p. 323.

23. FO371/41924, Postal and Telegraph Censorship, Report on France, 26 May 1944.

24. Alex Danchev and Daniel Todman (eds.), *War Diaries, 1939–45: Field Marshall Lord Alanbrooke* (London, 2001), p. 557.

25. William Hitchcock, *Liberation: The Bitter Road to Freedom in Europe, 1944–5* (London, 2008), pp. 23–7, 43; Wiéviorka, *Normandy*, p. 32.

26. Richard Overy, *Why the Allies Won* (London, 1995), p. 167; Tombs and Tombs, *That Sweet Enemy*, p. 592.

27. Churchill, *Triumph and Tragedy*, p. 35.

28. Nigel Nicolson (ed.), *Harold Nicolson, Letters and Diaries, 1939–45* (London, 1967), p. 394.

29. Foot, *SOE in France*, p. 423.

30. Douglas Porch, *Hitler's Mediterranean Gamble* (London, 2004), p. 591; Martin Gilbert, *Road to Victory* (London, 1986), pp. 817–20, 29–30; David Reynolds, *In Command of History* (London, 2004), pp. 449–50.

31. Reynolds, *In Command of History*, pp. 249–50; Andrew Roberts, *Masters and Commanders* (London, 2008), p. 493.

32. Jackson, *Dark Years*, p. 555; Foot, *SOE in France*, pp. 412–3, 442; Mackenzie, *Secret History of SOE*, pp. 617–25.

33. Foottit and Symonds, *France*, p. 116.

34. Foot, *SOE in France*, p. 414.

35. Reynolds, *In Command of History*, p. 303; Wiéviorka, *Normandy*, p. 315; Cobb, *Resistance*, p. 265.

36. John Harvey (ed.), *The Diplomatic Diaries of Oliver Harvey* (London, 1979), p. 354; François Kersaudy, *Churchill and de Gaulle* (London, 1981), p. 366; Crémieux-Brilhac, *Ici Londres*, vol. V, pp. 220–1; Luneau, *Radio Londres*, p. 290.

37. John Wheeler-Bennett, *Special Relationship* (London, 1975) p. 186.

38. Mackenzie, *Secret History of SOE*, p. 584.

39. Foot, *SOE in France*, p. 420.

40. Foot, *SOE in France*, p. 421; David Stafford, *Secret Agent* (London, 2000), pp. 214–15; Roderick Bailey, *Forgotten Voices of the Second World War* (London, 2008), p. 237.
41. A. B. Gaunson, *The Anglo-French Clash in Syria and Lebanon* (London, 1987), p. 151.
42. John Charmley, *Duff Cooper* (London, 1986), pp. 175–6.
43. Charmley, *Duff Cooper*, p. 181; Max Egremont, *Under Two Flags* (London, 1997), pp. 257–62.
44. André Béziat, *Franklin Roosevelt et la France* (Paris, 1997), p. 363.
45. FO371/ 41958, tel., Washington, 10 July 1944; Campbell to Halifax, 10 July 1944.
46. Béziat, *Roosevelt*, pp. 396, 489.
47. Harvey, *Harvey War Diaries*, p. 347.
48. Woodward, *British Foreign Policy*, vol. III, pp. 72–3.
49. Woodward, *British Foreign Policy*, vol. III, pp. 72–3.
50. Warren F. Kimball (ed.), *Churchill and Roosevelt: The Complete Correspondence*, 3 vols. (Princeton, NJ, 1984), vol. III, pp. 171–2, 237.
51. FO371/42060, Halifax to Foreign Office, 17 August 1944.
52. Woodward, *British Foreign Policy*, vol. III, pp. 75–8; FO371/41882, Churchill to Eden, 18 August 1944.
53. Hansard, 2 August 1944.
54. Kimball, *Churchill and Roosevelt*, vol. III, p. 338.
55. Kimball, *Churchill and Roosevelt*, vol. III, pp. 355–6.
56. Woodward, *British Foreign Policy*, vol. III, pp. 76–80; Béziat, *Roosevelt*, pp. 407–9.
57. Kersaudy, *Churchill and de Gaulle*, p. 370; David Dilks (ed.), *The Diaries of Sir Alexander Cadogan, 1938–45* (London, 1971), p. 673.
58. Dilks, *Cadogan Diaries*, p. 674; Kimball, *Churchill and Roosevelt*, vol. III, p. 369; Béziat, *Roosevelt*, p. 411.
59. Dilks, *Cadogan Diaries*, pp. 674–5.
60. Julian Norwich (ed.), *The Duff Cooper Diaries* (London, 2005), pp. 328–30; FO371/ 42025, Letter, Paris, 24 October 1944; Woodward, *British Foreign Policy*, vol. III, pp. 82–5.
61. Churchill, *Triumph and Tragedy*, p. 217.
62. *Le Figaro*, 5 October 1944.
63. Anthony Beevor and Artemis Cooper, *Paris after the Liberation* (London, 1994), p. 131.
64. Norwich, *Duff Cooper Diaries*, pp. 334–5.
65. De Gaulle, *Complete War Memoirs*, p. 723.
66. Reilly Papers, c.6919, unpublished memoirs, p. 167; Gilbert, *Road to Victory*, p. 1061.
67. Gilbert, *Road to Victory*, p. 1063; Elizabeth Barker, *Churchill and Eden at War* (London, 1978), p. 112.
68. Martin Gilbert, *Finest Hour* (London, 1983), p. 483.
69. Lord Ismay, *Memoirs* (London, 1960), p. 140.
70. Peter Mangold, *The Almost Impossible Ally* (London, 2006), pp. 141–3.
71. De Gaulle, *Complete War Memoirs*, pp. 726–7.
72. De Gaulle, *Complete War Memoirs*, pp. 726–7.
73. Mark Pottle (ed.), *Champion Redoubtable* (London, 1998), pp. 312–13.
74. De Gaulle, *Complete War Memoirs*, pp. 727–8.
75. De Gaulle, *Complete War Memoirs*, p. 728.

## 17 Rights and Wrongs

1. R. T. Thomas, *Britain and Vichy* (London, 1979), p. 117.
2. Arthur Funk, *Charles de Gaulle* (Norman, Okla., 1959), p. 139.
3. FO660/85, Foreign Office to Washington, 16 January 1943.
4. PREM3/182/6, Macmillan despatch, 3 January 1944.
5. Nigel Nicolson (ed.), *Harold Nicolson, Letters and Diaries, 1939–45* (London, 1967), p. 359.
6. Martin Gilbert, *The Road to Victory* (London, 1986), p. 971.
7. Warren Kimball, *Forged in War* (London, 1997), p. 191.
8. Harold Macmillan, *War Diaries: The Mediterranean, 1939–45* (London, 1984), p. 335.
9. Anthony Montague Brown, *Long Sunset* (London, 1995), p. 160.
10. Jean Lacouture, *De Gaulle* (London, 1984), vol. I, pp. 373–4.
11. Nicholas Atkin, *The Forgotten French* (Manchester, 2003), p. 252.
12. Philip Bell, *France and Britain* (Harlow, 1997), vol. II, p. 64.
13. Sean Greenwood, *The Alternative Alliance* (London, 1996), p. 298; M. R. D. Foot, *SOE in France* (London, 1966), p. 424.
14. Gerald Mansell, *Let Truth Be Told* (London, 1982), p. 146.
15. FO898/420, 'Postmortem on Political Warfare,' April 1945, BBC, WAC, April 1945; E2/193/6, European Intelligence Report, 2 October 1944; Institut Charles de Gaulle, *La France Libre* (Paris, 2005), p. 109.
16. E. H. Cookridge, *Inside SOE* (London, 1966), pp. 114, 274; Sarah Helm, *A Life in Secrets* (London, 2005), p. 426; Letter from Caroline Pinder Cracraft, *Times Literary Supplement*, 28 July 2006.
17. Sir Stephen Wall, address, 'The UK, the EU and the United States: Bridge, or Just Troubled Water?,' Royal Institute of International Affairs, 8 November 2004; BBC, Radio 4 News, 6 June 2009.
18. FO371/41882, Mack minute, 30 August 1944.
19. *Times Literary Supplement*, 11 October 1963; CAB103/572, Trend to Wilson, 26 March 1964.
20. Lord Ismay, *The Memoirs of Lord Ismay* (London, 1960), pp. 380–1.
21. BBC, WAC, E2/193/5, European Intelligence Reports, April 1943.
22. Olivier Wiéviorka, *Normandy* (Cambridge, Mass., 2008), p. 131; W. J. M. Mackenzie, *The Secret History of SOE* (London, 2000), p. 600; AIR14/1021, Harris to Bomber Command; Martin Middlebrook and Chris Everill, *The Bomber Command War Diaries* (Leicester, 1996), pp. 245, 292–3.
23. Robert Tombs and Isabelle Tombs, *That Sweet Enemy* (London, 2006), p. 563; Arthur Marder, *Operation Menace* (Oxford, 1971), p. 159; Christopher Buckley, *Five Ventures* (London, 1954), p. 137; Paul Auphan and Jacques Mordal, *La Marine française pendant la seconde guerre mondiale* (Paris, 1958), p. 254; Douglas Porch, *Hitler's Mediterranean Gamble* (London, 2004), p. 352; François-Georges Dreyfus, *Histoire de Vichy* (Paris, 1990), p. 444.
24. Michael Portillo, 'The Things We Forgot to Remember,' Radio 4, 9 April 2006; Dominique Lormier, *Mers-el-Kébir* (Paris, 2007), p. 16.
25. Arthur Marder, *From the Dardanelles to Oran* (Oxford, 1974), p. 288; Alain Peyrefitte, *C'était de Gaulle* (Paris, 1994), vol. I, p. 154.
26. Montague Brown, *Long Sunset*, p. 160.
27. FO660/113, Vice-Consul Marrakesh, 15 January 1944.
28. Charles de Gaulle, *The Complete War Memoirs* (New York, 1972), p. 231.
29. De Gaulle, *Complete War Memoirs*, pp. 57–8.

30. De Gaulle, *Complete War Memoirs*, pp. 57–8.
31. Institut Charles de Gaulle, *La France Libre*, p. 182; Philippe de Gaulle, *De Gaulle mon père* (Paris, 2003), p. 180.
32. Piers Dixon, *Double Diploma* (London, 1968), p. 313.
33. François Kersaudy, *Churchill and de Gaulle* (London, 1981), p. 428.
34. Alistair Horne, *Macmillan* (London, 1989), vol. II, p. 319.
35. PREM11/4831, Caccia minute, 6 February 1964.
36. Peter Mangold, *The Almost Impossible Ally* (London, 2006), pp. 199–200; Peyrefitte, *C'était de Gaulle*, vol. I, pp. 153–4.
37. D. R. Thorpe, *Eden* (London, 2003), p. 275.
38. PREM11/4230, Macmillan to de Gaulle, 15–16 December 1962.
39. De Gaulle, *Complete War Memoirs*, p. 162; FC033/1007, 'The Death of General de Gaulle,' 14 December 1970.

# Select Bibliography

### Official Archives

The relevant files in the National Archives, Kew, are extensive. The main series consulted are: ADM199; CAB21, 65, 66, 121; FO371, 660, 892, 954; PREM3; HS6.
BBC Written Archives Centre, Caversham.

### Unpublished Papers

Sir Patrick Reilly, unpublished memoir (Bodleian Library, Oxford).
Sherfield Papers (Bodleian Library, Oxford).
Spears Papers (Middle East Centre, St. Antony's College, Oxford).

### Published Documents

Addison, Paul and Jeremy Crang (eds.), *Listening to Britain: Home Intelligence Reports on Britain's Finest Hour, May–September, 1940* (London, 2010).
Crémieux-Brilhac, Jacques, *Ici Londres: Les Voix de la liberté, 1940–44*, 5 vols. (Paris, 1975).
*Documents on German Foreign Policy, 1918–45*, series D, vols. X–XIII (London, 1956–62).
*Foreign Relations of the United States 1940, vol. II: Germany and Europe* (Washington, DC, 1957).
*Foreign Relations of the United States 1941, vol. II, Europe* (Washington, DC, 1959).
*Foreign Relations of the United States 1942, vol. II, Europe* (Washington, DC, 1962).
*Fuehrer Conferences on Naval Affairs, 1939–45* (London, 1990).
*La Délégation française auprès de la Commission Allemagne de l'Armistice* (Paris 1947).
Martin Gilbert, *The Churchill War Papers, vol. II: Never Surrender, May 1940–December 1940* (London 1994).
—— *The Churchill War Papers, vol. III: The Ever Widening War, 1941* (London, 2000).
Jacobsen, Hans-Adolf, *Kriegestagebuch des Oberkammandos der Wehrmacht, vol. I, 1 August 1940–31 Dezember 1941* (Frankfurt, 1965).
Noakes, J. and G. Pridham, *Nazism, 1939–45*, vol. III: *Foreign Policy, War and Racial Extermination* (Exeter, 1988).
*The Papers of Dwight D. Eisenhower: The War Years*, vol. II (Baltimore, Md., 1970).

## Autobiographies, diaries, letters and memoirs

Alphand, Hervé, *L'Etonnement d'être* (Paris, 1977).

Annet, Armand, *Aux heures troublées de l'Afrique française, 1939–43* (Paris, 1952).

Auphan, Paul, *L'Honneur de servir: Mémoires* (Paris, 1978).

Baudouin, Paul, *The Private Diaries of Paul Baudouin* (London, 1948).

Benoist-Méchin, Jacques, *De la défaite au désastre* (Paris, 1984).

Bertram, Barbara, *French Resistance in Sussex* (Pulborough, 1995).

Béthouart, Marie-Emile, *Cinq années d'esperance: Mémoires de guerre, 1939–45* (Paris, 1968).

Burchik, Charles and Hans-Adolf Jacobsen, *The Halder War Diaries, 1939–42* (London, 1988).

Bouthillier, Yves, *Le Drame de Vichy: Face à l'ennemi, face à l'allié* (Paris, 1950).

Butcher, Harry, *Three Years with Eisenhower* (London, 1946).

Casey, Richard, *Personal Experiences, 1939–45* (London, 1962).

Catroux, Georges, *Dans la bataille de la Méditerranée* (Paris, 1949).

Charles-Roux, François, *Cinq mois tragiques aux affaires étrangères* (Paris, 1949).

Churchill, Winston, *The Second World War*, vol. II: *Their Finest Hour* (London, 1949).

—— *The Second World War*, vol. III: *The Grand Alliance* (London, 1950).

—— *The Second World War*, vol. IV: *The Hinge of Fate* (London, 1951).

—— *The Second World War*, vol. V: *Closing the Ring* (London, 1952).

Cunningham, Andrew, *A Sailor's Odyssey* (London 1951).

Colville, John, *The Fringes of Power: Downing Street Diaries, 1939–55* (London, 1985).

Danchev, Alex and Daniel Todman (eds.), *War Diaries, 1939–45: Field Marshal Lord Alanbrooke* (London, 2001).

Delavenay, Emile, *Témoignage: D'un village savoyard au village mondial* (Aix-en-Provence, 1992).

Dilks, David (ed.), *The Diaries of Sir Alexander Cadogan, 1938–45* (London, 1971).

Eccles, David, *By Safe Hands: Letters of David and Sylvia Eccles* (London, 1983).

Eden, Anthony, *The Eden Memoirs: The Reckoning* (London, 1965).

Frenay, Henri, *La Nuit finira: Mémoires de résistance, 1940–45* (Paris, 1973).

De Gaulle, Charles, *The Complete War Memoirs* (New York, 1972).

—— *War Memoirs, Documents*, vol. I, *The Call to Honour* (London, 1955).

—— *War Memoirs, Documents*, vol. II, *Unity, 1942–44* (London, 1959).

—— *Lettres, notes et carnets*, vols. III–V (Paris, 1981–3).

De Gaulle, Philippe, *De Gaulle mon père* (Paris, 2003).

Giraud, Henri, *Le seul but – la victoire: Alger, 1942–44* (Paris, 1949).

Glubb, John, *The Story of the Arab Legion* (London, 1948).

Godfroy, Vice-Admiral, *L'Aventure de la Force X à Alexandre, 1940–43* (Paris, 1953).

Groussard, Georges, *Service secret* (Paris, 1964).

Hart-Davis, Duff (ed.), *Kings Counsellor: Abdication and War – The Diary of Sir Alan Lascelles* (London, 2006).

Harvey, John (ed.), *The War Diaries of Oliver Harvey* (London, 1978).

Hoare, Samuel, *Ambassador on Special Mission* (London, 1946).

Hull, Cordell, *The Memoirs of Cordell Hull*, 2 vols. (London, 1948).

Ismay, Hastings, *The Memoirs of Lord Ismay* (London, 1960).

Kennedy, John, *The Business of War: The War Narrative of Major-General Sir John Kennedy* (London, 1958).

Kimball, Warren F. (ed.), *Churchill and Roosevelt: The Complete Correspondence*, 3 vols. (Princeton, NJ, 1984).

Kirkbride, Sir Alex, *A Crackle of Thorns: Experiences in the Middle East* (London, 1951).

Leahy, William D., *I Was There* (London, 1950).
Macmillan, Harold, *The Blast of War, 1939–45* (London, 1967).
—— *War Diaries: The Mediterranean, 1943–45* (London, 1984).
Marjolin, Robert, *Architect of European Unity: Memoirs, 1911–86* (London, 1986).
Monnet, Jean, *Memoirs* (London, 1978).
Muggeridge, Malcolm (ed.), *The Ciano Diaries* (London, 1947).
Murphy, Robert, *Diplomat among Warriors* (London, 1964).
Muselier, Emile-Henri, *De Gaulle contre le Gaullisme* (Paris, 1946).
Nicolson, Nigel (ed.), *Harold Nicolson: Diaries and Letters, 1939–45* (London, 1967).
Norwich, John Julius (ed.), *The Duff Cooper Diaries* (London, 2005).
Paillole, Paul, *Services spéciaux* (Paris, 1975).
Parker, Dodds, *Setting Europe Ablaze: Some Accounts of Ungentlemanly Warfare* (Windlesham, 1983).
Passy, Colonel, *Souvenirs*, vol. I: *Le Deuxième Bureau, Londres* (Monte Carlo, 1947).
—— *Souvenirs*, vol. II, *10 Duke Street, Londres* (Monte Carlo, 1950).
Piétri, François, *Mes années d'Espagne, 1940–48* (Paris, 1954).
Pottle, Mark (ed.), *Champion Redoubtable: The Diaries and Letters of Violet Bonham Carter, 1914–45* (London, 1998).
Rémy, *On m'appelait Rémy* (Paris, 1951).
Rougier, Louis, *Les Accords Churchill–Pétain: Histoire d'une mission secrète* (Montreal, 1946).
Schroeder, Liliane, *Journal d'occupation, 1940–44* (Paris, 2000).
Soustelle, Jacques, *Envers et contre tout*, vol. I: *De Londres à Algers* (Paris, 1947).
—— *Envers et contre tout*, vol. II, *D'Algers à Paris* (Paris, 1950).
Spears, Sir Edward, *Assignment to Catastrophe*, vol. I: *Prelude to Dunkirk, July 1939–May 1940* (London, 1954).
—— *Assignment to Catastrophe*, vol. II: *The Fall of France* (London, 1954).
—— *Fulfilment of a Mission: The Spears Mission to Syria and Lebanon, 1941–44* (London, 1977).
Teissier du Cros, Janet, *Divided Loyalties: A Scotswoman in Occupied France* (London, 1992).
Weygand, Maxime, *Recalled to Service* (London, 1952).
Wilson, Henry, *Eight Years Overseas, 1939–47* (London, 1948).
Young, Kenneth (ed.), *The Diaries of Sir Robert Bruce-Lockhart*, vol. II: *1939–65* (London, 1980).

**Secondary works**

Albertelli, Sébastien, *Les Services secrets du général de Gaulle* (Paris, 2009).
Alméres, Philippe, *De Gaulle à Londres* (Paris, 2001).
Amouroux, Henri, *La Grande Histoire des Français sous l'occupation*, vol. IV: *Le People réveille* (Paris, 1979).
Aron, Robert, *The Vichy Regime, 1940–44* (London, 1958).
Atkin, Nicholas, *The Forgotten French: Exiles in the British Isles, 1940–44* (Manchester, 2003).
Auphan, Paul and Jacques Mordal, *La Marine française pendant la seconde guerre mondiale* (Paris, 1958).
Azéma, J. P. and François Bédarida, *Le Régime de Vichy et les français* (Paris, 1992).
Bailey, Roderick, *Forgotten Voices of the Second World War: An Inside History of Special Operations during the Second World War* (London, 2008).
Barker, Elizabeth, *Churchill and Eden at War* (London, 1978).

Bell, P. M. H., *A Certain Eventuality: Britain and the Fall of France* (Farnborough, 1974).

—— *France and Britain, 1900–40: Entente and Estrangement* (Harlow, 1996).

—— *France and Britain, 1940–94: The Long Separation* (Harlow, 1997).

Berthon, Simon, *Allies at War* (London, 2001).

Béziat, André, *Franklin Roosevelt et la France, 1939–45: La Diplomatie de l'entêtement* (Paris, 1997).

Briggs, Asa, *The War of Words: The History of Broadcasting in the United Kingdom* (London, 1970), vol. III.

Brooks, Tim, *British Propaganda to France* (Edinburgh, 2007).

Brown, David, *The Road to Oran: Anglo-French Naval Relations, September 1939–July 1940* (London, 2004).

Buckley, Christopher, *Five Ventures* (London, 1954).

Burrin, Philippe, *Living with Defeat: France under the German Occupation, 1940–44* (London, 1996).

Butler, J. R. M., *Grand Strategy* (London, 1957), vol. II.

Callil, Carmen, *Bad Faith: A Forgotten History of Family and Fatherland* (London, 2006).

Cave Brown, Anthony, *The Secret Servant: The Life of Sir Stewart Menzies* (London, 1988).

Charmley, John, *Duff Cooper* (London, 1986).

Cobb, Matthew, *The Resistance: The French Fight against the Nazis* (London, 2009).

Cointet, Jean-Paul, *La France à Londres: Renaissance d'un état* (Brussels, 1990).

Cointet, Michèle, *De Gaulle et Giraud: L'Affrontement* (Paris, 2005).

—— *Marie-Madeleine Fourcade: Un chef de la Résistance* (Paris, 2006).

Cookridge, E. H., *Inside SOE: The Story of Special Operations in Europe, 1940–45* (London, 1966).

Corbett, Anne and Douglas Johnson, *A Day in June: Britain and de Gaulle* (London, 2000).

Coutau-Bégarie, Hervé and Claude Huan, *Dakar: La Bataille fratricide* (Paris, 2004).

—— *Darlan* (Paris, 1989).

—— *Lettres, notes et carnets de l'Amiral Darlan* (Paris, 1992).

—— *Mers-el-Kébir: La Rupture Franco-Britannique* (Paris, 1994).

Crémieux-Brilhac, Jean-Louis, *La France Libre: De l'appel du 18 Juin à la Libération* (Paris, 1996).

Cruickshank, Charles, *The Fourth Arm: Psychological Warfare, 1938–45* (London, 1977).

Davet, Michel-Christian, *La Double Affaire de Syrie* (Paris, 1967).

Dinan, Desmond, *The Politics of Persuasion: British Policy and French African Neutrality* (Lanham, Md., 1988).

Dixon, Piers, *Double Diploma: The Life of Sir Pierson Dixon, Don and Diplomat* (London, 1968).

Dockrill, Michael, *British Establishment Perspectives on France, 1936–39* (Basingstoke, 1999).

Dreyfus, François-Georges, *Histoire de Vichy* (Paris, 1990).

Duchêne, François, *Jean Monnet: The First Statesman of Interdependence* (New York, 1994).

Duroselle, J. B., *L'Abîme, 1939–45* (Paris, 1982).

Eck, Hélène (ed.), *La Guerre des ondes: Histoire des radios des langues françaises pendant la deuxième guerre mondiale* (Paris, 1985).

Egremont, Max, *Under Two Flags: The Life of Major General Sir Edward Spears* (London, 1997).

Ehrman, John, *Grand Strategy* (London, 1956), vol. V.

Ferro, Marc, *Pétain* (Paris, 1987).

Fondation Charles de Gaulle, *La France Libre* (Paris, 2005).

Foot, M. R. D., *SOE in France: An Account of the Work of the British Special Operations Executive in France, 1940–44* (London, 1966 and 2004).

—— *Resistance* (London, 1976).

Foot, M. R. D. and J. M. Langley, *MI9: Escape and Evasion* (London, 1980).

Footitt, Hilary and John Symonds, *France, 1943–45* (Leicester, 1988).

Fort, Adrian, *Wavell: The Life and Times of an Imperial Servant* (London, 2009).

Funk, Arthur, *Charles de Gaulle: The Crucial Years, 1943–44* (Norman, Okla., 1959).

—— *The Politics of Torch: The Allied Landings and the Algiers Putsch, 1942* (Lawrence, Ks., 1974).

Garnett, David, *The Secret History of PWE: The Political Warfare Executive* (London, 2002).

Gates, Eleanor, *End of the Affair: The Collapse of the Anglo-French Alliance, 1939–40* (London, 1981).

Gaunson, A. B., *The Anglo-French Clash in Lebanon and Syria, 1940–45* (London, 1987).

Gibson, Robert, *Best of Enemies: Anglo-French Relations since the Norman Conquest* (London, 1996).

Gilbert, Martin, *Finest Hour: Winston S. Churchill, 1939–41* (London, 1983).

—— *Road to Victory: Winston S. Churchill, 1941–45* (London, 1986).

Gildea, Robert, *Marianne in Chains: In Search of the German Occupation of France, 1940–45* (London, 2002).

Ginio, Ruth, *French Colonialisms Unmasked: The Vichy Years in French West Africa* (London, 2000).

Gwyer, J. M. A., *Grand Strategy* (London, 1964), vol. III.

Helm, Sarah, *A Life in Secrets: The Story of Vera Atkins and the Lost Agents of SOE* (London, 2005).

Hinsley, F. H., *British Intelligence in the Second World War,* 2 vols. (London, 1979 and 1981).

Hitchcock, William, *Liberation: The Bitter Road to Freedom in Europe, 1944–45* (London, 2008).

Horne, Alistair, *Macmillan,* vol. I: *1894–1956* (London, 1988).

—— *To Lose a Battle* (Harmondsworth, 1979).

Howard, Michael, *Grand Strategy,* vol. IV (London, 1970).

Hytier, Adrienne Doris, *Two Years of French Foreign Policy: Vichy, 1940–42* (Paris, 1958).

Jackson, Ashley, *The British Empire in the Second World War* (London, 2006).

Jackson, Julian, *The Fall of France: The Nazi Invasion of 1940* (Oxford, 2003).

—— *France: The Dark Years, 1940–1944* (Oxford, 2001).

Jaeckel, Eberhard, *Frankreich in Hitler's Europa: Die Deutsche Frankreichpolitik im Zweiten Weltkrieg* (Stuttgart, 1966).

Jeffery, Keith, *MI6: The History of the Secret Intelligence Service, 1909–49* (London, 2010).

Kammerer, Albert, *La Passion de la flotte française* (Paris, 1951).

Kedward, H. R., *In Search of the Maquis: Rural Resistance in Southern France, 1942–44* (Oxford, 1993).

—— *La Vie en Bleu: France and the French since 2000* (London, 2005).

—— *Resistance in Vichy France: A Study of Ideas and Motivation in the Southern Zone, 1940–42* (Oxford, 1978).

Keiger, J. V., *France and the World since 1870* (London, 2001).

Kent, John, *The Internationalisation of Colonialism: Britain, France and Black Africa, 1939–46* (Oxford, 1992).

Kersaudy, François, *Churchill and de Gaulle* (London, 1981).

Kershaw, Ian, *Fateful Choices: Ten Decisions that Changed the World, 1940–44* (London, 2007).

Kitson, Simon, *The Hunt for Nazi Spies: Fighting Espionage in Vichy France* (Chicago, Ill., and London, 2008).

Lacouture, Jean, *De Gaulle*, vol. I: *The Rebel, 1890–1944* (London, 1984).

Laffargue, André, *Le Général Dentz, Paris 1940–Syrie 1941* (Paris, 1954).

Langer, William, *Our Vichy Gamble* (New York, 1947).

Lean, E. Tangye, *Voices in the Dark: The Story of the European Radio War* (London, 1943).

Lormier, Dominique, *Mers-el-Kébir: Juillet 1940* (Paris, 2007).

Lukacs, John, *Five Days in London: May 1940* (New Haven, Conn., and London, 1999).

Luneau, Aurélie, *Radio Londres: Les Voix de la liberté* (Paris, 2005).

Mackenzie, W. J. M., *The Secret History of SOE: The Special Operations Executive, 1940–45* (London, 2000).

Maguire, G. E., *Anglo-American Policy towards the Free French* (Basingstoke, 1995).

Mangold, Peter, *The Almost Impossible Ally: Harold Macmillan and Charles de Gaulle* (London, 2006).

—— *Success and Failure in British Foreign Policy, 1900–2000* (Basingstoke, 2001).

Mansell, Gerald, *Let Truth Be Told: Fifty Years of BBC External Broadcasting* (London, 1982).

Marder, Arthur, *From the Dardanelles to Oran: Studies of the Royal Navy in War and Peace, 1915–40* (Oxford, 1974).

—— *Operation 'Menace': The Dakar Expedition and the Dudley North Affair* (Oxford, 1971).

Marlow, James, *De Gaulle's France and the Key to the Coming Invasion of Germany* (London, 1940).

May, Ernest, *Strange Victory: Hitler's Conquest of France* (New York, 2000).

Mayne, Robert, Douglas Johnson and Robert Tombs (eds.), *Cross Channel Currents: 100 Years of the Entente Cordiale* (London, 2004).

Medlicott, W. N., *The Economic Blockade* (London, 1952), vol. I.

Melton, George E., *Darlan: Admiral and Statesman of France* (Westport, Conn., 1998).

Mikes, George, *Darlan: A Study* (London, 1943).

Mockler, Anthony, *Our Enemies the French: Being an Account of the War Fought Between the French and the British, Syria, 1941* (London, 1976).

Ousby, Ian, *Occupation: The Ordeal of France, 1940–44* (London, 1999).

Overy, Richard, *Why the Allies Won* (London, 1995).

Paxton, Robert, *Parades and Politics at Vichy* (Princeton, NJ, 1966).

—— *Vichy France: Old Guard, New Order, 1940–44* (New York, 2001).

Piketty, Guillaume, *Français en résistance: carnets de guerre, correspondances, journaux personnels* (Paris, 2009).

Pimlott, John, *The Viking Atlas of World War Two* (London, 1995).

Playfair, I. S. O., *The Mediterranean and Middle East* (London, 1951), vol. II.

Porch, Douglas, *Hitler's Mediterranean Gamble: The North African and the Mediterranean Campaigns in World War II* (London, 2004).

Reynolds, David, *In Command of History: Churchill Fighting and Writing the Second World War* (London, 2004).

—— *Rich Relations: The American Occupation of Britain, 1942–45* (London, 1995).

Richards, Brook, *Secret Flotillas: The Clandestine Sea Lines to France and French North Africa, vols. I and II, 1940–44* (London, 1996 and 2002).

Roberts, Andrew, *The Holy Fox: A Life of Lord Halifax* (London, 1991).

—— *Masters and Commanders: The Military Geniuses Who Led the West to Victory in World War Two* (London, 2008).

Roshwald, Aviel, *Estranged Bedfellows: Britain and France in the Middle East during the Second World War* (Oxford, 1990).

Roskill, Stephen, *The War at Sea* (London, 1954), vol. I.

Roussel, Eric, *Charles de Gaulle* (Paris, 2002).

Sachar, Howard, *Europe Leaves the Middle East, 1936–54* (New York, 1972).
Sainsbury, Keith, *The North African Landings, 1942: A Strategic Decision* (London, 1976).
Salewski, Michael, *Die Deutsche Seekriegsleitung, 1935–45* (Frankfurt, 1970), vol. I.
Schmitt, G., *Les Accords secrets Franco-Britanniques de novembre-décembre 1940* (Paris, 1957).
Shennan, Andrew, *The Fall of France, 1940* (Harlow, 2000).
Smith, Colin, *England's Last War Against France: Fighting Vichy, 1940–42* (London, 2009).
Spears, Sir Edward, *Two Men Who Saved France: Pétain and de Gaulle* (London, 1966).
Stafford, David, *Britain and European Resistance, 1940–45: A Study of the Special Operations Executive* (London, 1980).
—— *Churchill and the Secret Service* (London, 1997).
Stenton, Michael, *Radio London and Resistance in Occupied Europe: British Political Warfare* (Oxford, 2000).
Stoler, Mark, *The Politics of the Second Front: American Planning and Diplomacy in Coalition Warfare, 1941–43* (Westport, Conn., 1977).
Sweets, John F., *Choices in Vichy France: The French under Nazi Occupation* (Oxford, 1986).
Thomas, Martin, *The French Empire at War, 1940–45* (Manchester, 1998).
Thomas, R. T., *Britain and Vichy* (London, 1979).
Tombs, Robert and Isabelle Tombs, *That Sweet Enemy: The French and the British from the Sun King to the Present* (London, 2006).
Tomkins, Peter, *The Murder of Admiral Darlan* (London, 1965).
Truchet, André, *L'Armistice du 1940 et l'Afrique du Nord* (Paris, 1955).
Tute, Warren, *Reluctant Enemies: The Story of the Last War between Britain and France* (London, 1990).
Unwin, Peter, *The Narrow Sea: Barrier, Bridge and Gateway to the World – The History of the English Channel* (London, 2003).
Verrier, Anthony, *Assassination in Algiers: Churchill, Roosevelt, de Gaulle and the Murder of Admiral Darlan* (London, 1990).
Wailly, Henri de, *Syrie 1941: La Guerre occultée* (Paris, 2006).
Waites, Neville (ed.), *Troubled Neighbours: British–French Relations in the Twentieth Century* (London, 1981).
Warner, Geoffrey, *Iraq and Syria, 1941* (London, 1974).
—— *Pierre Laval and the Eclipse of France* (London, 1968).
Webster, Charles and Noble Frankland, *The Strategic Air Offensive against Germany, 1939–45* (London, 1961), vol. III.
Weinberg, Gerhard, *A World at Arms: A Global History of World War II* (Cambridge, 1994).
Whitcomb, Philip (ed.), *France during the Occupation, 1940–44: A Collection of 292 Statements on the Government of Marshal Pétain and Pierre Laval* (Palo Alto, 1958).
Wiéviorka, Olivier, *Normandy: The Landings to the Liberation of Paris* (Cambridge, Mass., 2008).
Williams, Charles, *The Last Great Frenchman: A Life of General de Gaulle* (London, 1993).
—— *Pétain* (London, 2005).
Woodward, Sir Llewellyn, *British Foreign Policy in the Second World War*, 3 vols. (London, 1970–1).
Ziman, Herbert David, *Instructions for British Servicemen in France* (Oxford, 2005).

## Articles

Atkin, Nicholas, 'De Gaulle et la presse Anglaise, 1940–43,' *Espoir,* June 1990.

Bédarida, François, '16 Juin 1940: Le Project d'union des deux peuples,' *Espoir,* Décembre 1990.

Bell, Philip, 'La Grande-Bretagne et les Français Libres: 1940–44 – Un bienfait oublié?,' *Espoir,* June 1996.

—— 'L'Opinion publique en Grande-Bretagne et le général de Gaulle, 1940–44,' *Guerres Mondiales et Conflits Contemporains,* June 1990.

—— 'Some French Diplomats and the British, 1940–55: *Aperçus and idées réçues,*' *Franco-British Studies,* autumn 1992.

Bennett, G. H., 'The RAF's Free Fighter Squadrons: The Rebirth of French Airpower, 1940–44,' *Global War Studies,* 7 (2) 2010.

Bouchinet-Serreules, Claude and Etienne Schlumberger, '23 Septembre 1940: Dakar,' *Espoir,* Décembre 1990.

Cairns, John, 'A Nation of Shopkeepers in Search of a Suitable France, 1919–40,' *The American Historical Review,* June 1974.

Charmley, John, 'Harold Macmillan and the Making of the French Committee of Liberation,' *International History Review,* November 1982.

Cornick, Martyn, 'The BBC and the Propaganda War against Occupied France: The Work of Emile Delavenay and the European Intelligence Department,' *French History,* September 2002.

—— '"Faut-il réduire l'Angleterre en esclavage?" A Case Study of British Anglophobia, October 1935,' *Franco-British Studies,* Autumn 1992.

—— 'Fighting Myth with Reality: The Fall of France, Anglophobia and the BBC,' in Valerie Holman and Debra Kelly (eds.), *France at War* (Oxford, 2000).

—— 'Fraternity among Listeners: The BBC and French Resistance – Evidence from Refugees,' in Hanna Diamond and Simon Kitson (eds.), *Vichy, Occupation, Liberation* (Oxford, 2005).

Crémieux-Brilhac, Jacques, 'Les Emissions françaises de la BBC pendant la guerre,' *Revue d'Histoire de la Deuxième Guerre Mondiale,* November 1955.

Crouzet, François, 'Problèmes de la communication Franco-Britannique au XIXe et XXe siècles,' *Revue Historique,* July–September 1975.

Delpla, François, 'Du nouveau sur la mission Rougier,' *Guerres Mondiales et Conflits Contemporains,* April 1995.

Dodd, Lindsey and Andrew Knapp, '"How Many Frenchmen Did You Kill?" British Bombing Policy towards France, 1940–45,' *French History,* December 2008.

Foot, M. R. D., 'British Aid to the Resistance,' *Franco-British Studies,* autumn 1986.

—— 'De Gaulle et les services secrets pendant la guerre,' *Espoir,* June 1990.

*Franco-British Studies,* spring 1989. Special edition: 'Operation Torch and its Political Aftermath: Franco-Anglo-American Relations in 1942.'

Funk, Arthur, 'The "Anfa" Memorandum: An Incident at the Casablanca Conference,' *Journal of Modern History,* September 1954.

Gaunson, A. B., 'Churchill, de Gaulle, Spears and the Levant Affair, 1941,' *Historical Journal,* 27 (3) (1984).

Hartwell, Laurence, 'De Gaulle's Free French Army,' *Newlyn Shipping News,* 24 February 1910.

Hitchcock, William, 'Pierre Boisson, French West Africa and the Postwar *Epuration*: A Case from the Aix Files,' *French Historical Studies,* spring 2001.

Huan, Claude, 'Les Négociations Franco-Britannique de l'automne 1940,' *Guerres Mondiales et Conflits Contemporains,* October 1994.

Jessula, G., '1943: De Gaulle à Alger – Les "Carnets" de Harold Macmillan,' *Revue d'Histoire Diplomatique,* 105 (1991).

Johnson, Douglas, 'De Gaulle, La Grande Bretagne et la France Libre, 1940–43,' *Espoir,* June 1983.

—— 'Britain and France in 1940,' *Transactions of the Royal Historical Society,* 5th series, 22 (1972).

Lasterie, Philippe, 'Could Admiral Gensoul Have Averted the Tragedy of Mers-el-Kébir?,' *Journal of Military History,* July 2003.

Lerner, Henri, 'De Gaulle et l'Angleterre,' *Espoir,* November 1990.

Marck, David, de Young de la, 'De Gaulle, Colonel Passy and British Intelligence,' *Intelligence and Security,* spring 2003.

Melka, Robert, 'Darlan between Britain and Germany, 1940–41,' *Journal of Contemporary History,* April 1973.

Mickelson, Martin, 'Operation Susan: The Origins of the Free French Movement,' *Military Affairs,* October 1988.

Noel, Léon, 'Le Projet d'union franco-britannique de juin 1940,' *Revue d'Histoire de la Deuxième Guerre Mondiale,* January 1951.

Paxton, Robert, 'Le Régime de Vichy était-il neutre?,' *Guerres Mondiales et Conflits Contemporains,* December 1994.

Reynolds, David, '1940: Fulcrum of the Twentieth Century?' *International Affairs,* April 1990.

Queille, Pierre, 'La Politique d'Hitler à l'égard de Vichy: Finessieren et machtpolitik,' *Revue d'Histoire Diplomatique,* 3–4 (1983).

Shlaim, Avi, 'Prelude to Downfall: The British Offer of Union to France, June 1940,' *Journal of Contemporary History,* July 1974.

Thomas, Martin, 'After Mers-el-Kébir: The Armed Neutrality of the Vichy French Navy,' *English Historical Review,* June 1997.

—— 'The Anglo-French Divorce and the Limitations of Strategic Planning over West Africa, June–December 1940,' *Diplomacy and Statecraft,* 1, 1995.

—— 'The Discordant Leader: General Henri Giraud and the Foundation of the French Committee of National Liberation,' *French History,* March 1996.

—— 'France in British Signals Intelligence,' *French History,* March 2000.

—— 'Imperial Backwater or Strategic Outpost? The British Takeover of Vichy Madagascar,' *Historical Journal,* December 1996.

—— 'Signals Intelligence and Vichy France, 1940–44: Intelligence in Defeat,' *National Security and Intelligence,* 14 (1) (1999).

Tombs, Isabelle, 'Scrutinising France: Collecting and Using Newspaper Intelligence during World War Two,' *Intelligence and National Security,* summer 2002.

Weinberg, Gerhard L., 'D-Day after Fifty Years: Assessments of Costs and Benefits,' in *Germany, Hitler and World War II* (Cambridge, 1995).

Zamir, Meir, 'An Intimate Alliance: The Joint Struggle of General Edward Spears and Riad al-Sulh to Oust France from Lebanon, 1942–44,' *Middle Eastern Studies,* November 2005.

—— 'General de Gaulle and the Question of Syria and Lebanon during the Second World War: Part 1,' *Middle Eastern Studies,* September, 2007.

# Index